# Dublin

**Polly Devlin**

Mespil HAel

0035316671222

**Mitchell Beazley**

## THE AMERICAN EXPRESS ® TRAVEL GUIDES

Published by Mitchell Beazley International Ltd, Michelin House, 81 Fulham Road, London SW3 6RB

Edited, designed and produced by Castle House Press, Llantrisant Mid Glamorgan CF7 8EU, Wales

A cataloguing-in-publication record for this book is available from the British Library.

ISBN 1 85732 967 8

The editors thank Mary Fox at the Irish Tourist Office, London, Neil Hanson and Alex Taylor of Lovell Johns, David Haslam, Hilary Bird, Sharon Charity, Sally Darlington, Anne Evans, Melanie Gould, Anna Holmes, Muriel and Alf Jackson and Andrea Thomas for their assistance during the preparation of this edition.

**FOR THE SERIES:**
**Series Editor:**
David Townsend Jones
**Map Editor:** David Haslam
**Indexer:** Hilary Bird
**Gazetteer:** Anne Evans
**Cover design:**
Roger Walton Studio

**FOR THIS EDITION:**
**Edited on desktop by:**
David Townsend Jones
**Art editor:** Eileen Townsend Jones
**Illustrators:**
Sylvia Hughes-Williams,
David Evans
**Cover photo:** David Reed/
Impact Photos

**FOR MITCHELL BEAZLEY:**
**Art Director:** Tim Foster
**Managing Editor:** Alison Starling
**Production:** Matthew Batchelor

**PRODUCTION CREDITS:**
**Maps** by Lovell Johns, Oxford, England
**Typeset** in Garamond and News Gothic
**Desktop layout** in Ventura Publisher
**Linotronic output** by Tradespools Limited, Frome, England
**Printed and bound** in Great Britain by HarperCollins Manufacturing, Glasgow

# Contents

## Basic information

# Culture and history

# Irish art

# Sightseeing

# Where to stay

# Eating and drinking

# Entertainments

# Shopping

# Recreation

# Excursions

# Maps

# How to use this book

Few guidelines are needed to understand how this book works:

- For the general organization of the book, see CONTENTS on the pages preceding this one.
- Unusually for the *American Express* series, the SIGHTSEEING and EXCURSIONS chapters are based on itineraries, which you can use in whole or in part. They were conceived not as exhausting odysseys but because the author realized that Dublin and the Dublin region "may not involve much leg-work [but do] demand a lot of eye-work."
- Other chapters are self-explanatory and wherever appropriate are arranged alphabetically.
- As you turn the pages, you will find subject headers, similar to those used in telephone directories, printed in CAPITALS in the top corner of each page.
- There is a comprehensive and exhaustively cross-referenced INDEX at the back of the book.
- Following the index, a LIST OF STREET NAMES provides map references for all roads and streets mentioned in the book located within the area covered by the main city maps.

## CROSS-REFERENCES
These are printed in SMALL CAPITALS, referring you to other sections or alphabetical entries in the book. Care has been taken to ensure that such cross-references are self-explanatory. Often, page references are also given, although their excessive use would be intrusive and ugly.

## FLOORS
We use the European convention in this book: "ground floor" means the floor at ground level (called by Americans the "first floor").

## VOCABULARY
We have used certain standard words in their local Irish-English form rather than their American-English equivalents. These include motorway (superhighway/expressway), dual carriageway (four-lane highway), crossroads and junction (intersection), coach (bus), bookshop (bookstore) and newsagent (newsdealer).

---

## AUTHOR'S ACKNOWLEDGMENTS
The author would like to thank the following for their help and advice: Ian Lumley, Emer O'Kelly, Sean O'Criadain and Joan Grohmann. Thanks too to the following publishers for their kind permission to quote from: *The Small Towns of Ireland* by John Betjeman — John Murray (Publishers) Ltd, London; *The Irish World* ed. by Brian de Breffny — Thames & Hudson Ltd, London; *Dublin: A Portrait* by V.S. Pritchett — Random Century Group, London. And finally, thanks to Peter K. Fox, Librarian at Trinity College Library, Dublin, for his kind permission to quote him verbatim.

## KEY TO SYMBOLS

| | | | |
|---|---|---|---|
| ☎ | Telephone | Ⓜ | MasterCard |
| Fx | Facsimile (fax) | VISA | Visa |
| ⇔ | Parking | ⌷ | Secure garage |
| 🏛 | Building of architectural interest | ⌂ | Quiet hotel |
| 🔲 | Free entrance | 📷 | Conference facilities |
| 🔳 | Entrance fee payable | ▦ | Air conditioning |
| ⳤ | Guided tour | ♦ | Elevator |
| ⚑ | Cafeteria | ☐ | TV in each room |
| ⅋ | Facilities for disabled people | ⌞ | Telephone in each room |
| ⬛ | Simple hotel | ⚞ | Dogs not allowed |
| 🏩 | Luxury hotel | ⇝ | Swimming pool |
| ✿ | Good value (in its class) | ☜ | Sauna |
| ☐ | Cheap | ⚘ | Gym/fitness facilities |
| ⫿ | Inexpensive | ⚲ | Golf |
| ⫿⫿ | Moderately priced | ☙ | Garden |
| ⫿⫿⫿ | Expensive | ⵏ | Bar |
| ⫿⫿⫿⫿ | Very expensive | ▱ | Mini-bar |
| AE | American Express | ⚌ | Restaurant |
| ⊕ | Diners Club | ⏃ | Nightclub |
| | | ♫ | Live music |
| | | ⚘ | Dancing |

---

## HOTEL PRICE CATEGORIES

These are denoted by the symbols ☐ (cheap), ⫿ (inexpensive), ⫿⫿ (moderately priced), ⫿⫿⫿ (expensive) and ⫿⫿⫿⫿ (very expensive). They correspond approximately to the following actual local prices, which give a guideline **at the time of printing**.

Naturally, prices tend to rise, but, with a few exceptions, hotels will remain in the same price category.

| **Price categories** | Corresponding to approximate prices for **hotels** and **guesthouses** *single room with bath or shower, plus breakfast* |
|---|---|
| ⫿⫿⫿⫿ very expensive | over IR£100 |
| ⫿⫿⫿ expensive | IR£70-100 |
| ⫿⫿ moderately priced | IR£40-70 |
| ⫿ inexpensive | IR£20-40 |
| ☐ cheap | under IR£20 |

# About the author

**Polly Devlin** was born in the 1940s in Ardboe on the shores of Lough Neagh in County Tyrone. She grew up there with her five sisters and one brother; her father was a farmer and her mother a schoolteacher. In 1964 she won the Vogue Talent Competition and left Ireland to work in London for *Vogue Magazine.* She became features editor on *Vogue* and did the first interview in England with Bob Dylan, the first profile of Seamus Heaney in the English press, a controversial portrait of Barbra Streisand and a long interview with the Empress Farah Dibah in Tehran. She was with John Lennon and Yoko Ono when they were setting up their Art Show in New York State and was given a treasured gift by Lennon, a Yoko *Box of Smiles.*

She traveled through the Trucial Oman States at a time when the city of Abu Dhabi did not yet exist, when the Bedu still lived their nomadic life and the Sheik ruled from a *Beau Geste* palace. She has worked with all the great photographers including David Bailey, Norman Parkinson, Lord Snowdon and Richard Avedon. At the age of 23 she had her own column in the *New Statesman* and at 24 her own page in the London *Evening Standard.* From there she went to Manhattan to work for Diana Vreeland, the legendary editor of *Vogue.*

She is the author of *Dora,* a novel; *All of Us There,* an account of an Irish childhood which was acclaimed for its lyricism; a collection of short stories, *The Far Side of the Lough;* and *A History of Fashion Photography.* She recently wrote a booklet on ceramics for the National Museum in Dublin and is working on a film script. In 1992 she was honored with the OBE for services to journalism and broadcasting.

In 1969 she married an industrialist, then living in Paris and Italy. Her wedding took place in Tuscany. She has three daughters, and divides her time between Somerset, London and Ireland.

# A message from the series editor

Months of concentrated work have gone into ensuring that this edition is as accurate and up to date as possible as it goes to press. But time and change are forever the enemies, and in between editions we very much appreciate our readers writing to advise us of changes that they discover. Please do so — but be aware, as I am sure you are, that we have no control over restaurants, or whatever, that take it into their heads to close after we publish. (The devils won't sit still!)

My serious point is that we are striving to tailor the series to the very distinctive tastes and requirements of our discerning international readership, and your feedback is therefore extremely valuable.

Please send your comments to me at **Mitchell Beazley**, Michelin House, 81 Fulham Road, London SW3 6RB; or, in the US, c/o American Express Travel Guides, **Prentice Hall Travel**, 15 Columbus Circle, New York, NY 10023.

*David Townsend Jones, Series Editor, American Express Travel Guides*

# Dublin

# Unique Georgian city

A traveler does not so much enter Dublin as sidle in and become part of it. Dublin is a sly and delightful city with a slightly forlorn quality. It has lost some of that charm for which it was so famous and which was compounded as much out of the placatory attitude bred into the Irish by their history, as by the fact that for long the city seemed left behind in the slipstream of time. For decades right up until the 1960s it was marooned in an age and space where gentler manners and courtesy prevailed, as though Dublin's serene and classic beauty had influenced its inhabitants. And why not, since increasingly environment is seen as an important factor in the social development of a people.

Irish history has been a sad one; such history leaves a legacy. No one needs to be placatory any more since the Irish are their own masters, but the good manners persist. Cecil Woodham Smith the historian has an explanation:

> *Irish dignity, Irish hospitality and the easy good manners which still charm the modern traveller have an historical explanation. Three times at least the native aristocracy was conquered and dispossessed; many fled from Ireland to exile in France or Spain, but many others remained to be forced down by poverty and penal laws to the economic level of the peasantry.*

Well, all Dubliners are not descended from kings; but they are descended from a courteous race, and whatever the reasons, the manners are still there.

Arriving by boat or air, one can see how beautifully situated Dublin is, set in the crescent of hills which give it so many vistas and which act as great natural parks for Dubliners; one can be in the beautiful solitude of the Wicklow Hills or out on a long deserted beach within 20 minutes. V.S Pritchett, in his remarkable book *Dublin: A Portrait,* wrote a description of Ireland that could only have been written in the 20th century, which yet explains much of its old history.

> *. . . to fly into Dublin from Europe (is to go) out to the tattered fringes where Europe is breaking up. There is startling evidence in the sky, and it is sky that rules Irish life . . . . We are looking down at a windy island rocking among the Atlantic isotherms and isobars, the spirit of meteorology, a place shaped by weather . . . . You have arrived at the beginning or the end of creation.*

## DUBLIN AND DUBLINERS

One of the things that must strike any visitor to Dublin is the number of young people. The population has trebled in this century to more than one million. More than 40 percent of its population is under 25, and the city shows it. To be in North and central Dublin or down the Leeson Street nightclub strip late on a Friday or Saturday night is to be overwhelmed by the numbers of vivid young people pouring out from the bars and discos and pubs. It could be a scene from one of Roddy

Doyle's brilliant chronicles disguised as novels, which reveal a kind of Dublin not easily seen nor understood by visitors and which capture the atmosphere of North Dublin exactly.

Dublin does not have that disconnected international air about it that blights so many capital cities, where you smile and get nothing back. In its blend of sordid, beautiful houses, faded gentility and, alas, its hideous new buildings, it retains an air that is uniquely its own.

At first sight this is difficult to believe. There is now something hectic and hot in that famous laid-back Dublin atmosphere, that air it always had (and which was beyond analysis, although countless writers tried) of being both agreeably slow and yet having sparkle and wit, of leisure, and business and preoccupation. The city now has a ramshackle air like a butterfly reversing back into its cocoon, unable to cope with its beauty. And yet after only a very short time in the city, most visitors succumb. Louis MacNeice, an Irish poet from the North, is always quoted:

> . . . *But yet she holds my mind*
> *With her seedy elegance*
> *With her gentle veils of rain*
> *And all her ghosts that walk*
> *And all that hide behind*
> *Her Georgian facades —*
> *The catcalls and the pain*
> *The glamour of her squalor*
> *The bravado of her talk . . . .*

Perhaps the real reason that you suspend judgment and are receptive to Dublin's beauty has to do with the Irish perception of visitors as *people*. Their response is always vivid, personal, imaginative. You exist as someone with all your wits and rights about you, and that is something that is missing in most capital cities, where the visitor is just another tourist.

The older people in the street still look at you as though they *must* know who you are and who your people were. In that respect Dublin still remembers that it is a small family city. There is almost a moral quality to their apprehension of the otherness of people. Dubliners are rarely rude, though they are witty at your expense — but generally at a price you can pay. They gauge that price nicely.

Dublin is a city in which there are no foreigners. This is not to say that it reveals its inner life easily; it holds its own integrity and intensity in a secretive way, and, while Dublin and Dubliners appear to be greeting you with openness and a desire to please, there is an undertow of reserve that is sometimes difficult to perceive, let alone penetrate, unless you are Irish yourself. The consolation is that, if you aren't Irish when you come to Dublin, you may feel you are by the time you leave.

Not everyone has always felt like that. When Gerard Manley Hopkins came to teach Classics at the new Jesuit University College in the 1850s, he wrote from what was to become Newman House (at 85 and 86 St Stephen's Green):

*The house we are in is a sort of ruin, and for purposes of study very*

*nearly naked . . . . I have been warmly welcomed and most kindly
treated. But Dublin itself is a joyless place and I think, in my heart,
as smoky as London is.*

Nearly 60 years ago a visitor wrote about "the terrible friendliness" of
Dubliners, and it still holds true. They are friendly because it is in their
nature to be so, and because they are interested. You would do well to
respond to that interest. No one likes being slighted, Dubliners least of
all. The Irish are thin-skinned. You can offend easily by loud or bad
manners or by being patronizing: it is extraordinary how many visitors
think it incumbent to don a stage Irish accent. Do not do so. The word
*begorrah* no longer exists in the Irish lexicon, if it ever did.

Dublin is a city that lay almost inert for years, and in the last 20 years
it has been running lickety-split to catch up with the rest of the world,
sometimes tumbling out of control into a young world, the world of the
future. The older generations perhaps feel menaced by this, and it is a
generalization containing truth that the national temperament does not
like change — not much wonder, since change, in the past, was usually
for the worst, and resisting it was a safety mechanism, a determination to
avoid the erosion of a certain way of life against the encroaching
international homogeneity.

In Dublin there is a taut vitality in the air that comes both from its
coherent origins and from the fact that it is simultaneously capital city
and parochial town. People may know one another as in a small town;
but the rest of the world knows many of them too, as poets, researchers,
painters, musicians, scientists and business people of world class.

You still see things in Dublin that make you pause; two young men
riding two to the one bicycle, one pedaling for dear life driving the double
weight, the other perched on the saddle whistling nonchalantly, languid
as though on a chaise longue, his legs trailing along the cobbles; a shop
called Junk and Disorderly; women in Henry Street selling bananas in
voices that would cut cold steel, and when you stop to buy, the voices
change to a croon; a child playing a penny whistle, sweet at first glance,
poignant at the second, for she has been set to begging.

There are women with babies at the breast curled up at the foot of
lampposts, begging, and it is hard to pass them by. Walk across a park,
any park, and you see so much of Dublin life. You go over a little
footbridge on the North side, across a canal: the DART train trundles by,
dogs tear about, children scream and play, a scene anywhere, often
melancholized by Larkin, but in Dublin it takes on an extraordinary vivid
quality, what Joyce called "only a fadograph of a yestern scene."

If there is a soccer, rugby or hurling match on (and there are many,
for the counties of Ireland play against one another, and the tension
reaches fever pitch in a Final), the crowds are enormous in the streets,
since the stadia are in the center of the city — Croke Park, just north of
the Liffey, and Lansdowne Road, south — but there is never any trouble.
The opposing teams' supporters meet, mingle and banter. There is only
anticipation, hurry, excitement before the match as the crowds stream
one way; and only gloom and despair or jubilation as they stream back.

13

From its beginnings, Dublin always had certain natural advantages: its foundations on a reef of outcrop rock, known as Standfast Dick, which marked the ancient limit of shipping; its admirable local building materials of limestone, granite and finest quality brick of a beautiful red and purple color (although a lot of the brick came in as ballast on ships on the Dublin-Bristol route).

Then too the chronology of its development was also auspicious. At a crucial stage in its evolution from a walled medieval city to a capital city, Dublin was populated by a stylish, witty and greedy ruling class who wanted new grand homes: enterprising architects, entrepreneurial builders, rich peers with grand and sometimes enlightened ideas, and wealthy merchants.

A healthy infrastructure supported this growth. The Wide Street Commission, founded in 1757, laid down admirable ground rules for spacious streets and pleasing buildings; there was plenty of room in the city (compared with London, land was ridiculously cheap); and, above all, there was a thriving body of craftsmen, both local and lately arrived from Italy, Switzerland and Germany, engaged in producing work of the very highest quality. Some wisps of this Augustan age still cling like cobwebs in the corners of the city, but they are fading in the new, harsh light.

## THE ASCENDANCY

There have always been two distinct segments of society: the Irish, and the Anglo-Irish, or Ascendancy, who were, on the whole, Protestant and had political power. One description of an Anglo-Irishman runs, "he who takes more out of Ireland than he puts in." Yet the people of the Ascendancy left behind the buildings and squares that adorn Dublin as well as an extraordinary legacy of genius: Berkeley, Swift, Goldsmith, Congreve, Sheridan, George Moore, Grattan, Wolfe Tone, Robert Emmet and George Bernard Shaw among countless other luminaries who were all Anglo-Irish.

(Bernard Shaw would have none of it. Obfuscating the whole issue even further, he thundered, "My extraction is the extraction of most Irishmen; that is, I have no trace in me of the commercially imported North Spanish strain which passes for aboriginal Irish. I am a genuine typical Irishman of the Danish Norman, Cromwellian and — of course — Scotch invasions . . . . ")

Eilis Dillon in her book *Inside Ireland* writes that "Dublin in the nineteenth century was simply a part of England . . . and was not a popular capital with the rest of the country, and sometimes it seems to have remained unpopular to this day." The Anglo-Irish were a class and not a race; and as a class they gave much to Ireland and took much, and lost in the final balance.

John Betjeman summed it up in his poem *The Small Towns Of Ireland*:

> But where is his Lordship, who once in a phaeton
> Drove out twixt his lodges and into the town?
> Oh his tragic misfortunes I will not dilate on;
> His mansion's a ruin, his woods are cut down . . .

*. . . His impoverished descendant is dwelling in Ealing*
*His daughters must type for their bread and their board*
*O'er the graves of his forbears the nettle is stealing.*
*And few will remember the sad Irish Lord.*

Dublin, "that gallant venal city," as Joyce called it, "the soul of which, his elders had told him, had shrunk with time to a faint mortal order," is connected with its history deeply and intimately. History and mythology are irredeemably mixed, and the city is dotted with monuments to heroes from both versions of the past.

It has to be said, indeed has been, that patriotism is bad for sculpture. For a monument to stay standing, the hero has to have fought on the winning side: in Dublin, wonderful monuments have perished through the bombs of patriotic fervor, including statues to George II, William of Orange and Lord Eglington. When, in what might be called a vicious circle, the statue of Eglington was blown up, its head flew into the card room of the University Club, where he had spent most of his time.

Patriotism is none too good for aesthetics either, it would seem, judging from some of the new monuments that have been erected since 1922. Dublin can boast more hideous statues to her fallen great than can most capitals.

## WATER

Dublin is bisected by its famous river, the Liffey, wrongly supposed to impart its unique taste to Guinness. It runs from west to east into Dublin Bay, and north and south of the river divide each have their distinctive characteristics. "No city neglects its river as Dublin does," wrote Oliver St John Gogarty. "There is not a pleasure boat on the Liffey from Butt Bridge to Lucan. If the rivers and towns were in England, there would be water-gardens and boat-houses and people delighting themselves in the lovely amenities of the water."

"And drowning themselves," Tim said. (Tim was Tim Healy, first Governor-General of the Free State and the man who ruined Parnell.) This has changed now; the river is used at Ringsend as a pleasure place, and sailing is more and more a popular pastime.

The river (personified as a female deity *Abhann na Life,* and written on early maps as *Anna Liffey*) rises in the peat and rock of the Wicklow Hills, which play such a magnificent part in giving Dublin its borrowed views. It then meanders 70 miles through Wicklow, Kildare and Dublin before it reaches the sea. Once it was twice as wide as it flowed through Dublin as it is now, lipping up to the old Library in Trinity and surrounding Dublin Castle.

There are other little river tributaries of the Liffey running through the city. There is the Poddle in the south and the Tolka in the north, for example, and, again in the south, the Dodder, which is crossed by the oldest bridge in Dublin, a narrow, twin-arched stone one.

And there are the great canals that girdle the city, the Royal on the North side and the Grand on the South, which were built during the 18th century to connect Dublin to the rich Midlands and the Shannon. These have been celebrated in poetry and folk-song ever since they were built. The Grand Canal bounds an area of Dublin called Ballsbridge or Dublin 4, much mocked for its gentility and the refined accents of its inhabitants. This, incidentally, is something that visitors to a city generally miss — the little snobberies, gradations of an accent, the quality of an area, the mix of housing and how it affects the district. But Dublin has less class consciousness and separation of demographic groups than most other European capital cities; housing is mixed-income all over the city.

## WALKING OUT

The old claim that it was an easy walk from city center to the open country is no longer true, but nearly all of the things one ought not to miss in Dublin are contained within a square mile of its center.

George Moore, the eccentric Anglo-Irish writer, who had been brought up in idyllic surroundings in the west of Ireland, came to live in Dublin at the beginning of the century. He who had lived in Paris and London trying to find his way to Bohemia, fell in love with Dublin and felt he had found the true place of the soul. He was not the first or the last to take Dublin at face value (for one of the city's most charming tricks is to turn a guileless and smiling face toward the visitor, as long as he or she remains a visitor). He wrote:

> *The truth is that I am in love with Dublin. I think it is the most beautiful town that I have ever seen; mountains at the back and the sea in front and long roads winding through decaying suburbs and beautiful woods. Dublin dwindles so beautifully; there is no harsh separation between it and the country; it fades away.*

The suburbs are no longer so decayed, and the North side now dwindles in a fairly slovenly fashion, although one of the most spectacular new sights in spring are the daffodils, thousands of them, lining the stretch of motorway from the airport into the city. It is a marvelously Wordsworthian flight of fancy.

To start to know Dublin, there is nothing more agreeable than just sallying forth and seeing what is around the corner. Walking along the Liffey, crossing and recrossing the bridges — there are 13 — will give you the feel of "dear dirty Dublin." The graceful little cast-iron tollbridge (the Ha' penny Bridge), dating from 1815, spans the Liffey at Merchant's Arch and is one of the earliest iron bridges in the world; and O'Connell Bridge is a marvel of town and riverscape, now sadly marred by pounding traffic.

Dublin is still a beautiful city. On a summer's evening when the traffic is stilled and the evening shadows gather around the long perspective of certain streets, in their harmony of red Georgian brick and intricate iron work, there is nowhere like it.

In Dublin, to walk from area to area and street to street is to be excited by the diversity, delighted by the vitality, shocked by the ugliness, elevated by the beauty, disarmed by the kindness, and tickled pink by the wit. Enjoy it while it lasts.

# IRELAND

- —·—·—·—  International Boundary
- — — — —  Provincial Boundary
- ············  County Boundary

N

DONEGAL

Londonderry
DERRY
ANTRIM

U L S T E R
Donegal
TYRONE
Belfast

FERMANAGH
ARMAGH
DOWN

MONAGHAN

SLIGO
LEITRIM
CAVAN
LOUTH

MAYO
C O N N A U G H T
ROSCOMMON
LONGFORD
MEATH

WESTMEATH

GALWAY
Galway
L E I N S T E R
DUBLIN
DUBLIN

OFFALY
KILDARE

LAOIS
WICKLOW

CLARE
TIPPERARY
Kilkenny
CARLOW

Limerick
KILKENNY
WEXFORD

LIMERICK
M U N S T E R
Wexford

KERRY
Waterford
WATERFORD

Killarney
CORK

Cork

| 0 | 50 | 100miles |
| 0 | 50 | 100 | 150km |

17

# Basic information

## Before you go

### DOCUMENTS REQUIRED
Citizens of the EC, the US, Canada and most other countries do not require **visas** to enter Ireland. Visitors from Cuba, the countries of the former USSR and Libya do. All visitors from overseas, other than from Great Britain, require a **passport**. It is prudent to carry **identification** if you plan to visit Northern Ireland.

**Vaccination certificates** are not required, but you should check if one is needed on re-entry into your own country.

If you bring your own car or motorcycle, you need a **vehicle registration certificate** (logbook), an **insurance certificate** valid for the Republic of Ireland, and a **driver's license** or **international driving permit**. A **national identity sticker** is also required.

Inform your car insurance company of travel plans, particularly if you want comprehensive cover. It is important to note that your vehicle may not be driven by an Irish resident during your visit, other than a garage hand with your written permission.

### TRAVEL AND MEDICAL INSURANCE
Be sure to take out an insurance policy covering loss of deposits paid to airlines, hotels, tour operators, etc., and emergency costs such as special tickets home and extra nights in a hotel.

Visitors from countries with no reciprocal health agreement are not covered for any medical help other than accidents or emergencies, and even then will be expected to pay if they have to stay the night in hospital. They should be properly insured. No charge is made for visitors from countries with a reciprocal arrangement, such as EC member countries.

The **IAMAT** (International Association for Medical Assistance to Travelers) is a nonprofit organization that has a directory of English-speaking doctors who will call, for a fixed fee. There are member hospitals and clinics throughout the world, including two clinics in Dublin. Membership is free, and other benefits include information on health risks overseas. For further information write to **IAMAT** headquarters in the US or in Europe *(417 Center St., Lewiston, NY 14092, USA, or 57 Voirets, 1212 Grand-Lancy, Genève, Switzerland)*.

### IRISH TOURIST OFFICES OVERSEAS
The **Irish Tourist Board** is the main source for information on all aspects of travel to and around the Republic of Ireland.

- **Irish Tourist Board (in the US)**   757 3rd Ave., New York, NY 10017 ☎(212) 418-0800 Ⓕⓧ(212) 371-9052
- **Irish Tourist Board (in Canada)**   160 Bloor St. E, Suite 1150, Toronto, Ont. M4W 1B9 ☎(416) 929-2777 Ⓕⓧ(416) 929-6783
- **Irish Tourist Board (in the UK)**   150 New Bond St., London W1Y 0AQ ☎(071) 493-3201 Ⓕⓧ(071) 493-9065
- **All Ireland Tourism (also in the UK)**   British Travel Centre, 4-12 Regent St., Piccadilly Circus, London SW1Y 4PQ ☎(071) 839-8416 Ⓕⓧ(071) 839-6179

For a list of hotels approved by the **Irish Tourist Board**, write, telephone or fax the **Irish Hotels Federation**, 13 Northbrook Rd., Dublin 6, Republic of Ireland ☎(010-353-1) 976459 Ⓕⓧ(010-353-1) 974613.

## MONEY

The Irish pound (the punt) is written **IR£** to distinguish it from the pound sterling. The coins used are 1p (penny), 2p, 5p, 10p, 20p and 50p. Bank notes are IR£1, IR£5, IR£10, IR£20, IR£50 and IR£100.

Sterling currency should be changed at banks into punts, as fluctuations in exchange rates make it unlikely that it will be exchanged on parity with the punt in shops and other businesses. British and European visitors require **check guarantee cards** to cash personal checks.

**Travelers checks** are necessary for other nationalities but have the advantage of being usable anywhere. Those issued by American Express, Thomas Cook, Barclays and Citibank are widely recognized; make sure you read the instructions included with your checks. **It is important to note separately the serial numbers of each check and the telephone number to call in case of loss.** Specialist travelers check companies such as American Express provide extensive local refund facilities.

The most commonly accepted charge and credit cards are American Express, MasterCard (Access/Eurocard) and Visa, but many smaller shops and guesthouses do not accept cards. Charge and credit cards do not guarantee personal checks anywhere in Ireland.

American Express also has a **MoneyGram**® money transfer service that makes it possible to wire money worldwide in just minutes, from any American Express Travel Service Office. This service is available to all customers and is not limited to American Express Card members. Payment can be made in cash, or with an American Express Card with a Centurion Credit Line, an American Express Optima (SM) Card, Visa or MasterCard. For the location nearest you ☎**1-800-543-4080** (in the US and Canada).

## CUSTOMS

If you are visiting the Republic of Ireland for less than six months, you are entitled to bring in, free of duty and tax, all personal effects that you intend to take with you when you leave, except tobacco goods, alcoholic drinks and perfume. Ensure you carry dated receipts for valuable items, such as cameras and watches, or you may be charged duty.

Since January 1993, the limits for goods bought duty-free and tax-paid within the EC have been virtually abolished. The much higher thresholds, above which you must be able to prove that the goods are for your own personal use, have been set at 800 cigarettes, 400 cigarillos, 200 cigars, 10 liters of liquor (spirits) or strong liquor, 90 liters of wine (no more than 60 sparkling), 20 liters of fortified wines and 110 liters of beer.

## Other allowances

For goods bought anywhere outside the EC, or duty- and tax-free within the EC, including purchases from a UK duty-free shop, the limits remain as follows: 200 cigarettes *or* 100 cigarillos *or* 50 cigars *or* 250g tobacco; 1 liter liquor (spirits) or strong liquor (more than 22-percent alcohol by volume) *or* 2 liters of alcoholic drink less than 22-percent alcohol, fortified wine or sparkling wine *plus* 2 liters of still table wine; 50g/60cc/2fl.oz perfume and 250cc/9fl.oz toilet water; and other goods to the value of IR£34.

## Restrictions and recommendations

- Travelers under 17 are not entitled to the allowances on tobacco goods and alcoholic drinks.
- The "other goods" allowance for travelers under 15 is IR£17.
- Prohibited and restricted goods include narcotics, weapons, obscene publications and videos, as well as animals and birds.
- If you have anything in excess of the duty-free allowances, pass through the channel with red "Goods to declare" notices; otherwise pass through the green "Nothing to declare" channel.
- For exemption from Value-Added Tax (VAT) on goods bought in Ireland for export to non-EC countries, see page 28.

## GETTING THERE

**Dublin International Airport** is 7 miles (11km) N of the city. **Aer Lingus**, the national airline, is also a major tour operator within Ireland and owns its own chain of Copthorne Hotels within the UK, Europe and Africa. Most major airlines fly to Dublin; the other Irish airline, **Ryanair**, flies within Ireland and has international flights.

There are flights from Dublin to Shannon, Cork, Knock, Sligo and Belfast. There are endless variations on the fly/drive theme, whereby you reserve a car with your flight; or you can have a chauffeur meet you at the airport. The Irish Tourist Board will provide all details.

**By ferry or boat:** Dublin is only 65 miles from Holyhead across the Irish Sea. **Sealink Stena Line** and **B&I** operate daily services between Wales, Scotland and Ireland, with more sailings available in summer than in winter. The Sealink ferry sails from nearby Dun Laoghaire; B&I direct from Dublin. The routes to both ports are well signposted. **Irish Ferries** operate from Rosslare (near Wexford) to the French ports of Le Havre and Cherbourg and from Cork to Roscoff, in Brittany.

For addresses and telephone numbers see page 33.

## CLIMATE

It has been said that the Irish weather shifts from damp to wet, and certainly Irish weather has always been fickle in its humors. Michael

Mac Liammoir pondered on the question he was so often asked, "What is the best time to visit Ireland?" and decided:

> *There is no best time on which to lay a finger; you may breakfast in your garden on a sunny golden morning of February or November or huddle over the fire on some icy summer's day when the calendar informs you that this is indubitably the month that some Irish-American writer whose years in New York or California had filled his head with memories of gold once called the miracle of an Irish June. A miracle indeed when June decided to behave like June but one never can tell.*

Certainly the weather is becoming more unpredictable, and there have been many long hot summers recently. But Ireland is still called the Emerald Isle because its grass is so green, and that is thanks to the quantities of rain that fall. Less rain falls in Dublin than in many other parts of Ireland, but this is not to say that Dublin is dry. No matter how prolonged the rainfall, you will be told that it's only a shower and will soon clear. Usually in a year about 28 inches of rain falls in the Dublin district; on some of the western mountains of Ireland, 90 inches may fall.

The climate all over Ireland is temperate: mild and damp. May and June are statistically the driest months, although in practice April is usually the driest. Dublin's July temperature averages between 60-70°F (16-21°C), the maximum average for the country, with an exceptionally high number of hours of sunshine.

Come to terms with the weather straight away. A sunny day in the city is lovely, giving the old stone and bricks an opalescent air partly induced by petrol fumes. A rainy day gives the city an entirely different feel, one that is more Celtic twilight than European, and you might as well go along with it. And if you go out for the day to Glendalough or Newgrange or any excursion, be prepared for changeable weather.

Be prepared too for how the light changes everything. A dark field becomes a livid green as the clouds roll over, then turns to jade, then purple. As you drive, a blue mountain becomes damson, the sea rolls from black to silver. Nothing will prepare you for the exhilarating beauty that opens before you, whether it is wet or dry when you are driving across country.

The exception to the rule is fog. Stay within the city and look at the buildings or the paintings. Dublin fog when it rolls in is like T.S. Eliot's fog that rubs its back upon the window-panes, licks its tongue into the corner of the evening, lingers upon the pools that stand in the drains, and lets fall the soot from the chimney (less now that the new antismoke laws have just been passed). But such days are rare.

Whatever the weather, enjoy, and as some of the Irish say, may your god go with you.

## CLOTHES

In winter you need warm, waterproof clothes and sturdy shoes; Dublin's cold weather is not dry and there is often a biting wind. Dublin is mild in the spring, but again, a whipping wind can blow along the quays with a high chill and irritant factor, and it can be chilly and damp in the evenings. In midsummer you will often need a cardigan or light jacket during the day; even hot summer days rarely go much above 75˚F (25˚C), and the temperature always drops in the evening. Carry a lightweight fold-up raincoat if you can — a day that dawns sunny doesn't necessarily stay that way.

Although Dublin is less morally thin-skinned than it used to be, high standards of decency and modesty prevail; avoid offending sensibilities, especially if you are sightseeing in churches.

Dublin is an easy-going city and there are no set rules for dress when eating out or going to the theater. However, fashion-conscious Dubliners like to look smart when they go out for the evening, so you will be just as comfortable in a cocktail dress or suit as in casual clothes. Men need not wear a tie except at the grander restaurants and, in Dublin, in the Shelbourne hotel, where the style is more formal.

## GENERAL DELIVERY (POSTE RESTANTE)

Mail marked "c/o Poste Restante" will be held for collection free of charge at any post office for up to three months. In Dublin, use the **General Post Office** *(O'Connell St., map 4 B4 ☎ (01) 8728888)*.

# Getting around Ireland and Dublin

## FROM THE AIRPORT TO THE CITY

Taxis from the airport cost about IR£12.00 to the center of the city and are meter controlled. Limousine services are also available at the airport.

Dublin Bus operates bus services between Dublin Airport, Busaras (Central Bus Station) and major hotels in the city every 20 minutes from early morning until midnight. The fare is IR £2.50; children under 16 pay half. Ordinary double-decker buses are less expensive and take 20-30 minutes.

## PUBLIC TRANSPORT

Dublin is linked with other Irish cities and provincial towns by its network of rail and bus services. Buses operate as **Bus Eireann/Irish Bus**; rail services operate under the title **Iarnrod Eireann/Irish Rail**. These two, together with **Dublin Bus** (within the greater Dublin area), are subsidiaries of **CIE** *(59, Upper O'Connell St., Dublin 1, map 4 C4)*, the national transport company.

Telephone information on public transport services is available from the following:

- **Irish Rail (Iarnrod Eireann)** ☎(01) 366222
- **Irish Bus (Bus Eireann)** ☎(01) 366111, Monday to Saturday 9am-11pm, Sunday 10am-7pm
- **Dublin Bus (Bus Atha Cliath)** ☎(01) 8734222

- **Airport bus**   ☎(01) 366111
- **Sightseeing bus tours**   Contact Dublin Bus

## RAILWAYS
**Irish Rail (Iarnrod Eireann)** operates trains to major cities and towns. There are two classes, standard and super standard.

**Connolly** *(map 4B6)*, **Tara Street** *(map 4C5)* and **Pearse Street** *(map 4D6)* stations serve the suburbs N and S of the city. Connolly Station is also the main-line station for trains to Northern Ireland, Sligo, Wexford and towns N of Dublin. **Heuston Station** *(Kingsbridge, Dublin 8, off map 3C1)* operates trains to the W and S of Ireland.

Irish Rail also operates the **Dublin Area Rapid Transit (DART)** train, a boon for visitors to Dublin. It is an electrified line running the entire span of Dublin Bay, from Bray in the S to Howth in the N, and the trains go right through Dublin, with stations at close intervals. It runs from 6am to 11.30pm, with extra trains at rush hours. You can buy a day-ticket that will take you anywhere on the line, getting on and off as often as desired.

There is a personally guided two-hour DART tour from Bray to Howth. See page 26 for details.

## BUSES
A national network of buses (**Irish Bus/Bus Eireann**) serves major cities, towns and villages outside Dublin. **Dublin Bus/Bus Atha Cliath** *(59 Upper O'Connell St., Dublin 1, map 4C4 ☎(01) 8734222)* controls all public bus services within the greater Dublin area. There is an extensive bus service threading its labyrinthine way all through the city and to the suburbs.

Timetables and bus maps showing all the routes are on sale at newsagents. *An Lar* on buses means City Center.

Airport and provincial bus services operate from **Busaras** (Central Bus Station), Store St., Dublin 1, map 4C5 ☎(01) 366111.

A special express bus service called **Nitelink** operates from the city center to the suburbs all over Dublin on Friday and Saturday night. Departures are at midnight, 1am, 2am and 3am from College Green *(map 4D4)*, D'Olier St. *(map 4C5)* and Westmoreland St. *(map 4D4)*, and passengers can disembark at any safe point along the route. Tickets can be bought during the day, or from the **Ticket Sales Bus** (a mobile ticket sales office) in Westmoreland St. on Friday and Saturday night, for IR£2.

## DUBLIN EXPLORER TICKET
With this 4-day ticket you can travel on all Dublin buses and suburban trains including DART. It is not valid before 9.45am, but there are no evening restrictions. Available from the **Dublin Bus Booking Office** *(59 Upper O'Connell St., map 4C4)* or from any Dublin Bus station.

## TAXIS
Taxis operate from ranks, which are within walking distance of most shopping centers and hotels. Taxis have identifying medallions or placards on their roof. The main ranks are:

- **St Stephens Green**   Map 4E4-5
- **Burlington Hotel, Leeson St.**   Off map 4F5
- **College Green**   Map 4D4
- **Westland Row**   Map 4D5
- **O'Connell St.**   Map 4B4-C4

There is a large fleet of taxis. Pubs and restaurants will always telephone for a taxi, and there are radio taxi services. The telephone directory has many taxi cab numbers. Fares are metered. Two leading companies are:

- **National Radio Cabs**   ☎(01) 6772222
- **Co-op Taxis**   ☎(01) 6766666

### DRIVING IN IRELAND

The best way of traveling around Ireland is by car. By European standards there are few motorways or even dual carriageways, so always leave more time for your journey.

Driving is on the left in Ireland, although sometimes one is given cause to wonder, especially in the country where you can find yourself behind an old farmer meandering up a road as though he were driving a horse and cart. (In his mind's eye he probably is.) His counterpoint (and your other hazard) is Ireland's answer to Nigel Mansell in an old Toyota and a mustache, lashing his car into a lather to pass you on a corner.

Speed limits are generally 55mph (88kph) on the open road and 30 mph (48kph) in urban areas. Seat belts are compulsory, and children under 12 must travel in the rear.

A straight road is a rarity in Ireland. Try not to be in a hurry. It really does take longer driving from place to place than you could imagine; always give yourself more time than you think, and not just from necessity.

The **AA** *(freephone ☎(1 800) 667788)* provides a 24-hour emergency breakdown service.

### DRIVING IN DUBLIN

In Dublin places are so near to one another that it is often easier to walk than to drive. In any case, parking is difficult. If you do drive then never leave your keys in a street-parked car in the city: the incidence of joy-riding in parts of Dublin is high.

One of the things you'll notice about Dublin if you are driving, is that the traffic lights take forever. They are geared to change by the minute, and a minute is a long time if you're impatient. So be warned — be patient. And *never* jump the lights . . . other people do.

### CAR RENTAL

Petrol in Ireland is expensive, as are insurance costs, so car rental prices are relatively high. All the major car rental agencies have offices in the main terminal at Dublin International Airport. The main companies are:

- **Avis**   ☎(01) 6776971
- **Hertz**   ☎(01) 6767476

- **Budget**   ☎(01) 379802
- **Murrays Europcar Ltd**   ☎(01) 6681777; at airport ☎(01) 8444179
- **Murrays Chauffeur Drive Ltd**   ☎(01) 6681777

## TRAVEL BY AIR

There are scheduled flights within Ireland from Dublin to Shannon, Cork, Knock, Sligo and Belfast. For addresses and telephone numbers, see page 33.

Private helicopters are provided by **Celtic Helicopters Ltd** *(Dublin Airport ☎(01) 8423366)* and **Irish Helicopters** *(Westpoint Hangar, Dublin Airport ☎ (01) 8444500),* or through **Elegant Ireland** *( ☎ (01) 4751665).*

## BICYCLES

Bicycles are available to rent in Dublin and arrangements can be made to deliver them to await you at the airport. Rates are about IR£7 a day. Bicycles must be returned to where they were rented. Ask the Irish Tourist Board for details.

## CITY AND OTHER TOURS

Dublin Bus run sightseeing tours in an open-top bus, taking in all major tourist attractions in Dublin. The **Dublin City Tour** bus stops to pick up passengers at many hotels and passes 55 recognized places of interest, with a stop for coffee at the Royal Hospital, Kilmainham. For part of the year there is also an evening tour which includes a short walk through "old" Dublin. Departures:

- January 12 to March 6, Tuesday, Friday, Saturday at 10.15am only
- March 9 to December 13, daily at 10.15am and 2pm
- Evening tour: June 7 to December 13, daily at 6.15pm

On the **Heritage Tour**, buses depart every hour on the hour and you can get on and off at any point along the trail and rejoin the bus as you wish. On rainy days a covered bus is used.

Dublin Bus also run tours N and S along the coast:

- **North Coast Tour** (duration $2\frac{1}{2}$ hours), passing the major sights and stopping at Howth Harbour. Departures daily from May 11 to September 19 at 10.30am.
- **South Coast Tour** (duration $3\frac{3}{4}$ hours) to Bray, stopping at Avoca and Weavers on the way. Departures daily from May 11 to September 19 at 2pm.

The **Ceoil agus Craic** tour is an evening of traditional music and dance at the Irish Culture and Music Centre (Culturlann na h-Eireann) in Monkstown; there is a lounge and bar at the Centre. The tour lasts $3\frac{1}{2}$ hours. Departures by bus from June 30 to September 3 on Tuesday, Wednesday and Thursday at 7.30pm. Pick-up points at the Shelbourne, Burlington and other hotels.

All details about departures for the above tours from **Dublin Bus** *(59 Upper O'Connell St., Dublin 1, map 4 C4 ☎ (01) 8720000 (ext. 3028) or ☎ (01) 8734222).*

There are other tours that head farther afield:

- **DART Tours – Views Unlimited** is a 43-mile journey from Bray to Howth and back, starting at 10am at Bray Station, taking approximately two hours plus an extra hour spent at Howth Harbour. A tour guide points out historic, cultural and scenic places of interest. Contact Felicity Manley at **Dart Tours** *(39 Shrewsbury Lawn, Dublin 4* ☎ *(01) 2862861, or 8 Prince of Wales Terrace, Bray, Co. Wicklow* ☎ *(01) 2860164)*. Price: IR£4 one-way.

- **Bus Eireann** have many different tours to areas in and around Dublin. All buses leave from central Dublin, often with pick up points at hotels along the way. Tours include **Glendalough and Wicklow** (March 30-September 26 daily except Fridays), **Boyne Valley** (May 12-September 27 on Sunday, Tuesday and Thursday), **Avondale, Glendalough and Wicklow Hills** (June 5-September 18, Fridays only) and **Russborough and Blessington Lakes** (Wednesdays June 24-August 26).

## WALKING TOURS

Dublin Tourism have recently published three walking-tour booklets covering the following "trails":

- **The Georgian Trail** follows streets in the city s of the Liffey, with particular attention to Georgian buildings and the features of that period, as well as buildings and events of note from other times.

- **The Old City Trail** starts from College Green, the historic site where the Vikings built their Thingmote and the 18thC parliament was located. Along the route are the places of power and influence that have shaped the history of Dublin. On this trail also are the Liberties, the markets and Temple Bar.

- **The Cultural Trail** visits the Four Courts, the Custom House and the King's Inns, the great buildings making up what may be described as "Gandon's Triangle," N of the Liffey.

Dublin Bus operate a **Heritage Trail Tour** of Dublin City in conjunction with the walking trail. The hourly service, using double-decker buses, stops at selected points along the way where passengers can alight and rejoin the bus to continue to the next stage of the trail. You can, for instance, travel by the bus from Trinity College to Merrion Square, stop to visit the National Gallery, and then take the next bus to another point on the trail. The ticket is good for a whole day, so you can get on and off as often as you like.

The **Rock 'N Stroll Trail** *(details from Tourist Information)* is a trail of significant sites in Dublin's more recent music history. Plaques are erected at designated sites along the route showing the artists associated with each one. A brochure is available to follow the trail, which will also include information to young people on where to go, what to see, the current music scene etc.

It is possible to hire a guide to show you Dublin and its environs for any length of time, either for groups or individuals. Guides are available in most languages including Russian and Japanese. Tourist information

(Bord Failte) have names of recommended agencies. It is also possible to hire a limousine and driver to guide you around Dublin in comfort.

- **Tourist Information Offices**   14 Upper O'Connell St., map 4C4 ☎(01) 8747733; Baggot St. Bridge, map 4F6 ☎(01) 6765871; Dublin Airport ☎(01) 8445387
- **The Federation of Irish Guiding Interests**   ☎(01) 941251
- **Tour Guide Ireland**   Glendenning House, Wicklow St., map 4D4 ☎(01) 6794291
- **Guides to Old Dublin**   ☎(01) 533423 or 532407 (two-hour guided walks)

# On-the-spot information

### PUBLIC HOLIDAYS
**New Year's Day**; **St Patrick's Day**, March 17; **Good Friday**; **Easter Monday**; **Whit** or **June Bank Holiday**, usually last weekend of May/first weekend in June; **August Holiday**, beginning of August (variable); **October Holiday** (**All Souls** or **Halloween**), last day of October or November 1; **Christmas**, December 25; **St Stephen's Day** (**Boxing Day**), December 26. If a bank holiday falls on a Sunday, the following Monday tends to be taken in lieu.

### TIME ZONES
Ireland follows Greenwich Mean Time (GMT) in winter and changes to European Summer Time (EST), one hour ahead of GMT, from the end of March to late October. In winter this puts Ireland 5 hours ahead of Eastern Standard Time and 6-8 hours ahead of other US time zones; in summer, add another hour's time difference.

### BANKS AND FOREIGN CURRENCY EXCHANGE
Banks are open 10am-12.30pm and 1.30-3pm. On Thursday they stay open until 5pm. The lunchtime closure is an anachronism that maddens everyone except the bank workers. However, more and more banks are now staying open during lunchtime.

Most banks have facilities for cashing travelers checks and exchanging currency. So too do the main travel service offices:

- **American Express Travel Service**   116 Grafton St., Dublin 2, map 4D4 ☎(01) 6772874
- **Thomas Cook** (main bureau)   118 Grafton St., Dublin 2, map 4D4 ☎(01) 6771721
- The **Foreign Exchange Counter** at Dublin Airport is open seven days a week: summer 6.45am-10pm; winter 7.30am-8.30pm

### OPENING HOURS
**Museums and galleries** are usually open from 10am-5pm or 6pm from Tuesday to Saturday, though the National Gallery is open 7 days a week. On Sundays, hours tend to be shorter, usually from 2-5pm.

**Shops** are mostly open Monday to Saturday from 9am-5.30pm. Some smaller city-center shops and speciality stores open on Sunday. Shops in the city center stay open until 8pm on Thursday, and some suburban shopping centers stay open until 9pm on Thursday and Friday. Many small grocery stores stay open daily until late.

## RUSH HOURS

Rush hours in Dublin are compounded by perpetual road repairs. Avoid even being on the streets between 8.15 and 9.30am and around 4.30 to 6.30pm, when the air gets very dirty from exhausts (unleaded gasoline is not much used in Dublin). It can take $1\frac{1}{2}$ hours to cover a distance of, say, 3 to 4 miles within the city at these times. All streets become congested, particularly at bridges — and there are many bridges in Dublin.

## POSTAL SERVICES

Most post offices are open from 9am-5.30pm Monday to Friday and 9am-1pm on Saturday. The **General Post Office** is at O'Connell St., map 4C4 ☎(01) 8728888. Postal charges to Britain are the same as within Ireland.

The **postal districts** in Dublin give a clue as to location. Odd postal numbers are N of the city and even numbers S of the river. The exceptions are Conyngham Rd., on the N side of the river on the way to Phoenix Park, and Aras an Uachtarain, in Phoenix Park itself, which are marked as being in Dublin 8.

## MAILING GIFTS FROM IRELAND

**To the United States:** Goods costing up to $50 at retail value in Ireland can be mailed home duty-free. You may send as many gifts as you like without affecting your personal allowance, but the addressee in the US will be required to pay duty if he/she receives gifts worth more than $50 in one day. Packages should be marked "Unsolicited gift" with the sender's name, the nature of the gift and its value marked clearly on the outside.

Note that perfumes containing alcohol, alcoholic beverages, cigars and cigarettes are subject to internal revenue tax and may not be included within this $50 retail-value gift privilege.

**To Canada:** The rules are similar to those for Americans, for goods costing up to $40. Packages should clearly state that contents are a personal gift. A number of gifts, each worth up to $40, individually wrapped and addressed to different people, may be included in one parcel.

Note that parcels may not contain advertising matter, tobacco or alcoholic beverages.

**To EC countries:** For goods sent by post which are not commercial in character and which do not exceed certain quantities for products such as perfumes, coffee and tea, there is a tax-free and duty-free allowance of up to 77 European Units of Account (equivalent approximately to IR£55).

**Further information:** If you require further details of mailing regulations and allowances, you should telephone your embassy (under "Diplomatic and Consular Missions" in the telephone directory) or inquire at any post office.

**Customs formalities:** Customs regulations change from time to time, so it may be as well to look on this section as a rough guide rather than cast-iron information. If you have any doubt at all about the goods you are sending back, check up in advance — it could save you a lot of trouble, money and embarrassment.

## TELEPHONE SERVICES

Telecom Eireann is the semi-state-owned telephone company. The telephone service was always notoriously poor in Ireland, bedeviled by busy lines and understaffed exchanges. But that has greatly changed and the service now operates, on the whole, to a degree of efficiency. A local call from a call box that is working costs 20p, although most boxes are being adapted to take charge cards, available at nearly all newsagents and convenience stores.

Most areas in Ireland can be dialed direct and the codes are listed in the front of the telephone directories. For **Directory Inquiries** ☎1190: there is a charge for each inquiry, but you can obtain up to three numbers on each call.

The code for **international calls** begins with **00** followed by the relevant code for the country. **Direct Dial** calls are charged at 85p per minute, or 60p per minute after 6pm and on weekends. (Prices may rise.) The code for the **International Operator** from a public phone is **114**.

- To call Ireland from mainland Britain, dial 010 353 + local code (minus the initial 0) + local number.
- To call mainland Britain from Ireland, dial 0044 + local code (minus the initial 0) + local number.

## NEW TELEPHONE CODES

Most Dublin (01) telephone numbers printed in this guide are 7-digit, but some of them will remain 6-digit until **April 24, 1993**. If you use this book before that date and need any help or information ☎**1-800-330-330** (freephone).

## PUBLIC LAVATORIES (REST ROOMS)

Dublin isn't famous for its sanitary arrangements. Most people nip into a pub if the need arises. The sign *Fir* means men, *Mna* means women.

## ELECTRIC CURRENT

220 volts is standard. Hotels usually have 220/110 voltage sockets for electric razors. If you need an adaptor, buy it before you leave home.

## LAWS AND REGULATIONS

In common with most capital cities, parking regulations are stringent in Dublin. There are meters in most major squares.

For years, the biggest discrepancy between Ireland and the rest of

Europe was the law on contraceptives. They could easily be bought or sold, but it was a furtive business. All that has changed, although Ireland is still morally sensitive about sex. You must not import books and magazines that could be deemed obscene.

In general, Ireland is a free and easy-going place: you can't tether a goat in St Stephen's Green, but you can roam unmolested over hills and countryside in a way that is well-nigh impossible in other countries.

## CUSTOMS AND ETIQUETTE
When invited to a private house for dinner at, say, 8pm for 8.30, you should arrive just before 8.30. At lunchtime you should be punctual.

The habit of kissing cheeks on meeting is not widespread among women in Dublin and is not practiced at all among men. If you are a man, do not attempt a Continental embrace with an Irishman. He will fall back ashen-faced. Even a handshake is an unbearable intimacy for most Irishmen unless they are in their cups together, in which case they twine themselves around each other like rugby players.

Do not talk loudly in churches or take photographs during services. Religion is important and private in Ireland.

There is great social interchange in everyday transactions — shopping, in banks, in restaurants. Irish people chat to one another and take their time. They respond more openly and in a more relaxed way to visitors than do the people in most capital cities. Respond back.

An absolute characteristic of the Irish is that they hate meanness, especially when it comes to hospitality. A most important part of etiquette in Ireland is how to behave in a pub or gathering. If you are in a group of people drinking together you must buy your round. Indeed, it is one of the reasons why people drink too much in Ireland; if each person in a group buys each of his or her companions a drink as their turn comes up, the drinks can pile up in front of you; so can your friends. If you don't go along with this then you drink alone. And a solitary drinker saddens an Irishman's heart.

## TIPS
The normal method of tipping, if service is not included, is to give between 10 and 15 percent of the total. Always tip doormen in hotels and the small men who look after parking meters in the squares. They expect at least IR£1. You don't tip in pubs, but you can offer the barman a drink.

## DISABLED TRAVELERS
There are two extremely helpful companies in Ireland, and any person with a disability seeking advice about and assistance with facilities should write in advance to them:
- The **National Rehabilitation Board (NRB)** *(write to: 25 Clyde Rd., Dublin 4* ☎ *(01) 6684181)* publishes an invaluable illustrated booklet, *Guide for Disabled Persons,* as well as an *Accommodation Guide for Disabled Persons.*
- The **Disability Federation of Ireland** *(write to: 2 Sandyford Office*

*Park, Dublin 18* ☎ *(01) 2959344)* can provide a list of all organizations in Ireland offering services for disabled people.

Other useful contact organizations are the **Mental Health Organization of Ireland** *(Mensane House, 6 Adelaide St.* ☎ *(01) 6765871)* and the **Union of Voluntary Organizations of the Handicapped** *(29 Eaton Sq., Monkstown* ☎ *(01) 6681855).*

## LANGUAGE
Most signs are in both languages so are self-explanatory, but it is useful to know that the sign *An Lar* on buses means City Center and that on public lavatories *Fir* means men and *Mna* means women.

## THE DAIL/IRISH PARLIAMENT
The Irish Parliament is officially called **Oireachtas Eireann** and is a two-chamber assembly with a Lower House: the **Dail** of 166 members voted for by the electorate of Ireland, and the **Seanad**, or Senate, of 60 members who represent various sectional interests. There are seven political parties represented in the Dail. There have been many distinguished senators — W.B. Yeats was one — but it was of this band of representatives in the old Irish Parliament that John Welsey cried, "Who will teach the Senators wisdom?"

The Dail may be visited on Tuesday, Wednesday and Thursday when the House is in session. Either write to a Member or obtain an admission card from the Superintendent of the House. When the House is not in session, visits can be arranged from the Kildare St. entrance *(map 4 E5).*

## THE OFFICE OF PUBLIC WORKS (OPW)
This is the government body entrusted with the conservation of nature and heritage in Ireland. It manages nature reserves, national monuments and national parks. The officers at its headquarters are most helpful, and the OPW produces fine, helpful booklets that are usually on sale at all its sites.

The OPW issues a Heritage Card giving unlimited admission for one year to all OPW sites. Charges are: adults IR£10, senior citizens (retirees) IR£7, students IR£4. The card may be bought at most sites.

Among the buildings and open spaces in the OPW's care are the Casino at Marino, Phoenix Park, St Mary's Abbey, Kilmainham Gaol and Pearse Museum (St Enda's). All these are described in SIGHTSEEING.

• **OPW**     51 St Stephen's Green, map 4E5 ☎(01) 6613111

## RESEARCHING IRISH ANCESTRY
While researching your own genealogy you will get a fine insight into Irish history as well as your own family background. There are good handbooks to start you on your search: *A Record Finder* edited by Donal F. Begley contains "Matheson's Special Report on Surnames" and therefore narrows down the groundwork.

To gain professional help, write to the **Association of Professional Genealogists** *(Genealogical Office, 2 Kildare St., Dublin 2).* Consultations are by appointment only.

## NEWSPAPERS

Most newsagents have nearly all editions of major UK dailies on sale, and most good hotels stock German, French, Italian and American newspapers. Foreign newspapers are available from **Bus Stop** (*52 Grafton St., map 4D4*), **Easons** (*40/42 Lower O'Connell St., map 4C4*), **Tuthills** (*Royal Hibernian Way, off Grafton St., map 4D5*) and many other newsagents.

There are three Irish morning papers and two evening papers. The best daily newspaper is *The Irish Times,* an international newspaper with good foreign coverage, arts reviews, fine columnists, and a gift for language. It also has a useful and comprehensive *Notices* section. Politically independent, *The Irish Times* is sometimes castigated as being self-regarding and holier than thou, but stands loftily above such criticism.

*The Irish Independent* is more Ireland-orientated, more nationalistic, with good local news and sports coverage. It tends to support the Fine Gael party, perhaps the more liberal of the two main political parties. It publishes an evening paper, *The Evening Herald,* and a Sunday edition.

The *Irish Press* has much coverage about Ireland and the North. Its roots are in Fianna Fail, the more right-wing of the two large parties. It publishes an evening paper, *The Evening Press,* and a Sunday edition.

## MAGAZINES

*What's On In Dublin* is published by Bord Failte (who also publish *Tourism News,* available free at all Tourist Information offices). There is a good street map of Dublin in *Tourism Dublin.* These publications give information about tourist attractions and buildings, reviews of restaurants and notices of special attractions. They are also well written.

*In Dublin* magazine comprehensively covers events and festivals, books, theater, jazz, film, and local media stories and personalities.

*Hot Press,* Dublin's answer to *Rolling Stone,* is witty and punchy, with comprehensive coverage of theatrical and music events, with especial emphasis on the music/rock scene.

*PHOENIX* is the Dublin satirical magazine. Nothing, fortunately, is sacred to its editors, and it is essential reading to get a different view of Dublin from the rosy one you may be getting as a delighted tourist. The Office of Public Works (OPW), for example, is designated the Office of Pillage and Wreckage, and Mrs Robinson, the Irish President and national hero, is addressed less than reverently as "Her Majesty."

*Dublin Event Guide* is a free listings newspaper with good coverage of all events. It appears every two weeks.

*Image* magazine is the best glossy monthly and consistently features the best in Irish fashion. *Social & Personal* is a monthly magazine featuring Irish personalities and fashion.

## RADIO AND TELEVISION

**Radio Telefis Eireann (RTE)**, the State Broadcasting Authority, broadcasts on two TV channels, **RTE 1** and **Network 2**, and three radio stations, **RTE Radio 1** (90.7 Mhz), the more serious channel; **RTE Radio 2 FM** (88.5 Mhz), geared to popular listening and younger music; and **FM3 Radio** (92 Mhz), short transmissions daily, mainly of classical music and programs of minority interest.

**Radio na Gaelteachta** is the Irish-language station.

The standard of radio broadcasting in Ireland is superb. Regular broadcasters such as Gay Byrne are national heroes, and most are articulate, funny and occasionally wise. The talk, both by professionals and by people ringing in, is often riveting, and the music on RTE Radio 1 and FM3 is splendid and well chosen. And the voices alone make the radio worth listening to.

The Network 2 TV channel broadcasts in the afternoon on sound only before the TV schedule opens.

*Lifestyle* is the name of the satellite channel available on **Cablelink TV** in Dublin.

# Useful addresses

### TOURIST INFORMATION
The **Irish Tourist Board** and **Dublin Tourism** are extremely helpful. The main office is in O'Connell St. It is worth going there to pick up pamphlets and information about current events in and around Dublin.
- **Irish Tourist Board (Bord Failte)**   Baggot St. Bridge, map 4F6 ☎(01) 6765871 🇫🇽(01) 6764764
- **Dublin Tourism**   14 Upper O'Connell St., map 4C4 ☎(01) 8747733 🇫🇽(01) 8786275
- **American Express Travel Service**   116 Grafton St., map 4D4 ☎(01) 6772874, a valuable source of information for any traveler in need of help, advice or emergency services

### AIRLINES
**Aer Lingus**   Flight information ☎(01) 7056705; reservations (Ireland and UK) ☎(01) 8444777, (Europe, North American and other destinations) ☎(01) 844747; for deaf callers ☎(01) 7053959
**British Midland**   Flight information ☎(01) 8422011 or (01) 6798733; reservations ☎(01) 2838833
**Ryanair**   Flight information ☎(01) 8427811; reservations ☎(01) 8444411

### FERRY COMPANIES
**B&I**   15 Westmoreland St., Dublin 2, map 4C4 ☎(01) 6778271 (ticket sales) ☎(01) 6606666 (24-hour information)
**Irish Ferries**   2/4 Merrion Row, Dublin 2, map 4E5 ☎(01) 6610511
**Sealink Stena Line**   The Pier, Dun Laoghaire, map 2D5 ☎(01) 2801905, or contact any travel agency

### DIPLOMATIC AND CONSULAR MISSIONS AND EMBASSIES
**Australia**   Fitzwilton House, Wilton Pl., Dublin 2, map 4F6 ☎(01) 6761517

**Belgium**   Shrewsbury House, Shrewsbury Rd., Dublin 4, map **1C3**
☎(01) 2692082 or 2691588
**Canada**   65 St Stephens Green, Dublin 2, map **4E5** ☎(01) 6781988
**Denmark**   121 St Stephens Green, Dublin 2, map **4E4** ☎(01)
4756404
**France**   36 Ailesbury Rd., Dublin 4, map **1D3** ☎(01) 2694777
**Germany**   31 Trimleston Ave., Booterstown, map **1D3** ☎(01)
2693011
**Greece**   1 Upper Pembroke Street, Dublin 2, map **4F5** ☎(01)
6767254
**Italy**   63 Northumberland Rd., Dublin 4, map **1C3** ☎(01) 6601744
**Japan**   22 Ailesbury Rd., Dublin 4, map **1D3** ☎(01) 2694244
**Netherlands**   160 Merrion Rd., Dublin 2, map **1D3** ☎(01) 2693444
**Spain**   17a Merlyn Park, Sandymount, Dublin 4, map **1C3** ☎(01)
2691640/2692597
**United Kingdom**   31 Merrion Rd., Dublin 4, map **1D3** ☎(01)
2695211
**United States of America**   42 Elgin Rd., Dublin 4, map **1C3** ☎(01)
6688777

**PLACES OF WORSHIP**
**Christchurch Cathedral** (Church of Ireland)   Edward Sq., map
**3D3** ☎(01) 6778099
**St Patrick's Cathedral** (Church of Ireland)   Patrick St., map **3E3**
☎(01) 4754817
**St Ann's** (Church of Ireland)   Dawson St., map **4D5** ☎(01) 2880663
**Pro-Cathedral** (Roman Catholic)   Marlborough St., map **4B4**
☎(01) 8745441
**University Church** (Roman Catholic)   87a St Stephen's Green, map
**4E4** ☎(01) 4780616/4751618
**St Teresa's** (Roman Catholic)   Clarendon St., off Grafton St., map
**4D4**
**Adelaide Road Synagogue**   37 Adelaide Rd., map **1C2** ☎(01)
6761734
**Buddhist Centre**   11 North Terrace, Inchicore, Dublin 8 ☎(01)
537427
**Church of Jesus Christ of Latter-Day Saints** (Mormon)   48
Bushey Park Rd., Terenure, Dublin 6 ☎(01) 905657
**Church of Christian Scientists**   21 Herbert Park, Dublin 4 ☎(01)
6683695
**Dublin Central Mission** (Methodist)   Abbey St., map **4C4** ☎(01)
8740691
**Mosque and Islamic Centre**   163 South Circular Rd., Dublin 8
☎(01) 533242
**Reading Room**   18 Grafton Arcade, map **4D4** ☎(01) 6716443
**Religious Society of Friends** (Quaker)   Morehampton Rd., Dublin
4 ☎(01) 668368
**Seventh Day Adventists**   47a Ranelagh Rd., Dublin 6 ☎(01)
974325

# Emergency information

**EMERGENCY SERVICES**
**Police**, **Ambulance**, **Fire** and **Coastguard**     ☎999 or 112 free of
charge on all pay and card phones.

**HOSPITALS**
**St Vincent's Hospital** *(Elm Park, Dublin 4* ☎ *(01) 2694533)* is situated on the Merrion Rd. about half a mile from Jury's Hotel. There are
public and private facilities and a casualty (emergency) department.
    The **Mater Hospital** *(Eccles St., Dublin 7, map 3 A3* ☎ *(01) 301122)*
is situated on the N of the city and has a private and public facility as well
as a casualty (emergency) department.

**LATE-NIGHT PHARMACIES**
**O'Connell Pharmacy** *(55 Lower O'Connell St., map 4 C4* ☎ *(01)*
*8730427)*, 100 yards N of the bridge, on the left, open until 10pm.

**DENTISTS**
**Irish Dental Association**     Richview, Clonskeagh Rd., Dublin 4
☎(01) 2830499.
**Dental Hospital**     20 Lincoln Pl., Dublin 2, map 4D5 ☎(01)
6794311. Training hospital for the Dental Department of Trinity
College. Daytime dental facilities.

**AUTOMOBILE ACCIDENTS**
* Do not admit liability or incriminate yourself.
* Ask any witnesses to stay and give a statement.
* Contact the police.
* Exchange names, addresses, car details and insurance companies'
  names and addresses with other driver(s).
* Give a statement to the police. Insurance companies will accept
  the police report as authoritative.

**CAR BREAKDOWNS**
Call one of the following from the nearest telephone:
* The nearest garage/breakdown service.
* The police, who will put you in touch with the above.
* The number you have been given if you rented the car.

**LOST PASSPORT**
Contact the police immediately, and your consulate (see pages 33-4)
for emergency travel documents.

**LOST TRAVELERS CHECKS**
Notify the local police at once, then follow the instructions provided
with your travelers checks, or contact the issuing company's nearest
office. Contact your consulate (see pages 33-4) or **American Express**
*(* ☎ *(01) 6772874)* if you are stranded with no money.

# Culture and history

## An Irish history

Dublin is more than a beautiful city; it is the capital of Ireland, and through Dublin has swirled Irish history leaving its marks and its impress at every turn.

In order to understand the meaning of Dublin or the people of Ireland, you need to know something about the history of a country which perhaps more than any other in Europe is the result of its history and the subject of dream and myth. Those who travel here bring with them their dream or idea of Ireland and they try to make their dream-template match what they see. But it is easier if you know what made the original template, the unseen life living below the surface. Thomas Davis the poet-rebel wrote:

*This country of ours is no sandbank, thrown up by some recent caprice of earth. It is an ancient land, honoured by the archives of civilisation, traceable into antiquity by its piety, its valour, and its sufferings . . . .*

History shivers through the atmosphere of Ireland. It is enshrined in Irish songs, ballads, stories and poems, as well as the buildings, ruins, artifacts and remains. Almost anywhere you stand, you can see the relics of its different eras, the sad and beautiful agenda of its past, the past that has such a hold on Irish people that it seems sometimes they can't let go.

For a country that lies at the heart of the imagination of the Western world, Ireland is a faraway place. Its history is puzzling, convoluted, heartbreaking. It is so extraordinary a history that it still bleeds through the texture of everyday life, faintly staining it all the time, underlying the dealings of many of its citizens.

Through all its vicissitudes no nation has kept such a fierce hold on its identity, insisted so passionately and jealously on the importance of its nationhood or kept so alive the hurt of its history. Arthur Young, the traveler and historian who made a tour of Ireland in 1776-78, wrote that the people "seemed not only tied to the country but almost to the parish in which their ancestors had lived," and he found, even as late as 1778, that the English language was spoken in only two places: in Dublin and in parts of Co. Wexford.

Yeats, that great poetic spokesman for the new nation of Ireland in the 1920s, wrote, "Cast your mind on other days / That we in coming times may be / Still the Indomitable Irishry . . . . " Yet Yeats was of the Ascendancy, a class that Louis MacNeice described as having "nothing but an insidious bonhomie, an obsolete bravado and a way with horses."

Despite or perhaps because of its sad past, Ireland remains, paradoxically, a relatively gentle place. Even in Northern Ireland, where old conflicts are still being resolved, the atmosphere nearly everywhere is one of tranquility and people are friendly beyond the dreams of cliché.

## PAGAN AND CELTIC IRELAND

For centuries before the coming of Christianity, Ireland lay on the outer edges of the Western world, geographically remote from the main currents of European life, its people living a culturally diverse and rich life. This period gave rise to the great sagas (see MYTH).

The dynasty that ruled Ireland had its capital at Tara, the most potent and evocative site in Ireland. Sheep roam across this high, empty, sad place now, with its trenches and the barely discernible outlines of its buildings lying under the sward. There was a thriving European Celtic culture, apparent from the many artifacts and stones found in Ireland decorated in what was known as the La Tène style, named after the site of a 19thC excavation in Switzerland.

The La Tène style became merged with the decoration of the Vikings, and the fusion brought the elaborate intertwined schemes of Irish medieval art so beautifully realized in the *Book of Kells* in Trinity (see DAY 1, page 113), and the magnificent gold workings of the Ardagh chalice and the Tara brooch (although it has nothing to do with Tara), two of Ireland's greatest national treasures (see NATIONAL MUSEUM, page 73).

Ireland was a country, rich in gold, besides being fertile and mild, and successive waves of invaders bore down upon it. But over and over again these invaders became so thoroughly absorbed that they became more Irish than the Irish themselves, each influx enriching the native culture. (Incidentally, gold has been rediscovered recently in working on the sacred site of the mountain of Croagh Patrick.)

In the **4th or 5thC BC** the Celts arrived, perhaps from the Caspian region, and the basic elements of their artistic conceptions, their originality, refinement and style underlie every page of Irish culture like a visible watermark. The full flowering of Irish art, the fusion of the Celtic heritage and Christianity, reached its apogee in the 7th and 8thC.

## THE CHRISTIAN GOLDEN AGE

Before the coming of Christianity, the Irish had evolved from a loose congery of tribal kingdoms into a heptarchy with semi-independent rulers and then into four provinces, Ulster, Connaught, Munster and Leinster, with each of their kings acknowledging the ultimate authority of the High King of Tara. Each had a complex and sophisticated social and legal system, known as the *Brehon laws,* which regulated most aspects of life.

Ireland was never conquered by the Romans. Indeed, the Irish raided the Roman settlements in England and brought home captives, among whom it is said was the shepherd boy who became St Patrick, the central symbol of Irish Christianity and patron saint of Ireland. He is reputed to have explained the theological mystery of the Trinity by using the analogy of a shamrock, and the little three-leaved plant has, in its turn, become a symbol for Ireland.

With the arrival of Saint Patrick opens a golden age, the one that most informs that vein of memory and nostalgia that pulses throughout Ireland. The early Christian period lasted from the **5th** to the **12thC**.

St Patrick showed his determination to conquer the Ireland of the spirit by lighting a Pascal fire on Slane hill at Easter in **432**, thus pre-empting the Sacred Fire at Tara, which it was the King's sole prerogative to kindle. The country quickly and peacefully capitulated to Christianity. Some scholars hold that St Patrick is not one but two men, Palladius and Patrick the Briton, but this is not a theory that holds much water in popular mythology. Patrick *the Briton?* Also St Patrick is no longer, officially, a saint: but this slur is ignored.

From that symbolic fire on Tara, still a place of pilgrimage, though now it is a lonely site grazed by sheep, blazed a light that illuminated Europe through the Dark Ages. Ireland sent out so many inspired monks and teachers that it became known as the Land of Saints and Scholars, and produced the first flowering of medieval art.

All over Europe, towns and monastic establishments bearing the names of Irish saints and monks testify to their influence, and they are reputed to have gone as far afield as America. Fired by piety and veneration, fueled by an earnest desire to cast light into darkness, the Irish monks laid the cornerstone of Western culture and established a tradition of the love of learning that obtains in Ireland to this day. G.K. Chesterton described their quest as "missionaries in the very midnight of the Dark Ages, like a multitude of moving candles, that were the light of the world."

Patrick Pearse, one of the heroes of the 1916 Irish Uprising, wrote that had the Renaissance been based upon early Irish literature, the Western world would have been inspired by a more noble, more humane, more heroic, and a gentler tradition than that of the Greek and Latin classics. There may be truth in the theory, though anyone who has read the *Annals of the Four Masters* or the great sagas of Ireland (see MYTH) would perhaps question its gentleness.

## THE VIKINGS

When the Vikings invaded Ireland in the **9th and 10thC**, they destroyed peace and magnificence in centuries of sad and often bloody history. From this period date the famous round towers — of which there are more than 70 — found near many monastic and ecclesiastical sites and built first as campaniles, but later used as refuges and strongholds against the Vikings. They destroyed the monasteries and plundered the libraries, not, as is popularly believed, simply as wanton destruction but to appease the Scandinavian gods and to make "cures" for diseases.

The Vikings have always been viewed as a disruptive and destructive force in Ireland, partly because they plundered the monasteries and churches: it was in the monasteries that the annals were written. (In one little note scribbled on the edge of a manuscript he was illustrating, an 8thC monk wrote, "The wind is rough tonight, tossing the white hair of the ocean; I do not fear the fierce Vikings coursing the Irish sea.")

Recently historians have advanced the view that the Vikings were a positive stimulus. They founded the first towns of Ireland — Dublin, Waterford, Wexford and Limerick — and the Scandinavian influence can be seen in Irish artifacts after the **12thC**. On the other hand, many Irish treasures are to be seen in Scandinavian museums, and the Vikings didn't ask could they borrow them.

In **1014** Brian Boru (Brian of the Tributes), the king of Munster, pushed the Danes back to the coast at Clontarf, N of the Liffey, and though he was mortally wounded, he won a victory that marked the end of their domination. The memory of the Viking invaders is curiously vivid in the memory bank of the Irish, who seem to have total recall of things that happened centuries back as though they happened yesterday.

One Irish writer observed that "the Irish mind hops back to the flood when discussing a leaking tap," and Eilis Dillon, a member of one of the distinguished Catholic Nationalist dynasties of 19th and 20thC Ireland, once witnessed a man being ejected from a pub in Dublin after a fight with a Danish tourist. "We drowned them in the Tolka in 1014," he was screaming, and sure enough when she researched her history she discovered that the Irish did indeed drown the Danes in the little Tolka, a tidal stream on the N of the city. And a folklorist, James Delaney, relates how some years ago he visited a storyteller in Cork who, when he heard Delaney's name said, "Ah, it was you and your crowd that attacked Brian Boru's army on the way back from Clontarf."

**THE ANGLO-NORMANS**

In the **12thC** an army of Anglo-Norman knights from England (invited by an Irish chieftain to fight his battles) captured Waterford, Wexford and Dublin, and their king, Henry II, assumed the Lordship of Ireland, deposing Rory O'Connor. From this time dates the English involvement in Ireland, and if Ireland suffered from the invasion then it was not wholly one-sided. (A Venetian Ambassador termed Ireland "the Englishman's grave.")

The Anglo-Normans (known as the Old English) succumbed, like their predecessors, to the spell of the country, and by the 14thC had been assimilated into Irishness. Many of the most resonant names in Irish history stem from that invasion, including the Fitzgeralds, Barrys, Carews, and the Ormonde, Butler and Desmond families.

This period was responsible for the innumerable cathedrals, castles, monasteries and fortified houses, whose ruins punctuate the landscape of Ireland as their building did its history. The authority of the Crown was by now established in and around Dublin and a small surrounding area known as "the obedient shires" and later as The Pale, a frail settlement, disconnected with its Celtic hinterland. It seethed away waiting for chances for rebellion, which when they came were inevitably fractured by internecine rivalry.

## THE TRIBAL AND BARDIC TRADITIONS

It is germane to the history of Dublin and Cork that the native Irish or Gaels never lived in towns. They were a tribal people moving through their own lands, meeting up at central gathering places and palaces, each tribe with its own great prince and traditions. There was an Irish proverb, "A land without a lord is a dead land"; and today the names of those tribes are still carried by the people who live in their original districts. The fact that each chieftain was king of his province is perhaps one of the most obvious reasons for Ireland's troubles. One historian, Paul Johnson, writes, "The English presence in Ireland arose from the failure of the Irish society to develop the institution of monarchy."

One of the treasured traditions throughout the centuries was that poets and bards were an important part of each princely establishment. They moved from princely house to house singing and composing and carrying news as they traveled. It behoved the lords to give good hospitality: if they did not, they might well be cruelly satirized in verse. One 17thC poet composed this little tribute:

> *A shrewish, barren, bony, nosy servant*
> *Refused me when my throat was parched in crisis.*
> *May a phantom fly her starving over the sea*
> *The bloodless midget that wouldn't attend my thirst . . . .*
> *A rusty little boiling with a musicless mouth*
> *She hurled me out with insult through the porch.*
> *The Law requires I gloss over her pedigree —*
> *But little the harm if she bore a cat to a ghost . . . .*

One of the very last of the great Court poets, Egan O'Rahilly, had to turn for shelter to a man he regarded as an intruder and betrayer, the Viscount Kenmare, Valentine Brown. He ended his moving lament for the dispossessed Irish nobility on a note of defiant despair:

> *Two old grey eyes that weep: great verse that lacks renown,*
> *Have made me travel to seek you, Valentine Browne.*

Each district had its own bardic school. They continued, in a hidden and underground way, as the Courts of Poetry until the 18th and 19thC. But true Gaelic Ireland always lay beyond the city walls, hidden from the administrators and from the new law-makers. The Gaels were pagan in the original sense of the word: dwellers of the *pagus,* or heath, moving across the hills and the woods with their own codes and mores and especially their own laws of hospitality, which prevail at some levels to this day.

> *Rich in cattle, reckless in the hunt, prompt to donate gold and jewels*
> *from their coffers to the Church, proud, rancorous, independent,*
> *recalcitrant, amorous, lustful, devout, superstitious, hospitable,*
> *loving fighting and loving poetry, the Irish chiefs lived roughly, an*
> *outdoor life, disdainful of alien manners and fashion, not so much*

*resistant to change as inconsiderate of it. Habitually the chief, his family and cohorts dined al fresco despite the inclement climate, sometimes under a bower of rushes, using a table and benches made of ferns; at night they slept on rushes on the ground. Consequently for them campaign life was little different from home life, and they took to the woods and hills with ease when necessary, to wage guerilla warfare.*

(From *The Irish World,* edited by Brian de Breffny, 1977)

## THE STATUTES OF KILKENNY

In **1366** the English had contrived enough power to be able to summon a parliament and to pass the Statutes of Kilkenny. This series of laws ushered in one of those painful periods of suppression and repression which are the only constant in Irish history and which have so haunted posterity. They were a rehearsal for the Penal Laws of 300 years later; and perhaps for the English they seemed the only defense against the curious way in which Ireland seemed to spirit its invaders into its soul.

The Statutes deprived the "mere Irish" of all rights other than those accorded them by English law. Conscious of the way in which Ireland seemed to seduce colonists into becoming wholly Irish, laws were passed forbidding colonists to speak Irish, to Gaelicize their names, to entertain Irish bards, to marry with the Irish, or "to play with great clubs at ball upon the ground from which great evils and maims have arisen" (hurling or hurly, the national game, in other words).

More significantly, every chief in every province had to sign a formal agreement with the Crown whereby he could hold no forces without the consent of the Lord Deputy. Most important, he had to surrender his lands to the English Crown to receive them back to be held by knight service. It was a stroke of masterly deviousness, since it nullified fundamental Gaelic laws under which a chief ruled only for his lifetime and there was no law of primogeniture.

These statutes legalized the concept of the Pale and carried within themselves all the seeds of its future, of futility and failure. They made wider the gap between the English and the Irish, which time and time again could have been closed.

Lytton Strachey's description of the foray into the Irish interior by the Elizabethan Lord Essex, the Lord Deputy, sums it up:

*The strange air engulfed him. The strange land, charming, savage, mythical, lured him on with indulgent ease. He moved, triumphant, through a new peculiar universe of the unimagined and the unreal. Who or what were these people with their mantles and their nakedness, their long locks of hair hanging over their faces, their wild battle cries and gruesome wailings, their kernes and their gallowglas? Who were these people with their ancestors? Scythians? Spaniards? Gauls? What state of society was this, where ragged women lay all day long laughing in the hedgerows, where wizards flew on whirlwinds and rats were rhymed into dissolution? All was*

41

*vague, contradictory and unaccountable; and the Lord Deputy, advancing forth and further into the green wilderness, began, like so many others before and after him, to catch the surrounding infection, to lose the solid sense of things and to grow confused over what was fancy and what was fact.*

In the years following the passing of the malignant Kilkenny statutes, many chiefs rebelled, most notably Art MacMurrough Cavanagh (still known throughout native Ireland as King of Leinster), who from **1394** drove the Anglo-Irish back and closed in on their territory. But before he could consolidate his gains, he was poisoned and died in **1417**.

The fighting and unrest continued sporadically, and to try to bring English law and order into the country a statute of Henry VI, passed in **1429**, provided £10 to every liege-man in Dublin, Meath, Kildare and Louth (the area of the Pale) who would build a fortified castle "to wit 20 feet in length 16 feet in width and 14 feet in height or more." The ruins of these Ten Pound Castles, as they were known, still stud the countryside like shafts pinning a shield to the ground. Limerick had over 400, Cork 325 and Tipperary nearly 300.

## TUDOR STRIFE

The political state of Ireland remained in a ferment throughout the **15th and 16thC**. A report submitted to Henry VIII in **1515** spoke of "more than 60 countryes, called regyons In Ireland, inhabytyd with the Kinges Irishe Enymyes."

The Fitzgerald Earls of Kildare rose to power in the Pale, and Garret More, the Great Earl, was made Lord Deputy in the name of the English king, if only as a way of constraining him. These Geraldine earls were so powerful in the area of the Pale — which stretched from Dundalk in the north to Dalkey in the south and into the Leinster hinterland as far as Kells and Naas and the bridge of Kilcullen — that they were kings in all but name. (Much later they were raised to Dukes of Leinster.)

The Earls of Desmond, another branch of the Fitzgerald family, ruled over a virtual palatinate of half a million acres in Munster. Between these two territories lay another great palatinate, that of the Butlers, earls of Ormonde, who controlled what is now Co. Kilkenny and Co. Tipperary. The rest of Ireland was still in the hands of the chieftains and their clans. The ruined banqueting halls in their ancestral castles still testify to the grandeur and power of the Fitzgeralds, the Ormondes and the Desmonds.

When Henry VII ascended to the throne of England in **1485** his new deputy Sir Edward Poynings summoned another parliament and passed yet another set of anti-Irish laws. These became even more punitive when Henry VIII succeeded to the throne of England in **1509**.

Rebellion broke out, led by Thomas Lord Offaly, the son and heir to the Earl of Kildare, who was the acting Lord Deputy in the absence of his father. Called Silken Thomas (the reasons for the name vary: some say it was after the fringes on his followers' helmets, others, for his dandified appearance and love of fine clothes), he was led to believe that his father had been executed in London, and at a State Council meeting he threw his sword on the table and mounted a rebellion. He was tricked into submission by the promise of a pardon, which Henry VIII then violated. With five of his uncles, he was hanged, drawn and quartered.

The plantation policies of Queen Mary (**1553-58**) were bitter in the extreme. She colonized the counties of Leix and Offaly, naming them Queen's County and King's Country respectively (today they bear their old names again). The few Irish chieftains still left in the country fought back like "furies of hell with flakes of fire on poles." The English invited them to a peace conference, massacred them and hanged their wives and children. The survivors who took to the hills again to wage guerilla war came to be known as Tories from the Irish *toraidhe,* meaning a pursuer.

Queen Elizabeth succeeded to the English throne in **1558** and continued the policy of subdual by force. The connection between the English throne and some of the greater Earls was close — Anne Boleyn's father was of Ormonde or Butler stock, and Queen Elizabeth playfully referred to Thomas, tenth Earl of Ormonde (who was more or less king of Munster), as "my great black husband." When Queen Elizabeth I laughed it was time to take notice, and Tom, instead of losing his head, sent her that of his greatest rival the Earl of Desmond's "pickled in a pipkin."

The Queen extended the plantation policies to Ulster and Munster. In Ulster she gave a huge estate, almost the whole of Co. Antrim, to the Earl of Essex, who set about subduing the province. In Munster, Lord Deputy Grey, acting on a speculation of his secretary Edmund Spenser (he of the ravishingly poetic epic *The Faerie Queen*), who hated and despised the native Irish, that the Irish problem might be solved if a short end were made to all of them, tried out a scorched earth policy with considerable success against those who defied the plantation clearings.

Spenser used his gift for language to deliver one of the most chilling descriptions ever written of the survivors, if one can call them that. "Out of every corner of the woods and glens they came, creeping forth upon their hands, for their legs would not carry them. They looked like anatomies of Death; they spake like ghosts crying out of their graves." Scenes, alas, that would be re-enacted nearly 300 years later during the Great Famine.

Throughout the **late 16thC** the Irish fought on. Essex tendered for peace with Brian O'Neill, his chief opponent, and arranged a banquet at which the O'Neill household was slaughtered, "two hundred men, women, youths and maidens," and O'Neill and his wife were publicly executed as traitors. Over and over again the native Irish were dispossessed, tricked and massacred in their own country, and over and over again they fought back.

In **1595** the Gaelic Chieftains O'Neill and O'Donnell, who were also Ulster Earls, rebelled. Hugh O'Donnell, Earl Of Tyrconnell, whose bravery and that of his indomitable force of Kernes was legendary, and the extraordinary Hugh O'Neill, Earl of Tyrone, who had been educated at the court of Queen Elizabeth, won a famous victory at the Battle of the Yellow Ford.

But in **1601**, hopelessly outnumbered, despite help from Spanish troops, O'Neill was defeated at the Battle of Kinsale and made submission to Elizabeth I on March 30, **1603**, not knowing that she had died six days before. The Earls with their followers went into exile to the continent of Europe, leaving Ireland leaderless at a turning point in her history. From this catastrophe, known as the Flight of the Earls, in **1603**, begins modern Irish history.

## CROMWELL'S JUDGMENT

Ireland was a devastated country. Ulster was a desert, Munster a ruination, Connaught barren, and the descriptions of starvation and cannibalism are painful to read. "When plough and breeding of cattle shall cease then will the rebellion end" was the strategy. James I, newly crowned in **1603** as King of England, Wales and now Scotland, allocated the best land in Ulster to Scottish settlers, thus creating the beginnings of the problems in the North today.

When Cromwell came to Ireland he began his campaign with an episode deeply and painfully engraved on the Irish national psyche: the sack of Drogheda on the night of September 11, **1649**.

Thomas Wood, one of Cromwell's soldiers, recounted what happened to his brother Anthony, an antiquarian, who wrote the account down. One tiny incident Thomas recalled was:

> . . . *when they were to make their way up to the lofts and galleries of the church, and up to the tower where the enemy had fled, each of the assailants would take up a child and use it as a buckler of defense, when they ascended the steps, to keep themselves from being shot or brain'd. After they had killed all in the church, they went into the vaults underneath, where all the flower and choicest of the women and ladies had hid themselves. One of these, a most handsome virgin and array'd in costly apparel, kneel'd down to Tho. Wood with tears and prayers to save her life: and being strucken with a profound pity, he took her under his arm, went with her out of the church, with the intention to put her over the works and let her shift for herself; but then a soldier perceiving his intentions, ran a sword up her belly or fundament. Whereupon Mr Wood seeing her gasping, took away her money, jewels, etc., and flung her down over the works.*

Cromwell justified his appalling slaughter as "a divine judgement." He ravaged Cork as well, and by the end of the Cromwellian wars, some 600,000 Irish had been massacred, starved, driven to Connaught or deported to the West Indies to be sold as slaves. Scholars, craftsmen, poets and teachers were hanged, schools destroyed, books burned and Irish learning made impossible, and even more of the native Irish were dispossessed.

"To Hell of Connaught" was Cromwell's policy. Connaught is the most beautiful province in Ireland, but it is cripplingly barren. The rich acres of Ireland were given to settlers of all kinds and classes. While the native Irish got poorer, their spirit seems to have been indomitable, and though poverty is hard to bear, insults and injustices have always been the hardest punishment for the Irish psyche. One of the bardic poets, Owen Roe O'Sullivan, Eoghan of the Sweet Mouth, a man who epitomized the plight of the dispossessed Irish, once wrote:

> *Tis not the poverty I most detest*
> *Nor being down for ever*
> *But the insult that follows it*
> *Which no leeches can cure.*

Many of the dispossessed Irish stayed near their lost homes, haunting them. Some became legendary figures, some the equivalent of Robin Hood — like Edmund O'Ryan, a famous Tipperary outlaw whose "confiscated lands and forfeited life fired him to the resolution of heading a band of robbers and committing many acts of desperation, which were frequently counteracted by a generosity almost romantic or performed with a spirit truly heroic." He was the subject of one of the most popular of all Irish ballads, *Ned of the Hill,* originally a love song, but Ned the outlaw came to symbolize Ireland itself.

## THE LAND PIRATES

As had so often happened before, the settlers began to think of themselves as Irish, though the Irish themselves did not concur. England was still the settlers' mother country even if Ireland was their native land; and it was English manners, mores and modes (albeit idiosyncratic versions) that prevailed. But in many respects the two ways of life were so closely linked that, as they later found, to tear one from the other was to rend both to pieces.

From their banishment among the hungry rocks of Connemara and the poor wastes of rich counties, or as tenants of the land pirates (now their landlords) who owned thousands of acres that once were their own, the Irish watched and waited and paid service, lip and otherwise. What was noticeable to visitors was that, in the midst of such privations, good manners and hospitality were universal:

> *The neighbour or the stranger finds every man's door open, and to walk in without ceremony at meal time and partake of his bowl of potatoes, a stool is offered or a stone is rolled that your honour may sit down . . . and those that beg everywhere else seem desirous to exercise hospitality in their own houses.*

Indeed, until the Famine, peasants in mud cabins would make wills bequeathing estates that had long ago been confiscated from their forefathers; and that figure of fun in cartoons in *Punch,* the Irish beggar, Paddy, who claimed to be descended from kings, was often speaking the truth. "I am descended from as good a family as any I address, though now destitute of means," runs a letter in the Distress Papers to a workhouse, and it was true of many such destitutes.

The writer, Elizabeth Bowen, whose ancestors had been granted the dispossessed land of the Curtins in Co. Cork, wrote at the end of her life,

"The stretches of the past I have to cover have been on the whole painful. My family got their position and drew their power from a situation that shows an inherent wrong. In the grip of that situation England and Ireland each turned to the other a closed harsh distorted face, a face their lovers would hardly know."

What always struck disinterested observers was the huge gulf between the rulers and the ruled in Ireland, the enormous chasm between the classes. Laws that had long been banished in England as being too hard on the poor — such as the hearth tax repealed in **1689** — obtained in Ireland until the end of the 18thC. Arthur Young, that reliable historian, wrote tellingly:

> *A landlord in Ireland can scarcely invent an order which a servant, labourer or cotter dares to refuse to execute. Nothing satisfies him but an unlimited submission. Disrespect or anything tending towards sauciness he may punish with his cane or his horsewhip with the most perfect security; a poor man would have his bones broke if he offered to lift his hand in his own defense. Knocking-down is spoken of in this country in a manner which makes an Englishman stare . . . By what policy the government of England can for so many years have permitted such an absurd system to be matured in Ireland is beyond the power of plain sense to discover.*

In their security the Ascendancy began to build the great houses that became such jewels in the Irish landscape, the Big Houses, those enclaves of peace and beauty and isolation, and devised for themselves lives that were so thoroughly enjoyable "that they generally became beggared in a few years' time by dint of hospitality and inadvertence."

"To entertain their neighbours and be entertained, by drinking and field sports," wrote the 20thC historian J.C. Beckett, "was almost the sum total of their activities and probably formed a fair index of their notions of social responsibility and public duty."

The cripplingly poor people who lived on the land suffered privations, but as the Cork writer and teacher Daniel Corkery (whose book *The Hidden Ireland* about the bardic poets of Cork and the Southwest is romantic, revelatory and condemnatory of the Ascendancy) wrote of this time, "the Irish had not yet learnt to emigrate."

The heart, destitute, was a good anchor. So the mass of the Irish stayed, living where they might, for the most part in vile poverty, without books, without art, without houses, with no chance of education. A whole history of a might-have-been Ireland was irrevocably lost, and all the potential and all the backlog of learning that Ireland might now enjoy was unrealized. Occasionally a poet springs out from the shadows of the time, a remnant of the Bardic schools, and in their poems we realize what we lost.

## THE BOYNE AND ITS AFTERMATH

The Irish by now were being governed by people who "measured law by lust and conscience by commodity," according to one observer.

However, when James II ascended to the English throne in **1685**, the Irish gained some hope for a better future. And in due course, in **1688**, when the English throne was offered jointly to Mary, the Protestant daughter of James, and her Dutch husband, William of Orange, the Irish fought for James. At the Battle of the Boyne, in **1690**, James, due, it must be said, in great measure to his own cowardice, was defeated:

Soon Dublin was full of the shattered and agonized army. James, in his flight, is reputed to have met Lady Tyrconnel, wife of the head of the Talbot family, who had lost 14 of her family fighting for him, and said to her, "Your countrymen, madam, can run well"; to which she replied, "Not so well as your majesty, for I see you have won the race."

James fled to France, but the real casualty in the battle was what was left of Gaelic culture and order and the old Catholic aristocracy.

The look of Ireland changed during the **17thC** too, and what had been a wooded and spectacularly beautiful country was ravaged by the plundering of the forests. The French traveler De Beaumont wrote, "It is now almost destitute of trees; and when, on a fine day in spring, it appears though bare full of sap and youth, it seems like a lovely girl deprived of her hair."

Youghal, near Cork, for example, actually means "oak place," but the great woods that had sheltered the Gael in every century were ruthlessly chopped. Timber was sold at sixpence a tree, and the Valentine Brown, Lord Kenmare, so despised by the poets, cut down £20,000 worth of trees on a single estate. The Irish and their poets lamented the loss of their woods:

> *What shall we henceforth do without timber?*
> *The last of the woods is fallen.*

The felled woods were seen everywhere, and the countryside was speckled with ruins: broken abbeys, "roofless churches, battered castles, burnt houses, deserted villages from which the inhabitants were being cleared to make room for beasts; and these ruins were still raw, gaping, sun bleached — not yet shrouded in ivy, nor weathered to quiet bones."

James' army was reorganized and given new morale by Patrick Sarsfield, created Earl of Lucan, one of Ireland's most beloved heroes, although contemporary accounts suggest that though he was very beautiful he was not very bright. (The portrait of him in the National Gallery shows a wonderfully effeminate beauty, but he was all the same a marvelously dashing and brave hero and leader.) His password *Sarsfield is the name and Sarsfield is the man* still rings through the history.

His resistance forced William to make terms at Limerick, including a guarantee of religious freedom and the restoration of Irish rights, and as part of the treaty 14,000 soldiers of the Irish arms left for Europe from Cork in **1691** in what is known as the Flight of the Wild Geese. They formed the Irish brigades of the French army, fighting against — and sometimes with — the English for a hundred years and more, earning a reputation for great bravery. (Sarsfield was killed in battle in Europe at Landen in 1693.)

## THE PENAL LAWS

But the English parliament repudiated the treaty, and, instead of the promised rights, the Irish got the degrading Penal Laws in **1704**, which forced the mass of the Irish into the poverty that so aroused the righteous indignation of Dean Swift, champion of the Irish poor. "The gentry" he wrote, "rack their tenants to such a degree that there is not one farmer in a hundred through the kingdom who can afford shoes or stockings to his children, or to eat flesh or drink anything better than sour milk or water, twice in a year."

His most famous comment was his satirical pamphlet published in **1729**, *A modest Proposal for Preventing the children of Poor People from being a Burden to their Parents,* in which he suggested that the babies should be boiled and eaten, thus killing, as it were, two problems with one stone. George Berkeley, his younger contemporary, had published in the **1730s** his book *Queries,* asking questions about Ireland, including "whether there be upon the earth any Christian or civilised people so beggarly wretched and destitute as the common Irish?"

Edmund Burke, aged 19 and while still at Trinity, produced a magazine, *The Reformer,* in which he wrote after traveling outside Dublin:

> . . . *as for their food it is notorious they seldom taste Bread or Meat; their diet, in Summer is Potatoes and sour Milk; in Winter when something is required Comfortable, they are still worse, living on the same Root made palatable only by a little Salt, and accompanied with Water; their Cloaths so ragged that they rather publish than conceal the Wretchedness it was meant to hide . . . .*

There was never any shortage of good people appalled by what was happening and ready to record it. But there was also no shortage of those prepared to prevent any alleviation, lest it wrench power from the Ascendancy, which Burke defined as "nothing more or less than the resolution of one set of people to consider themselves as the sole citizens of the commonwealth and to keep a dominion over the rest, reducing then to slavery under a foreign power." Burke is one of the heroes of Ireland and relatively unsung. Of him, Dr. Johnson said, "You could not be in a shed with him, sheltering from the rain, for ten minutes without becoming aware that he was a great man."

In the years that followed, more than a million people emigrated to North America. In the American War of Independence (**1775-83**), over 30 of Washington's generals were of Irish descent.

Though they had no legal rights and were not allowed to attend places of learning, the Irish cultivated their oral gifts, and those brilliant traditional skills of storytelling and language that remain with them, and are commonly supposed to be genetic. They also formed a network of secret armies with one objective — the unshackling of Ireland from England.

In **1783** the Irish parliament was formed in Dublin, partly through the passionate eloquence of Henry Grattan, a Member of Parliament for the city of Dublin and a champion of great energy, who stood for patriotism and the cause of Catholic relief. Professor Roy Foster has described him thus: "the unparalleled Henry Grattan, barrister, polemicist, failed poet and opera fanatic, [who] also produced the ultimate in florid rhetoric and cleverly never undertook any duties more pragmatic than oratory."

## THE 1790s

In **1791** a new generation of rebels arose led by a Kildare lawyer, Theobald Wolfe Tone, who was neither Catholic nor Protestant but a Deist, Henry Joy McCracken, and other liberal-minded Protestants. Fired by the French Revolution, they tried to organize a Society of United Irishmen in which those of every religious persuasion might come together to establish a social order based on civil, political and religious liberty.

Frightened by the prospect of such a unified Ireland, the English government hastily repealed some of the Penal Laws. But even such concessions sparked bitter reprisals from secret Protestant organizations such as the Peep O'Day boys, and there was a revival of the Orange Order in which the most fanatical of Protestants banded together in lodges and, supported by the government, began a reign of terror.

There are horrible stories told of those days, and still remembered in lore. To obtain information from captured rebels, a sergeant known as Tom the Devil invented the "pitch cap," a mixture of pitch and gunpowder which was rubbed into the victim's head and then set alight. One of the United Irishmen was Lord Edward Fitzgerald, son of the Duke of Leinster, who wore his hair in a ribbon and had devised for himself a uniform of a bottle-green braided suit with crimson cape, cuffs, silk lace, and a cap of liberty; he was informed upon and was surprised at a meeting by Major Sim but fought to the death. Sir Jonah Barrington described how he saw the bodies of the rebel dead piled in the Lower Yard of Dublin Castle, "the most frightful spectacle that ever disgraced a royal residence . . . ."

Wolfe Tone had gone to France to seek aid against England, but as the first French fleet drew near to the Irish coast in **1796** it was scattered by a series of freak storms ("The Protestant Wind"). The second flotilla arrived too late. By then the United Irishmen had risen and been defeated, and its leaders were executed or died in prison.

Wolfe Tone, that charming, humorous, attractive hero whom the people loved so (though not the Catholic bishops), was captured wearing the uniform of a French colonel with blue coat and pantaloons, heavy gold epaulettes and a tricolor cockade. He asked to be tried as a soldier, but the court refused, condemning him to be hanged as a common felon. He said, "I wish not for mercy . . . The favourite object of my life has been the independence of my country and to that object I have made every sacrifice."

There are various versions of his terrible death, including the theory that his throat was cut by his jailers, but it is generally thought that he tried to commit suicide rather than face the ignominy of being hanged, and severed his windpipe mistaking it for the artery. He died after a week of suffering. "I would have sewn his neck up and finished the business," one of the Ascendancy softies, a certain Sir George Hill, declaimed in public. It is easy to see where Swift got his ammunition from. (Brendan Behan called Tone the greatest Irishman ever borne, and, with good cause; he is held in the highest esteem as the archetypal Irish hero.)

## THE FASHIONABLE 1790s

All the same, at this time a greater spirit of religious tolerance prevailed, and Dublin reached the peak of its importance with a thriving social and mercantile life. It also became architecturally one of the most beautiful cities in Europe, built in the Classical idiom, but with the imaginative verve that so informs it to this day.

In the **1790s**, there were a hundred peers living in the capital, in addition to countless lesser gentry. The rich and powerful peers built great mansions, the middling peers occupied elegant terrace houses like those in Merrion Square, and the professional classes lived in the new speculative buildings being put up all over the city. From this era dates Dublin's appearance, until recently one of the glories of Europe.

Fashionable Dublin was a witty, corrupt, optimistic, cosmopolitan, gamey city, riddled with snobberies and peopled by dandies who cared little for the rest of the country and its condition.

Dublin's heyday lasted a very few years, until the Dissolution of the Irish Parliament and the infamous Act of Union in **1801**, which brought the country under London's direct rule. Yet if those years left behind in Dublin a legacy of sadness and banishment, it also left a legacy of beauty, untampered with until recently. All commercial development stopped. With political power gone, the city slowly moldered and fell into an economic decline that created the worst slums in Europe.

## THE UNION

Ireland suffered under the new government, convened after the Act of Union. It had been contrived by despicable means, chicanery, corruption, bribery and larceny on a grand scale. Grattan said of it, "To find a worse government you must go to Hell for your policies and Bedlam for your methods." Grattan was a famous orator who used his way with words to sway a nation, but he could not stem the tide of corruption that bought a country into subjection. The Lords Castlereagh and Clare organized the sell-out.

Some £50,000 was paid out directly, mainly in bribes. There was direct compensation for parliamentary seats and suppressed offices (peers received hand-outs totaling £1.26 million), and there were a large number of peers created to load the vote against the anti-Unionists. Making his last speech in **1800** to the Irish Parliament, after the Act of Union reduced his dreams of a thriving semi-autonomous Ireland to ruins, Grattan at his most unctuous said, "Yet I do not give up my country: I see her in a swoon but she is not dead; although in her touch she lies helpless and motionless, still on her lips is the spirit of life and on her cheeks the glow of beauty."

It so happened that Thomas de Quincey was visiting Dublin just at this time and went to the House of Lords, where he witnessed the historic and terrible moment when the Act of Union became Law. Lord Castlereagh, so violently anti-Irish, had been the chief architect.

*Gradually the house filled: beautiful women sat intermingled amongst the peers . . . . Then were summoned to the bar — sum-*

*moned for the last time — the gentlemen of the House of Commons;
in the van of whom, and drawing all eyes upon himself, stood Lord
Castlereagh . . . .*

*At which point in the order of succession came the Royal Assent
to the Union Bill, I cannot distinctly recollect. But one thing I do
recollect — that no audible expression, no buzz, nor murmur, nor
susurrus even, testified the feelings which, doubtless, lay rankling
in many bosoms.*

*Setting apart all public or patriotic considerations, even then I
said to myself, as I surveyed the whole assembly of peers, 'How is it,
and by what unaccountable magic, that William Pitt can have
prevailed on all these hereditary legislators and heads of patrician
houses to renounce so easily with nothing worth the name of a
struggle, and no reward worth the name of an indemnification,
the very brightest jewel in their coronets? This morning they all rose
from their couches Peers of Parliament, individual pillars of the
realm, indispensable parties to every law that could pass. Tomor-
row they will be nobody — men of straw — terrae filii.*

*'What madness has persuaded them to part with their birth
right, and to cashier themselves and their children forever into
mere titular Lords?'*

The sorry state of Irish affairs provoked another rising, in **1803**, this
time led by the disorganized but passionate patriot young Robert Emmet.
It failed miserably — indeed it hardly happened. But there was nothing
miserable about Emmet, who remains almost the most loved of all great
national heroes.

**THE LIBERATOR**
For the next 20 years many influential figures tried without success to
get some form of Catholic emancipation passed by the British Parliament. Then from Derrynane in Cork rose "the Liberator," a member of
a landowning family, Daniel O'Connell, who became the champion of
the Irish Catholics. He was the first Irishman to see that nationalist
objectives could only be obtained through organizing the Catholics
into a potent civil force in a legal mass campaign.

A man of massive energy, principle, conceit, sex appeal and charm
(when asked who was the greatest Irishman, he replied, "Why, after me I
suppose old Harry Grattan was"), he was determined to keep within the
law in the fight for the rights of his people; and he differs from other Irish
patriots in that he would not fight to the death. "Irish freedom was not
worth the shedding of a single drop of Irish blood." He had been to school
in France, had seen at first hand the horrors and excesses of the French
Revolutionary Army, and wanted never to see more blood spilled.

O'Connell united the rural Irish and by manipulating and conserving
their meager resources turned them into a powerful force. In **1823** he
formed the Catholic Association representing tenant farmers, who paid
a subscription of a penny a month (the "Catholic Rent"). With the money
amassed from all over Ireland, he was able to finance organizing the

Catholic vote. In **1826** his candidate, a Liberal protestant, defeated the landlord's candidate, Lord Beresford, by a huge, shocking margin.

O'Connell himself was elected in **1828** by a similar margin, and the Prime Minister of the time, the Duke of Wellington (who had been born in Dublin), passed the Emancipation Bill in **1829** seeking to avoid the civil war that he thought must ensue were the Catholics yet again to be put down by force. For the first time, Irish Catholics could go to Westminster.

O'Connell began similar agitation for a repeal of the Act of Union and the restoration of "The old house in College Green" (the Irish Parliament). He organized what *The Times* called "monster" meetings, where he spoke to 250,000 people at a time, most memorably on the hill of Tara. But before the biggest meeting, due to be held at Clontarf, he backed down from the threat of violent clashes with the government, who had sent their forces out seeking a confrontation. He was arrested and his power from then on waned. The forthcoming Great Famine was in any case such a catastrophe that it transformed political life. O'Connell died of the plague on a ship on his way to Genoa, and when his body was brought back to Dublin, Ireland seemed physically to rock with grief.

John Mitchell, a nationalist associated with the Young Ireland movement of the 1840s, who was transported to Australia (he later escaped), wrote an epitaph that must rank as one of the most ambivalent elegies of all time:

*Poor old Don! Wonderful, mighty, jovial and mean old man! With silver tongue and smile of witchery and heart of melting truth. Lying tongue, smile of treachery, heart of unfathomable grand! What a royal yet vulgar soul!*

## THE GREAT FAMINE

There was an uneasy truce in the country. Thackeray, who visited Ireland in **1842** and was very rude about it, wrote, "I wonder who *does* understand the place? Not the natives certainly, for the two parties so hate each other that neither can view the simplest proceedings of the other without disrupting, falsifying and abusing it."

In **1845** the first of the devastating potato blights struck Ireland. There had always been isolated areas of famine, but Trollope, for example, who worked as an Inspector of Postal Service, wrote that, "It never struck me there was much distress in those days. The earth gave forth its potatoes freely and neither pig nor man wanted more." But this new blight was widespread. It was first noted in a garden near Cork: *Phylophthora infestans*. Terrible years of famine followed hard on one another.

The famine was a blow from which Ireland psychologically has only just recovered. Every day corn was exported in tons and cattle in droves, but nothing was done to divert this free-enterprise trade to help the starving population. The famine was the greatest disaster of its kind to befall a European nation in a time of peace. At least one million people died and another million emigrated, often sailing in coffin ships where they died in horrible conditions.

By the turn of the century the population had dropped from 8 million to $4\frac{1}{2}$ million, although this should not wholly be blamed on the famine. All over Europe, **1848** was a year of insurrection, and a militant movement of romantic nationalists of both religions, known as Young Ireland, made a futile rebellion under William Smith O'Brien, a Protestant landlord of old Irish lineage. It was wholly defeated and the movement collapsed, but its ideal of the union of the "orange" and the "green" in a sovereign nation gave Ireland its national tricolor flag.

Many hundreds of thousands of the emigrants carried with them a lasting bitterness and anger at what they had left behind and how they had to flee their country. By **1858** the Irish Catholics in North America had organized themselves into the Fenian Brotherhood, called after the *Fianna,* the army of the legendary Irish hero Finn MacCool (see MYTH). Fenianism became a powerful force in both Ireland and the United States.

Rebellion and force might be one way to liberalism, but Home Rule and the activities of the Land League were the political preoccupations of the next generation of Irishmen and Englishmen concerned with Ireland's fate. Ireland, as Marco Polo once said of China, is a sea that salts all rivers that run into it.

## HOME RULE

Charles Parnell, an Irish Member for Parliament and a Protestant landlord, an extraordinarily complex and rather charmless man, led the demand for Home Rule and the activities of the Land League. By **1890**, at last, it seemed that Ireland would get Home Rule. But Lord Frederick Cavendish and T.F Burke the Under-Secretary were murdered in Phoenix Park by two members of The Invincibles, a small secret organization, and the cause was set back. It was further damaged by Parnell's involvement with Kitty O'Shea and her subsequent scandalous divorce case. Parnell was cited as co-respondent, which caused many of the Irish to withdraw their support.

The indomitable Gladstone forced the Home Rule bill through the House of Commons in **1893**, but it was defeated in the House of Lords and had to wait nearly 20 years until it was passed in the Commons again. In the intervening years the House of Lords had its powers curtailed and there was every chance the bill would become law; but in Ireland the Unionists led by Edward Carson resisted with violence and threats, and the Ulster Volunteers were formed. The Irish Republican Brotherhood, which had been formed after the Fenian Uprising of **1867** and which had, in the years between, become a powerful secret organization, opposed Carson and his followers by launching the Irish Volunteers.

One month after the outbreak of the World War I in September **1914**, the Home Rule bill finally became law but, through political chicanery, was suspended for the duration of the war. If it had gone through, the future sad history of division in Ireland might have been averted.

## IRISH REVIVAL

All this time alongside the political turmoil another kind of revolution — a cultural renaissance — was taking place. The famine had weakened the Gaelic language, and now the Irish Revivalist Society began to encourage a pride in Gaelic legends, poetry and tradition.

There was a sudden upsurge of interest in all things ancient and Gaelic, which in turn led to an interest among certain members of the Ascendancy in Irish folklore, the idea of the revival of the Gaelic language, and the concept of the Celtic Twilight. Michael Mac Liammoir wrote, "To Yeats . . . the supreme moment of Ireland was revealed at the hour of twilight, and its mood, that hovers between day and night, between light and dark, between, in so many familiar cases, sobriety and intoxication, is at the heart of Ireland's being." It also led to the foundation of the Abbey Theatre (originally called the Irish Literary Theatre), whose leading lights were Lady Gregory, W.B. Yeats and Edward Martyn (see DUBLIN'S THEATRICAL HERITAGE, page 75).

Even during the worst of times in the 19thC, a thriving and parallel life was being led in Ireland — that attractive social life organized by and exclusive to the Anglo-Irish. Among so much that is extraordinary about Ireland is this perpetual Janus-faced culture and life: patriots and poets could be nationalist and Protestant, long for the Gaelic revival but speak English (it was Shaw who said that English was the native language of Irishmen), and be famous as Irishmen, but be counted as English in the pantheon of English literature. And for centuries the two classes, or as some might say, the two races, the Anglo-Irish and the Irish, each considered themselves to be living the "real" life of Ireland in which the other played bit parts.

Stephen Gwynne, an ardent Irish nationalist born in a rectory and certainly a member of the Ascendancy, who considered himself to be Irish to the backbone, wrote, "The new nationalism describes me and the likes of me as Anglo-Irish. So all my life I have been spiritually hyphenated without knowing it."

For the gentry, the native Irish supplied the local color and the local labor. For the Irish, the Anglo-Irish were still intruders, their erstwhile masters, there by default, and remaining only on sufferance.

There was loyalty, but only of a kind. The conquered Celt has never been straightforward in his dealings with those who consider themselves to be socially superior. This attitude is perhaps best summed up in David Thompson's great book *Woodbrook* in which he speaks about the servants of a real Irish house in the early 20thC: "They secretly cherished hatred for the major, their present landlord and employer, whom in day to day relationships they loved; cherished this hatred because of his ancestors and theirs and because it might help their advancement." What in truth was anathema to most of the native Irish was that the class that had endowed them with a sense of social inferiority and, as they believed, taken their land should also claim the same national identity, yet despise it in its purest form.

## THE RISING
One of the most dramatic acts in the Irish drama — or tragedy — began on Easter Monday, April 24, **1916**, when the Irish Volunteers and the Citizens Army, 2,000 in all, led by Patrick Pearse, a half-English

poet, barrister, teacher and idealist, seized 14 strategic buildings in the center of Dublin and proclaimed an Irish Republic. The other leader was James Connolly, the founder of Irish socialism. They took over the General Post Office in O'Connell Street (then called Sackville Street) and made it their headquarters, simply by walking in and ordering the staff and customers out. Pearse read out the Proclamation of Independence, calling on all Irish men and women to fight for their freedom. At first no one believed what was happening, but over six days there was bitter street fighting between the rebels and 20,000 British troops. By the end, 64 Irish soldiers had died and 134 police and British soldiers were dead, many buildings were in ruins and the Rising, which was in fact deeply unpopular, had been quelled.

It might have been no more than another of the abortive attempts that litter the pages of Irish history had not the British executed 15 of the leaders. Connolly, wounded and fatally ill, was placed in a chair to be executed; another was married in the prison chapel and was executed 12 hours later. Yet another, Eamonn De Valera, was reprieved because he was an American citizen, and later went on to become leader of the Irish Republic. (It is typical of something that he was educated at Trinity.)

The executions made martyrs of the leaders, outraged the Irish and fanned their long-suppressed and smoldering anger and pain into a full-scale movement, which led to secession, and this, in one horrible twist of fate, led to a brutal Civil War.

In the general election of **1919** an overwhelming number of Republican and Home Rulers were returned to Parliament, including Constance Gore-Booth, one of the two beautiful sisters at the heart of the Literary Revival, both of whom had inspired Yeats. As Countess Marciewicz, she was the first woman ever to be elected to Parliament (not Nancy Astor as is popularly believed). The British government would not recognize Dail Eireann, the new Irish Parliament, and to quell the country brought over a temporary security force known as the Black and Tans (because of their black and khaki uniforms). They speedily superseded in outrageous acts all the vicious mercenaries who had ever been imported to quell the Irish.

## CIVIL WAR

In **1921** a Partition Act was passed, permitting the six counties of Northern Ireland to opt out of a treaty that established the independence of the rest of Ireland. In **1922** a disastrous year-long civil war broke out in the South, between those who were prepared to support a treaty signed by de Valera (who was to become leader of the Irish Republic) with the British government and those who repudiated it.

As many as 200 of the 2,000 good country houses occupied at the beginning of the Troubles were burned. The ruins are beautiful and haunting. Ireland, after the Treaty and for many years after, might be likened to China in the throes of the Cultural Revolution save that the killing was finished. The way of life that loomed ahead had no place in it for gracious living, or at least not until everyday existence got back to what it had never been — normal.

The burning of their houses was an enormous shock to the Anglo-

Irish, who believed themselves to be Irish and also believed that they commanded the loyalty of those around them. They deceived themselves.

If now it seems an act of vandalism that such beautiful monuments should have been put to the torch, one must remember that to the mass of the Irish whose forebears had been dispossessed to make way for the great demesnes over which these houses presided, where their owners lived "at the end of long avenues far away from one's fellow creatures," they were more than just great buildings. It was not easy simply to perceive them as beautiful artifacts and ornaments to the countryside. They were symbols of the establishment, more like Residencies than residences, and as such, when the smoldering resentments of centuries flamed into the open, they became targets for the flame in every sense. And the simile of the Residency can be carried further, since the English government regarded the Irish uprising as mutiny and executed nearly all its leaders.

(Yet it has to be said that many more great houses of Ireland — what should have been part of the national treasury — have been lost through neglect, greed and stupidity since 1922 than were ever burned.)

In **1923**, after deep wounds had been inflicted on both sides and with the loss of some of the finest leaders, including the pro-treaty leader Michael Collins, the Irish Free State came into being. In **1937** De Valera drew up a new constitution for Ireland which declared Ireland a republic.

## A SEAT AMONG NATIONS

Since **1923** Ireland has not had an altogether happy history. The narrow-mindedness and repressive attitudes of many of the new leaders made the new republic for years an oppressive provincial place.

De Valera became a *shaman* for many of the Irish, and his attitude and vision, however awry and idealistic, is perhaps best summed up in a famous speech he made in **1943** in which he saw Ireland as "a land whose countryside would be bright with cosy homesteads . . . the romping of sturdy children . . . and the laughter of comely maidens." Ireland at the time was on its knees. (Incidentally, De Valera, who was tall, gaunt and ascetic, was described by the Dublin wit, Oliver St John Gogarty, as looking like something "uncoiled from the *Book of Kells.*")

But Ireland has taken her seat among nations, and the last 30 years have seen a flowering of talent among poets, painters, musicians and writers, which guarantee her identity. The new president Mary Robinson, who keeps a light always burning night and day in a top-floor window to show concern and continuing thought for Irish emigrants, is a symbol of the new Ireland, emerging and free. It has been a long incubation.

# Myth

*For Ireland is abroad, a country of greetings but of hundreds of years of goodbyes. You begin to think that your large early Victorian room in Dublin has only three walls to it; and that where the fourth wall should be, there is rain, air, space, whispering and the chaos of myth . . . .*

(V. S. Pritchett, *Dublin: A Portrait*)

There is a parallel history to Ireland that in a sense has as much veracity as the chronological one; it shivers through the atmosphere of Ireland, lies at its nationalistic heartland and has had a potent influence in the shaping of Irish spiritual and cultural life. This history is a mosaic composed of oral legends, of tales of the Other World, mysteries and myths, sagas and annals, showing that the Irish poetic imagination has a history going back thousands of years, a coiling lifeline into the legendary and mythological past.

The telling and retelling and indeed the making of myth and legend comes from an energy that discovers itself as vision and is often the inspiration for great art.

In earlier times Ireland had not four but five provinces (indeed the Irish word for *province* means five), and this vanished province is often used as a poetic metaphor, as indeed is so much of this mythological history. It also reminds of a time when Ireland had an underworld and upperworld, although contrary to most mythologies the people of the Irish underworld were benign, although if crossed they could be destructive. From this springs the belief in the **shidhe** (the fairies) who play such a part in that magical world implicit in Irish country customs and belief. The **Banshee** (the white ghost) was much believed in as a wailing herald of death until well into the 20thC. (It was also the name of *The Journal of Irishwomen United*, an early feminist magazine in which Irishmen refused to believe.)

## THE EPIC SAGAS

All over Ireland the names of places and of men and women are linked to the scenes of epic dramas and encounters, battles and momentous happenings, as well as the names of gods and heroes and heroines: **Maeve**, the queen of Connaught; **Aengus**, the love-god, son of the **Dagda** (signifying *good god*) who was leader of the **Tuatha de Danann**; the Hound of Ulster, **Cuchulain**, greatest of the heroes of Irish legend, and **Setanta**, his real name (which connects him with the Setantii, a British tribe); and **Deirdre**, supreme in beauty, the Helen of Troy of Ireland, whose tragic history is one of the three Sorrowful Tales of Ireland.

Irish mythology, complicated by its very nature and intricacies, is made more so because it was transmitted by the clergy, who modified and transmuted it to make it more acceptable to their creed.

The series and cycles that relate the prehistory of Ireland form one of the great heroic traditions of European literature and are interlinked with it, many of the gods and goddesses and their functions being paralleled in other sagas. In Ireland the sagas were kept alive, first through the tradition of bardic story-telling, then by medieval monks' scholarship, then almost by stealth through the years of official proscription. So they passed in memory and in script from generation to generation until once again they became part of the official heritage of the country.

Among the most potent of the bardic sagas was the **Tuatha de Danann** (the Tribe of Dana), about an ancient race of gods who inhabited Ireland in pre-Celtic times. This is one of the great mythologies of Ireland and predates Christianity by thousands of years, but in the intervening centuries, as Christianity became so powerful in Ireland, the ancient gods of the Tuatha de Danann were downgraded from the status of gods to that of members of a prehistoric race.

The sons of Mil, known as Milesians, or Gaels, who wrested Ireland from the Tuatha de Danaan, became the permanent inhabitants of Ireland. The Tuatha de emigrated to that ever-present but invisible other world beyond human time, reached by certain entrances in the world: the *sid* or fairy mounds, often surrounded by thorn trees, which were also associated with magic. (Until very recently no farmer would plow up or cut down a fairy thorn tree and would not disturb a *sid*.) And until the present day there was a belief in charms, or cures, which were handed down from one member of a family to another and were secret. One never paid for a charm to be used but gave a gift. One love charm went:

> . . . *the charm Mary put on the butter is the charm for love and lasting affection. May your body not cease to pay me attention, may your love follow my face as the cow follows her calf from today till the day I die.*

The great epics of the Milesians fall into three cycles: the **Ulster Cycle**, which contains the **Tain bo Cualnge** (The Cattle Raid at Cooley), concerning the heroic Cuchulain who plays the same role in the Irish myth as Siegfried in the German or Achilles in the Greek epic; the **Fenian Cycle**, which deals with **Fionn MacCumhaill**, one of the greatest warriors and captain of the legendary race the **Fianna**; and the **Cycle of the Kings**, which contains a hard core of historical truth.

### THE TALES OF OISIN

The story goes that **St Patrick**, at the end of his mission when he had converted Ireland to Christianity, bade **Oisin**, last of the Fenian warriors and son of **Fionn MacCumhaill**, to relate the old tales, of feats and heroes, stories of hunting over mountains and plains, of fabulous creatures and glorious battles, and chivalry, betrayal and death.

Oisin had just spent 300 years in **Tir na Nog**, the land of youth, and when he returned had found the world changed unutterably and Fionn MacCumhaill's great white mansion on the Hill of Allen crumbled into a series of grass-covered mounds. (Oisin's odyssey is significant. From the very beginnings of memory in Ireland it seems as if the Irish must emigrate to the land of dreams knowing that when they get there the land of dreams is the one they have left behind. Certainly there seems, for a nation so rooted in its past, to be an addiction to restlessness.) Of Fionn MacCumhaill, the author of the 12thC *Colloquy of Old Men* wrote:

> *He left no women without bride-price and he left no servant without his fair due, and he left no man without his wages, and he promised nothing at night which he would not fulfil in the day and nothing in the day which he would not fulfil in the night.*

**Brogan**, Patrick's annalist, transcribed the tales as Oisin poured them out, in a threnodic stream of imagist prose and poetry, and Patrick listened to the old history of the country he had so transformed into another life. The old story was of heroes and gods; the new one was to be one of saints and scholars. Patrick, listening to these stirring and poetic epics, took fright at the pleasure he gained from listening and thought to destroy them. Happily for us he was reassured by his guardian angel, who directed him to allow the sagas to be recorded, that they might delight the people of Ireland till eternity arrived. Certainly they delight, but they also confuse.

This pious and poetic explanation would account for the way in which mythology and magic is mixed with Christian piety, and from this mingling of myth, religion and actual events over the following centuries came the cycles and legends as we know them today.

Monks, scribes and annalists continued to record the legends. As each century passed more legends were added to the store — legends of Patrick's follower **Brigid** (she is a great saint in the Irish pantheon, but the original Brigid was a powerful pagan goddess, daughter of the Dagda, and kept the perpetual flame burning); parables about **Columba**, one of the greatest of the Irish saints, who founded the great monastery of Iona (see DAY 1, page 104); and stories of Vikings, raiders and heroes, monks and monasteries.

And there were the intensities of such stories as the **Children of Lir**, one of the most powerful of stepmother stories, a work of enduring genius, which vaults the pagan and Christian ages, borne aloft by symbolism. In this compressed elegiac tale of four children turned into swans for 900 years, who are changed back into humans by the bells of Christianity, lies a history of the Irish race, its complexity, ambiguities, yearnings and wanderings.

As you walk though Dublin and its environs you will see many monuments and sculptures depicting these creatures of myth and faith. In the General Post Office in O'Connell St. there is a monument to Cuchulain; in the Garden of Remembrance in Parnell Sq., the Children of Lir at the moment of metamorphosis rise out of a fountain. Once every seven years the **Earl Gerald** (who had been given the secrets of the black arts and could change himself into any creature he chose, but was trapped in the form of a goldfinch) returns to earth as a man and rides around the Curragh of Kildare on a steed whose silver shoes are half an inch thick; when these shoes are worn as thin as a cat's ear he will be restored to fight Ireland's battles.

On the Hill of Allen, crowned by the ramparts and ring fort of Fionn's stronghold, are still to be seen, on a moonlit night, **Bran** and **Sceolan**, his two favorite hounds, running through the heather whining with impatience for the vanished hunt. Wherever the name Bull appears in a place name, all over Ireland, it was there that the **Brown Bull of Cooley** and the **White-Horned Bull of Connacht** fought their epic contest.

## THE FOUR MASTERS

By the beginning of the 17thC, the old traditions were being systematically destroyed and the old fabric began to tear and decay and was in danger of perishing. The defeat of the old Irish at the Battle of Kinsale in 1601 and the subsequent Flight of the Earls were catastrophic for the national aristocratic order, which by its intricate system of patronage had encouraged poetry, music, and the retelling of sagas and legends.

Then in a brilliant show of ecclesiastical scholarship and massive antiquarian research, the **Four Masters**, monks from Donegal, began in 1627 to assemble manuscripts and annals, compiling them into an extraordinary and valuable record, *The Annals of the Four Masters,* one of the greatest manuscripts in the canon of Irish literature. (The original is in the Royal Irish Academy Library in Dawson Street — see page 103).

In roughly the same era, **Geoffrey Keating**, a priest, historian and poet, began to collect and collate the history of his island and its past from any source he could find, to produce the seminal *Basis of Knowledge about Ireland.*

After the national calamity of Kinsale, certain people, in communities denied books and learning, memorized whole stories and became the "memory-man" for their districts, as did the official story-tellers, the *seanachies,* a kind of shaman. The tradition obtains to this day, and you can hear the *seanachies* at any *feis* at fairs and festivals; contact **Culturlann na hEireann** (Irish Cultural Institute), Belgrave Sq., Monkstown ☎(01) 2800295 for details.

## THE CELTIC TWILIGHT

Toward the end of the 19thC, the era of the revival of interest in all things Gaelic, that passion for magic, goblins and ghosts which Yeats characterized as the Celtic Twilight, led writers and researchers to travel to the most remote parts of the country gleaning stories and songs. There is a wonderful story concerning **Standish O'Grady**, one of the first of the Gaelic revivalists, listening and transcribing at the elbow of an old man scything in the fields, who was reciting, in courtly language, an epic poem of chivalrous love dating from a thousand years before — a poem that he had never read and indeed may never have been written down, but, minted in his voice, was as fresh as the day the great court poet had composed it. Such discoveries reopened the long perspectives.

Myth is a retaining structure for the spirit of a nation. In music, in rock, in poetry, in prose, in drama, the mythologies of Ireland are a rich reservoir for poets, painters and musicians. (They are, too, for chancers who want to give an instant whiff of Olde Ireland to their projects —

witness shopping centers called after the ancient gods, or the Cuchulain Coffee Bar.) But at their best, the Irish legends still yield new images, which shine like opals in the different lights of time.

The legends and myths of Ireland are constantly being added to as new heroes emerge; each poet, each hero shapes an individual myth. One remarkable recent example is the story of **Michael Mac Liammoir**, actor, writer and founder of the Gate Theatre (see DUBLIN'S THEATRICAL HERITAGE, page 75), a man revered as a great if eccentric archetypal Irishman.

In the given and accepted legend he was the Cork-born son of parents who had emigrated to England but had returned to his native country, there to enrich it immeasurably. In what people took to be his thinly disguised autobiography *Enter a Goldfish,* that story seemed to be wholly underwritten. But in a new biography it transpired that this man, more Irish than the Irish in his devotion to and fanatical pride to the country, was born Alfred Lee Wilmore in Willesden, North London, and had no links with Ireland until he founded the Gate Theatre in 1928. (Of course, for certain people the story will be a verification of the mythic thing called an Irishman, since Mac Liammoir was a homosexual and one other powerful Irish legend is that there are no gay men in Ireland.) His story is a wonderful metaphor for Ireland in which enduring myth, legend, poetry and fierce belief merge into something that tells a truth independent of each separate fantastical element.

It is worth reading one of the many good books on Irish sagas or a translation of *The Tain* to appreciate the symbolism of Irish life. Even so whimsical a concept as the wee folk or leprechauns and fairy mounds *(sid)* comes straight from the idea of the race who were banished to the underworld by the Gaels and who continued to live in great beauty and style in their own underworld kingdom.

There are many versions and explanations of all the sagas, which, as one commentator puts it, "provide Ireland with a mythological prehistory, a kind of genealogical charter for all the dynasties and tribes of Ireland. The material, then, is rich; what it means is another matter."

For an inspired look at how myth and the folk tales of Ireland can be used imaginatively, hilariously and passionately, you could do no better than to read **Flann O'Brien's** great masterpiece *At Swim-Two-Birds* (1939). The narrator is a young Dublin student who takes the reader on an unforgettable journey through Irish mythology. And most of all, read Irish poetry.

> *This is our fate; eight hundred years' disaster,*
> *crazily tangled as the* Book of Kells:
> *the dream's distortion and the land's division,*
> *the midnight raiders and the prison cells.*
> *Yet like Lir's children banished to the waters*
> *our hearts still listen for the landward bells . . . .*
> *(An Irishman in Coventry* by John Hewitt)

# Irish art

## Fine arts

### ARTISTS' GROUPS AND SOCIETIES

The Irish are not the best at working in groups — especially not Irish artists and writers. They are too touchy and fiercely individualistic. But when they do get together for a common purpose they have an uncommon vision and energy.

Among the most influential of the artistic groups formed this century were and are the following.

### ROSC

The name ROSC means "poetry of vision" and was chosen to embody the ideals for the series of exhibitions held at four-yearly intervals in Dublin at different exhibition halls. It was founded in 1967 for the purpose of showing substantial group exhibitions of important contemporary art from around the world. An international selection committee chooses work by a group of artists which they consider to represent the most significant trends of the moment. The next exhibition is in 1995.

### Irish Exhibition of Living Art (IELA)

This influential society was founded in 1943 as a reaction to the conservatism of the Irish art establishment of that time. It ceased to hold exhibitions in the 1980s, when the cultural climate had sufficiently changed to render them redundant — exactly as the founders would have wished. Founding members included **Evie Hone**, **Mainie Jellett**, **Norah McGuinness** and **Louis Le Brocquy**, among the finest artists Ireland has produced this century.

### The Great Book of Ireland

In 1991 the idea of the *Great Book of Ireland* was conceived as a way of raising money to help literary projects and to build a **National Poetry Centre** in Temple Bar. Initially 120 artists and 140 poets were commissioned to make contributions directly onto the huge vellum pages, bound between elm boards taken from a tree planted by Yeats at his tower in the w of Ireland, Thor Ballylee. The finished and remarkable artifact is both an anthology and an exhibition and is for sale for IR£1.2 million. It is hoped that one day it might be shown next to the *Book of Kells* in the Library at Trinity.

## IRISH ARTISTS
### Harry Clarke (1889-1931)
The great stained-glass artist and one of Ireland's finest 20thC artists died when he was only 41 years old. Clarke's work, at first glance, seems derivative but is transfigured by his singular, passionate spirit and blazing, fanatic energy. His windows are a mixture of Aubrey Beardsley decadence and Rimbaud-inspired symbolism, Celtic motifs and Art Deco, holy innocence and fantasy, fused into a remarkable unity. They are to be seen in churches in and around Dublin and all over Ireland. (Ask the Irish Tourist Board for information.) Most accessible of all are his ravishing windows in Bewley's Oriental Café in Grafton St.

His illuminated volumes of the Roll of Honour of men killed in the 1914-18 war is in the **National War Memorial** at Islandbridge (see DAY 3, page 159). Some wonderful examples of Clarke's work can also be found at **Belcamp College** in Darndale (see EXCURSIONS, page 250).

### Paul Henry (1876-1958)
A landscape and figurative painter born in Belfast, who studied in Belfast and Paris, Paul Henry became one of the most famous Irish modern artists. He worked in Paris and London, and settled in Achill Island, Co. Mayo in 1912. His paintings of the west of Ireland, the people, the horses, the mountains and sea and bogs, and particularly of the western Irish sky, have become definitions of the landscape. His wife **Grace Henry** (1868-1953) was a fine painter whose work is in many public collections.

### Evie Hone (1894-1935)
One of the family of famous Irish artists, the painter and stained-glass designer studied with Mainie Jellett in Paris, where she was much influenced by Georges Rouault. She later worked at *An Tur Gloine* (see page 53). Her most famous work is the huge *Crucifixion* and *Last Supper* stained-glass window for Eton College Chapel, England (1949).

### Nathaniel Hone the Elder (1718-84)
Nathaniel Hone was one of the earliest of the famous dynastic Dublin family of artists. He worked in London where he was a founder member of the Royal Academy (in 1768) and became a successful and fashionable painter. But he quarreled with and left the Royal Academy. He seems to have understood and certainly painted children beautifully, and the portrait of his son playing the flute is one of the most popular in the **National Gallery**.

### Nathaniel Hone the Younger (1831-1917)
The landscape painter, born in Dublin, was related to Nathaniel Hone the Elder. He left Dublin, where he was a successful engineer, in 1854 and went to Paris to study painting. He moved to Barbizon, in the forest of Fontainebleau, where he became friends with the great French artists of his time, including Corot, who greatly influenced him.

His paintings are warm, often of rural subjects, sunlight and shadow on fields and woods.

### Mainie Jellett (1897-1944)

Born in Dublin, Mainie Jellett, like so many Irish artists of the first decades of the 20thC, attended the Metropolitan School of Art in the city. She studied in Paris under André Lhote and became the foremost Irish proponent of abstract and Cubist art. She was a wonderful colorist with a brilliant and inventive sense of style and design and became the first Chairman of the IELA (Irish Exhibition of Living Art — see page 44) in 1943. Her paintings can be seen in the **National Gallery** and the **Hugh Lane Municipal Gallery of Modern Art**, and her work is much sought after by collectors.

### Sean Keating (1889-1978)

The Limerick-born landscape and figurative painter expressed in his vivid and realistic paintings a romantic vision of heroic Ireland and the spirit of nationalistic fervor, and became almost the official artist of the new Irish Free State. An academic painter of the school of heroic realism, he focused on national rather than international themes. In his work, Irishmen and women are portrayed as noble in adversity, and he took an idealized and sentimental view of the poverty that crippled Ireland. His best-known work, *Men of the West,* is in the **Hugh Lane Municipal Gallery**.

### Oisin Kelly (1915-81)

A sculptor, born in Dublin, who worked in Germany and England, he spent two years working under Henry Moore at Chelsea Polytechnic before becoming a teacher at St Columba's Rathfarnham, where he taught for many years. He designed for the Kilkenny Design Workshop and was commissioned to make many sculptures for religious and civic sites. Many of his large monuments are in Dublin and Cork.

### Louis Le Brocquy (1916- )

In the 1950s and '60s an expressive semi-abstract mode of painting emerged in Ireland. Painter, designer and graphic artist Louis Le Brocquy is the foremost painter working in this idiom, painting abstract poetic interpretations of nature and people. His portraits, in their prismatic, fractured beauty, reveal the essence of the sitter. He was one of the founders of IELA and has often represented Ireland at exhibitions abroad, including the Venice Biennale. Since 1958 he has lived in France and there began his most famous series, the ethereal white paintings of heads of literary and poetic figures (Beckett, Joyce, Yeats). His designs for tapestries depicting episodes from *The Tain,* the Irish folk saga, are much admired.

### Norah McGuinness (1903-80)

A Cubist, landscape and subject painter, she studied in the Metropolitan School of Art under Harry Clark and later went to Paris, where she studied under André Lhote. Her delightful, loose, highly decorative paintings are much sought after. She was a founder member of the IELA and after the death of Mainie Jellett became its president.

### F.E. McWilliam (1909-1992)

Born in Banbridge, Co. Down, he was one of Ireland's greatest modern sculptors. He studied at the Slade and in Paris and was much influenced by Picasso, the Surrealists and Brancusi. His monumental works in wood, granite or metal are full of resonance and meaning. His heads, though highly abstracted, are menacingly powerful metaphors.

### James Malton (1760-1803)

Among the most famous images of Dublin (reproductions appear framed and hung in hotel lobbies and bedrooms, are used as book jackets or as endpapers, and are for sale in many galleries) are those taken from aquatints by James Malton, one of a famous family of artists, a pupil of James Gandon and the son of Thomas Malton, an architectural draftsman.

In 1797 he published his famous series of views, *A Picturesque and Descriptive View of the City of Dublin,* consisting of a set of 25 views of the principal buildings. They ran to a great many editions and display a world lost to us, one that has many familiar features — 23 of the depicted buildings still stand today. The original watercolors for the aquatints are in the **National Gallery** collection. Reproductions can be bought in galleries and shops, and occasionally a complete edition comes up for sale at auctions.

### James Arthur O'Connor (1792-1841)

Although he was self-taught, O'Connor became one of Ireland's most important landscape painters. His topographical views of Ireland and its great houses are celebrated and important documents as well as fine pictures. He was much influenced by Dutch 17thC landscapes and by the Romantic movement.

### Sir William Orpen (1878-1931)

The famous portrait, landscape and genre painter was the dominant Irish artist in early 20thC Ireland. Although he lived mainly in London, he taught at Dublin's Metropolitan School of Art and influenced a generation of young painters including Sean Keating. He was commissioned by Sir Hugh Lane to finish the series of portraits of well-known Irishmen intended as the basis of the collection for the foundation of the **Hugh Lane Municipal Gallery of Modern Art**. He was an important influence in the rise of the native tradition in early 20thC Irish painting. His works are in all Irish public collections, as well as the Tate Gallery, London and the Metropolitan Museum of Art, New York.

### Walter Osborne (1859-1903)

Walter Frederick Osborne, the son of William Osborne, another famous Dublin painter, worked in France at Pont-Aven and painted in the *plein-air* style. He was much influenced by Continental painters and became known as the Irish Impressionist. His paintings of Dublin life are imbued with the look of someone who knew every inch of the city from the inside out but saw each scene afresh; his narrative paintings of absorbed children are among the most famous and loved in the **National Gallery**. His work was much influenced by the Impressionists, but he rendered his subjects in his own vision of lush light.

### Sarah Purser (1848-1943)

The painter, designer and stained-glass artist Sarah Purser was one of the most powerful and influential Irish artists of the 19th and early 20thC. She trained in Dublin, Paris and Italy and had formidable organizational powers as well as formidable talent. Responsible for mounting a joint exhibition of works by John Butler Yeats and Nathaniel Hone, she helped inspire Hugh Lane to found his gallery of modern art in Dublin, and also to persuade the government to hand over Charlemont House as the gallery's future home. Besides being a fine portrait painter, she ran studios, classes and *An Tur Gloine* (see page 53).

### Edward Smyth (1749-1812)

Among the best sculptors Ireland has produced is Edward Smyth, who embellished so much of James Gandon's great buildings. Among his finest works are the **Riverine Heads** (see below) on the **Custom House** and sculptures of Dublin worthies in the **City Hall**. He was the first head of the Dublin Society's School of Modelling in 1811.

### Jack Butler Yeats (1871-1957)

Both painter and writer, Jack B. Yeats was one of the foremost 20thC Irish artists. The brother of W.B. Yeats was born in London but spent his childhood in Sligo, and its landscapes and seascapes and the faces of the Irish of the rugged west figure largely in his strong, vivid, painterly canvases.

## ART GALLERIES

Dublin is well served by its galleries, which cover the whole spectrum of art from the treasures of the Renaissance in the **National Gallery** to the contemporary shows at the **Douglas Hyde Gallery**. One of the striking things about Dublin's museums is their staff: they are interested and informative and take an interest in the paintings and the artists. All in all the galleries of Dublin are a delight. Nearly all Dublin's art galleries are within walking distance of the centre. The **Chester Beatty Library** and the **Royal Hospital Kilmainham** are farther afield so it would be best to take a taxi.

### Chester Beatty Library and Gallery of Oriental Art

*20 Shrewsbury Rd., Ballsbridge. Map 1C3* ☎*(01) 2692386* 🖭 *Open Tues-Fri 10am-5pm; Sat 2-5pm* ✗ *Wed and Sat at 2.30pm or by prior arrangement.*
This is a treasure house. There are three buildings within the old walled garden house.

The **Old Library Building**, dating from 1953, houses among other things the Chester Beatty library, a group of codices dating from the 2ndC BC. It also has one of the best small collections of Oriental manuscripts and miniatures in the world, and boasts a rare collection of Western bindings and manuscripts, including some exquisite Continental Books of Hours.

The **Chinese Room** contains Oriental furniture and lanterns. The ivy-draped New Gallery, built in 1956 and extended in 1975, consists of a lecture theater and a gallery with changing and varied exhibitions of treasures from the Far Eastern collection. Finally, there is **The Annexe** with its **Reference Library**, where students and scholars come from all over the world.

See also DAY 4, page 171.

### Gallagher Gallery, Royal Hibernian Academy

*Ely Place. Map 4E5* ☎*(01) 6612558* 🖭 *(but*🖭 *when RHA Summer Exhibition is showing). Open Mon-Sat 11am-5pm (Thurs till 9pm); Sun 2-5pm.*
The Academy was founded in 1823 by Royal Charter and held its first exhibition in 1826. In 1916 its premises were destroyed by fire with all its records. Now its headquarters are the RHA Gallagher Gallery in Ely Place, and here there are regular exhibitions of the work of the Academy's members, traveling shows, group exhibitions and shows of new works by young Irish artists, as well as an annual watercolor exhibition.

See also DAY 1, page 94.

### Douglas Hyde Gallery of Modern Art

*Nassau St. entrance to Trinity College. Map 4D5* ☎*(01) 6772941, ext. 1116* 🖭 *Open Mon-Thurs 11am-6pm; Fri 11am-7pm; Sat 11am-4.45pm. Closed Sun.*
The Douglas Hyde Gallery in Trinity College is the most important space in Dublin for international and Irish avant garde works and retrospectives of art and photography from all over the world. Its program includes lectures, performances and events.

### Irish Museum of Modern Art (IMMA)

*Royal Hospital, Kilmainham. Map 1C1 ☎(01) 6718666. Open Tues-Sat 10am-5.30pm; Sun noon-5.30pm ✗ of North Range of buildings ☛ Bookshop.*

This is an enormous and spectacular building, recently restored. As well as the permanent Modern Art Collection, there are changing exhibitions, retrospectives of the work of international artists, and musical, theatrical and operatic events.

The basis of the museum's collection was 50 pictures donated by the Australian painter Sir Sidney Nolan and Gordon Lambert's collection of Irish and international art. This nucleus is being expanded by acquisitions, donations and loans — for example, the **O'Malley Collection**, on permanent loan from the Irish American Institute, which includes work by Evie Hone, Mainie Jellett, Jack Yeats and Louis Le Brocquy.

See also DAY 3, page 157

### Hugh Lane Municipal Gallery of Modern Art 血

*Charlemont House, Parnell Sq. North. Map 4B4 ☎(01) 8741903. Open Tues-Fri 9.30am-6pm; Sat 9.30am-5pm; Sun 11am-5pm. Closed Mon ✗ by arrangement ☭ (closes 30mins before gallery closing time). Musical events (🎦) frequently at noon on Sun: check listings. Lectures (🎦) every Sun at noon, or 2pm if there is a concert.*

Lord Charlemont seems to have been a delightful creature, vain, witty, clever, a bibliophile and patron of art, architecture and theater. His new mansion in what was then Rutland Square was built for him by Sir William Chambers in 1765 and was a gathering place of the cognoscenti. He commissioned a long library from James Gandon and filled it with so many books that when the books were sold at Sotheby's in 1864 the auction went on for ten days.

Little of the original interior of Charlemont House now remains, and an unattractive porch was added to the exterior in the 1930s. But the gallery is a beautiful building with its lofty stairs, lovely door overmantels and, in some rooms, delightful fireplaces, blue- and white-tiled.

The collection is fascinating, its nucleus made up of paintings from Sir Hugh Lane's personal collection. There are wonderful Constables, Manet's *Eva Gonzales,* Renoir's *Les Parapluies.* (Some of this collection goes to the National Gallery in London every seven years but is in Dublin now until 2000.) There are paintings by Jack B. Yeats, Picasso and Rouault, and in the **Portrait Room**, there are fine portraits of some great figures from Ireland's poetic and turbulent past.

See also DAY 2, page 126.

### National Gallery of Ireland

*Merrion Sq. West. Map 4D5 ☎(01) 6615133 🎦 Open Mon-Sat 10am-6pm (Thurs to 9pm); Sun 2-5pm ✗ Sat 3pm, Sun 2.30, 3.15, 4pm. Closed Christmas; Good Friday ☭ Bookshop.*

The National Gallery of Ireland, at the back of Leinster House, was founded in 1854 and opened to the public in 1864. The committee running it faced a difficult task, trying to put a collection together with little money and no basic endowment. The gallery acquired its first treasures when Henry Doyle, the first director, bought many works of the Dutch 17thC masters of landscape at a time when they were underrated. It was also Doyle who bought the three Rembrandts displayed here and the painting generally regarded as the centerpiece of the collection, Fra Angelico's *Martyrdom of Saints Cosmas and Damian.*

In 1900 Henry Vaughan, a London collector, bequeathed his collection of drawings and watercolors by Turner to the National Gallery of Ireland on condition that they should be exhibited only in January, the darkest month of the year; they may be shown to individuals at other times on request. The greatest benefactor was Sir Hugh Lane, a cultivated, generous man at the center of Dublin life, who in his later years became Governor and Guardian of the gallery. Lane's collection of 39 paintings by Continental artists, including Manet and Renoir, is now divided between the HUGH LANE MUNICIPAL GALLERY and London's National Gallery.

Over the years there have been important bequests, including a fine collection of Irish works from artist Evie Hone, and from that obsessive collector, Sir Chester Beatty, who donated a revelatory collection of 19thC pre-Impressionist French painting. In 1986 Sir Alfred Beit bequeathed to the gallery 17 paintings from his private collection. The bequest of royalties from one third of George Bernard Shaw's estate has allowed the gallery to acquire certain works that would otherwise have been beyond its financial reach. His statue — tiny in scale — stands outside the gallery.

Among the gallery's treasures are paintings by Goya, El Greco *(St Francis in Ecstasy),* Rembrandt and Brueghel, as well as the Fra Angelico. A large English section includes paintings by Reynolds, Stubbs, Constable and Gainsborough, and there is a fine collection of Irish masters. Many of these are connected with the people, events and history of Dublin. Look out for *The Earl Bishop of Derry with Lady Caroline Crichton* (1788) by Hugh Douglas Hamilton to see what the epitome of the Ascendancy at both its most arrogant and delightful looked like; *Cupid and Psyche,* a most erotic picture by the same artist; and a ravishing picture of the *Ladies Catherine and Charlotte Talbot* by John Michael Wright (1679). If anything would want to make you visit Malahide Castle, their home, this picture would; look too for the depiction of an *Irish Interior* in Philip Hussey's painting of the 1750s and George Barret's dramatic rendering of the *Waterfall at Powerscourt* (1760).

Also in the gallery is the **Milltown Collection**, from the contents of Russborough House (see EXCURSIONS, page 236) presented in 1902 by the Countess Milltown, the last descendant of the original brewing family who built the great house.

See also DAY 4, page 167.

### National Portrait Gallery

*Malahide Castle, Malahide. Off map* **2***A4. Open all year Mon-Fri 10am-12.30pm, 2-5pm; Apr-Oct Sat 11am-6pm, Sun, bank holidays 2-6pm; Nov-Mar Sat, Sun, bank holidays 2-5pm*

The portraits in Malahide Castle, before the disastrous sale of the collection and contents to pay death duties, were regarded as the most complete record of any one family in the British Isles. The National

Gallery purchased 31 of these portraits of the Talbot family, whose fate and history is closely linked with that of Ireland, and rehung them in the castle. There are many other portraits, including those of Irish notables like Henry Grattan, Oliver Goldsmith, Carolan the harper, Hone the Elder and Hester Van Homrigh (Swift's Vanessa).

See also EXCURSIONS, page 253.

## IRISH CRAFTS

### Pottery and porcelain

There is a long tradition of pottery and porcelain in Ireland. In the early 18thC an immigrant Quaker called **Jonathan Chamberleyne** set up a pottery at Wexford, and creamware was produced at Rostrevor in Co. Down from as early as the 1740s. All over Ireland in the 18thC glazed wares, stoneware and earthenware were being produced in quantity from small potteries. By the end of the 18thC the craft seems to have disappeared and pottery had to be imported. But by the middle of the 19thC there was a new impetus, and blue and white earthenware and delftware in distinctive style was being produced.

An Irishman, **Thomas Frye**, is credited with being one of the first to discover the secret of hard paste Western porcelain. He added bone ash to his porcelain mix, which made the clay less liable to disintegrate in the kiln. A remarkable man born near Edenderry in 1710, Thomas Frye was a brilliant all-round artist and engraver and could have been one of Ireland's foremost painters; but at the height of his career he went to manage a small china factory at Bow in London's East End, where he carried out his experiments and ruined his health. Among his most charming works are the white figurine portraits of famous actors and actresses of his day: there are examples in the National Museum. The notice of his death read: "The inventor and first manufacturer of porcelain in England to bring which to perfection he spent 15 years amongst the furnaces till his constitution was near destroyed."

**Belleek China**, made in a small village in Fermanagh, has an international reputation, which derives from its covetable and rare 19thC feldspar pottery with its extreme translucence and delicate glaze. The modern pieces, though employing the skill of talented workers, do not match the original standard of design. The factory is open to visitors.

Fine examples of Irish pottery and porcelain are on show in the fine arts section of the **National Museum**, which also has a comprehensive range of Irish **silver and glass**.

### The Revival movement

The great seminal iniative in the arts and literature at the turn of the century was the Revival movement. This was the response of artists in different disciplines to the renewed interest in Irish mythology, legend and the struggle for national independence. The **Irish Industries Association** and the **Arts and Crafts Society**, along with their offshoot, the **Guild of Irish Art Workers**, encouraged activity in furniture-making, wood-carving and especially stained glass and painting, which achieved a high level of excellence.

Among the best were **Harry Clarke** and **Wilhelmina Geddes**, working in stained glass, **Oswald Reeves**, making beautiful pieces in enameled metalwork, and **Nan Holland** and **Alice Brittain**, whose jewelry is memorable. The style they worked in was generally a fusion of Celtic/La Tène with New Art (Art Nouveau) and produced lovely, distinctive artifacts, imbued with a richness and sense of place, time and atmosphere.

One of the most famous projects was *An Tur Gloine* (the Tower of Glass), a studio that still exists, albeit in a different dispensation, behind Upper Pembroke St. in Dublin. From it stems the strong tradition of modern stained glass in Ireland. There are many churches, including Loughrea Cathedral and the Chapel Royal (the Church of the Most Holy Trinity, Dublin Castle), where the work of graduates of the famous glass studio can be seen, including work by Evie Hone.

### Cut glass and crystal

The Irish tradition in cut glass and crystal is also notable, and **Waterford Glass** in particular has long been world-famous. The factory at Waterford is open during the working week. Now other towns produce cut crystal, including **Tyrone Crystal** in Dungannon, which is available in Dublin.

Much glass design in Ireland is curiously old-fashioned and ornate and rarely wholly pleasing. However, the glass made by **Simon Pearce** is simple, classic and beautiful. He now makes it in the United States, but his work is sometimes available in Pearce shops in Naas and Cork.

**Jerpoint glass** is attractive and well designed and is available in many shops around the country, including the Kilkenny Centre (see SHOPPING).

### Craft workshops and exhibitions

The remarkable organization, **Kilkenny Design Workshops**, was set up in April 1963 to raise the standard of design in Ireland and to give craftworkers a haven in which to experiment and make prototypes. Work done by its affiliated craftworkers and artists can be bought in the workshops in the old stables at Kilkenny Castle or from the Kilkenny Centre in Dublin (see SHOPPING).

One of the best places to see the work of independent young artist-craftsmen is the Crafts Council of Ireland's outlet in **Powerscourt Town House**, where there are exhibitions and displays of imaginative new work being produced in Ireland (see SHOPPING).

Temporary exhibitions of arts and crafts, painting and sculpture produced in Ireland are held in the **Exhibition Hall** on the ground floor of the Baggot St. headquarters of the Bank of Ireland.

The **Irish Life Exhibition Centre** in the Customs House Development holds changing exhibitions of new Irish art, and the Craft Potters Society of Ireland hold their annual exhibition there. There is a vague proposal to open a **Decorative Arts Museum** branch of the National Museum in this development.

## NATIONAL TREASURES

### Illuminated manuscripts

Trinity College's most precious possessions — the illuminated medieval manuscripts, the **Book of Durrow** and the famous **Book of Kells** — are both on display in Trinity Library. Every year new research reveals more about this extraordinary work, the *Book of Kells*. No one knows how many scribes were employed — but with over 600 wonderfully illuminated pages it obviously took years to complete and was a huge investment in time and resources. For example, 185 calves had to be slaughtered to produce the vellum. (See DAY 1, page 113.)

The symbol of St Mark from the **Book of Kells**.

The point about the *Book of Kells* is not just its intrinsic beauty, but its spiritual value. When you look at it you see the visual expression of what Christianity *meant* — the new, essentially simple but extraordinary ideas of kindness as love, duty as a virtue, and labor as a means of praise.

These books were regarded as miraculous objects. Indeed, at some point in its history the *Book Of Durrow* was in the keeping of an "ignorant man [who] when sickness came upon cattle, for their remedy putt water on the book and suffered it to rest there awhile and saw also cattle returne thereby to their pristin state and the book to receive the loss." Alas, this diagnosis was optimistic, for the book suffered from its immersions.

In 1989 a limited edition of 1,480 copies of the *Book of Kells* was produced at $15,000 a copy.

### National Museum of Ireland

*Kildare St. Map 4E5 ☎(01) 6765521 ⬚ (but ⬚ for Treasury Section except on Tues). Open Tues-Sat 10am-5pm; Sun 2-5pm. Closed Mon.*

The National Museum of Ireland, which is regarded as one of the three best in Europe (with Athens and Budapest), has three distinct sections: the main museum on the Kildare St. side of Leinster House, with the Treasury, silver, glass, ceramics, costumes, Irish lace, coins and medals, and a room devoted to the 1916 Rising; the Merrion Street Zoological Collection; and the Merrion Row Viking Exhibition.

In the **Treasury** section, a new view of old Ireland is revealed, in all its virtue and glory. In 2000BC a staggering amount of gold jewelry and ornament was produced, executed with the highest degree of craftsmanship. Much of what has been discovered from this era forms the collection. Here are wonderful treasures, forming a priceless and unrivaled collection of Irish antiquities and artifacts from Stone Age times to the Middle Ages.

The most dazzling of all of Ireland's golden ages was the Dowris phase of the Late Bronze Age, and at its apogee during the 8th-6thC BC so much gold was produced that there was an export trade from Ireland. The amazing richness of this period was revealed by the discovery in 1854 of what is known as the **Clare Hoard**, found during the building of the West Clare railway. Many of the pieces had already been melted down before Sir William Wilde made his inventory. The weight of the surviving gold was 174 ounces and was the greatest find of prehistoric gold ornaments ever discovered in Western Europe.

Among other superb objects in the **Antiquities Department** is the exquisitely fashioned **Ardagh Chalice**, found in a field near Limerick in 1867 by a boy digging potatoes. Most renowned of all in Ireland, most revered, and certainly most reproduced, is the bronze, gold and copper **Tara Brooch**, made in the 8thC and found in 1850 in material that had collapsed from a cliff at Bettystown in Co. Meath. It has a diameter of 8.2 centimeters ($3\frac{1}{4}$ inches) and the length of the pin is 22.5 centimeters ($8\frac{7}{8}$ inches). It was given the name Tara by a dealer through whose hands it passed, and has no connection with the Hill of Tara.

The brooch is made of cast silver gilt and is enormously sophisticated in construction. It so much recalls the work and skill of the Ardagh Chalice that it may have come from the same workshop, and one is moved almost to love for the medieval enameler who cared not a whit about himself or his signature but only for the intricate perfection of what he was doing for the glory of God.

The **ceramics gallery** is a delight, full of small interesting piece as well as some huge decorative statues. One of the most important and extraordinary things in this room, dating from the 13thC, is the **Fonthill Vase**, from the Yuan Dynasty whose most famous emperor was Kublai Khan, he of the stately pleasure dome. This celadon vase, once festooned with gold or bronze and made in the emperor's own pottery, was in royal collections all over Europe and was bought at auction in 1892 by the trustees of this museum soon after it was founded in 1877. It cost IR£27.35. Now it is priceless, or if you had to put a price on it would run into millions. There is also lovely Irish glass tracing the history of Irish glass-making, with some superb rare examples, and an informative booklet (by your author!).

See also DAY 1, pages 99-100.

### Dublin Civic Museum

*58 South William St. Map 4D4 ☎(01) 794260 or (901) 794260 ▣ Open Tues-Sat 10am-6pm ( ✗ Wed at 1.15pm); Sun 11am-2pm. Closed Mon.*
The museum, in an 18thC house, has a collection of ephemera, prints, pictures and coins, which give a clear idea of a vanished Dublin. (See DAY 1, page 105.)

## INTERIOR DESIGN

One of the most rewarding houses to visit in Dublin for its free and fantastical plasterwork is that built for himself at **20 Lower Dominick St.** in North Dublin by the master builder and stuccodore, Robert West. He had a marked partiality for birds, and the house contains a full and striking collection of them in various poses. This is the headquarters of the National Youth Federation, but groups are admitted by appointment. More of West's work (and another 63 birds) can be seen on the s side of St Stephen's Green at **86 Newman House** (see DAY 1, page 98).

The **Royal Hospital Kilmainham** has been restored at enormous expense over the past decade and is now the center for the **Irish Museum of Modern Art**. It is well worth visiting for the ceilings alone.

The building at **73 Merrion Sq.**, which houses the **Irish Architectural Archive**, is a fine example of a Dublin town house with superb plasterwork and original fittings. Here you will see a splendid overall view of Irish architecture through the ages.

**Life in a Georgian House** at **29 Fitzwilliam Sq.** comprises two houses owned by the Electricity Supply Board. The ground and first floors of nos. 29 and 40 have been redecorated to show the typical furnishings of a Dublin house of the period 1790-1820. The National Museum has loaned much of the paintings and furniture.

For good examples of fine 18thC stucco and a collection of Irish and Continental furniture, visit the **State Apartments** in **Dublin Castle** (see DAY 3, page 143).

# Dublin's theatrical heritage

*In this Theatre they has plays*
*On us, and high-up people come*
*And pays to see things play in here*
*They'd scut and run from in the slums.*
(L.A.G Strong, on the Abbey Theatre)

Dublin has long been famous for its theater, ever since the literary revival engendered the idea of a national theater at the turn of the century, an ideal that became a reality at the **Abbey Theatre**. From its beginnings, the Abbey Company was extraordinary, with a cast of stars who became world renowned. On its stage, many new plays have been first presented that have since become part of the international repertoire.

Not that Dublin audiences, always deeply fascinated by theater, were wholly appreciative. When Synge's *Playboy of the Western World* was staged there, there was uproar because it was thought to insult Irish people. Audiences broke up in disorder both at the word "shift" and at the appearance of a prostitute as a character in the play, and there was a week of rioting.

W.B. Yeats had been determined that the new theater would not put on political plays. But in Ireland, then as now, everything is political. Sean O'Casey's plays were perhaps the most famous, and the premiere of *The Plough and the Stars* occasioned another riot.

Augusta, Lady Gregory, one of the cofounders of the Abbey with Yeats and Edward Martyn, was a legend while still alive, a small, dartingly energetic woman who kept the theater going on sheer willpower. Dublin, according to Joyce, was suffering from "hemiplegia of the will," and Lady Gregory resisted such passivity with all her considerable might.

She was 51 years old when she had her first play presented. By the end of her life she had written over a hundred, and it was said that her play *The Rising of the Moon* made more rebels than any political speech or movement. Shaw consulted her when writing *St Joan,* and it was she who succeeded in getting a grant from the government so that the Abbey became the first state-subsidized theater in the English-speaking world.

She had a finger in every pie, almost literally; before a performance the cast would gather in the Green Room for tea to eat a monumental barm-brack, an enormous fruitcake made by her own cook, so heavy it took two men to carry it. God knows what it did to the performances — added substance perhaps. Years later, Yeats, when visiting the Municipal Gallery, came upon Lady Gregory's portrait by Mancini, and mused: "a great ebullient portrait certainly; / But where is the brush that could show anything / of all that pride and that humility . . . "

The Abbey building was given in a grand quixotic gesture by Anne Horniman, an English heiress, who over the years financed the theater to a generous extent. One evening after a performance, Yeats, feeling particularly beleaguered, came on stage in the makeshift theater where they were creating history as well as staging plays, and made an impassioned speech about the necessity of theater. She came backstage, said, "I will give you a theater," and did. She paid for the old music hall in Abbey St. to be converted into a proper theater holding 600 people.

This famous building burned down, but a new theater without any visual appeal was opened in 1966. (See DAY 2, page 123.)

The other "great" Dublin theater, the **Gate Theatre Company**, stages classic and international productions and is an integral part of Irish theater life. It was founded in 1928 by Michael Mac Liammoir, a visionary who believed he was Irish, and his partner Hilton Edward. "Our beginnings in 1928, like the beginnings, almost thirty years previously, of Yeats' National Theatre Society that was later to become the Abbey, were at once wildly ambitious and severely, almost ostentatiously small," wrote Mac Liammoir.

A great actor in his own right, Michael Mac Liammoir had worked in the international theater before he came to Dublin, his fine head "filled with the thoughts of Ireland's need for a theatre in the capital city that could show something more than the Abbey, where only a portion of Irish life was interpreted."

Michael Mac Liammoir's one-man show *The Importance Of Being Oscar,* based on the life and work of Oscar Wilde, was a huge international success (he gave 1,384 performances). At the last performance in the Gate when he was 76, nearly blind but utterly indomitable, the audience was in tears. The then President of Ireland, Cearbhall O Dalaigh, led the standing ovation.

The Gate Theatre still flourishes and for years outstripped the Abbey in its imaginative production of new and classic drama. Now they both have a fine repertoire.

For further information on Dublin's contemporary theater scene, see PERFORMING ARTS.

# Irish music

Music is important to the Irish. The harp is the national emblem of Ireland. From traditional to rock to classical, music runs through the country, keeping it on its toes. And it has always been important. Throughout the ages people gathered to sing and to dance at cross-roads, to hold impromptu concerts and *ceilis* (dances), but because of the twists of history the instruments used were simple and solo: a voice, a fiddle, a harp. (There is little chance of forming an orchestra if all you've got is a pipe fashioned from a reed or a drum from a goat-skin.) There was nothing simple though about the melodies and counterpoint — they were complex, formal, sophisticated.

It all goes back a long way; the music of Ireland weaves and wavers in and out of its history, a lament, a threnody, a hymn, a lilt, a jig. In the Ulster dialect of Irish the word *Ceol* means or signifies both music and poetry, and this intermingled dependence of word with rhythm, sound with sound, is a given in all Gaelic music, and what is now called traditional music.

As early as 1183 the skills of Irish harpers were being extolled by Giraldus Cambrensis, the Welsh historian and cleric who visited Ireland in 1183, and in 1580 an Irish poet wrote that he had written a poem, "that will often be recited by merry people on many a grassy sward and will be a solace in every gathering with a harp obligato of equal extent."

The harpers were powerful people and revered, and this still obtains (groups like **U2** and the **Saw Doctors** are new gods). Great traditional singers and groups are honored, their names entered in that pantheon reserved for those the Irish love without jealousy or derision. It is the only one, save for the saints. (The tenor John MacCormack was a superstar in Ireland and is still spoken of with pride, and there are those who think that James Joyce should have stuck with his original plan to be a singer.) You can still hear the sound of authentic ancient harp music in Ireland, since there are replicas of the old harps, played by modern masters, which sound quite different from gut-strung newer harps.

What in other nations goes under the rather disheartening title of folk music is here living and real and part of everyday life, though there never were any folk in Ireland, wherever else that curious race may be found. Of course there is a passion for Country and Western music, and the unwary may find themselves of an evening besieged by a mixed choir in green and gold costumes from Upper Ruritania singing *Danny Boy,* and if you have chosen to go to a banquet this is what you will have bought, and my sympathy is unnecessary. Then too there are the endlessly repetitive reels and jigs (what is derisively called *diddeley-aye* music as if the melody had been caught in a loop, with the phrase endlessly recurring), though this same music in the hands of a master can sound as moving as any raga or lament.

Irish music is sad, diverse, sometimes comic. It can take the form of a John Field nocturne (although to be honest that romantic composer left Ireland when he was 11 in 1793 and never returned). It can be a moving lament *(My Lagan Love),* or full of irresistible zest (Sir Arthur Sullivan of Gilbert and Sullivan fame was the son of an Irish bandmaster and wrote an *Irish Symphony in E minor;* and Micheal Balfe, composer of the *Bohemian Girl* in 1843, was Irish born). And there is a long tradition of opera singers and a fervently enthusiastic audience for classical music in Ireland. Dublin led the way in recognition of Handel's *Messiah,* for example, when the composer was not being given a hearing in England, and the review in the Dublin newspaper spoke of "the exquisite delight afforded to the admiring audience, the Sublime, the Grand and Tender conspiring to transport and charm the ravished Heart and Ear . . . . "

## TRADITIONAL MUSIC

But the music most people want to hear when they visit Dublin is traditional Irish music, and there is plenty of opportunity. The Irish love their music. Yet for years in this century, after the advent of radio and "modern" music, it was disregarded and kept alive only by the old practitioners. In the early 1950s, in the vanguard of the folk boom, music producers from **Radio Eireann**, the Irish State radio, went around the country to record the fiddlers, the tin whistlers, the pipers and the singers of the countryside. They found an enormous reservoir of talent. But they also found that some people were reluctant to reveal themselves as traditional musicians, because such music was despised; and some fiddle players went to join fellow musicians with their fiddles hidden under their coats because they didn't wish to be seen.

In 1951 a group of musicians who met regularly at the Pipers Club in Thomas St. in Dublin planned a *Fleadh Cheoil* (Feast of Music), which was so successful that *Fleadhanna Cheoil* are now popular events in towns and villages all over the country, with a glorious culminating event held in a different town each year. And from this sprang the *Comhaltas Ceoltoiri Eireann* (the Fellowship of Musicians of Ireland), which organizes events, teaching and activities all over Ireland and abroad, as well as producing recordings of Irish traditional music.

An enormous resurgence followed; new composers appeared who drew on traditional music to create a contemporary Irish music. Most notable was **Sean O'Riada**, director of music at the Abbey Theatre at the time, who, in 1961, founded the group **Ceoltoiri Cualann**, which had a profound influence on subsequent Irish traditional music in group form. (Once, spontaneously, he on the fiddle, and the inimitable Paddy Moloney on the uilleann pipes, ripped through 26 variations of the traditional song *The Blackbird* without consultation and without repetition.) O'Riada's music for the film *Mise Eire (I am Ireland)* caused a sensation in Ireland. In 1969 he and the Ceoltoiri Cualann (who became **The Chieftains**) were recorded at a concert they gave at the Gaiety Theatre. The album is still one of the most fervently exciting things you could listen to: *O'Riada Sa Gaiety* (Gael Linn CEF027) — try to buy it.

The uilleann pipes are so called because *uilleann* is Gaelic for elbow and the bellows of the instrument are pumped by the arm and elbow. Leo Rowsome was, with Seamus Ennis, the great uilleann piper of his time. When the **Claddagh** label was launched in 1959, he was the first to be recorded on it. But it seemed that he was the last of a long dispensation, for there were then only 70 uilleann pipers left in Ireland. Now, after this extraordinary revival of the last decades, it is a popular instrument — and no wonder. It is widely regarded as producing the loveliest sound of any of the world's many pipes. For an orchestral sound with the uilleann pipes, listen to Shaun Davy's interpretation of *St Brendan's Voyage to America,* played by Liam O'Flynn.

The hammer dulcimer and pipes is another wonderful meeting of instruments: on the album *The Long Finger* you can hear two masters, Joe McHugh and Barry Carroll, play old airs.

Then various singers and groups appeared. **The Clancy Brothers** and **Tommy Makem** in Aran sweaters sang songs that everybody knew and which lacked apparent distinction. But they were singing them to international acclaim and their distinction became apparent. **The Dubliners**, with the extraordinary rough voice of Luke Kelly, lifted ensemble playing and singing of popular folk and traditional music into new realms.

Traditional music is still alive and developing. **The Chieftains** were a national institution almost from the start: with their full-bodied sound and traditional repertoire they swept the boards. New energy was injected into the music scene in the 1970s, when young musicians fused rock and Celtic influences. From this fusion came such bands as **Horslips** and **U2**, and later groups like **The Pogues** and **Hothouse Flowers**, bringing an Irish tradition to rock, with an anarchic element added.

In the 1990s, **Sinead O'Connor**, with her extraordinary vocal range, has become famous both for her sound and her unconventionality. The **Saw Doctors**, a young, unpretentious group of accomplished musicians with a wonderful energy, have brought a new awareness of Irish songs and music to a wide audience; their *The N17* has become almost an Irish anthem, *the* emigration song.

For who to see and where to see them, turn to PERFORMING ARTS.

## A SELECTION OF RECORDINGS TO BUY

The records you could buy to give you a real taste are:

- *The Long Finger (Am Mhear Fada),* Joe McHugh and Barry Carroll (the hammer dulcimer and uillean pipes: JMB001)
- *Claddagh's Choice,* an anthology of traditional Irish music.
- *The Best of De Danann,* with Dolores Keane's *The Rambling Irishman*
- *The New String-Harp,* Maire Ni Chathasaigh

- *Ancient Music for the Irish Harp,* Derek Bell (Ceirnini Claddagh: CC59CD)
- *Van Morrison and The Chieftains*
- *The Tain,* Horslips
- *The King of the Pipes,* Leo Rowsome
- *O'Riada sa Gaiety*
- *After Hours,* The Bothy Band
- *Nocturnes of John Field,* John O'Conor
- *Sharon Shannon,* Sharon Shannon
- *Mise Eire*

# Ancient sanctities: Dublin's architecture

The architecture of the Irish capital has always been one of its great glories along with its people and its literature, its canals and its river, its bridges and monuments and the myriad other glorious things that make it still, against all the odds and against the current of the 20thC, such a captivating place to visit, to stay in, to live in. How did it and how does it happen?

What makes it so remarkable is that this lovely city and this quality among the Dublin people has come out of the most tragic history of any in Europe. Their art was annihilated, their language suppressed, their leaders banished and slain, their population diminished and scattered. Yet people who could well be embittered or resentful appear to have little rancor, and the only glint of steel in the South is a sharp tongue tempered with irony and humor.

That word *still* in the opening paragraph is used with regret. Until recently the inner city of Dublin was a lovely Georgian city, intact as though caught in a time-warp, a felicitous delight to walk through and enjoy. That was the problem. It was lovely to look at, but parts of it were hard to live in because of insidious decay. It is easy with hindsight to know that the city could have been preserved and restored; that the old buildings in the more derelict great squares and streets could have been modernized without damaging their intrinsic structures — although the practice of keeping a facade and inserting a modern block behind it never properly works, and produces something meretricious.

One of the saddest things is to read mouth-watering descriptions of houses or streets in one of the many guide books to Dublin written in the 1940s and '50s by fine writers such as Kate O'Brien, Olivia Manning and Frank O'Connor, only to find, when one seeks them out, an empty space, like a snaggletooth, or a hideous office block. **Mespil House**, for example, which reeked with history and had some of the best plaster-work and ceilings in Ireland, has disappeared and a complex of flats stands in its place. The ceilings were saved, and transferred to **Dublin Castle** and to **Aras an Uachtarain** in Phoenix Park, once the Vice-Regal's lodge and now the house of the President, but there is never the same resonance to these relics in their new surroundings.

## "WE ARE NOT INTERESTED IN HISTORY"

In the 1960s and '70s a new brutalism stalked the land. Parts of Georgian Dublin were butchered and its unity splintered, and not just by property speculators: the State Electricity Board led the way. City planners with the best will in the world, and developers and speculators with none, wreaked havoc, and these are still at large, beavering away, sewing destruction on Dublin's remarkable and valuable heritage and continuing to spread concrete and plastic and aluminum over whatever doesn't move.

Maurice Craig, the doyen of architectural historians, has called cement "Ireland's national disease." And the businesses and people who occupy the houses that survive put in inappropriate aluminum double-glazing, remove the glazing bars that are so intrinsic to the windows and thus the proportions of the Georgian house, render the front of the house and finish the brickwork with colored rendering.

The **Irish Georgian Society (*An Taisce*)** — Ireland's national trust — and other conservation groups do what they can to forestall the destruction or to influence design, but on the whole the quality of the buildings put up in place of the lost buildings is dismal and tacky.

Until after World War II there was no equivalent of Great Britain's National Trust, and even now *An Taisce* has no government funding. The Vikings' reputed destructiveness has been well enough matched in this century in the example of **Wood Quay**, where a Viking site of historical and archeological consequence was discovered. Dublin Corporation refused to preserve it as a site, refused even enough time to explore it thoroughly ("We are not interested in history," in their infamous words) and instead commissioned the most controversial buildings in Dublin, a pair of massive bunker-like civic buildings which bulk like thugs over Christ Church Cathedral, ruining scale and perspective all around.

An official in the Corporation's Planning Department, when asked, at a public meeting, why there was so much dilapidation in the inner city, attributed it to the fact that "much housing stock was more than 70 years old and thus was well past its prime . . . . " This, in an 18thC city!

Ireland is the only country in Western Europe that makes no significant sum available to individuals committed to buying or repairing historic buildings. There is no statutory legislation comparable with the "listed building" designation in other countries. Dublin Corporation makes available £60,000 *per annum* for the repair of the capital's historic buildings: that sum would hardly repair and re-roof one building.

Against this neglect, the forces of conservation are not great. *An Taisce*, as stated, receives no government funding. It was founded in 1948 and owns and cares for many properties around Dublin, including Booterstown Marsh and Tailor's Hall. It is a voluntary body and is strapped for money, and hampered by lack of staff and backup.

A **National Heritage Council** was established in 1988, and makes a small number of annual grants to historic buildings on condition they are accessible to the public. The Council's remit includes all aspects of conservation, including wildlife and landscape, so it is stretched beyond its resources.

But the fault lies not so much with Dublin Corporation (though it has never been a loved body) as with national attitudes. Too much is left to the goodwill of private citizens.

A stretch of lovely 18thC houses on **Bachelor's Walk**, with magnificent interiors, were demolished around the turn of this decade; terraces have been demolished on **Arran Quay**; half of **Mountjoy Square** is lying rotting; **Henrietta Street** is neglected; even houses on **St Stephen's Green**, notably **no. 88**, have been gutted. Stretches of **Upper Merrion Street** lay empty for years, while in government ownership, and these houses are now being sold off to private developers, without any proper control over their architectural treatment.

**St George's, Hardwicke Place**, the most outstanding Regency Church in Dublin, has been sold for "entertainment use"; **St Mary's**, built in 1700, has had all its wonderful internal joinery destroyed or stolen. **St Catherine's**, Dublin's greatest Palladian church, with the best facade, stands abandoned, its organ smashed, and Dublin Corporation is reluctant to let interested parties in to view it.

Worst of all, the authorities seem to learn nothing from other cities, from Birmingham, England, for example, which is having to rebuild its disastrous central Bull Ring road. Here, the Corporation is still smashing dual carriageways through inner city areas including **Parnell Street** and **Patrick Street**, the historic heart of Dublin.

The streetscape is blurred and mutilated by paving stones not being replaced. When a street has been dug for construction work, it is often filled in with tar or concrete and simply left to shape itself as it may. The simple omission of paving stones and their grid lines gives the sidewalks even in the prettiest streets a squalid air. The traffic too is uncontrolled. Walking along Bachelor's Walk is not to be advised at rush hours as container trucks and cars huff and puff and belch their oil an inch away from your nose. There are no tunnels, few diversions and hardly a restriction. And cars drive up the broad streets at 60 miles per hour.

For years influential people have been trying to get the destruction stopped. Yeats wrote " . . . a spirit suffers because of its share when alive in the destruction of an honoured house; that destruction is taking place all over Ireland today. I know of old houses, old pictures, old furniture that have been sold without apparent regret . . . . Sometimes it is the result of poverty, but more often because a new individualistic generation has lost interest in the ancient sanctities."

It may be that the generation who came after the founding of the Irish Free State associated the magnificent heritage of Georgian architecture in Dublin too much with the Ascendancy, that it was not what they thought of as an *Irish* creation. It is hard to love something that is a symbol of your own deprivation. "The taste that created Dublin," unequivocally observed a man who much loved Dublin, the writer Richard Hayward, "was the taste of an aristocratic governing class that was entirely alien to Ireland and all things Irish and that was . . . fiercely and often cruelly impatient of the Irish people and the Irish way of life." He was exaggerating, but it underpins the disregard that has been shown for a unique heritage.

81

## THE GREAT ARCHITECTS

The fact is that although many of the buildings we admire and which you will look at while you are in Dublin were built by English or Continental architects, many more are by Irish architects. Nearly all of the plasterwork, painting and sculpture that you will see in the great houses and museums were done by Irishmen and women who had been given the chance to get at the tools of their trade. For centuries, over and over again, Irish men and women were deprived of the conditions to become artists, or the education and input to be able to look at and appreciate objects for their own worth. When they got the chance, they seized it and produced their own vivid versions of the particular art or craft.

Finally, it doesn't matter what nationality the architects and artists were. They beautified Ireland, and for that they should be honored and celebrated. The great architects are as much heroes of Ireland as are the singers and poets and the men who fought over the buildings. But whereas monuments are erected to the bravery of fighters and the achievements of writers, the beautiful monuments that comprise Dublin itself were hardly recognized as the expression of their creators' genius. There is nowhere in Dublin a blue plaque to James Gandon.

Among the great architects are **Sir William Robinson** and **Colonel Thomas Burgh**, both of whom were Surveyor-Generals of Ireland, Robinson from 1670 to 1700 and Burgh from 1700 to 1730. Robinson's masterpiece is the Royal Hospital Kilmainham. Thomas Burgh, from a landed family in Co. Kildare (his father was a bishop), was a soldier by profession, and is most famous as the designer of Trinity Library.

**Sir Edward Lovett Pearce**, who is sometimes described as "the Inigo Jones of Ireland," was also a soldier. A dragoon officer by training and an intellectual and dilettante by inclination, he was a friend and indeed a cousin of the gifted John Vanbrugh who designed those two great English palaces, Castle Howard and Blenheim. Pearce is one of the greatest of Irish architects, yet oddly enough he disappeared for a long time from architectural history; in the records, all mention of his work was erased, and his buildings were not reattributed to him until well into the 20thC.

Pearce, who knew and admired the work of Hawksmoor, had done the equivalent of the grand tour, traveling widely in Europe, and brought to his commissions a civilizing erudition. He worked for only a few meteoric years, from 1726 until his mysteriously early death in 1733, but in those few years he transformed the face and course of architecture in Ireland. Among his greatest buildings are the Parliament House, now the Bank of Ireland, parts of Dublin Castle and Henrietta Street, and the fine wings of Castletown House.

Perhaps most significant of all is **James Gandon**, an English architect of Huguenot parentage. He had been a pupil of **Sir William Chambers**, who never came to Ireland but designed the miraculous, perfect Casino at Marino for Lord Charlemont. The story goes that Gandon was "smuggled in" against opposition from England, as well as from the Dublin merchants and grandees who believed that their trade would be ruined if the Customs House was moved farther downstream — in which case he was one of the best pieces of contraband ever to reach Ireland's shores.

His three great contributions are the Corinthian front to the Parliament House (1785), the Custom House (1789-91) and the Four Courts (1786-96), both these latter now largely restored.

Gandon, already middle-aged when he became a Dublin immigrant, acquired some of its wit. He was overseeing the building of the Corinthian portico at Parliament House, when a stranger, rounding the curved screen from the Ionic colonnade in front, stopped and asked him what the order of the new column was. Gandon said, "A very substantial order, being an order of the House of Lords."

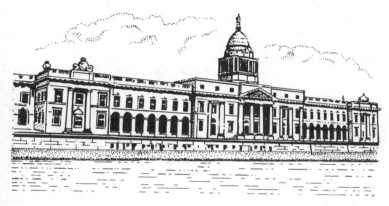

The **Custom House**: the south or river front.

James Gandon never left Dublin, and the city is the better for it. He died aged 80 in 1824 and was buried in the same grave as his friend the antiquarian Francis Grose. Grose's epitaph reads that he died while in "cheerful conversation with his friends," and the addendum reads, "Also his friend James Gandon, Architect. Born in 1742 — Died in 1824." Like Christopher Wren, if you seek his monument, look around you. But if you want to see what he looked like, there is a delightful portrait in the National Gallery, showing him holding his plans for the Customs House, with his great buildings ranged behind him.

One of the greatest architects to work in Ireland was **Richard Castle**, born Cassels and often referred to under that name, born in Hesse-Kassel in what is now Germany in the last years of the 17thC. A military engineer by profession, he met and worked with the Englishman William Kent and his great patron Lord Burlington, one of the four great English Earls of Creation. He may have already had some family living in Ireland, or else was persuaded to come to Ireland by Edward Pearce or by Sir Gustavus Hume, for whom he designed his first house in Ireland, Castle Hume in Co. Fermanagh, destroyed by fire soon after it was built.

Castle introduced his robust version of the Palladian style to Ireland; and when Edward Lovett Pearce died, Castle took over where he left off and over the span of his career built many of the great palaces and civic buildings of Ireland, beginning with the little jewel that is the Printing House in Trinity College. He died at Carton, which he designed in 1739 for the Earl of Kildare (see EXCURSIONS, page 245), while scribbling a letter to his carpenter.

There were many other relatively unfeted but brilliant Dublin builder-architects. There were men like **Robert Mack**, for example, who built Powerscourt Town House in 1771 to his idiosyncratic interpretation of Palladian design and made of it one of the finest houses of the period. In so doing he showed that an architect can work within the Classical orders, indeed the ancient sanctities, and still contrive to make something new and suitable, worthy and redolent of its city. (It is now a fine shopping center off Grafton St.)

Then there was **George Semple**, who designed Swift's Hospital (see DAY 3, page 153), or **Nathaniel Clements**, the architect of Henrietta St. and Aras an Uachtarain. Another architect who left his mark on Dublin was **John Ensor**, who came from Coventry and was a pupil of Richard Castle. He laid out Gardiner's Row and Merrion Square. (He was sent to prison for gross prevarication "in the building of a barrack in Carrick-on-Shannon." If only such draconian legislation were available now for those people who impose their tawdry designs on the city.)

Skilled plasterers had always been part of the workforce of Dublin since medieval times. But in the mid-18thC Lord Kildare brought over the brothers **Paul and Philip Lafranchini**, from Switzerland, who had already worked on the great Castle Howard in Yorkshire, to decorate his house at Carton, which Richard Castle had designed. Under their influence, the native Irish craftsmen became so skilled in this exuberant and fantastic new style that their fame spread.

(It could get out of control. At Russborough House — see EXCURSIONS, page 236 — where Irish pupils of the Lafranchini brothers were given their head, they seem to have lost it and produced a startlingly dense clotted staircase hall, which closes in on the unwary climber like something out of a baroque fairy tale.)

By the 1770s the influence of the Adam brothers had brought Classical restraint to the exuberance of the Lafranchini style, and the native craftsmen added their own elements and interpretations to produce a style that is recognizably Irish. The greatest stuccodores were **Michael Stapleton** (Powerscourt House, Belvedere House and Trinity Examination Hall) and **Robert West**, who created the extraordinary swirling motifs and birds — positive aviaries — in his own house at 20 Lower Dominick Street (see DAY 2, page 133) and at 86 St Stephens Green, Clanwilliam House, now part of Newman House (see DAY 1, page 97).

The jobbing builders were Irish. They followed plans and followed them well, but often added their own individualistic touches, much as the monks who worked on the illuminated manuscripts scribbled little comments about their state of mind or composed a quick *haiku* on the edge of their manuscript — or as the **O'Shea brothers** carved monkeys playing billiards on the outside of the Kildare Street Club as a metaphor, it was whispered, for what was going on inside.

Among the architects were **Thomas Cooley**, the young London architect, who won the competition to design the City Hall; **Thomas Ivory**, who designed the Bluecoat School; the **Ensor brothers**, mainly involved in house-building; and **John Semple**, who built curious spiky churches all over Dublin.

In Victorian times, the architects **Deane & Woodward** were responsible for many of the Neo-Gothic/Venetian buildings of Dublin. **Benjamin Woodward**, born in 1817, was the son of a captain in the army, and his apprenticeship to a civil engineer made him perhaps a better architect and certainly one who knew how to construct. His significant career lasted really only about 12 years, but when he died at Lyon at the age of 44, he too had changed the look and direction of Irish architecture. The Museum Building for the Engineering Faculty in Trinity, with its Venetian-Lombardesque look and use of colored stone and decoration, was imitated in many of the new commercial buildings of Dublin, and the Kildare Street Club was a daring building to produce for the ruling class in Classical Dublin.

**Patrick Byrne**, a Dubliner, built many of the 19thC churches of Dublin, including St Audoen's in the High St. and Adam and Eve's Franciscan Church. (Incidentally, the real name of Adam and Eve's is the Church of the Immaculate Conception, but during Penal Days a hidden Mass House stood where the church is sited; to reach it, one went through an inn called the Adam and Eve.)

There were many other good architects through the centuries who worked in Dublin, including **Edward Parke**, **William Murray** and **Edward Welby Pugin**, who designed the Augustinian Church in Thomas St. The McCabe Memorial (1887) in Glasnevin cemetery, with carved decoration by **C.W. Harrison**, is a Victorian gem.

## THE 20TH CENTURY

In this century most architecture has been, with a few admirable exceptions, little short of vandalism. The most famous architect was **Micheal Scott** of the firm **Scott Tallon & Walker**, who were responsible for many buildings including the Bus Station in Central Dublin (Busaras) and the Abbey Theatre. **Sam Stephenson and Associates** were responsible for the Civic Offices of Dublin Corporation on Wood Quay, about which more people seem to feel more strongly than almost any other thing that has happened in Dublin since the loss of Fitzwilliam St. in the early 1960s (see DAY 4, page 168).

The irony is that the citizens of those European capitals that were devastated by World War II have worked painstakingly, meticulously over the years to reconstruct the beauty that was so violently lost. In Dublin, which never suffered the war, the enemy is within.

Perhaps one heartening development is that in 1989 a developer knocked down, in breach of the law, the Grammar School, the finest 18thC buildings in Drogheda. The High Court issued an order requiring them to salvage and store all the demolished materials for its rebuilding. This was the first time a developer has been literally stopped in his tracks, and it created a fine precedent.

Perhaps the most cheering thing of all is that the younger generation is fighting back. One of the most influential and certainly the richest sections in Irish society, the music and rock groups, are doing their bit. The huge warehouse by the docks which could so easily have been demolished has been turned into The Point, a huge concert hall, and U2 has chosen a fine Victorian warehouse for use as their headquarters. And Temple Bar, once earmarked for a bus station, is now one of the most congenial areas of Dublin.

A footnote: there are many private houses both N and S of the Liffey that have been restored by private individuals or have been preserved intact. Many of these are open at the owners' discretion, and a list may be obtained from the Irish Tourist Board.

James Gandon's masterpiece, the **Four Courts.**

# Guide books and background reading

Ireland has produced so many writers of genius that there is a wealth of all kinds of literature about the country. And there has been such an extraordinary upsurge of interest in all things Irish in the last ten years that in almost every bookstore in Dublin, large sections are devoted to matters of Irish interest and every aspect of Irish life.

The best general history is *Modern Ireland 1600-1972* by R.F. Foster (Allen Lane/The Penguin Press). For a quick incisive fix on the modes and mores of modern Ireland from a witty acute writer who misses nothing and has a peerless sense of humor, read *The Best of Nell,* a selection of work over 14 years by Nell MacCafferty, who has played a valuable role in shaping modern Ireland's consciousness (Attic Press). She also writes a column in the *Irish Press* newspaper on Thursday, and if you read her and Nuala O'Faolain in the *Irish Times* on Monday you will not only get the best eye-view of daily Irish life, you will get the best prose. And Kevin Meyer's *Diary* in the *Irish Times* is a must.

One of the best guidebooks to Ireland as a whole is *The Companion Guide to Ireland* by Brendan Lehane, which is comprehensive on Dublin (Collins). Another invaluable background book is Maurice Craig's *Architecture of Ireland* (Batsford) and his *Dublin 1660-1860* (Penguin).

*The Ultimate Dublin Guide: An A-Z of Everything* by Brian Lalor (O'Brien Press) is a factual gazetteer in alphabetical format about Dublin, which is informative and easy to use. *Heritage: A Visitor's Guide* is a well-designed book published by the Office of Public Works, describing all the monuments in their care.

For insight into the Anglo-Irish aspect, the most informative books are *The Anglo-Irish Tradition* by J.C. Beckett, *Ascendancy to Oblivion* by Michael McConville and *Twilight of the Ascendancy* by Mark Bence-Jones. *Ireland Observed* by Desmond Fitzgerald and Maurice Craig is an informative and revealing book, as is the lavish *Great Irish Houses and Castles* by Jacqueline O'Brien and Desmond Guinness (Weidenfeld).

Recommended background reading includes *Celtic Dawn* by Ulick O'Connor, *The Houses of Irish Writers* by Caroline Walsh, and *The Houses of Ireland* by Brian de Breffny and Rosemary FFolliott.

V.S. Pritchett's *Dublin: A Portrait* (with photographs by Evelyn Hofer) is a brilliant and imaginative jump into the inner life of the city, as valid now as when it was written 20 years ago. It has recently been republished as a text piece by Chatto and Windus. *Where They Lived in Dublin* by John Cowell is an idiosyncratic guide to famous denizens of Dublin (The O'Brien Press).

*Dublin: A Traveller's Companion,* selected and introduced by Thomas and Valerie Pakenham (Constable), is an interesting and often amusing anthology of writings about Dublin from the 16thC to the present day.

Oliver St John Gogarty's books *It Isn't This Time of the Year at All* and *As I was Going Down Sackville Street* are a trifle heavy-handed, but full of nuggets about the famous literary age of Dublin from the turn of this century (Sphere). *Dead as Doornails* by Anthony Cronin is a fascinating account of the literary life and characters of Dublin in more recent years (Oxford University Press).

The slender, well-illustrated pamphlets in the *Irish Heritage Series* are well worth collecting. Accurate, precise and elegant, these little compendiums, written by experts in their field, are invaluable (Eason & Son Ltd).

*The Complete Wicklow Way,* a step-by-step guide by S.B. Malone, is a comprehensive signposted walking trail from Marley Park over the hills and glens of Wicklow (see EXCURSIONS, page 225) by the man who thought up the idea of the way (O'Brien Press).

The story of one of the most celebrated heroes in Irish mythology, literature and story-telling, *Fionn MacCumhaill — Images of the Gaelic Hero* by Daithi O h-Ogain is a scholarly account (Gill and MacMillan).

For a comprehensive dip into the best of writing in Ireland past, read *Irish Literature: A Reader* by Maureen O'Rourke Murphy and James MacKillop, an anthology of Irish writing from the 8thC to the present day. It is an unusual and delightful selection (Syracuse University Press).

Any books by Roddy Doyle give a unique view into proletarian Dublin life. *The Commitments* and *The Van* are two of his best.

*Cuisine le Mairin* is a delightful food-book, a bilingual collection of recipes and anecdotes, which give instant access to the food and food customs of Ireland: there is hardly a better way to read a secret history of its country than to know how its people ate (Attic Press). *The Land of Milk and Honey* by Brid Mahon is a clever culinary guide straying through centuries and across the regions of Ireland, full of fascinating information about traditional Irish food and drink. A mix of myth legend, fact and recipe (Poolbeg Press).

In the past few years there has been a renaissance in Irish poetry, a quite extraordinary flowering. There are good anthologies of modern Irish poems available everywhere and the poetry sections in most bookstores are bulging. Seamus Heaney, Paul Muldoon, Derek Mahon, Ciaran Carson and Medbh McGuckian are among the best Irish poets.

Claire Boylan's novel *Home Rule* (Hamish Hamilton) is an extraordinary depiction of Dublin at the turn of the century; and Paul Durcan's *Crazy about Women* is a unique book — a collection of poems inspired by, and in response to, paintings in the National Gallery (The National Gallery Publications).

In James Joyce's *Ulysses* his view of Dublin is so intricately linked with what he called its actualicity that sometimes it seems as if it only half existed before he added its missing dimension in his great novel. His attitude toward the city of his birth was a characteristically Irish one: on the one hand, he despised both it and its inhabitants; on the other, he loved it with a passion that was translated into an obsessive life's work. And it has to be said that he also produced a work that many people can't or won't read. If you really want to know more about Dublin than Dubliners themselves, and haven't already read it, then this is the book that transfixed the city in the world's imagination.

The originating British publisher is given for most of the books mentioned above.

For books of Irish interest, go to:

- **Cathach Books**    10 Duke St., Dublin, map **4D4**  ☎(01) 6718676
- **Carraig Books**    73 Main St., Blackrock, Co. Dublin, map **2D4**  ☎(01) 2882575
- **De Burca Rare Books**    27 Priory Drive, Blackrock, map **2D4**  ☎(01) 2882159

# Sightseeing

## How to use this chapter

I have divided sightseeing into daily itineraries, and some involve longer walks than others: Dublin is so full of things worth seeing that even a short walk can take up pages of this guide. So, walking around Trinity College, for example, may not involve much leg-work, but it does demand a lot of eye-work. If you wander off the routes suggested in these daily excursions you will never be far away from the center of Dublin or another itinerary; just take up where you left off.

There are four itineraries: the first and last involve close-quarter exploration, and the middle two would demand more energetic walking if you followed them to the letter. Whether you do so, or whether you treat them as a lucky dip, is entirely up to you. The itineraries are:

- **DAY 1** (page 90): St Stephen's Green to College Green
- **DAY 2** (page 116): Dublin north of the Liffey
- **DAY 3** (page 137): Old Dublin
- **DAY 4** (page 160): The Merrion area and the Pembroke estate
- The chapter ends with a special feature on **PHOENIX PARK**.

### MAPS

City maps of Dublin available commercially are not well detailed. They are based only on the national grid, whose primary role is not the orientation of visitors. There is no good A-Z street directory.

The **Dublin Street Guide** is published by the Ordnance Survey. Be warned — it is difficult to use, because rather than looking up the street name and then turning to the relevant page, you are referred to a grid in the middle of the book, and having found the grid, you turn to the map, and search . . . and search . . . and search . . . . Those without perfect 20:20 vision will need glasses to see anything, and the text includes 20 pages of streets not named on the map. Grown men are found whimpering trying to find, for example, Henrietta St. However, Dubliners are kind and will often lead you out of their way to where you thought you wanted to go.

This lack of street direction has been kept in mind in this volume. Here, in the back of the book, are **maps of Dublin**, and a LIST OF STREET NAMES starting on page 276. And each DAY has its own enlarged area map, with additional detail relevant to the text.

# Day 1
## St Stephen's Green to College Green

*See Dublin City map **4**, and DAY 1 map opposite.*

How you see Dublin depends on the light. Dublin is governed by its sky and its light, and the Custom House, for example, looks different when it is retracting under the "yellow rain guttering down" and its dome looks like a shivering goose pimple, from when it lies placid under a blue and pearly sky. The material world of Dublin is a prime trick, varyingly repeated, of that old Gaelic magician, the light.

**College Green**, in the center of Dublin, is a fine focus for any architectural tour of the city. You could start by wending your way from **St Stephen's Green** down to College Green. There is a popular song that goes: "Dublin can be heaven, with a coffee at eleven and a stroll around Stephen's Green." But starting there can make you pause, since one genteel section of Dublin society traditionally called it Stephens Green and the other St Stephen's. Whichever, it is a lovely oasis in the middle of Dublin.

St Stephen's Green is two distinct entities: the buildings around the Green, and the green heartland, the oldest park in Ireland, laid out in 1664. For a small city park it is agreeably varied and secretive (well, not *that* small: it extends to 27 acres).

It was always a public park "wholie kept for the use of citizens and others, to walk and take the open air," save for a period in the mean 19thC when it was closed to everyone but residents with keys. The railings were put up in 1815 to commemorate Waterloo.

Lord Ardilaun, the chairman of the Guinness brewery which has played such a large part in the life of Dublin, bought out all the keys from the residents around the green, landscaped it, and presented it to Dublin in 1880, since when it has become essential to this area, the lungs of this part of the city.

It is a well-tended municipal place with good shrubs and plantings and, in the summer, bedded-out flowers in such livid colors as to rattle the eyes in your head. There are noble trees, shrubberies, bridges, islands, secret lawns, plantations and curving paths meandering from one corner of the square to the other, opening up many a vignette of Dublin life, from old men with their grandchildren, to businessmen earnest in discussions about where to buy the next drink, to respectable middle-aged women furtively snipping plant cuttings with nail scissors and hiding them in their bags; a whole gamut, and they don't come much more gamuty than Dubliners taking their time and their leisure. There are wide lawns, a large lake, and a bandstand where live music is often played during the summer months, anything from a brass band to a group appearing that night at the Olympia Theatre. One minute the bandstand is empty and there is hardly anyone about; the next a rock group has struck up and the whole scene is *en fête*.

One could spend a lot of time in St Stephen's Green just looking at

# DAY 1

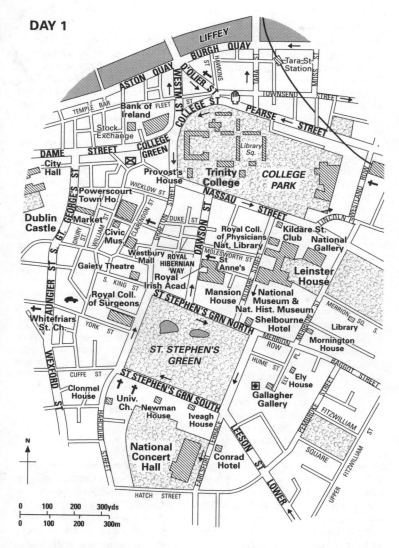

people and the houses that surround it. But "doing" the monuments and statues is a mini-tour in itself and a nice game of hide-and-seek, or perhaps connections in the Forsterian sense, since the monuments in the green commemorate events and people connected to the green and its environs. And if you sit down to observe the world going by, there are many benches dedicated to famous Dubliners. Forget about judging the aesthetic merits of the monuments — there is no point.

## Clockwise around St Stephen's Green

Start at the NW corner of the Green. The entrance arch facing Grafton St. is **Fusiliers' Arch** (1907), also known as Traitors' Arch, a memorial to the members of the Royal Dublin Fusiliers killed in the Boer war. Along from here on the N side is a decorative trough and drinking fountain for refreshing parched horses, presented by Lady Laura Grattan in 1880. This is not just a handsome memorial to vanished days: in the summer months, horse-drawn jaunting cars and carriages line up along the N side waiting to take people on a tour of the surrounding streets.

Just inside the Green, on the Grafton St. (W) side, is a **memorial to O'Donovan Rossa**, fighter and general rebel, Fenian leader and editor of the *United Irishman*. He died in New York but is buried in Dublin, and Patrick Pearse's panegyric at his funeral is seen as an early warning and a blueprint of the ethos of the 1916 Rising: "Life springs from death and from the graves of patriotic men and women spring living nations." The monument, by Seamus Murphy, that fine Cork sculptor, looks almost megalithic, but was erected in 1954.

Paid for by public subscription, Thomas Farrell's **statue of Lord Ardilaun**, who presented St Stephen's Green to the nation, stands, or rather sits — for he is seated on an elaborate chair — on the W side of the Green, gazing in the direction of the Guinness brewery.

The **bust of James Clarence Mangan** — the strange, melancholy poet who was born in Fishamble St., lived in direst poverty in York St., taught himself many languages, and died of drugs, alcohol and cholera in the Meath Hospital — rests on a pedestal bearing a curiously blanched representation of *Dark Rosaleen*. This was the title of his most famous poem, a lament, hymn and anthem to this most romantic of all personifications of Ireland, once again, of course, steeped in blood.

> *Oh the Erne shall run red*
> *With redundance of blood.*
> *The earth shall rock beneath our tread.*
> *And flames wrap hill and wood.*

Poor old Ireland, constantly threatened with rape and pillage, constantly under siege: no wonder James Joyce with his modest ambition to glorify ordinariness and redeem a nation through *words* has become a national hero. A **bust of James Joyce** by Marjorie Fitzgibbon, with his long, mean face and beautiful be-ringed fingers, faces no. 86, now part of **Newman House**, wherein he set the famous and illuminating conversation between Stephen Daedalus and the Dean about the use of the word tundish (meaning funnel) in *A Portrait of the Artist as a Young Man*.

This particular piece of sophistry has become talismanic in Irish literature: "His language, so familiar and so foreign, will always be for me an acquired speech . . ." The college is now open to the public (see page 97). There is also a bench nearby dedicated to Joyce and to his father, the feckless John, who once said of his son that if you dropped him in the Sahara he would make a map of it. One can't help speculating on how much he would have relished his son's fame and how *very* much he would have claimed credit for it.

Nearby is a **bust of Thomas Kettle**, the Irish poet who was killed at the Battle of the Somme in the 1914-18 War and who is widely known in Ireland for his poem, which ends:

> *So here, while the mad guns curse overhead,*
> *And tired men sigh, with mud for couch and floor,*
> *Know that we fools, now with the foolish dead*
> *Died not for flag, for king nor Emperor —*
> *But for a dream, born in a herdsman's shed,*
> *And for the secret scripture of the poor.*

It was Kettle, a classmate of Joyce's, who defined the modern way forward for Ireland: "If Ireland is to become truly Irish, she must first become European," though his pronouncement was not particularly popular, since the Irish are generally only concerned with finding out what being Irish means.

Nearby is the **bust of the Countess Markiewicz** (again the work of Seamus Murphy), who fought at the head of her battalion in the Green, in the 1916 Rising — just marched in, in her cockaded hat, and barricaded herself and her troops into the little hillocks and dells, to the perfect astonishment of the Easter Bank Holiday revelers, who suddenly found themselves in the middle of a war. She, with her sister Eva Gore-Booth, inspired the marvelous poem by Yeats, which begins:

> *The light of evening, Lissadell,*
> *Great windows open to the south,*
> *Two girls in silk kimonos, both*
> *Beautiful, one a gazelle.*

Nearby is the **W.B. Yeats memorial** by Henry Moore, *Knife Edge*, unveiled in 1967 in Moore's presence, which in no way inhibited the usual Irish relish for controversy about modern art. This piece is often the focal point for poetry readings and events in the square. (A trustee of the Municipal Gallery of Modern Art, looking at a new Henry Moore sculpture, observed, "That figure has got leprosy.")

Perhaps the most prominent monument is on the NE corner, just across and down from the Shelbourne Hotel. It is the memorial to **Wolfe Tone** by Edward Delaney, which, because of its shape, was immediately christened *Tonehenge* by Dublin wits. Behind it is *Famine*, also by Delaney, a sad representation of the specter that for so long haunted Ireland. There are many other telling monuments to be discovered in the Green, and if you make a little pilgrimage here into busy Merrion Row, you will find the modest Huguenot graveyard, dated 1693, behind its railings, lately restored by the French government. Here lie the relics of a people who enriched Dublin, whose other memorials are in their names interwoven with those of Dublin streets and Dublin life — D'Olier, LaTouche, Le Fanu, and many more.

All this area is rich in every sense. Impressive houses ring the Green on all four sides, although the felicitous unity has been disrupted on the W and NE sides in particular by shopfronts. Every house has a special history.

The N side used to be called **Beaux Walk** in the 18thC, since this is where the dandies strolled — "hellfire bucks, drinking brandy and claret wine" — and the Pinkindindies, whose pointed swords pricked passers-by as they strode along. Many of the large houses, which are now clubs, contain fine plasterwork. On this side too is the **Shelbourne Hotel**, the most famous hotel in Dublin and a meeting place for Dubliners and visitors all day long.

The E side has lovely houses stretching its length in unity. Halfway along, just off Hume St., is **Ely Place**, rich in lore and history. But perhaps no street in Dublin should have a more emotive ring than **Hume Street**, for it was here in 1969 that architectural students from universities and colleges occupied a group of Georgian buildings that a property developer was about to demolish. It was almost the first time that battle had been joined on such an issue in Dublin, and though the developers got their way, they had to revise their proposed new building so that it was more in keeping with the area. Since then, public awareness of the value of such buildings has been greatly increased.

**Ely House** *(8 Ely Place, map* 4E5 ☎ *(01) 6761835/6762839),* which faces down Hume St., was built for the Earl of Ely in 1771. Today it is occupied by the Knights of Columbanus, a religious lay-order, spoken of with a certain *frisson* in Dublin as a kind of Catholic freemasonry. It is a noble seven-bay building, unique in Dublin, with an interior graced by fantastic Rococo plasterwork by Michael Stapleton. The decoration on the staircase is by an unknown genius.

At the foot of the stairs is a life-sized figure of Hercules in stone, and the bronze panels on the stairs depict his labors in metaphorical devices. Connoisseurs point out that it is copied from one in the Musée d'Art Moderne in Brussels. Frank O'Connor, the writer, who was a director of the Abbey Theatre, visited it 40 years ago and wrote:

> *We stepped inside, and made the acquaintance of Hercules. Hercules, lifesize, was acting as newel post of the great staircase which, instead of banisters, had long gilded beasts who slunk up the stairs to the first-floor landing. Against the Venetian window which lit the well of the stairs was a shadowy figure supporting the cross, and on the wall on our left a big picture of the Pope looking at Hercules.*

Many guide books say that Ely House can be visited at reasonable hours by arrangement. But I have tried to gain access many times and have always been thrown back from the barricades by an entry phone, and the voice of a querulous office worker on the third floor who will never open the door. This, all the same, is one of the most famous interiors in Dublin. Groups may visit by prior arrangement only.

Also on Ely Place is the **Royal Hibernian Academy's Gallagher Gallery**, an inappropriate building out of keeping with this street and sporting a plaque that thanks a building speculator for its squat red existence on the site of Oliver St John Gogarty's house and George Moore's garden. The plaque drips gall. St John Gogarty, a famous Dublin wit, a fine lyric poet and writer and a surgeon, was perhaps most famous of all (and this would surely have made him furious) as the prototype for Buck Mulligan in *Ulysses*. Inside, the Gallagher Gallery has fine exhibition space both for sculpture and for painting and kinetic art. The Irish Watercolour Society exhibits here, and their work is extremely interesting. (For further details see ART GALLERIES, page 67.)

The adjacent gardens used to belong to no. 4, where lived the writer and poet George Moore, who teased his neighbors dreadfully and was generally Moore-ish, that is to say either totally odious or mildly winning. (Oscar Wilde, who hated him — it was mutual — said, "Moore has not an enemy in the world, and none of his friends like him . . .") He wrote two books of verse, whose titles, *Flowers of Passion* and *Pagan Poems*, perhaps hint at their flavor.

It was here that he wrote his autobiographical *Hail and Farewell*, which gives such an evocative, invaluable and somewhat jaundiced account of Dublin in his day, at the turn of the century. (Sarah Purser, a Dublin artist — see FINE ARTS, page 66 — said of him, "Most men kiss and don't tell: Moore doesn't kiss and tells.") Moore was delighted that the windows of his house overlooked the back garden of the Loreto convent, where he could see, he said, the nuns' knickers drying on the line. He turned against Dublin later in life, and when a shop opened in St Stephen's Green, he cried, "Other shops will follow and this beautiful city of Dublin will become in a very few years as garish as London."

In this street, a century before, lived the hated Earl of Clare (1750-1817), who so relentlessly opposed reconciliation in Ireland, and John Philpott Curran, the lawyer, whose daughter was romantically involved with the rebel leader, Robert Emmet. The latter, high in the pantheon of Ireland's young heroes, was born at no. 124. **Emmet's statue** by Jerome Connor, presented to the people of Ireland in 1966 by Irish-American admirers, stands opposite his house. His famous speech from the dock, which ended with the words "When my country takes her place among the nations of the earth, then, and not till then, let my epitaph be written. I have done . . ." is still a rallying cry in Ireland.

When Curran learned of the affair he banished Emmet from the house and refused to defend him when he was on trial fighting for his life. Emmet was beheaded, and the sad story of the young lovers was immortalized in Moore's song: "She is far from the land where her young hero sleeps." In fact, Sarah married an Englishman and died in India. (The house is open only by appointment).

**Leeson St.** is a main thoroughfare leading into the SE corner of the Green. It is lined with new, obtrusive buildings, and their detailing, with their backs turned on the street, is a national disgrace. The other street meeting at this main junction is **Earlsfort Terrace**, where battles for the new university were waged and lost and won.

The history of Catholic higher education in Ireland is not a happy one. Catholics and dissenters were barred from taking degrees in Ireland, and those few Catholics who could afford higher education had to go to the Continent. The first Catholic University was set up under John Henry Newman in 1854 in the building of an older institute, but in a spirit of absolute meanness it was not given any funds or the right to grant degrees. It faltered, Newman resigned, and in 1879 the Royal University was set up in its stead.

The Royal and Catholic became University College Dublin. In 1908 an act allowed a National Catholic University and the buildings in Earlsfort Terrace were taken over for that purpose. The main block, with its long limestone facade and Doric pillars, was designed by R.M. Butler in 1912. **Alexandra College** in the same street was one of the most famous girl's schools in Dublin and pioneered the fight for the admission of women to university, finally achieved at Trinity in 1903. It was demolished in 1972 and the **Conrad Hotel** stands in its place.

The University moved out to its new campus at Belfield in Stillorgan, and the old Examination Hall in Earlsfort Terrace was expertly and successfully converted into the **National Concert Hall**, something that formerly Dublin had sadly lacked. In a short space of time, with concerts, shows, opera and recitals, this has become integral to Dublin's musical life. Incidentally, the same acoustic expert, V.C. Jordan, who worked on the Metropolitan Opera House in New York and the Sydney Opera House, designed the acoustics. *(Earlsfort Terrace, map 4F5* ☎ *(01) 6711533, booking office open Mon-Sat 11am-7pm* AE ⊕ ⊙ VISA *Sunday concerts open from 7pm; tickets cannot be exchanged.)*

In a building on Earlsfort Terrace is stored the State Coach of the Lord Mayor of Dublin in 1791, where it had lain disregarded for decades. Now wonderfully restored, you can see it if you're in Dublin for the St Patrick's Day Parade.

**Iveagh House**, formerly nos. 80 and 81 on the s side of St Stephen's Green, incorporated a smaller house designed by Richard Castle and given to the Irish nation in 1939 by Rupert Guinness, the second Lord Iveagh. It is now the Department of Foreign Affairs, and little of the original facade remains. Mrs Clayton, wife of the Archbishop of Dublin who lived here in 1731, described it thus:

*First there is a very good hall well filled with servants, then a room of eighteen foot square, wainscoted with oak, the panels all carved, and the doors and chimney finished with very fine high carving, the ceiling stucco, the window-curtains and chairs yellow Genoa damask, portraits and landscapes, very well done, round the room, marble tables between the windows, and looking glasses with gilt frames. The next room is twenty-eight foot long and twenty-two broad, and is as finely adorned as damask, pictures, and busts can make it, besides the floor being entirely covered with the finest Persian carpet that ever was seen.*

This is all changed now, but the rooms on the first floor are important. The music room is decorated with charming motifs of musical instruments, and there are three romantic views of Roman Antiquities by the

Irish painter George Barret, who had in his youth been apprenticed to a stay-maker. He studied art with Robert West and had a great success in London exhibiting Irish landscapes "done from life." He made a fortune, squandered it and was rescued by Edmund Burke, that great Irishman, philosopher and orator. Burke was a man of supreme intellectual integrity who knew so much about so much and was deeply interested in art and esthetics. His book, *A Philosophical Enquiry Into The Origin of Our Ideas of the Sublime and the Beautiful* (more familiarly called simply *The Sublime and the Beautiful*) was a powerful influence on the sensibility of generations of readers and painters.

The ballroom in Iveagh House was added by Sir Benjamin Lee Guinness, that same benefactor who caused St Patrick's Cathedral to be restored out of all knowing (see DAY 3, page 150), and father of Lord Ardilaun, who presented St Stephen's Green to the nation. The ballroom was one of the wonders of Dublin, with its onyx and marble. Katherine Everett, the Irish writer who was once secretary to Lady Ardilaun, noted that although she owned many great houses, nothing gave her as much pleasure as her house on St Stephens Green. "She was touchingly delighted when connoisseurs admired her rooms . . . for she had never before enjoyed informed appreciation of her great possessions." Alas, for security reasons Iveagh House is not open to the public.

Richard Castle's other buildings to the s side are w of Iveagh House. He was responsible for **no. 85**, now part of Newman House (nos. 85 and 86), which belongs to **University College, Dublin** *(Newman House, 85-86 St Stephen's Green, map 4E4* ☎ *(01) 4757255/4751752, open June-Sept Tues-Fri 10am-4.30pm, Sat 2-4.30pm, Sun 11am-2pm, closed rest of year except for guided groups, by appointment only* ☎ *)*. No. 85 was one of the earliest buildings on the Green, built in 1740 for Hugh Montgomery in order to show his neighbors that he was a man of some substance. The house was detached and was called Clanwilliam House and was very grand. It still is: its saloon, on the first floor, is graced by an elaborate Rococo ceiling by Paul and Philip Lafranchini, which is a smaller version of the famous one at Carton House in Co. Kildare (see EXCURSIONS, page 245).

Downstairs, also by the Lafranchini brothers, is the **Apollo Room**, a small reception room off the entrance hall, with a life-sized figure of Apollo over the mantle accompanied by Nine Muses. This astonishing piece of roomscape, to put it mildly, has been beautifully restored; in fact, both houses, after years of wear and tear of university life, are being brought back to felicitous grandeur, although as yet there is no furniture to speak of in any of the rooms. But with interior decoration like this *in situ,* one hardly needs anything so prosaic as furnishings.

**No. 86** (the other part of Newman House) was also designed by Richard Castle for Richard Chappel "Burn-chapel" Whaley, an 18thC bigot whose nickname arose from his little way of hunting priests and burning their Mass-houses. He, it is said, had his house built in a different idiom in order to aggravate Hugh Montgomery next door. But he must have had some redeeming features, if only a sense of humor, judging by a check he wrote to his banker, the Huguenot grandee David LaTouche, whose daughter married a cousin of Henry Grattan (Dublin was a small inter-related city), which was duly honored: "Mr Latouche open your pouch / And give unto my darling / Five hundred pounds sterling / For which this will be your bailey / Signed Richard Chappel Whaley."

(There is a beautiful memorial nearly 25 feet high, with Mr LaTouche aboard a large sarcophagus, clutching his left bosom like Napoleon, in Delgany Church near Greystones: see EXCURSIONS, page 231.)

The plasterwork in no. 86 was done by Robert West, who had a studio near the Liffey and thus had plenty of opportunity to observe birds whirling and cresting. This is a rococo and fantastic event, an aviary of over 60 birds frozen in mid-perch, ranging over ceilings, walls and staircases. Nothing could be in greater contrast to the chaste stillness of the Lafranchini plasterwork next door, although the ceiling in the magnificent saloon or *piano nobile* on the first floor is also by them. During the occupation by the Catholic University, the room was used as a chapel and was painted soup-brown, perhaps to help the students meditate on the next world.

Whaley's son Thomas (Buck) Whaley, who also lived at no. 86, sounds an even more hair-raising member of society than his father. Having inherited a fortune at an early age, he dissipated it in gambling and general debauchery and then, bored, wagered that he could travel to Jerusalem and back within a year, set off, played handball against a wall in the Holy City, returned within nine months, and is reputed to have won a fortune on his bet — estimates vary from £7,000 to £20,000. ("The only instance in all my life before," he said, "in which any of my projects turned out to my advantage.")

Visiting Newman House is a great pleasure, not least because of the knowledgeable and charming guides. They point out that while the houses were used as rooms for the students of the Catholic University, the goddesses, cavorting and reclining nakedly, were subject to censorship, and Juno, for the moment, still wears a rough plaster throw covering her ruder bits.

Newman House, with its lead lion slumbering above the main door, has undergone a transformation and is already one of the sights of Dublin. (In the basement below is one of the best restaurants in Dublin, **The Commons** (see EATING AND DRINKING).

Next door is the Byzantine-style **University Church**, commissioned by the famous Doctor John Henry Newman, later Cardinal Newman, who, as rector of the new Catholic university, fought a dispiriting battle against the repressive attitudes of his Dublin superiors. He brought John Hungerford Pollen over from England in 1853 to build his church, which might have strayed from Constantinople via Oxford to settle, Russian Orthodox-fashion, in the square. With its mysterious atmosphere, gleaming Irish marble (from Connemara and Kilkenny), highly decorated apse and rich polychromatic decorations, it is both fascinating and soothing after a heavy spell of sightseeing. It is now a fashionable church for Dublin weddings, and one of the best oases in Dublin.

Nearly every Georgian house in Dublin has good plasterwork, and one of the pleasures of walking along the streets at dusk is looking in at the cornices and ceilings. St Stephen's Green is one of the best places for plaster-spotting. The two houses that make up **Newman House** are among the finest you will see in Dublin, certainly the finest you will see without difficulty, because although there are other houses being restored and reconstituted and their owners will show you around, they do not always appear in guide books.

**Harcourt Street** runs from the SW corner of the Green, but its unity has been scarred. W.B. Yeats went to school here in the High School, since demolished. Still, here is the rail station, with an interesting Roman Doric facade designed by George Wilkinson in 1859, now used as an office, although people dream about it being reopened as a station. It would certainly make sense. Dublin traffic is terribly congested and renders street life less agreeable than it should be.

A possible detour is down Harcourt St. to its junction with Harcourt Rd., where you turn right. Follow the road some 350 yards along and turn left into Synge St. At no. 33 is **Shaw's Birth Place Museum**, rescued at the last minute by the Irish Georgian Society. The Irish Tourist Board has now taken it over and when restoration is finished (scheduled for 1993) it will be part of the Dublin Writers Museum (see DAY 2, page 126). Shaw wrote the inscription on the plaque himself: *Bernard Shaw, author of many plays, was born in this house 26th July 1856.*

Back on the Green, the W side is dominated by the pedimented and pillared bulk of the **Royal College of Surgeons**, designed by Edward Parke in 1806. Its N front was lengthened in 1826 by William Murray, a nephew of the great Francis Johnston who built so many of Dublin's fine buildings. In the tympanum are representations of *Medicine* and *Health,* and there are bullet marks on the facade, memorials to the fierce fighting in 1916 when Countess Markiewicz occupied the building. (She searched for scalpels in case it came to hand-to-hand fighting.) Heading N, the rest of the Green from here down to Grafton St. is mostly shops and restaurants and new shopping centers.

### Kildare Street

Leading off St Stephen's Green on the N side, Kildare St. was built at about the same time as Merrion Square (see DAY 4), and almost as its counterpoint. Ten peers had their houses in this street at the time when **Leinster House** was at its peak as the town house of the Duke of Leinster. The great iron gates of the palace that now houses the **Dail Eireann** are guarded by the *Garda Siochana,* the Irish police, and occasionally are picketed by voters with a grievance, although the grievances are only manifested by placards: the picketers generally look fairly content.

On either side of the gates are the entrances to the **National Library** to the left (as you face into Leinster House) and the **National Museum,** which faces the Library. Both buildings with their pavilions and semicircular porticos, twin images, were designed in the 1880s by the confusingly named Sir Thomas N. Deane and his son Sir Thomas M. Deane of the famous firm Deane & Woodward, who built so many of Dublin's great Victorian buildings.

The Library houses a massive archive of information about Ireland and is treasure trove for scholars — books, maps, periodicals, paintings and much else besides. Tickets are needed for the reading rooms. To gain access, telephone ahead stating your requirements ( ☎ *(01) 6618811)*.

The National Museum has a permanent, mouth-droppingly wonderful display of Irish gold, as well as an exhibition showing the growth of Dublin, and Irish glass and ceramics. There are wonderful things in this museum, with its intimate and gentle atmosphere (see page 72). It is being completely refurbished and it is hoped that its unique appeal will be preserved.

At the bottom of the street is the **Royal College of Physicians**, a porticoed building by W.G. Murray, which contains a fine collection of portraits of surgeons and physicians. An Irishman, Dr Barry O'Meara, was Napoleon's doctor, and his collection of Napoleonic memorabilia is here. This College of Physicians was one of the first to admit women to medicine. Of the first 50 women on the medical register, 80 percent were licentiates of the college. *(Not open save by special arrangement.)*

Nearby at no. 2 is the **Kildare Street Club**, built 1859-61 by the firm of Deane & Woodward. This High Victorian building is one of the best architectural manifestations of the devout interest of the mid-Victorians in medieval architecture, fueled by the work of Augustus Pugin and the writing of John Ruskin. It is often described as "Lombardo-Venetian-style," but with its red-brick walls, stone dressings and corbeled cornice, is too solidly anchored into the ground to have any Venetian lightness.

There are other Ruskinian Gothic buildings scattered throughout Dublin: they seemed to have the right gravitas to match up to the lordly aspirations of the Victorian merchants and administrators who built them. Unfortunately the merchants and administrators in charge these days do not have the same sensibility or aspirations for Dublin's future. Not overmuch bothered about preserving these buildings, they seem unaware of the national treasures they have in these magnificent monuments.

Some are well looked after, notably the **Museum Building** in Trinity, and some of the major banks, but many more have suffered through planning disasters and official vandalism. It is part of the old story; and although Georgian architecture is being perceived at last as an asset, Victorian architecture, still, is not. In 20 years' time the city will grieve for the Victorian buildings it has lost, as it occasionally grieves now for the Georgian ones it once cast away. Breast-beating never did anyone any good. (An honourable exception is the **National Irish Bank** in College Green, built by W.G. Murray in 1867 and beautifully restored.)

The Kildare Street Club is a self-consciously grand building, a kind of alderman in its Dublin street, and is redeemed from pomposity by its carved windowsills with their delightful little carvings of whimsical beasts done by the O'Shea brothers, famous stonemasons from Cork. They were men of "pronounced character, insubordinate to a degree." In other words they were independent Irish artists; but in their work they seemed to Ruskin to justify his faith in the "genius of the unassisted Workman." The club was the last bastion of the Ascendancy, and famously, unrepentantly philistine. Founded in 1782, it seems to have mummified from its very beginning. (In 1938 the writer Claud Cockburn overheard the Earl of Wicklow mulling over the news that some kind of international conflict might be starting. He told anyone who would listen that they could take it from him that it was all nonsense.)

George Moore wrote, "The club is a sort of oyster bed into which all the sons of the landed gentry fall as a matter of course . . . there they remained spending their days drinking sherry and cursing Gladstone in a sort of dead language which the larva-like stupidity of the club has preserved . . . . " Moore had a pen that could be deadly, although not as deadly as W.B. Yeats, who was half-friend, half-enemy to Moore and wrote that he looked like an umbrella left behind at a party and was "more mob than man."

The history of the club makes for a certain teeth-grindingly amusing reading. One story concerns the saintly Edward Martyn, a cousin of George Moore, who was also a writer, though not a very good one. Although a fully paid-up member of both the landed gentry and the Kildare Street Club, he fervently espoused the cause of Irish nationalism and, what was worse, broadcast this in the Club, where the very word could bring on apoplexy among the more choleric members. The Club moved to have him expelled; a court case followed, which Martyn won, and he returned to the Club in great good humor. His cousin Daisy, Countess of Fingall, asked him how he could bear to return to a place where he was so publicly unpopular, and he replied "I like the food."

In fact he was a abstemious man. The (perhaps apocryphal) story goes that afterwards, of an evening, he enacted an elaborate tease whereby he would kneel in the main window of the Club and, as the Angelus was rung from the bells of the city, would intone the Rosary to a receptive crowd outside, who were more than happy to respond to the familiar religious mantra. This did not best please the members as they pushed their way into the bar. (The Angelus is a peal of three bells rung thrice; at its signal the work of the country paused for prayer. It is still broadcast on State radio, Radio Eireann, daily at 6pm, though many listeners find this a sectarian habit.)

The Kildare Street Club still exists, but is amalgamated with the University Club in a different building in St Stephen's Green.

Whatever the Club's role in Irish history, one mourns the vandalization of Benjamin Woodward's building and its interior, so steeped in incident and history that it ought to have been kept as a national treasure. Its unique staircase with pierced stone balustrades and its marvelous interiors were torn out as late as 1972 and were so badly remodeled that the new floors bisect the old windows and ruin its appearance.

The **State Heraldic Museum** (2 Kildare St., map 4D5 ☎ (01) 6614877, open Mon-Fri 10am-4.30pm; Genealogical Consultancy open Mon-Fri 10am-12.30pm, 2-4.30pm) is in the building now, and the office of the Chief Herald (formerly the office of Ulster King of Arms). The Museum is in what was the coffee room of the old Club and is hung with the heraldic banners of the Irish Chiefs. Also here are the blue robes and badges of the **Order of the Knights of St Patrick**, who for so long had their place in Dublin Castle (see DAY 3). On display is armorial china made for the use of entitled families, and objects decorated with heraldic devices, some of them so beautifully drawn they are small works of art in their own right and desirable little *objets de vertu.* The Museum illustrates the significance and display of heraldry down the ages.

### Dawson Street

At the bottom of Kildare St. is Nassau St., one of the busiest thoroughfares in Dublin, once known as Patrick's Well Lane. Straight ahead you can see the wall and trees that surround Trinity College.

The next major street left off Nassau St. is Dawson St. In earlier days this was known as Mynchen's Fields and was the property of the nunnery of St Mary's de Hogge. Then Joshua Dawson, a Dublin worthy and speculator (the two are rarely synonomous in Dublin), leased the land and in 1705 laid out and built the new street and gave it his own name. He built his own grand house paneled in oak in 1710, and five years later sold it to Dublin Corporation for £3,500.

Since then it has been the Lord Mayor's official residence, the **Mansion House**, and is reputed to be the oldest house in continuous occupation in Dublin. Formerly a refined, austere red-brick building, it is now ornamented with a bib and tucker of frilly ironwork, much despised by purists, disliked by Yeats, but Dublin likes it like that. Inside is the chair in which Handel is reputed to have conducted the first performance of *The Messiah,* that miraculous expression of faith first performed in Dublin in Fishamble St. in 1792 (see MUSIC, page 77).

Beside the Mansion house is the **Round Room**, designed by John Semple and built in a vast hurry for George IV's visit in 1821. This was not the most edifying event in Ireland's history. He is reputed to have arrived drunk, and though the death of his wife was the official reason for his canceling the anticipated country tour for which half the families in Ireland had beggared themselves, rebuilding and redecorating their houses, it was widely held that the real reason was that he was not fit to travel due to inebriation. It was noticed, all the same, that he could hurry straight enough to his mistress, the formidable Lady Conyingham in Slane, and that a new straight road had been built to facilitate his ardor. In 1919 the First Irish Parliament adopted the Declaration of Independence here.

Dawson St. is a busy commercial street. There are offices and good shops, and a large shopping center, **The Royal Hibernian Way**, under a covered arcade built on the site of the old Royal Hibernian Hotel, the scene of many a social and sporting memory. Within the precinct there are cafés, a pub and a buttery.

Just off the E side of Dawson St. in Molesworth St., the big Victorian porticoed building is the **Freemasons' Hall** *(Molesworth St., map 4 D5* ☎ *(01) 6761337, open June-Aug Mon-Fri for video show followed by ✗ at noon, 1pm, 2pm, 3pm; closed rest of year, but may be shown by appointment).* It is the headquarters of the Grand Lodge of Freemasons in Ireland, the second oldest Grand Lodge in the world. Inside is an extraordinary series of rooms decorated in four different styles: Ancient Egyptian, Classical, Gothic and Tudor. A small museum holds artifacts, documents and regalia of the Movement.

**St Ann's Church**, halfway up Dawson St., faces busy Molesworth St. and closes the view beautifully from Grafton St. Once one of the most fashionable churches in Dublin, it is an 18thC building with a Victorian-Romanesque facade added by Thomas Deane in 1868. It has a strange little oddity inside, in the form of shelving placed near the altar, to fulfil the terms of a bequest made by Theophilus, Lord Newtown, who bequeathed £13 a year for loaves of bread to be displayed there before being distributed to the poor of the parish.

The church is open daily all the year round. The memorial to Elizabeth Phibbs is by Edward Smyth, the great Irish sculptor (see FINE ARTS, page 66). The stained-glass windows are by Wilhelmina Geddes, one of the first of the Dublin stained-glass artists (see FINE ARTS, page 71). There are lunchtime concerts and recitals in the church now, a most tranquil way to spend a quiet lunch-hour ( ▓ *details of concert program on board beside the door*).

Academy House, or Northland House, is the **Royal Irish Academy** *(19 Dawson St., map **4E5** ☎ (01) 6762570; library open Mon-Fri 10.30am-5.30pm; membership essential, but can be applied for at any time; ground floor open for viewing during library hours)*. Founded in 1785 to promote the study of "Science, Polite Literature and Antiquities," its first president was the remarkable Earl of Charlemont. It is still a leading scholarly institute, and holds concerts and chamber music recitals. The building, designed in 1769 by John Ensor, who designed so much that is felicitous in the surrounding areas, has a magnificent ceiling, fine plasterwork in the Chinese style (white on a green background) and a good staircase.

It also has a glorious collection of those ancient manuscripts and incunabula which are among the chief treasures of Ireland and which have had such extraordinary vicissitudes and journeys through time before coming to rest in the two beautiful libraries of Trinity College and the Royal Irish Academy. (In many of these lovely objects, scholars have found little footnotes, almost doodles, like *haiku*, which leap across the centuries: "I ask your Beatitude, holy presbyter Patrick, that whoever holds in his hand this little book may remember (me) Columba the writer who wrote this little gospel for myself in the space of twelve days by the grace of our Lord.")

Here the manuscripts include the *Cathach* (or *Battler*) *Psalter of Columba*, the *Stowe Gospel* and the early 17thC *Annals of the Four Masters* (see MYTH, page 60). Here too are the *Book of Ballymote* and the *Book of Lecan*, two of the greatest medieval manuscripts, which somehow crept out of Trinity College Library at the end of the 17thC and made their way into this library, where they nestle very nicely. (Equally mysteriously, nine leaves of the *Yellow Book of Lecan* became detached and are back in the possession of Trinity.)

The *Cathach Psalter* dates from the middle of the 6thC (the sixth century!), and erroneous legend has it that this manuscript started a bloody war, was the making of a great saint and gave rise to the homily that is related and recited to each generation of Irish schoolchildren. The Abbot Finnian, Columba's master, returned from a pilgrimage to Rome

103

with a beautiful book of psalms, which took pride of place in his church. During the year 560, Columba crept into the church, night after night, and painstakingly and secretly copied the precious manuscript.

When the abbot discovered what he had done he demanded the copy, but Columba refused to give it up. The case was brought before the King who ruled that he yield the book to the Abbot, with the words, "To every cow its calf; and to every book its copy." Columba refused the judgment, called on his kinsmen the O'Neills of the north to avenge him, and went to battle. (The battle was held at Drumcliffe, where W.B. Yeats is buried, and his strange, beautiful epitaph, "Cast a cold eye / On life, on death / Horseman, pass by!" may refer to the ghosts of the slain in the battle.)

The story continues that in the court that tried Columba after the battle, he was sent into perpetual exile and commanded to convert as many pagan souls as the number slain in battle. He left Ireland forever, sailed to Iona in Scotland, founded the monastery there and became one of the greatest of the early saints.

### Grafton Street

When you reach the top of Dawson St., you are back on the N side of St Stephens Green. If you turn right, you reach Grafton St., named after a viceroy, the Duke of Grafton, whose wife was Henrietta and had a street named after her as well.

This is *the* center, what Anthony Cronin, a Dublin writer, called "Dublin's main boulevard of chance and commerce." His book *Dead as Doornails* is a mordant, amusing account of a certain kind of Dublin literary life, one that Cyril Connolly described as "as warm and friendly as an alligator pool." Many of its scenes are set in **McDaid's**, a pub in Harry St. just off Grafton St., famous for its old literary associations (very old and mostly buried). James Joyce (of course) walked down Grafton St., and found it "gay with housed awnings . . . muslin prints silk dames and dowagers jingle of harnesses hoofthuds lowringing in the baking causeway."

Grafton St. was always the smartest shopping street in Dublin. In the 1970s and '80s it went through a sad and shabby period, but now that it has been pedestrianized it has gone in the opposite direction to become overcrowded, garish and busy. It is enjoyably vivid, can be oppressively busy or full of entertainment, or simply noisy.

This is literally street theater. As well as the shops and cafés and hustle and bustle, there are street musicians and entertainers. In terms of shopping it has to some extent been overshadowed by the adjacent new shopping centers, like the **Powerscourt Town House Centre**, a lovely building with a covered courtyard that takes up a whole block, with its main entrances in Clarendon St. and William St., just parallel to Grafton St., only 50 yards away on the W side. Another is the **St Stephen's Green Shopping Centre**, near the top of the street.

The Powerscourt Centre is an imaginative conversion of Lord Powerscourt's 18thC many-storied mansion house, built by Robert Mack, an Irish architect in 1771, using granite from the Powerscourt estate in Co. Wicklow, and with wonderful plasterwork by Michael Stapleton. The St Stephens Green Centre looks ersatz Victorian, which is what it is, with its enormous vaulted glass roof like an antique rail station and its huge clock. It was built in 1989 and is crammed with shops.

The Powerscourt Centre is varied and enjoyable, with a whole floor devoted to small antique stores, and access to the original great rooms of the mansion. There are little cafés and art galleries, and boutiques and craft stores on many floors.

Just before you come to the back of Powerscourt Centre from Grafton St., you pass **St Teresa's Church** in Clarendon St., an unremarkable Carmelite church built in 1793 and enlarged over the next century, set behind handsome gates; what *is* remarkable is the hustle and bustle inside. People pop in and say a quick prayer as they pass, and there is nothing of that elegiac quiet you get in so many churches in other capitals, where you can almost hear religion dying. This was the first church legally to be erected in Dublin after the repeal of the Penal Laws, which might account for its low-profile position. Beneath the altar is a confrontational sculpture of the *Dead Christ* (1829) by the Irish sculptor John Hogan, and it was this uncompromising piece that first made him famous.

The Carmelite churches of Dublin are popular in Dublin; there's something about the atmosphere of pure reverence.

In the **Whitefriars Street Church**, which is now in Aungier St., since the entrance to the church was reversed in 1951, is a wonderful carved medieval statue of *Our Lady of Dublin,* which, tradition holds, belonged to St Mary's Cistercian Abbey N of the Liffey (see DAY 2, page 131). The right arm of the Child Jesus has been evidently restored, but given that it was supposed to have been used as a pig trough during the Reformation (the back was hollowed out) and was bought by a priest of the church for pennies from a junk shop in Capel St., covered in whitewash, in 1834, it is in remarkable condition. Originally it was beautifully painted, but crude stripping of the whitewash in the early 19thC removed the original paint as well. It is a wonderful piece of work, and although the long-held belief that it was carved by Dürer is now discounted, it was certainly done by a master carver.

If you're in the mood for another shopping center, near here to the w is the **South City Market Arcade** (1892) in South Great George's St., a charming arcade of stalls and shops under a vaulted roof designed in a competition in 1878; and on the way back to Grafton St. is another large shopping center, the **Westbury Mall**, with little winding streets crammed with shops, restaurants and cafés.

Back in South William St. next to the Powerscourt Town House is the **Dublin Civic Museum** (for details see MUSEUMS, page 73), an 18thC building in what was the City Assembly House, built for the Society of Artists in 1765. This is a modest, agreeable museum with many floors of idiosyncratic exhibits that give different insights into the past and contemporary life of Dublin. Permanent displays illuminate the history of the city and its people — not necessarily famous or celebrated ones, but those who have made their mark on Dublin, and the exhibits are all the more fascinating and relevant for that. There is also a set of Malton aquatints (see FINE ARTS, page 65), and regular exhibitions of particular events that cast an illuminating light on different facets of Dublin life.

At the heart of Grafton St. are the long-established names of Dublin trade, especially **Brown Thomas**, first opened as a haberdashery in 1848, **Switzers**, opened by a Swiss immigrant in 1838, and **Weirs** the jewelers, with its glass-engraved windows and doors. There are an inordinate number of shoe shops in the street, an Imelda Marcos dream.

The street has always been a commercial center, but it has other associations. Samuel Whyte's Academy was situated at no. 79, and among its alumni were Arthur Wellesley (the future Duke of Wellington), Robert Emmet and R.B. Sheridan. This is the site of **Bewley's Oriental Cafe**, which is one of Dublin's institutions. The smell of coffee coming from the Grafton St. interior was the equivalent of Proust's madeleine to many a Dublin child. This, the most famous of a chain of cafés, was started over a century ago by a well-known Dublin Quaker family who originally fled England at the beginning of the 19thC. It has a fine Art Deco front and windows by one of Dublin's most original creative geniuses, the stained-glass artist Harry Clarke (see FINE ARTS, page 63). The James Joyce room has a splendid view of the street theater below as you eat the renowned barm-brack, a rich tea cake ("brack" means speckled). On the top floor is a small museum devoted to the history of the Bewley dynasty and the coffee trade. The museum is open when the café is open. The chain was bought from Bewley's some years ago and in summer is often so noisy and crowded that its much-vaunted atmosphere curls up and creeps out.

All around, off the little adjacent streets, are famous Dublin pubs (see EATING AND DRINKING). (The fact that a pub is well known in Dublin is no reason to suppose that it remains the same as it was before it became well known, if you follow me.) Curiously, there isn't a pub in Grafton St. itself, which alone would make it a unique thoroughfare in Dublin. (A passage in *Ulysses* concerns Leopold Bloom musing on the puzzle of crossing Dublin without passing a pub.)

At the junction of Nassau St. and Grafton St., across from **The Provost's House**, is a statue by Jeanne Rynhart (1988) commemorating the famous Dublin character celebrated in the song *Molly Malone,* who sold "cockles and mussels alive, alive oh," and all one can think on viewing her is that if any street trader came out in a *décolletage* like that on a winter's day she would frighten the horses, never mind catch her death of cold. In fact Molly died of the Liffey fever, which used to decimate the poor of Dublin. The statue is called, with the Dubliners' penchant for the nicknaming of things, *The Tart with the Cart.* (Not far away up O'Connell St. is a fountain to Anna Livia, known either as *The Floozie in the Jacuzzi* or *Anna Rexia.* Near Liffey St., a sculpture of two women with shopping bags officially named *Meeting Place* is now *The Hags with the Bags.* All these monuments have become rendezvous points.)

### The Bank of Ireland

Whichever way you walk to College Green, you arrive at two of the greatest buildings in Dublin, **Trinity College** and the **Bank of Ireland**, with between them the statues of two great patriots, Henry Grattan by John Henry Foley (1871), and the memorial to Thomas Davis by Edward Delaney, erected in 1966.

The Bank of Ireland, previously known as **Parliament House** and built in 1729, stands on the site of the old Chichester House, where early parliaments had always been held. It has a monumental splendor and, although it appears to be a uniform and dignified building, is in fact an intricate jigsaw, composed of the work of various architects.

Sir Edward Lovett Pearce, who was a Member of Parliament, designed the core of the building, the first building in the world intended to be a two-chamber legislature. The first stone was laid in 1729. Arthur Dobbs, another Member, completed that part of the building. James Gandon designed the Corinthian portico as a separate entrance to the House of Lords, and united it to Pearce's main facade by the curved screen wall with its niches. Then Robert Parke added the other portico on the w side. Finally, Francis Johnston came along and remodeled the interiors and unified the whole. Alas, no one could so easily unify the country that the parliament never properly represented. "Tell us what the pile contains," wrote Swift, "Many a head that holds no brains."

The building was sold to the Bank of Ireland in 1802 for £40,000 with a proviso that it should never again be used for public debating. After Independence, in the 1920s, plans were drawn up for restoring the building to its original use, but Leinster House was chosen instead, a choice deeply regretted by many. Everyday banking business is still carried on within the building, but it is open to view during office hours.

The paneled room, which was the House of Lords, remains much as it was in the 18thC. Nothing gives such an idea of the power, exclusivity and size of the cartel that was the ruling class than this small, intimate room, with its carved oak fireplace, magnificent chandelier (made in 1788 with 1,233 pieces of sparkling glass, at Ballybough Bridge), and the two huge and fine Huguenot tapestries celebrating the Siege of Derry and the Battle of the Boyne.

These tapestries were designed by Johann van der Hagen, a landscape, marine and scene painter working in Dublin, woven by "ye famous tapestry weaver" John van Beaver and his assistants, and completed and hung in 1733. He worked these for Robert Baillie of Dublin, and they cost £436 6s 3d (say $500). That they are still here is a miracle, since their backs are badly charred from the fire that swept through the building in 1792. In 1971 the building was cleaned and restored, and the heads of the statues on the s pediment by Edward Smyth of *Fidelity, Hibernia* and *Commerce* were newly carved by a Dublin sculptor, Paddy Roe of Sandyford, Dublin. The statues on the E pediment were also restored.

In a little cul-de-sac behind the bank is the **Bank of Ireland Arts Centre** *(Foster Place, College Green, map 4 D4* ☎ *(01) 6711488/6711671, open May-Sept Mon-Sat 10am-5pm, Sun noon-5pm),* traditionally known as the Armoury, where there are changing exhibitions and concerts.

### Trinity College

Immediately opposite is one of the great focal points of Dublin: the facade of **Trinity College Dublin** *(map 4 D4-5, open Mon-Fri 9.30am-5pm, Sat 9.30am-12.30pm),* dominating College Green. (You will look in vain for a hint of green.)

It is hard to convey the importance of Trinity College in the historic life of Dublin. Yeats made a famous remark to the effect that the only evidence of religious veneration in the Irish Protestant mind was directed toward Trinity College; and in some ways the gibe conveys the almost sacred place it held in the minds and hearts of what was the Ascendancy, and which so colored Dublin's history and indeed made and shaped it. Now it is a much-loved university for all creeds. (You are not allowed to say the word *classes* in Ireland.)

Trinity College was founded as a university for the perpetuation of a ruling class in 1592 on the site of an Augustinian monastery "near Dublin" dispossessed by Henry VIII 50 years previously.

The original charter aimed for a college "whereby Knowledge, Learning and Civilitie may be increased, to the banishment of barbarism, tumult and disorderly living," although it didn't always work out like that (the students once murdered a tutor).

It is a wonderful site in its own right, a mixture of over 40 acres of buildings and squares, lawns and trees, retaining an air of seclusion and tranquillity, although the traffic of Dublin roars around its perimeters. The whole center of Dublin is vivified by the stream of students passing in and out of its various gates. Remember when you visit during the trimester that it is a university as well as a famous monument and that certain rooms may be closed to fulfil their functions. Remember also that things that the visitor might admire may have their own secret life: for example, there is a portrait of Queen Elizabeth in the Examination Hall under which it is supposed to be unlucky to sit.

Anyway, part of the pleasure of being there while the students are around is looking at, listening to and observing the inadvertent pageant. Many students still live within the precinct in what one graduate remembered as "a series of warm, homely, lino-covered little burrows behind its magnificent facade . . . in the summer it was the huge green expanse of College park where we sunbathed and crammed for our exams and where early regulations had expressly forbidden the shooting of snipe." The cleaners who "do" the students' rooms must not be of "foul visage," and they are still called "skips."

Ireland has high educational standards, and a Trinity education is recognized as remarkably good; but in earlier times a disenchanted observer recorded that "Trinity fellows made up in bad manners for what they lacked in learning". There were Hooray Henrys even then; a notice to students in the dining rooms warned that during Commons Dinner "No student shall walk over the dinner table" and "There shall be no throwing of bread."

But for all these *canards* the alumni include Burke, Grattan, Swift, Congreve, Goldsmith, Wilde, Synge, Samuel Beckett and countless other luminaries such as those heroes of Irish resistance, Robert Emmet and Wolfe Tone. (It is reputed that when Beckett became a lecturer in French, he delivered a series of lectures on a group of imaginary French poets.) There has always been a rich mixture of piety, fantasy and debauchery in the legend of Trinity graduates, a feeling of something slightly high and raffish. Bram Stoker, the author of *Dracula,* graduated from there (his house is just yards away), as did Nahum Tate, who wrote *While Shepherds Watched Their Flocks By Night* (I remember hearing an Irish child lustily caroling *While leopards watched their flocks by night*), and Frances Lyte, author of *Abide With Me*.

Trinity is traditionally associated with great names in literature, but there are equal luminaries from the other disciplines, including Professor E.T.S. Walton, who was awarded the Nobel prize in physics for research on splitting the atom at Cambridge University.

For centuries after its founding, Trinity remained an enclave of the Ascendancy, and was almost exclusively Protestant until the 19thC. Described as a museum where "there are stored all sorts of educated eccentrics in a seat of learning," it was taken for granted that the sons of the gentry would go there if they were not academically ambitious or able enough to go to Oxford or Cambridge, or simply chose to stay "at home."

All that has quite changed, no thanks to the Roman Catholic hierarchy, who proscribed it for years so that no Catholic could attend without a dispensation. It wasn't that the Catholic hierarchy finally saw sense; rather that Trinity offered courses that no other Irish university could match. Now, no one enters Trinity other than on academic merit. It is a hugely popular and over-crowded university.

By the end of the 17thC, the faculty numbered about 340 persons. The student body now numbers nearly 10,000, and Trinity Trust is in contact by its newsletter with 40,000 graduates all over the world. The first women students were admitted in 1904.

The layout of the College is essentially 18thC. The spectacular w front, a 300-foot Palladian facade incorporating **Regent House**, dates from 1752 and was designed by the English architect Theodore Jacobsen. The facade reflects the self-confidence of the city and its society. As you enter between the gates and John Henry Foley's statues of Edmund Burke and Oliver Goldsmith (both educated here) and under the main arched entrance past the Porter's Lodge, walking across a paving of oak setts, you find yourself in an 18thC green and gray square, lit by lamps at night.

It is a felicitous grove of academe, this **Front Square** and **Parliament Square**, surrounded by fine buildings, including the **Chapel**, the **Theatre** (also known as the **Examination Hall**), the **Dining Halls** and the **Reading Room**, and closed by the great punctuation point of the **Campanile**. Parliament Square was given its name in the 1750s when it was rebuilt with the aid of grants totaling £40,000 — the equivalent of millions in modern currency, all defrayed by the Parliament of the day.

The **Dining Hall** was designed by Richard Castle, but because of chronic trouble with the foundations it began to disintegrate only ten years after it was finished in the mid-1740s. It has been shored up and rebuilt periodically ever since. In 1984 a disastrous fire destroyed the roof and ceiling of the Hall and Common Room, but it has been impeccably restored, and various additions to the building have made it a center of college life. Most notable perhaps is the **Atrium**, built in 1985 and designed by de Blackam & Meagher, and the new **Fellows Bar**, which is a re-creation of Adolf Loos' bar at 10 Kärtner Strasse in Vienna designed in 1907.

There is a **Buttery** beneath the dining hall where students have traditional Irish meals (like baked beans and chips). Fairly lugubrious portraits of famous Trinity denizens hang aloof on the high walls of the Dining Hall, including three that hung in Castle's original building: Frederick Prince of Wales, Provost Baldwin (he was Provost for an unprecedented 41 years) and Archbishop Price (who first employed Richard Guinness to brew beer for his servants: see EXCURSIONS, page 243). Below them, the diners are often a couple of workmen who remain quite undisturbed in their lunch by one's passing.

To the NE of the Buttery is a residential square and tennis courts called **Botany Bay**. There is a certain debate as to whether it is named after the penal colony in Australia or the kitchen garden that was once here.

The beautiful little multi-denominational **Chapel**, with its vaulted ceiling, fine plasterwork and stained-glass windows behind the altar, was built between 1779 and 1790 to the designs of Sir William Chambers. A beautiful organ restored in the 20thC is still housed in its 18thC case, and the whole building, hushed and gleaming with care, has a rare and tranquil atmosphere to be savored.

Opposite is the **Theatre or Examination Hall**, also designed by Chambers between 1777 and 1791, with a fine ceiling by Michael Stapleton, the friend and executor of Robert Adam and one of the finest stuccodores in Europe. This is closed when examinations are in progress. Look out for notices of the concerts that are held in this unique setting. The Hall is the setting for all great University occasions, and degrees are conferred there in a ceremony that is still conducted in Latin.

It is a wonderful room, lofty and light, with a half-cupola and noble windows and fairly horrid modern lights quarreling with a gilded oak waterfall of a chandelier, which used to hang in the Irish House of Commons. On the walls are nine portraits, most of them commissioned from Robert Home at the end of the 18thC. They include Dean Swift, George Berkeley and Archbishop James Ussher, the scholar antiquarian and bibliophile who gave the *Book of Kells* to the Library.

There is also a black-and-gold sarcophagus depicting **Provost Baldwin**, larger than life on the point of death (in 1758) on a white marble mattress, being comforted by a grieving woman emblematic of the University while an interested angel holding a wreath of palm hovers around. The scroll in the left hand of the effigy is thought to be Baldwin's will, in which he bequeathed £80,000 to Trinity. The monument was made by Mr Hewetson, an Irishman who lived in Rome, and it cost £2,000, so there was a fair balance left.

Between these buildings is the **Campanile**, 100 feet high, a temptation to abseiling students designed by Sir Charles Lanyon. Built in 1853, it houses the great bells of the college. It is reputed to stand on the same place as the original medieval monastery bell tower. The bronze statue nearby is of W.E.H. Lecky, a 19thC professor at Trinity whose *History of Ireland in the 19th Century* is a definitive work of its kind, although in common with many of his contemporaries, the whole vital area of what one might call the secret Gaelic bardic history seemed closed to him. The library in the Arts building is named after him.

The 1911 marble statue of Provost Salmon is by John Hughes, a fine Dublin sculptor who died in 1941, and the wonderful monumental shape dominating the space around it is *Reclining Connected Forms* by Henry Moore. In Fellows' Square there is a sculpture, *Cactus,* by the American sculptor Alexander Calder, better known for his mobiles. This is one of his later works, called, logically enough, *Stabiles.* A sculpture by Pomodoro, *Sphere Within a Sphere,* was presented to the College by the Italian government and sits — if that is the word for so round and delightful an object — in the center of the Berkeley podium like something lately fallen from outer space.

Between the Museum building and the old Library is the **Berkeley Library**, built in the 1960s by Paul Koralek, winner of an international architectural competition. It now contains over a million books. The 1960s were not a good time for architecture anywhere, and this building has actually been praised for making so few concessions to its surroundings. Certainly it has no manners.

The quadrangle to the N is **Library Square**, with the terraced **Rubrics** on the E side, intrinsically the oldest buildings in Trinity, dating from 1700, which include Oliver Goldsmith's rooms. The rooms once occupied by ugly, attractive Oliver were given such a thorough restoration in Victorian times that little of the original is left. On the S side is the **Old Library** *(map 4D5; three areas of the Old Library are open to visitors: the Colonnades, the Treasury, and the main chamber of the Long Room, Mon-Fri 9.30am-4.30pm, Sun noon-5pm (last admission 4.30pm)* 🔲 *(IR£2.50, and students and senior citizens/retirees IR£2.00); a multimedia audiovisual exhibition relating the history of Dublin is on display, for which translations are available, open May-Sept daily 10am-5pm).*

The Library was begun in 1719 to the plans of Thomas Burgh, who sadly did not live to see it completed and who, with Sir Edward Lovett Pearce, was the founding father of the Irish architectural profession.

The Library with its **Long Room** is one of the glories of Ireland. Opened in 1732, it cost over £15,000, and its 209-foot-long single room, canopied by its barrel ceiling and lit by 100 windows, is a triumphal space, the equal of any room of learning in the world. It still has an aura of learning for the *love* of it, for all its daily stream of tourists. Its symmetry, its polish, the light filtering in through the protective holland blinds, the glimmer and texture of the binding on the books, the general luminosity of the room even on a dark day, the luminosity darkening to shadow as it drifts up to the great barrel-vaulted roof, add up to great allure. What it delivers is the effect of a cathedral, not of learning but of the exclusive worship of learning.

Lining both sides of the room in an impressive pedagogic symmetry are the busts of scholars, a major collection of sculpture, as well as being fascinating portraits of such luminaries as Robert Boyle, the scientist, son of the great Earl of Cork, James Ussher and Jonathan Swift. This guard of honor is a most felicitous addition to the room.

When it was first built, the Long Room had a gallery and two magnificent oak staircases, but so strong was the fear of fire that there was no provision for heating or lighting. In fact the real threat of fire came during the Williamite Wars, when the college was occupied by the troops of James II, who were only prevented from sacking the library by the anguished appeals of the Provost, the Rev. Michael Moore.

The designers of the library were not much interested in creature comforts. George Berkeley, Bishop of Cloyne, theologian, philosopher and Fellow, after whom the new Libraries at Trinity are named, wrote crossly, "I am lately enterd into my Citadell in a disconsolate Mood, after having passd the better part of a sharp and bitter day in the Damps and mustly [sic] solitudes of the Library without either Fire or any thing else to protect Me from the Injuries of the Snow that was constantly driving at the Windows and forceing it's Entrance into that wretched Mansion, to the keeping of which I was this day sennight elect'd under an inauspiciary Planet." In his book *The Querist*, written with the practical objective of provoking discussion among his contemporaries by raising issues and querying assumptions, he asked, "whether a gentleman who hath seen a little of the World and observed how men live elsewhere, can contentedly sit down in a cold, damp Sordid habitation, in the midst of a bleak country inhabited by thieves and beggars." So quite often cross.

The library was originally built over an open colonnade, a precaution designed to protect the books from damp, for in the days when the Library was built, the Liffey lapped much nearer the College. The colonnade was bricked over in 1892 to give more room for books, which changed the elegant lines of the exterior. The original interior had been altered in 1859 by Deane & Woodward, the great Victorian-Ruskinian architects of Dublin, who replaced the spine wall with a double row of granite columns. Now the Colonnades have been remodeled to create new book stacks, a library shop, and a new exhibition gallery for changing displays of treasures from the Library. The revised layout includes **The Treasury**, a new exhibition area for the *Book of Kells* and other Early Christian manuscripts, placing them within their true setting and context: that of monastic life.

The library has an extraordinary collection of incunabula, manuscripts and printed books, altogether 2.5 million volumes, and is one of only four libraries entitled to a free copy of every book published in Britain and Ireland. Among its treasures are a copy of the first German Bible, a First Folio of Shakespeare, and an ancient harp connected by romantic legend with Brian Boru. But perhaps its most famous and glorious possessions are the illuminated medieval manuscripts, including the

***Book of Durrow*** and the most famous of all, the ***Book of Kells***. Both are on display in the Treasury, and four different pages, protected by glass, are revealed each day. At least 300,000 people come to see the manuscripts every year: they elevate humanity and illustrate the divine, and therein lies their appeal. "People are drawn by the beauty," Peter Fox, Chief Librarian at Trinity, explained. "No page is the same and none is ordinary. Major manuscripts like this one were done to glorify God. The *Book of Kells* seems to retain that ancient power."

Elbow the school children aside and pore over these wonderful works. The *Book of Kells* contains the Four Gospels and is profusely illustrated, measures $13\frac{1}{2}$ inches (34 centimeters) by $9\frac{1}{2}$ inches (24 centimeters), and dates from the early 9thC. It illustrates not only the Gospels, but the peerless skill and devotion of the monks in the art of illumination and illustration, which made their books objects of veneration. Such is their perfection that an initial letter or decorative panel, when magnified, reveals wild and varied flights of the imagination, intense color, and often a delicious sense of humor. (See MUSEUMS, page 72.)

There is a moving little story connected with this book and the Plunkett family, whose name, like those of so many Norman families, runs through Irish history like a thread. At the time of the Dissolution of the Monasteries, Richard Plunkett was the Abbot of Kells. When the monastery and all its land was wrested from him in 1539, he rescued the precious Book (already damaged by being stripped of its jeweled shrine cover).

The story then goes that it passed secretly from one Plunkett house to another, pursued by someone in authority who knew about it and was determined to have it but could never quite get it within his reach, until it came to a member of the Plunkett family in Dublin, who delivered it to Archbishop Ussher the famous bibliophile. There was no one more worthy to receive it than this remarkable man, James Ussher, one of the first graduates of Trinity. He loved books and Trinity with a passion, and his collection formed the nucleus of the library. There are various romantic stories about how the collection was started, including his quest in England for rare books, always trying to keep a step ahead of his friend Sir Thomas Bodley, founder of the Bodleian Library in Oxford.

Ussher's scholarship was legendary, based on the teaching given him by his two blind aunts, who knew all of the Scriptures by heart. He became Archbishop of Armagh, but was most famous as the author of a history of the world written in Latin, in which he calculated that the world began in 4004BC, said to be the source of the dates later inserted into the margins of the Authorised Version of the Bible.

Toward the end of his life he suffered terrible vicissitudes; his traveling library was confiscated by Parliament, and though it was returned, it was plundered by soldiers. At his death in 1656, Ussher left his library of books (over 10,000 volumes) to his daughter Elizabeth. The King of Denmark and Cardinal Mazarin of France both expressed interest in buying it, but it was purchased for Ireland on the orders of Oliver Cromwell for £2,500, the money being raised, it is said, by the army, which seems fairly unlikely, given their previous behavior in Ireland.

The library was further enhanced by the addition of the 20,000 books from the fabled collection of a Dutch nobleman, Hendrik Fagel. His library was about to go to auction in March 1802 when Trinity made a successful bid for the entire collection. It cost £8,000. In today's terms that is a little over a million pounds. A bargain, certainly.

We know with certainty that both the *Book of Kells* and the *Book of Durrow,* which dates from the middle of the 7thC, were donated to the library by Henry Jones, Bishop of Meath, in the early 1660s. These books are like living things, and looking at them one is powerfully reminded of John Milton's great declamation: "Books are not absolutely dead things, but do contain a potency of life in them to be as active as that soul was whose progeny they are; nay they do preserve as in a vial the purest efficacy and extraction of that living intellect that bred them."

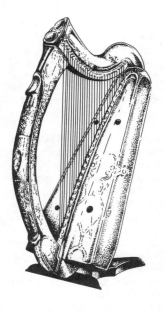

Perhaps the most cherished object in the library after the great books is the elaborately carved harp long associated with Brian Boru, who died in 1014. In fact, the harp, hollowed from a single piece of willow, was presented to the College by William Conyingham in the 18thC and dates from the 15th or 16thC, making it the oldest known medieval harp in existence.

In 1961 a craftsman from Cork re-strung the harp and the sound was recorded.

Within Trinity's precinct, at the sw end, is the **Provost's House**, said to be "the most perfect house in Dublin" and certainly one of the grandest and, at the time of its building, the most expensive: it cost £11,000. It was started in 1759 and is a copy of General Wade's house in London, which was designed by Lord Burlington but inspired by Palladio. The facade is attributed to John Smyth, the interior to Henry Keene, and the plasterwork is by Patrick and John Wall.

It was built for and by Francis Andrews, the Provost of the time, who was a rubicund, worldly bachelor with subtle and expensive tastes, a fine intellect and a penchant for adventure. He became a Fellow of Trinity when he was a tender 21 years old, and he was also a member of the Irish House of Commons.

He owed his appointment to the then Lord Lieutenant, the Duke of Bedford. When the Chancellorship of the University became vacant in 1756 the Duke in his turn was installed. Jobs for the Boys. The Duke graciously presented the College with his full-length portrait by Gainsborough, which still hangs in the Saloon, one of the finest reception rooms in Dublin, with an elaborate coffered ceiling and lovely proportions.

Provost Andrews traveled all over the Continent, which is perhaps ironic in view of the avowed aims of the founder, Queen Elizabeth I: "whereby knowledge and civility might be increased by the instructions of our own people there, whereof many have usually heretofore used to travaill into Ffrance, Itally and Spaine to gett learning in such foreign universities, whereby they have been infected with poperie and other ill qualities and soe become evil subjects."

When Provost Andrews was in Vienna in 1767, he was shown as much respect as if he had been the Viceroy of Ireland, and he liked such style. The house he built is in effect a small palace, connected to the Front Square by a covered passage, with a magnificent pillared saloon extending the full length of the w front. It is the only great 18thC house still used for its original purpose. *(Closed to the general public.)*

This paragon was human. In his will he left his collection of colored prints to a Miss Dolly Monroe as being "a fitter ornament for her dressing room than any library."

Other buildings within Trinity include the **Museum Building**, on the s side of New Square (now the School of Engineering), designed in Venetian-Byzantine style by Deane & Woodward and built in 1853-57. It was loved by John Ruskin not least for the free carvings done by Irish masons, among them the famous and turbulent O'Shea brothers whose imagination Woodward never attempted to curb, nor their behavior. A selection of Irish marble was used in the interior, especially in the elaborate arcaded staircase and the finely worked intricate cupola.

This building, with its colored stone and surface decoration, its embellishments and ostentatious air of wealth and pride in achievement, had a profound effect on the look and public taste of Dublin. Ireland was and remains a conservative nation, and, in architecture, Classical forms remained the accepted convention far into the middle of the 19thC. The Museum Building, which was more overtly showy than any other public building in Dublin, influenced much subsequent commercial and public display in the city.

Opposite the Museum Building is the little **Printing House**, given by John Stearne Bishop of Clogher, a general benefactor. It was built in 1734 by Richard Castle and was his first independent work in Dublin. (In 1602 the New Testament had been printed in the old Printing House.) The Doric portico of this pretty new Printing House became the logo on its publications, which ranged from a translation of Horace, printed in 1745, to 20thC editions. The building is now part of the Micro Biology Department of the University.

In 1989 the **O'Reilly Centre for Communications and Advanced Technology** was opened, and there are plans for another center linked by a science complex, with new buildings tucked behind the facade of Westland Row.

Trinity College celebrated its quatercentenary in 1992, and the lasting contribution to the general celebrations was another major building program along its N frontage on Pearce St., including the reconstruction of 19thC brick terraces, rejuvenating what was a blighted area, and the 400 student residences planned for the Temple Bar area (see DAY 3, page

139), which will connect the living spaces of the city with the great beehive that is Trinity.

To walk through the arched entrance of this magical enclosure on a golden summer's day or the veiled gray of the winter is a valuable experience. In its intricacies and multitudinous lives, its color, the interweaving of building and passages with foliage and space and sky, the feeling of timelessness and the haste of the students, one gets an echo of the intricate maze revealed in the beauty of the *Book of Kells,* held within the enclave.

# Day 2
## Dublin north of the Liffey

*See Dublin City maps **3** & **4**, and* DAY 2 *map on pages 118-9.*

The North side of Dublin has always had its detractors and its admirers, and for centuries there was a battle over which would be the smartest side. Dublin Castle and the High Street — the Old City — had always been the strategically important defensive areas of the city, but fashion forsook those narrow streets and heights for the broad sweeps N of the Liffey when, in the reign of Charles II, during the Duke of Ormonde's sumptuous vice-royalty, there was a wave of expansion northward, which included the building of four new bridges and the laying out of Capel St.

Fashion moved north, and Dorset St. (named after the Earl of Dorset, Lord Lieutenant of the time) became the main artery of a new residential district. It was only after Sackville St. and the Carlisle Bridge (now O'Connell St. and O'Connell Bridge) were completed that the whole axis of the city changed. The impetus was set by Luke Gardiner, a property speculator, who bought the huge Mary's Abbey estates belonging to the Earl of Drogheda and launched an expansionist building program beginning with Henrietta St., which was an immediate success. Three generations of Gardiners left their names scattered across the North side, their main townscape achievement being the creation of Mountjoy Sq. (the second Luke Gardiner was created 1st Baron Mountjoy in 1779).

Lord Fitzwilliam of Merrion, s of the river, observing the success and the fortune Gardiner was making with his venture, set about wresting the glamor of the city away from this *nouveau* Gardiner family. Fitzwilliam was greatly assisted when the powerful Earl of Kildare chose to build his town house s of the river. In one sense the battle has never really ended, and in effect both sides lost when Dublin declined after the Act of Union of 1800.

During the 18thC Dublin underwent a transformation from a small, somewhat beleaguered city, still connected to the Pale rather than to the country as a whole, into one of the most glorious townscapes of Europe, and capital of a unified, though not wholly happy, colony — which also happened to be an entirely separate country. Crippling trade restrictions that had obtained for centuries had been lifted (the building of the Custom House testifies to the growth of trade), and Dublin became a boom city.

It was thronged with high-living power-brokers, rakes, bucks, gorgeous courtesans (not to say whores), dashing playwrights, politicians and parliamentarians, and a great many peers. In their train came speculators, middlemen and bailiffs. Here was all the motley and trappings of the capital of what was becoming, for a certain stratum of society, a prosperous nation. A thriving and sparkling social life blossomed, and to service the whole edifice came the craftsmen and artists, stuccodores and silversmiths, portrait-painters and cabinet-makers, sculptors and potters, seamstresses and lace-makers, glassblowers and shoemakers, and, of course, bankers. Dublin became one of the most handsome Georgian cities imaginable; yet just outside its limits lay huddled cabins and hovels that looked like buildings out of the Stone Age.

In 1757 the first Commissioners for making "Wide and Convenient Streets" had been appointed. The consequent ample streets and beautiful squares, with their buildings in that flushed rose-red-to-pink-to-salmon brick that is so warmed by light, the beautiful doors with their characteristic fanlights, the detailing and glazing of the windows, made Dublin into one of Europe's finest capitals. (The tracery of ironwork balconies that add such distinction to many buildings tend to be Victorian additions.)

Among the chief reasons why the street architecture of this time is so comely is that it was often designed by masons and bricklayers who knew how brick stood on brick and how to handle stone. The work was thus informed by the spirit and thought and genuine knowledge of the people who built it, rather then translating it off a drawing board.

One of the best Irish social historians, Terence de Vere White, made the observation that between 1760 and 1860 "It was almost impossible, seemingly, to build an ugly house in Ireland . . . builders and their foreman had all had an instruction in the rudiments of Classical design; they knew no other way to go about their work."

There were houses built as great set pieces — **Tyrone House** designed by Richard Castle, **Belvedere House** by Michael Stapleton, **Charlemont House**, built for the Earl of Charlemont (the "Volunteer" Earl) by Sir William Chambers in 1767 — all to be seen in this area. But the town houses of Dublin, no matter how grand, fitted into the streetscape, the only external decoration being their beautiful doors with fanlights and pillars.

With the growth of trade and prosperity came the loosening of old angers and hostilities, and in Grattan's parliament there seemed to be a chance for Ireland to become a viable, thriving country. Transport improved, industries built up, and the great canals were built; and even here the rival areas of the city vied with each other. There was no need for two canals, but two were built: the **Royal Canal** on the North side of the Liffey, cutting through Ireland like a cheese knife from Dublin to Shannon between Lough Ree and Derg; and the **Grand Canal** on the South side, following much the same route but linking Loughs Allen and

Ree. The canals were important thoroughfares: the Grand Canal carried 100,000 passengers a year up to the 1850s and was in commercial use up to the 1960s. (Both canals are now being restored all along their lengths.)

Now some of the dilapidated great houses are undergoing rehabilitation and certain streets regaining their chic — a slow, expensive process.

## Crossing the Liffey

The North has history on its side and its inhabitants. Brendan Behan was an archetypal North-sider and bore an amiable, vivifying and fairly abstract hatred for the softies who lived s of the Liffey, though such abstract feelings didn't prevent him from loving them even unto marriage. The people he liked, he said, lived between the Custom House and Glasnevin cemetery ("between birth and death, come to think of it"), and his beloved area covers most of the great sights of the N of the city.

The North city has for many people a more authentic "Dublin feel" than the South — perhaps because it is older, grittier and, some would say, less smug.

To explore it, set of from College St., just to the N of College Green, and the base of the triangle formed by Westmoreland St. and D'Olier St. where *The Irish Times* is published. Dublin abounds in characters, but people still remember with wistfulness one of the greatest editors of recent (Irish) Times, Robert Maire Symllie, who wore a green sombrero, weighed 308 pounds, sang parts of his leading articles in operatic recitative, grew the nail of his little finger into the shape of a pen nib like Keats, and edited a great paper.

The traffic is unremitting in this absolutely central area, but in Westmoreland St. there is a traffic island to which you can cling and on which stands a statue of Thomas Moore, who was idolized as a national poet in the early 19thC, as feted for poems like *Lalla Rookh* and his lyrical verses in his day as, say, John Lennon was in his. *Moore's Melodies* were universally sung in the Victorian era and are still popular in Ireland, although purists frown at their ersatz Irish and sentimental content. One of the most feeble Dublin jokes derives from the congruence of the Moore monument standing over an underground public lavatory, and his most famous song being called *The Meeting of the Waters*. James Joyce used the joke in *Ulysses,* though there is hardly a thing in Dublin that Joyce didn't devour

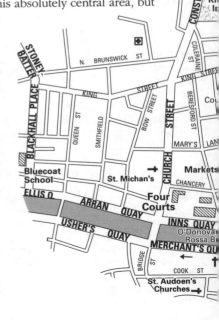

for his own ends. He also wrote in *Portrait of the Artist as a Young Man* of coming upon "the droll statue of the national poet of Ireland; it seemed humbly conscious of its indignity."

There is a sculpture called *People's Island* by Rachel Joynt on West-moreland St., a busy commercial thoroughfare with good Victorian buildings and a Bewley's Oriental café with perhaps the best-preserved interior of all.

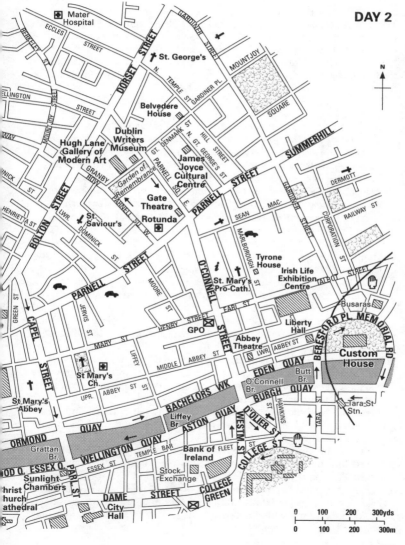

As you walk N you will see, indeed you will see from any view along the Liffey, the strange turquoise umbrella-like canopy on top of **Liberty Hall**, the headquarters of the Transport and General Workers Union, standing on one of the most prominent sites in central Dublin and a graceless building, typical of its period and bearing all the marks of the School of Spindly Modern — the slapdash detailing, the plastic finish, the horrible height. It all ill becomes the site: town planning at its worst.

## The Custom House

The great jewel of the area, of course, is the **Custom House**, completed in 1791 and designed by James Gandon, who was persuaded to come to Dublin by John Beresford, Chief Commissioner of the Irish Revenue. Although Ireland may not owe very much to the same Beresford, it owes him this: that Gandon was about to leave England for Russia before Beresford lured him to Dublin.

> *Dublin, 15th January, 1781*
> *Sir — I have the pleasure to inform you, that I have at length obtained an order from Government for the building of a new Custom House, with all possible expedition, and I have proceeded so far as to send to take possession of a large lot in the lower situation. I expect to accomplish this in the course of this week, and the sooner afterwards we can settle our plans the better. This business must be kept a profound secret, as long as we can, to prevent clamor, until we have everything secured.*

The clamor was not prevented. Beresford built the Custom House in the teeth of violent opposition from the merchants and citizens who thought the old Custom House, farther upstream from what is now called Grattan Bridge, a perfectly good enough building; and Gandon was prudent and found "a good cane sword" to protect him as he went about on his rounds.

Beresford was famous as a ruthless place-seeker, whose style of living was so ostentatious that he became known as John the Magnificent. In the Custom House, Beresford was in effect building himself another palatial residence; his apartment and offices were unusually grand even for the time and position. Someone wrote in about 1805, "It is in every respect a noble edifice in which there is no fault to be found except that Beresford is sumptuously lodged in it."

He was a kind of Irish de Borgia. His relatives and dependants were given office through his efforts, and he ruthlessly bent the rules to gain wealth and position.

The Custom House is one of the glories of Dublin, one of its most perfect 18thC buildings. It dominates a whole quarter of the city and is comparable to only one other building in architectonic importance, and that one within view upriver: the **Four Courts**. Classical but rhythmically animated, derivative in detail but original in conception, it aligns itself so well along the Liffey and the lie of the river that it looks as if the water was added as a final touch.

Built on slob or reclaimed land, to replace the old Custom House up at Essex (later renamed Grattan) Bridge, it cost the then unheard of sum of £400,000, although the headlong decline in trade after the Act of Union (see HISTORY, page 50) meant that it was hardly used for its original purpose.

In 1921 during the Troubles it was raided by the Dublin Brigade of the IRA to destroy government records, and it blazed for five days. It took weeks to cool down, and the cracks of the stone as it expanded and burst could be heard for long distances.

It was restored, but alas, with that hubris so peculiar to bad architects, certain details that gave the building its overall distinction were omitted, and everyone always points out that the pale Portland stone of the original dome was substituted by Ardbraccan stone, which has darkened over the years and given the lines a different emphasis, although no one now remembers the original.

In the famous series of aquatints of *Views of Dublin* by James Malton, produced, as he explained, "to display the beauty of Dublin to the world," the dome appears to be in a much less pronounced color and the building seems to float. Or perhaps it is Malton's genius that makes it look so ethereal (see FINE ARTS, page 65).

The building (illustrated on page 83) is 375 feet long and 205 feet wide, with a central front projection joined by colonnaded arcades to end pavilions. The four statues along the North Front, at the back of the building, represent Europe, Asia, Africa and America, and were carved by Joseph Banks, a London sculptor.

But these have little of the energy and genius of the other sculptures ranged along the building, carved by Edward Smyth, the best of Dublin's fine sculptors. He sculpted *Commerce,* the figure on top of the copper dome resting on her anchor, and the keystones above the windows and entrances on the river front, representing 14 river god heads: the Riverine Gods, of extreme diversity and variety, of extraordinary strength and ferocity, and covered in ornament and details. They represent the Atlantic Ocean, the 13 main rivers of Ireland, and the one female head among the 14, in the central position overlooking the Liffey, represents old *Anna Livia Plurabelle* herself (pictured on page 66). The coat of arms, so vital, so crisp, on each end pavilion are the arms of the kingdom of Ireland, with the harp of O'Carolan (pictured above).

The Custom House has just undergone a six-year conservation, restoration and cleaning program and is not open to the public (it houses the Department of the Environment). But the garden often is, so you can get close up to see the details.

What is so remarkable is that although regret is voiced that the hideous Loop Line Railway Bridge, built in 1891 to connect stations on each side of the river, still obscures the Custom House from any good vantage point upriver, there are no plans to tunnel the railway under the river. All solutions must be expensive, but the daily price that Dubliners pay for this defacement of one of their great buildings is surely too high. If the Custom House were in Paris, the Parisians would not suffer the railway to be there one day longer. And then, to compound the injury, Liberty Hall, the tallest building in Dublin, breaches the whole skyline and throws the scale of the Custom House completely out of true.

This dock area has changed, and not always for the better, since the building of the high glass-walled financial center and the **Irish Life Exhibition Centre**, where there are changing exhibitions of new Irish arts and crafts. (There is a proposal to open a Decorative Arts Museum branch of the National Museum in the Custom House Development.) This area, so quiet at night save for traffic on both sides, used to have scenes of immense activity throughout the day. Even as late as 1950, a writer, John Harvey, described the docks here with the sad little vignette of families saying goodbye to their emigrating children:

> *In the evening they take on their own special character, with the pale clear air casting its magic over the grimy pubs and warehouses and the noisy clanging of cranes and derricks giving place to the cheerful mudlarking and fighting of Dublin's irrepressible youngsters. On the nights when the Liverpool boats leave from the North Wall with their crowds of modern emigrants — lured by England's streets paved with gold — there is always a silent group on the opposite quays to watch and perhaps to follow slowly as the ship moves down the channel.*

Forty years on and emigration is still the curse of Ireland. Now all that is here is a single tethered Guinness boat, either the ***The Lady Patricia*** or the ***Miranda Guinness***, named after Guinness daughters — an old tradition and why not?

In the original plan for the area, Beresford planned a great square set with trees and lined on three sides by magnificent houses for the merchant princes of Dublin, all of whom were related to one another. It was a lost opportunity. Instead the Custom House at the back faces up to the dilapidated and battered remnants of Gardiner St.

### From the Custom House to St Mary's Pro-Cathedral

Just N of Beresford Place, which curves round the back of the Custom House, is **Busaras** (1953), the Central Bus Station, designed by Michael Scott. He was one of Ireland's best-known architects after the war, and his work, though some may think this odd, is much admired.

Scott also designed the **Abbey Theatre** in Lower Abbey St., which leads off from Beresford Place: the theater is at the junction with Marlborough St. Founded in 1904 as the Irish National Theatre by Lady Augusta Gregory, W.B. Yeats and Edward Martyn, Yeats wrote of "an excellent little company which plays both in Gaelic and English. I may say that we have turned a great deal of Irish imagination towards the stage." The first performance took place in 1904, and over the years the theater has become part of the nation's heritage, its history embedded in the national psyche (see DUBLIN'S THEATRICAL HERITAGE, page 74).

The original theater looks from photographs to have been a decent building with proper and welcoming entrances. But it was burned down in 1951, and the new building (1966) has mean little entrances and repellent proportions. It was altered in 1989, perhaps to try to bring some charm to its sour countenance, but the smile isn't there.

But inside it beams, and new generations of playwrights have kept the flame burning. There are two auditoria: the Abbey with 638 seats and the Peacock with 157 seats. On the walls of the foyer and stairs are fascinating photographs and portraits of celebrities connected with the theater, and, of course, Dublin wit being what it is, there is the story of a theatergoer gazing at Brendan Behan's utterly distinctive photograph and murmuring "the unbearable likeness of Behan." The great actor-director Micheal Mac Liammoir wrote that "the work of the Abbey Theatre was, and is, fundamentally to reveal Ireland to herself and then to the world," and the theater still carries on the work.

Farther along Abbey Street Lower is the Greek Revival **Trustee Savings Bank**, and this pastiche shines out in the street like a good deed in a naughty world.

Up Marlborough St. on the right is the Catholic **St Mary's Pro-Cathedral**, designed by John Sweetman of Raheny (a suburb of North Dublin) and built between 1816-25 with a somewhat dauntingly cold and Classical Doric exterior. It was based, it is said, on the Temple of Theseus in Athens, and crowded into its little space it looks as if it really ought to be shimmering under blue skies among olive trees. It was sited here because of religious prejudice, having been designed for the loftier spaces of O'Connell St., which it would have graced.

Inside, the high, devout and pillared interior with its lofty central dome is somewhat lugubrious, with little of the cheery bustle of so many of Dublin's city churches. In the foyer at the back, where a little shop sells Mass-cards, postcards and pamphlets, there is a remarkable sculpture of a plump man in a toga surrounded by lambs, his plow leaning against the tree. It is uniquely ugly.

Edward Martyn (see DAY 1, page 101), a wealthy Galway landowner and writer and co-founder of the Abbey Theatre, endowed a choir composed of boys and men, the Palestrina Choir, to specialize in music by the great classical composers of polyphony. The choir, with its purity and sweetness of tone and a strength and vitality that many larger choirs lack, is still going strong. One of its most famous members was the tenor John McCormack.

The choir sings the 11am Mass each Sunday in the cathedral and on major Holydays throughout the year. The Pro-Cathedral Folk Choir also sings with the Palestrina Choir at certain events and ceremonies, and no matter how skeptical the listener, it is uplifting to hear these voices raised in this harmony. The huge organ with its big warm tone was rebuilt 20 years ago.

The church has some elaborate treasures, including a fine parcel-gilt monstrance that is used for Exposition. On Sundays there are as many visitors to the church as there are parishioners.

Just opposite the Pro-Cathedral is **Tyrone House** (*Marlborough St.*), designed by Richard Castle in 1740 for the Beresford family, later Earls of Tyrone and further ennobled as Marquesses of Waterford. The exterior has been remodeled, but the interior is fine, with plasterwork by the Lafranchini brothers in the Saloon; in fact, every room is reputed to have wonderful plasterwork. A replica block was built just to the N when the house became the Headquarters of the Department of Education. Sad to say, the house is not open to the public. The marble Pietà, *La Deposizone* by Ermenegildo Luppi, was presented to the Irish people by the Italian Government in gratitude for the relief supplies sent to Italy by Ireland after World War I.

### Around Parnell and Mountjoy Squares

From Marlborough St. it is a short walk NW to **Parnell Square** and **North Great George's Street**, and all the other seats where some of the greatest of the North Dublin grand houses were built. What happened, partly as a result of the Act of Union in 1800, was extraordinary.

Houses that had just been built suddenly became redundant as the center of power moved to London and the aristocracy and politicians followed. The country and the city were governed from Westminster, overseen by a viceroy who brought in his own discriminatory ways to the conduct of social life. Only the Anglo-Irish participated: to be native Irish was seen to be vulgar. Much of Dublin went into decline. The great houses of the nobility were left empty of their grand occupants, and the cosmopolitan glory faded, leaving behind the glory of their plasterwork and furnishings.

The greatest of the houses was **Belvedere House** in Great Denmark St., off the N corner of Parnell Sq., on a wonderful site facing down North Great George's St. It was built in 1786 for the second Lord Belvedere and was one of the last great houses built before the surge to the S. Michael Stapleton, sometimes described as "an Irish Adam," was both architect and stuccodore here, and he reached a peak of achievement, creating what is considered the finest Neoclassical plasterwork in Dublin. The ceilings are exquisite, airy, the staircase a flight of fancy. The **Diana Room** and the **Apollo Room** are superb of their kind.

The house has been a Jesuit school since 1841; James Joyce attended it briefly and got the fright of his life when he listened to the hell fire sermon. Thanks to the continued occupation of this house, the original fireplaces made by Peter Bossi, a Venetian who worked in Dublin for 13 years until 1798, have remained *in situ*. These distinctive surrounds, with fragments of colored stone set into white marble rather like *pietra dura*, are perfectly matched to the weight and amplitude of the rooms in which they were placed, and were so in many of the great houses all over Dublin. Alas, many were casualties in the years of neglect.

Off the NW corner of Parnell Sq. in Granby Row, the **National Wax Museum** *(map* 4B4 ☎ *(01) 8726340, open Mon-Sat 10am-5.30pm, Sun noon-5.30pm)* is a truly lifeless museum that is not a national institution in any sense. About 200 wax exhibits include leading politicans (thin as they are on the ground in Ireland), pop stars, fantasy figures and the *pièce de resistance,* Christ and the Twelve Apostles.

Beyond the far side of the square, in North Great George's St., is the new **James Joyce Cultural Centre** *(map 4B4* ☎ *(01) 8731984),* run by the charming and knowledgeable Ken Monaghan, who is James Joyce's nephew. The Centre, a fine old house, is being restored bit by bit as funds become available.

Just a few dozen yards away, Temple St. leads into **Hardwicke Place**, where stands **St George's Church** by Francis Johnston, which many consider to be his greatest contribution to Dublin. Johnston must have loved it too, for when it was completed he presented a peal of bells to the church. This is a splendid edifice, with its great ordered facade and soaring steeple looking as though it is trying to lift off and leave the severe Ionic portico behind. Under the portico are three carvings by Edward Smyth of *Faith, Hope* and *Charity.* Johnson gave the roof of St George's the enormous span of 65 feet but didn't quite get round to doing the necessary engineering, so that it nearly collapsed in 1836 and was only saved by the deft work of two Dublin engineers, John and Robert Mallet, who inserted iron arches. The Duke of Wellington was married here. It is now used as a conference center. A crude handwritten notice hangs on the noble door: HALL FOR HIRE.

**Eccles Street** nearby (the continuation of Temple St., heading NW) is famous as the home of Leopold Bloom in *Ulysses.* But it was the real home of Francis Johnston, who lived at no. 64 and built a miniature church tower with bells in his garden, the same ones he presented to St George's after objections from his neighbors.

This great architect died in 1829 and is buried in the cemetery of St George's at Whitworth Rd., but his headstone is almost impossible to find as the inscription is faded away.

(The real front door of the putative house in which Leopold Bloom and Molly lived is now in **The Bailey**, a pub in Duke St. — see PUBS.)

Just a little N of Eccles St., some 500 yards away, is the **Royal Canal**, restored and fully navigable in the city stretches. Sections of the towpath have been landscaped to make an agreeable walk cutting through a varied townscape that is almost rural at times and very far removed from these elegant, patrician, civic streets.

The same distance away to the E is **Mountjoy Square**, where Brian Boru is reputed to have pitched his tent before the Battle of Clontarf. Half of it is dilapidated or in ruins; the other still shows that elegance of height and line that made this the only true square in Dublin — each side being exactly the same size — and one of its most beautiful before the bulldozers moved in. And let no one think that Dubliners did not resist.

They did; indeed, some went on living in the houses that were threatened until they were practically lifted out in the machine's grab.

The square was laid out by Luke Gardiner between 1789 and 1800 and was meant to have a church in the middle, but St George's was built just around the corner in Hardwicke Place, so the plan was dropped. The plasterwork in nos. 25 and 26 is by Charles Thorp, who later became Lord Mayor of Dublin and who also made the ceiling of the **Blew** or **Bluecoat School**, beyond the Four Courts (see page 133). The central park in Mountjoy Sq. is beautifully looked after.

**Parnell Square** (previously known as Rutland Sq.) is just N of O'Connell St. Once known as **Palace Row**, the terrace of Parnell Sq. North was laid out by John Ensor. The central plot was purchased by the influential and fashionable Lord Charlemont, which immediately assured the success of the development. Lord Charlemont was a bibliophile and patron of art, architecture and theater, and his new house, built by Sir William Chambers, who also built for him the Casino at Marino (see page 248), was a gathering place for the learned cognoscenti in the 1780s.

**Charlemont House** is now the **Hugh Lane Municipal Gallery of Modern Art** (see page 68 for further details). This is one of the finest galleries in Dublin, with a wonderful collection of 19th and 20thC Irish and Continental works, and it seems appropriate that Charlemont's salon should metamorphose into a place filled with lovely things, with people admiring and discussing them. *Plus ça change* . . .

The nucleus of the collection is made up of paintings from Sir Hugh Lane's personal collection, and in the Portrait Room there are fine portraits of some of the figures from that very past you have been walking through in the squares and streets around the house. (For more about the Hugh Lane Gallery, see GALLERIES, page 68.) Perhaps the greatest tribute was written by Yeats, who was inspired to write the great poem *The Municipal Gallery Revisited* after seeing the portraits of the dead heroes who had been his friends. The poem ends, "Think where man's glory most begins and ends, / And say my glory was I had such friends."

At nos. 18 and 19 Parnell Sq. North, next door to the Municipal Gallery, is the **Dublin Writers Museum** *(18/19 Parnell Sq., map 4 B4* ☎ *(01) 8722077, open Apr-Sept Tues-Sat 10-5pm, Sun, bank hols 1-5pm; Oct-Mar Fri-Sat 10am-5pm, Sun 1-5pm* ▨ ✗ *by advance arrangement; 'Books Upstairs' bookshop* ☎ *(01) 8722239; 'Chapter One'* ⇥ ☎ *(01) 8732266).* This is a lofty, almost sumptuous museum opened in 1991, with ceilings by Michael Stapleton and fine restoration, all surprisingly colorful.

Lord Farnham bought no. 18 in 1780. There followed a succession of owners until the building was taken over by the City of Dublin School. When they moved out and while it was standing empty in the 1980s, the original fireplaces were ripped out.

Back in the 19thC, George Jameson, a member of a Dublin distilling family, purchased the building and commissioned a Manchester architect, Alfred Derbyshire, to improve the interiors. This he did, as he acknowledged, "with the help of Irish workmen and Irish artists." Between 1891 and 1895, Derbyshire created a magnificent saloon or *piano nobile* on the first floor, with an ornamental colonnade and richly gilded frieze, which was added onto the original elaborate plasterwork. The end result was both extravagant and eccentric. Derbyshire also added stained-glass windows with allegorical figures of *Music, Literature, Science* and *Art,* and painted the walls in a neo-Pompeian style. As a remarkable Victorian interior imposed on a structure with Georgian lines, this is fairly worth looking at.

The museum itself is not wholly satisfactory. There are displays of memorabilia relating to Irish writers, including three Nobel prizewinners, Samuel Beckett, George Bernard Shaw and W.B. Yeats, yet the place is curiously empty — perhaps because it is so new. One can't help wishing that the other museums of Dublin would lend more of their literary treasures — it seems ridiculous to have copies of portraits, when the originals are in a museum a mile away. There are traveling exhibitions, special exhibitions, lectures and visiting writers. For all its limitations, this a delightful place to spend an hour, although school parties can be fairly distracting. There is a good restaurant, coffee bar, bar and bookshop.

Next door at no. 19 is the **Irish Writers Centre**, part of the Museum, where writers and visitors can meet and talk and work. It is next door to the Municipal Art Gallery, with all its glories.

Just a short walk away is **St Mary's Chapel of Ease**, John Semple's Gothic creation (1829), in St Mary's Place, which joins Dorset St. with Mountjoy St. Built of black calp (a black limestone found in Ireland), the building is known as the **Black Church** for obvious reasons. It looks like something from Grimm's Fairy Tales. More like a fortress than a church because of one archbishop's paranoid conviction that Protestant congregations were in constant danger of massacre, its interior was one enormous parabolic vault, much admired by John Betjeman. Dublin children used to frighten themselves by repeating the folklore even as they ran around the building that "if you go twice around the Black Church you will see the Devil." Austin Clarke, a fine Dublin poet, called his autobiography *Round the Black Church.*

Semple was the official architect for the Board of First Fruits, a form of Queen Anne's Bounty, a fund consisting of the first fruits and tithes formerly paid to the Pope but annexed to the crown by Henry VIII. It flourished for over a century until its dissolution in 1833, and built churches and glebe houses for the established church (the Church of Ireland) all over Ireland. During the time of the Penal Laws, when churches for worshipers in the Catholic faith were proscribed, the building of Church of Ireland churches was promoted by the State even in places where there were hardly any Protestants, and large quantities of public money were spent in this way. All the same, hundreds, perhaps thousands, of "Mass houses" were built by the unaided resources of people always hovering on the brink of famine.

No longer a church — it was deconsecrated in 1962 — Semple's Black Church has now been chopped up into offices. It owes even this shaky survival, as so many buildings do, to the Irish Georgian Society.

The **Garden of Remembrance** is within Parnell Sq., with its lake in the form of a cross and monument of the *Children of Lir*, by Oisin Kelly, dedicated to all who died in the cause of Irish freedom. Here the Irish

Volunteer movement was formed in 1913, and here the survivors of the subsequent 1916 Rising were held before being transferred to prison.

## O'Connell Street

The Rising was sparked off in O'Connell St., the main thoroughfare of Dublin. Formerly Sackville St., it was named after the Great Liberator and until the end of the 18thC was a quiet backwater, since there was no bridge over the Liffey at that place.

Luke Gardiner and Dr Bartholomew Mosse planned a grand tree-lined mall, Gardiner's Mall, later renamed Sackville St., which they hoped would become a profitably fashionable area. At the top of the street, where it ran into Parnell Sq., Dr Mosse acquired the site of Madame Violante's famous music hall and built the big complex of buildings commonly called the **Rotunda** *(Parnell St. & Sq., map 4B4; for hospital, individuals who call at reasonable times during the day will be admitted, but groups need previous permission from Matron; in chapel, public services on Sun; shop ( ☎ (01) 8728165 run by the Friends of the Rotunda).* This landmark building is now so hemmed in by traffic and later additions that its overall plan is somewhat obscured.

The Rotunda's *raison d'être*, so to speak, was the **Lying-in Hospital**, built in 1750 and celebrated in the annals of obstetrics not only as the first purpose-built maternity hospital in the world (still used for the same purpose), but also as one of the healthiest and most progressive hospitals since its conception (old Dublin play on the word). Between 1829 and 1849 in Paris, about 4 percent of mothers died in childbirth; in Vienna, 5 percent; at the Rotunda, a little over 1 percent. Long before it was fashionable or common practice to do so, the Rotunda encouraged mothers to have their newborn babies with them at all times, the babies sleeping in cradles hung at the foot of the bed.

At the E end of the Hospital is the Rotunda after which the hospital is now named. It was erected in 1764 as an Assembly Room to the designs of John Ensor and was improved by James Gandon in 1786. It was the scene of many notable events: John Field played in public here for the first time; Franz Liszt gave a concert, and the 1783 Volunteers held their Convention here.

In 1910 the interior was brutally adapted as a cinema, the Ambassador. It is now disused and its future is undetermined. The Supper Room, once known as the New Rooms, designed in 1784 by Richard Johnston, brother of Francis, with advice from Gandon, is now the **Gate Theatre**. Under the Gate Theatre is the **Pillar Room** *( ☎ (01) 8722729),* recently restored and often used for opera and orchestral recitals.

The **Gate Theatre Company** is an integral part of Irish theater life, founded in 1928 by Micheal Mac Liammoir, a visionary writer, myth-maker and great actor, and his partner Hilton Edward. His aim was to present an international repertoire of foreign masterpieces that Dublin was unlikely to see unless he and his company brought them there. (Among the foreign masterpieces was the teenaged Orson Welles, who made his first appearance here.) To this day the Gate Theatre continues to flourish (see PERFORMING ARTS).

The private **Rotunda Chapel** is a charming Baroque fantasy reached by a staircase above the main entrance. Its famous ceiling by Bartholomew Cramillion (1755), which cost a fortune for those days (£585 9s 9d), has four recesses, for allegories of *Faith, Hope* and *Charity* and an organ; the large panels were intended for paintings by Cipriani that were never executed. The ceiling is painted, deep-corniced, with extravagant leaves and branches and generally animated plasterwork, and with a flying nursery of *putti:* bold babies, demure babies, angelic babies, little long-legged cherubim holding up gilded canopies and peering over the edges of the folds and drapes at the allegorical figures.

Access is limited, as this is still a hospital and there are maternity wards on each side, as if Bartholomew's babies so long frozen in mid-flight have suddenly taken wing and escaped next door. (Looking at these delicious infants, I was reminded of Brendan Behan's wonderful found remark when he was walking through the old **Daisy Market** near Capel St. and overheard a stall-holder say, "Keep the baby's bottom off the butter.")

This whole area was radically changed only 40 years after Gardiner had conceived his dream of making the area the playground of the idle rich by the building of the wide Carlisle Bridge, now called **O'Connell Bridge** (though the name has never officially been changed), which made it the hub of Dublin and the province of the hard-working merchant class. O'Connell Street's great width, 150 feet from side to side, makes it unusually grand in concept, although the concept has sadly vanished in reality. "Neon-Classical," Maurice Craig, the doyen of Irish architectural historians, called it, but even that hardly applies any more; somehow, the street has the rakish air of a boulevard.

In the center of O'Connell St., and a monument more than a building to Dubliners, is the **General Post Office**, perhaps the most famous building in Dublin and always called the **GPO**, with its Ionic portico of six fluted columns and pediment surmounted by skyline sculptures of *Hibernia, Mercury* and *Fidelity* by Edward Smyth. Designed by Francis Johnston, it was completed in 1814 and is enshrined in the national consciousness as the focal point of the proclamation of a free republic. About 60 rebels led by Pearse and Connolly rushed into the main office, which had only just reopened after major restoration and redecoration, and barricaded themselves in (see HISTORY, page 54). The interior was gutted during the fighting; indeed, most of O' Connell St. was destroyed but was restored in the 1920s.

O'Connell St. was dominated until 1966 by **Nelson's Pillar**, a handsome high Doric column of mountain granite erected in 1808, with a statue of Nelson leaning against a capstan on top by the Cork sculptor Thomas Kirk. The Pillar, designed by William Wilkins of Caius College Cambridge, under the direction of Francis Johnston, was built at a cost of £6,856 to commemorate Nelson's victory at Trafalgar. It gave a focus to the street, to climb the 168 narrow twisting steps was every child's treat, and from its balcony there was a wonderful panoramic view.

It was in every way an addition to the townscape, but for someone whose brain had hurried off in the opposite direction it was an unbearable imperialistic monument, so it was brought down by a bomb on the

50th anniversary of the 1916 Rising — yet another of the philistine, misguided effects of the ersatz patriotism that has so defaced Ireland. (After the explosion, two identical stone heads of Nelson went on sale as the genuine article. The real one is now in the Dublin Civic Museum: see MUSEUMS, page 73.)

One of the most knowledgeable writers on Dublin, John Harvey, wrote in 1949: "O'Connell Street is the only street in the inner city which runs for a considerable distance in a straight line; it is redeemed from the soulless frigidity of gridiron planning by its great width, one hundred and fifty feet, and by the Nelson Pillar at its centre . . . . The Nelson Pillar is a grand work, without which the long stretch of O'Connell Street would lose much of its vitality . . . it is a convenient and intrinsically valuable focal point . . . . " Prophetic words indeed.

There are many other monuments and statues in the street, with the tall monument at the N end taking precedence: **Charles Parnell** by Augustus Saint-Gaudens, erected in 1911. Parnell is wearing two overcoats — apparently his habit, in life. Behind him on his pillar are his famous warning words spoken in 1855, which every Irish schoolchild can recite: "No man has the right to fix the boundary to the march of a nation. No man has a right to say to his country, 'Thus far shall you go and no further . . . . ' "

A huge Irish harp is depicted on the monument, but harpers and purists, generally the same thing, recoil on seeing it, since the strings are not attached as they should be, and the man who carved it had obviously never really looked at a harp. The question of the harp is not simply academic. The harp, with the shamrock and the color green, is the great symbol of Ireland, and as such appears everywhere. (It was also the symbol on the label of Guinness.) On the day after the unveiling of the monument in 1911 the name of the street behind was changed from Great Britain St. to Parnell St.

All down the central island of the street are other monuments of varying quality. Among them is Oisin Kelly's 1987 monument to **Jim Larkin**, with his powerful upraised arms and huge hands, an image that has become wholly associated with this fervent, brave socialist. Born in Liverpool of Irish parentage, he was the first successful organizer of the Worker's Union of Ireland. In 1913, at the height of his power and threatened with arrest, Larkin disguised himself as an old priest and made his way to the balcony of the Imperial Hotel, which was opposite where his statue now is, beside the site of Clery's, Dublin's largest department store, and managed to address the crowd before the police moved in. They then charged the crowd with batons, and 400 people were injured.

By dint of successful strikes he reorganized the dock labor of Dublin. In just three months in 1913 there were 30 separate disputes, and to glance down the list gives a unique view of working-class Dublin in that year:

*Involved in strikes, lock outs and sympathetic strikes were agricultural laborers, bill posters, biscuit makers, bottle makers, box makers, brass finishers, brick layers, builders' laborers, cabinet makers, canal loaders, carpenters, carriers, carters, coach makers, confectioners, dockers, electricians, engineers, farm workers, gas workers, glaziers, hair dressers, farriers, iron founders, linen workers, manure workers, market gardeners, match workers, millers, news-boys, painters, paviors, plasterers, plumbers, poplin workers, seamen and firemen, soap makers, stevedores, stone cutters, tobacco workers, tramway employees, van drivers, wood machinists — even school-boys at the national schools in Rutland Street.*

Around the base of the Larkin statue are inscribed his words: "The great appear great because we are on our knees; let us rise."

Farther down, nearly at the center of O'Connell St., is the **Anna Livia Fountain** by Eamon O'Doherty and Sean Mulcahy, unveiled in June 1988 as part of the Dublin Millennium Celebrations and immediately estab-lished as a city rendezvous. The enormous statue of **Daniel O'Connell** by John Henry Foley was hit by army sniper fire in 1922; you can see the marks on the ample bosom of Courage with the laurel wreath of Victory in her hair.

When Yeats, who was a senator in the new Parliament, was resisting the measures to prohibit divorce that the repressive Free State Govern-ment wished to introduce, he remembered the three great stone men on O'Connell St., Nelson, Parnell and O'Connell, each deeply associated with notorious love affairs, and wrote in angry irony: " . . . for intellect would make us proud / and pride bring in impurity: / the three old rascals laugh aloud . . . "

The pageant that is O'Connell St. is a show in itself. Here the young seem to congregate like a step-out of cassowaries meeting under the canopy of those big old London plane trees with their chattering pied wagtails in the branches above. Somewhere there is a band or street musicians, and always the habitués claiming the end is nigh or declaiming some mysterious faith of their own.

### West of O'Connell Street

Walking down O'Connell St., getting on toward the Liffey, you come to **Middle Abbey Street**, on the right. It follows the line of an ancient monastic route that led w to **St Mary's Abbey** *(Mary's Abbey, map 3 C3* ☎ *(01) 8721490; interpretative exhibition in the Chapter House open mid-June to Sept Tues-Sun noon-6pm),* about ½ mile away. Founded in the 12thC, the abbey was once the largest Cistercian foundation in Ireland; the medieval vaulted Chapter House with its rib moldings is the surviving remnant. It was here that Silken Thomas threw the State Sword on the table and declared his revolt against Henry VIII, which ended in his own death and that of most of his family (see HISTORY, page 42). The Abbey was sacked under the Dissolution of the Monas-teries by that same king in 1539, and the stone from the building was used to build Essex Bridge.

Nearby in Mary St. (up Capel St., then right) is **St Mary's Church**, dated 1697, designed by Thomas Burgh the master architect of Trinity Library. The churchyard is dedicated to Wolfe Tone (see HISTORY, page 49), who was born near here. This is one of the few places in Dublin that actually tells you about its own history. On a board outside are listed some of the people associated with the church, including Richard Brinsley Sheridan and Sean O'Casey. The future of the church is uncertain.

Continuing E, Mary St. elides into **Henry Street**, off which on the left leads **Moore Street**. These two, now pedestrianized, are the most famous of Dublin markets, with their street traders and vegetable and fruit stalls. The cries of Dublin are to be heard here at all hours of the day, curiously repetitive like some strange hydra-headed bird selling bananas and Swiss chocolate. The enormous covered shopping center **ILAC** also houses a Central Library with a daily program of lectures, films, and imaginative exhibitions that give insight into Ireland, like the one in which a thousand amateurs sent in their snapshots to make the biggest family photograph album in the world. It is a thriving, vibrant part of Dublin and extremely enjoyable to visit.

### From O'Connell Street to Blackhall Place

In the opposite direction, Mary St. leads E into St Mary's Lane, which in turn leads to the **Dublin Corporation Fruit and Vegetable market** in St Michan's St. The market was established in 1892 and is housed in a grandiose pillared building, with the City arms displayed over the archway at the main entrance.

Just behind the Four Courts in Church St. is **St Michan's** *(Church St., map 3 C3* ☎ *(01) 8724154* ✗ *of church and vault Mon-Sat between 10am and 12.45pm; late Mar-Oct also between 2 and 4.45pm* ☎*)*, one of Dublin's oldest church sites, dedicated to a Danish saint in 1095. The medieval-looking tower with its crude Classical doorcase in fact dates from 1686. (Incidentally, the <u>ch.</u> is pronounced hard as in Mi<u>ch</u>ael.) It is famous for its vaults cut from magnesian limestone, a rock so absorbent as to prevent decomposition and to cause a form of soft mummification. In these vaults are preserved corpses, probably dating from the 17thC, many of which have eerily soft-looking skin and malleable joints.

The display of bodies has been tidied up and laid out in one small, rather too well-lit vault, so that one might be looking into a cyclorama in a museum rather than the real thing. One corpse is that of a very tall man with his legs broken to fit in the coffin. The whole effect is not so much gruesome (although it is that too) as sad; you feel that these poor bones should be left in peace. But then, visitors form a necessary part of the revenue for the upkeep of the church. There has always been controversy over whether or not such exploitation of the dead should be allowed. One writer and historian of Dublin, John Harvey, was fierce in his denunciation:

> *But what is objectionable about St Michan's is that the visit to the vaults has been made a highly publicised function for tourists, from which the parish derives a large revenue. Such exploitation of the private dead is even more disgraceful than the filthy state of desecration which is the lot of many older graveyards of Ireland. It is hard to understand the insensitive mentality of the ghouls who carry on this lucrative show.*

Near here, still farther w, and best reached by walking along the quays, is **Blackhall Place** in which, sudden and surprising in an unprepossessing area, is the beautiful **Blew-Coat** or **Bluecoat School**, by Thomas Ivory. It was originally founded by Royal Charter in 1672 with no less an object than to give shelter to *all* the poor of the city — "but this extravagant project was relinquished for one more rational and feasible, namely, to educate and maintain the sons of freemen who had been unsuccessful in trade . . . . " Life doesn't change much over the centuries. The official name is **The King's Hospital**. It was built in 1773 to replace the old building, and the lovely old blue uniform worn by the boys was only abolished in 1923; the building remained a school until 1970.

This is a handsome building, although the pepperpot dome on the building was only added in 1904, Ivory's original one having been left unfinished due to the money having run out, and a bad fist they made of the new one. In the boardroom, which has a fine reproduction ceiling copied from the original made by Charles Thorp the Elder in 1778 for £72 and which was burned, there is a painting by John Trotten showing a fairly bored-looking Thomas Ivory, attending a cost-cutting meeting, at which presumably he was told his cupola was not going to be built after all. The building is not open and is now the Solicitors' Training College and Offices of the Incorporated Law Society of Ireland, which assures it of its future.

Two blocks E of Blackhall Place is **Smithfield**, the old Haymarket of Dublin. Immediately to the N, a continuation of Blackhall Place, is the curiously named **Stoneybatter**, which is simply a mixture of languages: English, and *bothar,* the Irish word for road. This was one of the earliest roads into Dublin and was part of the *Slighe Cualann,* one of the five great highways from Tara, the hill of the kings.

**Lower Dominick St.** was another of the most fashionable streets of the same epoch, and no. 20 was one of the first houses to be built in the street and one of the longest to survive. It was the home of Robert West the great stuccodore, who used birds as his motif and who taught Michael Stapleton (Stapleton later took over West's practice and was his executor). Much of West's work was freehand (a lot of later plasterwork was done using molds, which produced a repetitive, much less vivacious effect), and he made some particularly ferocious-looking birds here in his own house. The plasterwork is exuberant and yet restrained and symmetrical, with great curlicued, fantastic elements. Tours are by arrangement only via the **National Youth Federation Organization** *(20 Lower Dominick St., map 4B4* ☎ *(01) 8729933).*

## Henrietta Street and the King's Inns

Nearby, heading w, is **Henrietta Street**, a street of sad old palaces waiting for their princes and princesses to kiss them back to beautiful life. Some of these quixotic people have arrived; the street is stirring. Closed off at one end by the **King's Inns**, this street was once described as the "grandest cul-de-sac in Europe." So many bishops and archbishops of the Established Church lived there that it was known as the "hill of primates." Looking up it to the angled Classical bulk of the

King's Inns, and trying to avoid the pox of parked cars that so defaces all of Dublin — they would hang them from the lampposts if they could — is to gaze upon a peerless Classical diminishing perspective.

Henrietta St., named after the Duke of Grafton's wife, was in the 18thC the most fashionable street in Dublin, "and of so palatial a caste," wrote Maurice Craig, "that one easily understands how it remained the most fashionable single street in Dublin till the Union, long after many rival centres had been created."

Sir Edward Lovett Pearce was involved in the building of a number of houses in the street. **No. 9**, commissioned by Pearce's cousin Thomas Carter, the Master of the Rolls, in 1731, is generally considered the finest, and looks much like the house built by Lord Burlington in Great Burlington St., London, including the fine staircase. Burlington was one of the noble English amateur-architects and dilettantes known to historians as the Lords of Creation. The building is now a hostel. This house and its neighbor **Blessington House** (which has been altered) retain the finest early 18thC domestic interiors in Dublin.

Over the years the street fell into terrible disrepair and housed slums that were among the most disgraceful in Europe. In the late 19thC Alderman Meade, Lord Mayor of Dublin, acquired many of the houses, ripped out the fireplaces and sold the interior fittings to whoever would buy them, letting the rooms out as tenements. The only buildings that stood in good repair were those that had been maintained by a convent or religious institution, or by the library of King's Inn in its separate building.

Sean O'Casey was born near here, and his plays *Juno and the Paycock* and *The Plough and the Stars* give a graphic sense of life as lived in these paradoxical tenements:

> . . . a long lurching row of discontented incurables smirched with the age-long marks of ague, fever, cancer and consumption . . . the doors were scarred with time's spit and anger's hasty knocking: the pillars by their sides were shaking, their stuccoed bloom long since peeled away and they looked like crutches keeping the trembling doors standing on their palsied feet.

Now the steady decline is beginning to be arrested. One house was bought in 1974 with the help of the Irish Georgian Society, by an extraordinary young husband and wife who have restored it year by year and floor by floor as their family grows. They probably know more about these houses and their construction than anyone else in Dublin.

The **King's Inns** were James Gandon's last great achievement. Although the foundation stone was laid by the dreaded Lord Clare in 1795, the buildings were not finished until 1817 and the work was carried on by H.A. Baker, one of Gandon's pupils. The residents of Henrietta St. were not best pleased when they discovered his masterpiece blocked off their view, but in fact its angled position gives great harmony to the street.

Strictly speaking, the King's Inns are the work of three architects. The central portion is by Gandon, the cupola by Johnston in 1816, and the two extensions are mid-19thC. This facade has two caryatid entrances representing *Ceres* and *Bacchus,* which seems fairly unlikely for a temple dedicated to Law and Order. (Indeed, its local nickname is the Temple.)

How you approach the King's Inns makes a difference to your initial view and concept of the building. From the Henrietta St. entrance you see it bit by bit; approaching from Constitution Hill on the other side you get the full impact.

The surrounding park is open to the public and has beautiful cast-iron benches. The building and Library may be visited by arrangement with one of the Benchers of the King's Inns.

**Constitution Hill**, formerly known as Glasmanoge, runs alongside an institution famous in Dublin annals, once known as the Richmond and later as the Grangegorman lunatic asylum. (Grangegorman was liberal for its time: "the only modes of coercion permitted here are the imposition of the arm-straps, the muff, strait-waistcoat, solitary seclusion and degradation from one class of patient to another . . . " The words "The Gorman" carried more heft than just the name of a place in Dublin; but as well as signifying nervous stress, they remind us of the great stretch of manors leading up Christchurch to the monastic grange of Gorman and as far as Glasnevin.

### The Four Courts

Walking due s down toward the quays leads to the **Four Courts** *(Inns Quay, map 3 C3, open Mon-Fri 11am-1pm, 2-4pm)*. The building (illustrated on page 86), with its great central block and portico of six Corinthian pillars, its lantern dome and its statues along the skyline, was designed to contain the Courts of the Exchequer, Common Pleas, King's Bench and Chancery. Started in 1774 by Thomas Cooley but completely redesigned in 1785 by Gandon after Cooley's death, it is now rated as one of Gandon's greatest buildings.

The building was set on fire during the Civil War and although it was reconstructed using Gandon's extant plans, the pavilion wings were flattened back to allow a freer flow of traffic, which changed the rhythm of the building. Purists also complain that the saucer dome is less satisfactory than its predecessor.

What can never be restored was the loss of all the official archives and public records, which blazed for five days. By a horrible irony the Public Records Office housed a vast amount of Irish archives sent from their great houses for safekeeping: priceless documents, medieval rolls and all the original maps of Ireland, surveys, fully detailed records of the Irish Parliaments, the deeds of Christchurch from its foundations . . . . So much was lost that it is not only heartbreaking to think of it but a severe embarrassment to historians and to the Irish nation. One historian unequivocally writes:

> *The Troubles brought much senseless and unnecessary loss on the country, and many a fair house and mansion with its treasures went up as a burnt offering to human folly and brutishness, but the destruction of the Record Office in the Four Courts was the greatest single disaster of this orgy of destruction and violence.*

135

What we have lost is evident from the quality of what has survived, including Sir William Petty's famous *Down Survey,* the first complete topographical survey of any country, which shows the boundaries of parishes and townlands. Its name has nothing to with Co. Down, as people generally believe, but is derived from the features of the country having been plotted *down* on the map. Oddly enough a set of the maps survives in the Bibliothèque Nationale of Paris, from which the present set in Dublin is copied. The set of maps in Paris was captured by a French pirate, carried off as booty and, in spite of many diplomatic protests, was never returned — fortunately, in view of the fire.

The Four Courts is an extremely busy legal beehive. The Law Library is an enormous area that can hold up to 700 people. Solicitors can meet barristers in the area outside the library, and often there are settlements being attempted in this area.

The most interesting part of the day for an onlooker takes place in the Round Hall at 11am, when the cases to be heard for the day are "called over." After the "call over," the barristers and solicitors and their clients wait for their turn in the Round Hall: this is not the time to visit if you only want to look at the architecture, as it is so busy. The public may attend the courts so long as there is no sign saying "in camera."

There is a restaurant in the basement where most of the people working in the Four Courts go for lunch; they also serve breakfast and coffee throughout the working day. There are two policemen on duty outside the Supreme Court, which is just off the Round Hall.

About $1\frac{1}{2}$ miles w of the Four Courts lies **Chapelizod**, a suburb that until quite recently was a separate village and whose strange name comes from a corruption of **Chapel of Izod** or Iseult, the daughter of Angus, King of Ireland, who was courted by Tristan King of Cornwall and whose tragic love story inspired Wagner's great opera *Tristan and Isolde.* Chapelizod was also the scene of Sheridan le Fanu's famous chiller *The House by the Churchyard,* one of those Gothic novels that 19thC Dubliners produced to such fantastic effect; another was *Dracula* by Bram Stoker. But Chapelizod itself is best left to memories of its romantic past.

### Back along the quays

The Four Courts are about a mile w of O'Connell Bridge. Walking back E along the quays on either side of the river may be a pleasure for the eyes but is a nightmare for the nose — traffic is continuous, enormous and unrestricted, especially at rush hours; dirty great container trucks on their way to or from the docks lash their tails and growl. Yet these fragile little quays, relics of Dublin's history, are the main E-W arteries for the traffic of the capital.

Nevertheless, you should walk, because whether you return along the N quays or the S, or crisscross the bridges back and forth, you see many delightful things. A statue, arms outstretched, perched high over the quays blessing the river city. The exterior of **Sunlight Chambers** on the corner of Essex Quay and Parliament St., a remarkable Arts and Crafts building with a tiled frieze showing scenes from a day in the life of soap, soap and more soap (the frieze needs a wash). The **Brazen Head**, down a side alley from Bridge St., charming especially when it is quiet, which it is during the day (there is traditional music there on weekends). The **Winding Stair** café on the North side. The view of **St Audoen's** and its pretty little park made out of what was the graveyard, with its access through Dublin's only surviving medieval gate. Ups and downs and little nooks to sit in; the look of the Liffey; the antique stores; the clothes market spilling out from Liffey street.

Elizabeth Bowen remembers that as a child living in what is now Dublin 4, her family thought that N of the Liffey was *terra incognita*:

> No swamp or jungle could hold more threats than the tacitly ruled-out parts of one's own city. Even along the verges of St Stephen's Green there were canyon-like streets that could intimidate me. My fear was not social, not the rich child's dread of the slum. It was a charnel fear, of grave-dust and fungus dust. I had heard of poverty-rotted houses that might at any moment crumble over one's head . . . .

There are occasional hints of that attitude from people living s of the river who speak darkly of Handbag Junction or warn you to weld your bag or pocketbook to your person and tell you not to leave your car with your keys in it — in other words, to behave in the perfectly normal way you would in any capital city anywhere in the world; here they warn as though they were telling you not to swim in a shark-infested bay. The North side of the Liffey is full of lovely things, and you walk in it as you do nowadays in any city. With respect.

# Day 3
## Old Dublin

*See Dublin City maps 3 & 4, and DAY 3 map on page 138.*

There are countless ways to see the old Town of Dublin, its cathedrals, the Liberties, and the quays, but if you are walking from **College Green** or thereabouts, walk via the streets behind the quays. Until recently one would have said at all costs to walk down the quays themselves, along the river, past the charming **Ha'penny Footbridge**, also known as the Metal Bridge, the Wellington Bridge and, its official name, the Liffey Bridge; it has recently been ornamented with arches and lanterns.

But the quays are so noisy with traffic during most of the day that walking them is no longer the pleasure it was. Also there is the hazard of Dublin buses, which make the unwary walker jump out of his or her skin. They run on diesel so that dirty black fumes spew out, and the noise of their engines is like a huge old witch taking off with a hiss. These should be the first thing that the City Fathers and Mothers should change, to help their city.

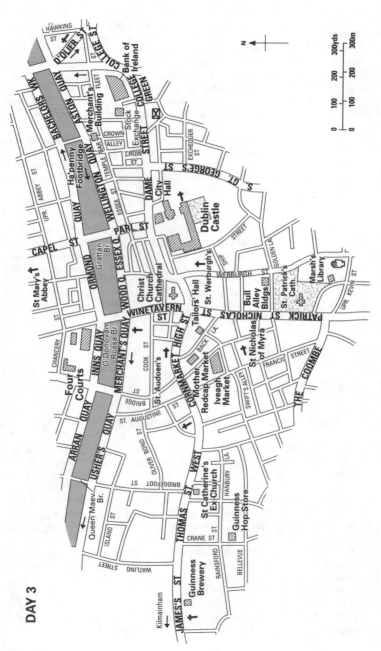

## Temple Bar

But besides the negative aspects, there are positive reasons for turning into the **Crown Alley** area of Temple Bar through **Merchant's Arch** under **Merchant's Building**, small but perfectly formed, and designed by Frederick Darley in 1821. In this little opening at almost any hour of the day or night you can hear exponents of any kind of music, good or bad, since it is a dry haven for street musicians.

Near here on Merchant's Quay is **Adam and Eve's Church** (or The Immaculate Conception), named after a Catholic Mass House that it replaced, which was reached by going through the Adam and Eve pub. The Franciscan church was built in 1829 by Patrick Byrne, and is mostly hidden by the friary building except for the large copper dome.

The **Temple Bar** area is fast becoming Dublin's Bohemian Quarter or Left Bank, having been saved from extinction at the last hour from its marked fate as the City Bus Terminal by the intervention of the then Taoiseach (or Prime Minister) Charles Haughey. Not that the threat has gone. The planners are still creeping around looking for likely sites, and rumor has it that they are gazing wistfully across the Liffey behind Lower Ormond Quay. While the plans for the terminal were being pushed through, the craftworkers and artists set up their shops without security of tenure, and now that the place is spick and span everyone hopes that they can afford to remain. The truth is, the area cannot afford to lose them.

Temple Bar owes its name to Sir William Temple, Provost of Trinity, whose 17thC house and gardens were here, and it is now a place of small lofts and vernacular architecture.

There was a wonderful scandal in 1992 when a new street guide to the area listed one house as a brothel. The media hurried round to knock on the door and were delighted when it was opened by husky-voiced women who coyly "no commented" when asked for their occupation. But a single house is a far cry from the days of Monto (short for Montgomery Street), the notorious red-light district of Dublin above the Custom House, where at least a thousand prostitutes plied their trade and of which Joyce wrote with fear and dread. When the district was cleaned up in the 1920s the names of the streets were changed, and Montgomery St. is now Foley St.

In **Crown Alley** there is a fine, fully restored 19thC warehouse, and in nearby **Crow Street**, one of Dublin's earliest theaters stood on the site of **Cecilia House**, the old Catholic University Medical School.

This area has a fine mix of cafés, music and record stores, co-operatives and clubs, art galleries and second-hand clothing stores, astrological read-outs and resource centers, and all that mixture of New Age trades and people that one meets in enclaves like these, which so contribute to the flavor of any city, cynics notwithstanding. (See SHOPPING and EATING AND DRINKING). There is minimal traffic, especially at night in summer, when people spill out from the pubs and cafés (see PUBS). Then cars venture down the narrow cobbled streets almost at their peril, and it is hard to see why they are permitted down here at all. Certainly the revelers feel hostile to them, and are slow to move out of their way.

**Street Art Temple Bar** is a new project to turn the whole area into one big art gallery with monumental pieces of sculpture set on under-developed sites, and street corners and empty shop windows used to display conceptual art and installations. These pieces make you do a double take: the display changes as the area develops and sites are taken over, but new ones appear. It's an interesting and imaginative concept. More on-site information about this whole revivified area can be had at the **Temple Bar Information Centre** *(23 Essex St. East, map 4D4)*, which also provides an excellent little guide (IR£3).

The new **Irish Film Centre** in Eustace St. is a brilliant conversion of a complex of old buildings, with delightful architectural references to the history of film — a pathway lit like a strip of film, for example — and containing two cinemas, a bookshop, bar, an archive and restaurant. Built around a courtyard, the complex is a remarkable use of a difficult site. The building was designed by architect Sheila O'Donnell and is a fine addition to the whole area and to film life in Dublin (see ENTERTAINMENTS).

Temple Bar is bounded by **Dame Street**, with its fine commercial Victorian buildings, many built as banks and some still used as such, with fine marble and porphyry columns and elegant carved finials — as well as a huge new bank, which looks like a great licorice allsort, plonked down in the 1970s.

## City Hall

Just down Palace St., past a tall house with its huge oxymoron lettered across its facade — *Sick and Indigent Roomkeepers Society, Founded 1790* — is a little entrance to the lower yards of **Dublin Castle**. Gazing at its new glassed-walled buildings, one wonders afresh at the vanity of architects who impose their lack of taste and history on such beautiful surroundings.

Leave this entrance and go up Dame St. to **City Hall** *(Lord Edward St., map 4D4 ☎ (01) 796111, open Mon-Fri 9am-1pm, 2.15-5pm; visits to the Council Chamber only by appointment)*, on its little eminence looking down Parliament St. A ten-jetted fountain with three stony-faced Fates presides over a small park beside the City Hall that marks Dr Barnardo's birthplace. The tribute simply reads, "Caring for children is his unending legacy." Down a little cul-de-sac nearby is a plaque to three men killed in the Civil War.

The City Hall, headquarters of Dublin Corporation, was originally built as the **Royal Exchange** and occupies one of the most important sites in the city, facing down over Grattan Bridge and the wide thoroughfare of Parliament St. (The **RiverRun** gallery with its interesting exhibitions of modern Irish art is on the corner here.) Capel St., across the bridge and one of the oldest streets in Dublin, has fine 18thC houses, with good paneling, ceilings and staircases, including a pair owned by Dublin Corporation left in limbo by their ever-confusing dual carriageway plans.

Because of the importance of the site of City Hall, in the center of the old city, on a hill abutting onto Dublin Castle, a competition for its design was organized in 1769. There were 61 submissions, and the prize was taken by an unknown young London architect, Thomas Cooley, who only lived for five years after the building was completed, but whose name was made by this building. Among the other entrants was James Gandon, who came second, and Thomas Ivory the Dublin architect, who was given a consolation prize and was not consoled.

For years I admired this cold building inside and out, but only began to love it after reading the description by the great architectural historian, Maurice Craig: "The detailing of the Royal Exchange is impeccable, the workmanship of the highest quality, the design suave if not genial. It suffers from facing North and from being, as a building, very evidently almost entirely useless." Not entirely. Dublin Corporation still meets here, and the interior is still remarkable and full of impressive architectural detail.

Apart from its architectural interest, City Hall is both famous and infamous in Dublin's annals. Daniel O'Connell made his first public speech here in 1800; the rebels were horribly tortured here after the 1798 rebellion (passers-by in the street could clearly hear their cries); and in 1824 the iron railings collapsed under the weight of people watching a public whipping. Three people were killed, and the railings were re-placed by a stone balustrade.

The interior contains some magnificent **sculptures** in the finest tradition of late Baroque sculpture by Edward Smyth, including one of Henry Grattan and Charles Lucas, MP, which won him a sculpture competition when he was only 23 and brought him to the attention of James Gandon. There is also splendid **stucco work** by Charles Thorp, who later became Lord Mayor of Dublin. Perhaps the chief glory is the carving by Simon Vierpyl (who showed his genius in the Casino at Marino, whose memorably glowering bust of Dr Gilbert is in Trinity College Library, and whose apprentice Edward Smyth was).

The large central **rotunda** has a spectacular dome and mosaic, surrounded by a wreath of shamrocks depicting the Arms of the City of Dublin with its three flaming castles, as someone said, but really depicting a symbolic city under siege, with the Latin legend underneath: "An obedient citizenry creates a happy city." Or if you wish, "Happy the city where citizens obey." Look out for this coat of arms on many lampposts and monuments: it lends itself particularly well to street furniture.

The **statues of Thomas Davis** (1853) and **Daniel O'Connell** (1846) are both by John Hogan, who, while a young man in Cork, had attracted so many admirers of his work that a public subscription was raised to send him to study in Rome. There he worked with considerable success for 20 years, and in 1849 returned to Ireland. Here he found himself caught between two ideologies: because he had lived and worked in Rome, he was tainted with popery, for one suspicious segment of society; and for the other, he was infected with nasty, foreign, liberal ideas. Poor Hogan was much bewildered. *Plus ça change.*

Just above the City Hall on its SE flank are the **Municipal Buildings**, originally **Lord Newcomen's Bank**, designed by Thomas Ivory (he of the consolation prize), who got his revenge by designing a more elegant building than Cooley's — according, again, to Craig: "On this highly sensitive site," he wrote, "facing the main gate into the castle using a repertoire of shallow arched recesses, a flute frieze, and delicate swags, he paid such respect to Cooley's building as to succeed, in the opinion of one modern critic, in making the Exchange look coarse." So much for Cooley. (The Municipal Buildings are not open to the public.)

## Dublin Castle

Through the Great Gate with the figure of *Justice* by John Van Nost with her tilted scales is **Dublin Castle** *(map 4 D4 ☎ (01) 6777580 or (01) 6777129, open Mon-Fri 10am-12.15pm, 2-5pm; Sat, Sun, bank holidays 2-5pm)*. When the scales were at one point seen to be dipping unequally (well, they still do), the authorities solved the problem by boring holes in the scales to let the rainwater escape. The blind flanking gateway supports *Fortitude,* also by Van Nost.

For seven centuries Dublin Castle was the mainspring of Dublin life, a symbol of power and panoply of Government, of the Ascendancy, of social life and, for some, of terror, for this castle, now so open and so fair, was for years a frightening place to many of the Irish and a symbol of British intransigence and insularity. It was a prison, an administrative center, and the quarters, during the Season, of the Viceroy. Nowadays it is mainly used for State ceremonial purposes and European Community meetings.

The castle was founded in 1204 by mandate of King John, who wrote to Lord Justice Fitzgerald of Ireland in 1205: "You have given us to understand that you have not a convenient place where in our treasure may be safely deposited and forasmuch as a fortress would be necessary for us at Dublin, we command you to erect a castle there in such competent place as you shall judge most expedient as well to curb the city as to defend it." It didn't just curb a city; it curbed a country.

In 1213 Henry de Loundres, Archbishop of Dublin, who quenched the fire in Kildare (see EXCURSIONS, page 259), began building the castle. He chose the most strategically valuable site in Dublin, a stretch of high ground where the River Poddle entered the pool of dark peaty water *(Dubh Linn)* from which Dublin got its name. The Poddle's course made a natural moat on three sides of the castle, a conventional four-square fortified bastion with drum towers at each corner. It has remained much the same shape ever since, although it has spread outward and downward. Little of the medieval building remains, although the Record Tower is a Norman building. The castle became a vice-regal residence in 1560 by order of Queen Elizabeth 1.

Now the castle is not so much a castle as a series of courtyard buildings of the early 18thC based on English Palladian originals. The **cupola** was taken from an illustration in William Kent's *Designs of Inigo Jones* (1727). The southeastern range of buildings in **Upper Castle Yard** (1740-50) were by Joseph Jarratt, although what we see for the most part is a modern reproduction, the building having been burned down in 1941, with a great loss of fine furnishings.

To cross the beautiful courtyard is to be reminded of "ploughing the half-acre," the phrase used to describe the activities of the middlemen, perhaps the most hated people in Ireland, who collected the rents of tenants for absentee landlords, and who were assiduous place-hunters, keeping their eyes open for the main chance, pushing their children forward, and petitioning the monarch not to grant relief to the Catholics.

Every century has laid its mark on Dublin Castle, every event, every hero. Their impress is here. Perhaps the 20thC has marked it most of all, with its destructive fires, the total change of government and change of use, and the latest restoration, most of which has been sensitive, although too much was demolished during the castle's restoration as a major conference center for the European Community.

Whenever you open the pages in the history of the castle some turbulent event leaps out. In 1534 the castle was subjected to a long siege by Silken Thomas, grandson of the great Earl of Kildare and acting deputy in place of his father. He was called Silken because of his own love of finery and because "his horseman's jacks were embroidered with silks." Defeated, he was later executed at Tyburn, London with five of his uncles.

In 1592 occurred the most celebrated escape in the history of the castle, perhaps in the history of Ireland. Red Hugh O'Donnell, son of the great northern chieftain, had been lured on board a ship, kidnapped and brought to Dublin and held as hostage to bring his father to submission. He escaped, was recaptured, and escaped again with the brothers Art and Henry O'Neill, sons of another great chieftain. On either Christmas Eve, 1591 or January 6, 1592, Hugh and his companion, without any outer garments, escaped into the Wicklow Mountains. Henry was lost in the darkness, Art O'Neill died in the cold and was buried on the mountain, and O'Donnell's feet were destroyed through frostbite, though he went on to fight many a gallant fight for Ireland.

Red Hugh was imprisoned in one of the original great corner towers, called the **Record** or **Wardrobe Tower**, where was kept "the royal robe, the cap of maintenance and other furniture of State preserved here by a patent officer who has a competent salary for that employment." The Record Tower was at the center of the Administration from the 18thC until 1922. (Now it is being restored and is to become a museum exhibiting the course of the castle's history.)

In 1684 there was a devastating fire, and new buildings were designed by the Surveyor-General Sir William Robinson. For the next century the castle was added to and improved, until by 1779 an observer could write that "this castle is far superior to the Palace of St James's as well in the exterior, as the size and the elegance of the apartments within." (The fear of fire was so widespread that the castle pastry cooks had their ovens outside the walls.)

Crossing the courtyard does not offer any real hint of the magnificence within. The guided tour begins in the hall, with its wonderful benches painted with family crests, and up a double staircase onto the landing that leads to the **State Apartments**.

Here some floors are covered in carpets in the color that the French call *caca d'oie,* which quarrel horribly with the furniture, including the superb set of French needlepointed chairs given by Lord Granard. Other floors are far more suitably covered in magnificent examples of Donegal carpets, adapted from Adam designs. The fine oval-shaped **Wedgwood Room** has beautiful sconces and a frozen waterfall of a Waterford chandelier. All over the State Apartments are noteworthy ceilings, especially the two removed from demolished Mespil House. The portraits of the Viceroys stare down at the public with hauteur.

In the **Drawing Room**, the tall chimney glasses, the pier glasses and the console tables were part of the original furnishings. The paintings are on loan from the Milltown Gift, originally from Russborough House, in the National Gallery of Ireland. The **Apollo Room**, a reproduction of the drawing room in Tracton House, which once stood on the corner of St Stephen's Green and Merrion Row, was incorporated into the State Apartments during the 1964-8 reconstruction. The ceiling, dated 1746, shows Apollo in the clouds with his lyre and the signs of the zodiac and, in the corners, groups depicting *Music, Agriculture, War* and *The Chase.*

To walk around the State Apartments is to gain direct access to colonialism, repression and privilege, but the young guides who show you around relate its history in a careful, detached and cheerful way. No mention is made of the Irish rebels' heads, spiked outside after various uprisings, or of the wife of an O'Neill suspended in a cage in full view as she starved to death in retaliation for her husband's insubordination.

Across the precinct is a fascinating guided tour to the layers of underground Dublin discovered when the restoration, costing millions of pounds, was undertaken in the last few years. In the **Viking and Norman Defences Exhibition**, visitors can descend beneath the rebuilt buildings and see the only remnants of the Viking town defenses visible in Dublin. It is beautifully shown, with glass walls and steel staircases and murals, a kind of instant dive into the magma of Dublin.

Also within the confines of the castle is the little jewel of the **Church of the Most Holy Trinity**, formerly the Chapel Royal, built between 1807-14 to the designs of Francis Johnston, who was by then Architect to the Board of Works. This lovely Gothic-Revival church, rather Strawberry Hill in feeling with its pointed, airy finials, and 90 historical figures representing British monarchs carved around the exterior, was the official chapel of the Viceroy. St Peter holds a key over the main door, and Dean Swift is perched over a window.

Within, there is a secular, almost theatrical atmosphere, with the wonderful fan-vaulted ceiling, much lavish oak carving, a high and handsome gallery overlooking the pews, painted with the names of the Viceroys of Dublin, and glowing stained-glass windows. On the front of the organ-loft are carved the Royal Arms, and on each side the arms of the Duke of Bedford, who laid the foundation stone of the Chapel, and of the Duke of Richmond in whose administration it was completed. The fine plasterwork and stucco ornamentation is by George Stapleton, son of the great Michael, who had died in 1801, and the stone carvings are by Edward Smyth and his son John.

The castle was considered unhealthy from the late 18thC onward, which in practice meant it was deemed to be unfashionable and insalubrious, so the Viceroys lived in the Viceregal Lodge in Phoenix Park and only moved into the castle for the Season, the period of official entertainment, starting in the first week of February and ending with a grand Ball on St Patrick's night.

Accounts of life at the castle differ according to the point of view. For the Ascendancy, the Season was the center of social life and the epitome of glamor. Invitations to levees, drawing rooms (formal court receptions) and balls were eagerly awaited, especially by what George Moore called "the muslin martyrs," the unmarried daughters in search of eligible bachelors. The various elaborate rules and regulations as to what was *de rigueur* in wear and behavior were strictly observed.

For the vast majority of the population, the castle was the hated symbol of the alien power (although the changing of the guard every day was one of the spectacles of Dublin, attended in great numbers by the people). The authorities did little to endear themselves to this underclass. During the famine of 1848 the round of parties and receptions continued apace. Elizabeth Grant, a Scotswoman who lived in Ireland and kept a revealing diary, wrote: "Mr Dennis . . . had been at the Levee, 1,300 people, Drawing room 1,600, Ball 1,200. No jewels, they are gone, but handsome dresses and apparently hearts as light as if the owners were not increasing their debts and were surrounded by a prosperous instead of by a pauper peasantry."

Eilis Dillon, distinguished daughter of a famous Irish dynasty, wrote that her grandfather, who held, among many other posts, the Curatorship of the National Museum and thus as a public servant was obliged to attend levees at Dublin Castle, found it distressing as he had never been anything other than a staunch Nationalist. Further insult was added by his having to wear a sort of uniform consisting of a black velvet embroidered jacket and knee breeches of white flannel lined with satin. He found the whole affair "shabby genteel with poor food and faulty ceremony."

Naturally, the personal fortune and glamor of the Viceroy governed the quality and tone of life at the castle. Lord Dudley, Viceroy at the turn of the century, spent £50,000 over and above his official salary on extravagant parties and events, and the members of the Kildare Street Club mourned as the Dudleys drove away for the boat to England. In their place came Lord and Lady Aberdeen, immediately nicknamed Jumping Jack and Blowsy Bella. (He fidgeted a lot, and she was not glamorous.) But they were good for Ireland and the Irish people and had their well-being at heart, and for the first time Irish music and an Irish play was put on at Dublin Castle, though at least one guest, Lady Alice Howard, thought it all too horrid and vulgar for words.

The Aberdeens were genuinely interested in the country they were living in rather than its surface glitter; and the Ascendancy teased and despised them for that and their more democratic way of entertaining. "Very common Lot," said the bold Lady Alice after a dinner party at the castle during the Aberdeen's first season. It is not related what the Common Lot thought of Lady Alice, who really wasn't pretty enough or clever enough to be quite so discriminating.

The **Genealogical Office**, built between 1750-60 and perhaps the most beautiful of the castle buildings, with its strange attenuated mid-18thC cupola, was designed by Joseph Jarratt. The **Clock** or **Bedford Tower** stands on the base of one of the original gate towers of the castle.

This was the scene of one of the most extraordinary jewel thefts of the century, when the regalia known as the Crown Jewels disappeared days before King Edward VII was due on a state visit. He was not best pleased with the various theories put forward by mortified officials. "I don't want theories," he snapped. "I want my jewels."

The solution propounded as most likely is that the theft was carried out by one of the three heralds who had access to the safe in which they were stored, who had notoriously extravagant tastes and, indeed, later went to prison for fraud. In his delightful book, *Twilight of the Ascendancy,* Mark Bence-Jones writes, "That the police chose to ignore so obvious a suspect can be explained by his having frequented a clique of high-placed homosexuals who included Lord Ronald Gower, the uncle and close friend of the King's brother-in-law the Duke of Argyll. The theft of the jewels occurred only a couple of months after the homosexual scandal involving the Kaiser's friend Prince Eulenburg; it is possible that the King was determined at all costs to avoid a similar scandal in which his brother-in-law might have been involved."

The fine **State Chambers** are now used for the inauguration of the President of Ireland. **St Patrick's Hall** was instituted in 1783 and is an impressive vast space with a magnificent painted ceiling and walls, decorated and frescoed, festooned with banners, and a frieze with the arms of the Knights of St Patrick, who were not, as one might suppose, standard bearers for the missionary saint, but staunch upholders of the conservative Ascendancy.

The **Throne Room** (or Presence Chamber), remodeled by Francis Johnston, houses a mighty throne reputed to have been presented by William of Orange and last used by George V in 1911. All the State Chambers are still in use, and open to the public when not required for State functions, which is not very often. But check before visiting.

The **Treasury** in the Lower Yard is the most recent part of the castle to be restored, happily with a more sensitive touch. There is an exhibition space, bookshop and coffee bar.

For a first-hand glimpse into social life during a drawing room, one can do no better than to read Elizabeth Grant's *The Highland Lady in Ireland* in 1848:

> *The entrance hall was lined with a double row. We were received in the anti-room where was a table spread with refreshments, tea, coffee, negus, lemonade, champagne, ices, sandwiches, cakes and white soup. The long drawing room soon filled and then the door was opened into the old men's hall in which one thousand people found room enough to leave abundant space for dancing. It was lighted by three rows of chandeliers, eight in number, containing in all one thousand candles. The recesses of the bay windows were lighted by lamps and carpeted and filled with sofas, charming, cool retreats for many a quiet flirtation. The recess of the folding doors held Kelly's quadrille band. Two regimental bands were in the gallery. The supper was quite splendid, in the large dining room, no seats; the company went in divisions and always found everything as at first. I heard the champagne alone cost one hundred*

*pounds. The Lord Lieutenant walked up the immense hall at eleven, followed by a poor enough suite, and Court, yet it was all very pretty. The company stood till he was seated on the throne, Lady Clarendon beside him. All around were Duke and Duchess of Leinster, Marquess and Marchioness of Drogheda, Earl and Countess of Milltown, Clonmel, Portarlington, and their belongings with half a dozen more. A good display of diamonds, glittering Aide de Camps etc . . . .*

## Old Dublin

Turning out of Dublin Castle by the back way brings you to Werburgh St. and to the oldest part of Dublin, a mixture of shabby and chic, run-down churches and upmarket antique stores, fine pubs, a good fish-and-chip shop and a dirty great dual carriageway rasping through, like a saw cutting velvet.

**St Werburgh's Church**, dedicated to Werburgh, daughter of the king of Mercia, designed by Thomas Burgh in 1715 and rebuilt in the 1760s after a fire, with a fine gallery by John Smith, has the best-preserved 18thC interior in Dublin. The excellent stucco work is by Michael Maguire, and the unusual Gothic pulpit carved by Richard Stewart originally belonged to the Chapel Royal.

This church had one of the few spires in Dublin, but it was demolished in 1810 for fear, so it is always said, that it should be used as an attack position on Dublin Castle (viz V.S. Pritchett: "It is as well to keep in the back of one's mind that Dublin was always an enclave or citadel with a well founded fear of the Celts or Gaelic raiders coming down from the hills . . . . "). But there is as much truth in the story that the spire began to tilt alarmingly. Although Francis Johnston undertook to secure it, the inhabitants insisted upon its coming down, which perhaps is prudent when you remember that his great church, St George's, Hardwicke Place (see DAY 2, page 125), fell apart at the seams fairly soon after he built it.

There are good and interesting monuments and memorials in the church, to members of the Guinness family among others, and Lord Edward Fitzgerald is buried in the vaults. Not far away in the adjoining graveyard lies Major Sim, who arrested him, wounding him mortally in the process. The entrance to the church is from the side through no. 8 Bristol Buildings.

This whole area was known as **The Liberties**, so called because it was outside the medieval city walls and exempt from local and civil jurisdiction, answerable directly to the representatives of the King and the Pope. As a consequence the area because a cosmopolitan quarter, as French, Dutch, Huguenot and Flemish settlers took refuge here from religious persecution and built up thriving trades that gave the area a distinctive look.

The area had a markedly anarchic atmosphere. This really *was* Bohemia. The Liberties suffered great decline and poverty with the punitive Trade Laws of the 19thC, and the pretty, old houses became appalling and dangerous slums; and corners survive to this day that still look Dickensian.

Continuing s, near St Patrick's Park is **Bull Alley Buildings**, behind Bull Alley school, an extraordinary edifice with a Classical facade and red-brick backing, like something from a Daumier etching. I was staring at the washing strung between the windows, at the genuine look of tenements, when two small children on bicycles rode up. "What are you looking for?" said one. "She's not looking for, she's looking at," said the other. "What at?" said the one. "At what she's come to see," said the other.

The city authorities, in their folly, have seen fit to cut dual carriageways on both sides of this area, so that crossing to Christ Church becomes positively hazardous, and have turned the Liberties and the great core of Dublin into a kind of frenzied race-track. The shortest stretch between two points for cars is the longest journey for pedestrians. This was an intimate, close, original part of Dublin, and it needs a Yeats to write a new poem about the terrible calamity, and the names of the men in the Corporation who sold out to the car at any price, to the eternal cost of Dublin. (He did write one about the death of a house: "But he killed the house; to kill a house / Where great men grew up, married, died, I hereby declare a capital offence." God knows what he'd say about this.)

There are still pockets of old Dublin hanging on for dear life, one peg on an old line. **Iveagh Market** in Francis St., about 200 yards w, built by Lord Iveagh in 1907 on the site of the medieval fair green to house street vendors, is much touted as a place to see Dublin vendors displaying their wares and their wit. But all I've ever seen are silent people picking up mounds of old clothes, minding their own business, which has nothing to do with tourists. There are bric-a-brac shops here too and a fish market. A carved stone head, particularly grotesque and winking, on the facade is said to be Lord Iveagh himself, but it looks most unlikely, given the general look of the Guinnesses. (For more points of interest in Francis St., see page 155.)

Near here on Back Lane, a short stroll N, is the congenial **Mother Redcap Market** *(Back Lane, near Christ Church, map 3 D3, open Wed-Sat)*, which has antique stores and exceptional food and cheese stores. This is worth visiting for these stalls alone, to get fresh Irish food at its best, but, really, here you must beware of "dippers" (pickpockets, in Dublin parlance).

Near Mother Redcap Market, also on Back Lane, is **Tailors' Hall** *(Back Lane, map 3 D3* ☎ *(01) 544794, open Mon-Fri 9.30am-4pm)*, the head-quarters of *An Taisce,* the Irish National trust, and a delightful building set back from the street overlooking a little parterre and herb garden. This beautiful 18thC guildhall, the oldest in Ireland, one of the few Queen Anne examples left, dating from 1707 and a deeply important building, was only just rescued by the Irish Georgian Society before it fell down.

Over and over again one hears of the last-ditch rescue of buildings by the Irish Georgian Society and that remarkable man Desmond Guinness. On seeing Tailors' Hall, rotting and neglected by Dublin Corporation, who owned it, it was he who set about saving it. With the help of the architect Austin Dunphy, who gave his services free, Desmond Guinness rescued it so that it now stands like a gem in this setting. Even if that philistine and narrow-minded argument that Ascendancy buildings have no place in a new Dublin is advanced and by such perverted thinking thus deserve to fall, then by the same token the Tailors' Hall stood out as one that surely deserved to be rescued. For it was here that the Catholic Committee of the United Irishmen (The Back Lane Parliament) had their meetings, and planned to free Ireland.

There are fine things to be seen inside the building, including a marble fireplace presented by guild members in the 18thC and a minstrel's gallery overlooking the hall.

A little way s, down toward St Patrick's Cathedral, is one of the prettiest sights in Dublin, the **Library of St Sepulchre**, always called **Marsh's Library** *(St Patrick's Close, map 3E3* ☎ *(01) 543511, open Mon, Wed-Fri 10am-12.45pm, 2-5pm; Sat 10.30am-12.45pm* 📷 *but donation of IR£1 expected)*, in St Patrick's Close near to the cathedral. Built in 1703 to the design of Sir William Robinson, it is tucked behind a high wall, through a little gate. Even walking up to it induces a sense of anticipation.

It was the first public library in Ireland when it opened in 1707, founded and endowed by Narcissus Marsh, Archbishop of Dublin, who had been Provost of Trinity and lamented the wearisome task of tending "340 young men and boys in this lewd and debauch'd town." One can see why he built this haven.

Archbishop Marsh had a head start in forming his library by buying 10,000 books for £2,500 from the collection of Edward Stillingfleet, Bishop of Worcester, in 1705, and it now contains 25,000 books, including examples from rare medical collections, early printing and travel books, and hundreds of manuscripts, the rarest of which is a volume of the *Lives of the Irish Saints* dating from 1400.

Toward the end of his life, Archbishop Marsh was looked after by his 19-year-old niece, Grace Marsh, and as he sadly recorded in his diary, her heart wasn't really in the job:

> *This evening betwixt 8 and 9 of the clock at night, my niece Grace Marsh (not having the fear of God before her eyes) stole privately out of my house at St Sepulchres and (as it is reported) was that night married to Chas Proby, Vicar of Castleknock in a tavern and was bedded there with him. Lord, consider my affliction.*

An old ghost story relates that before she eloped she slipped a note between the pages of a book she believed he would read the next morning. But he never found it and spent his nights flicking through the pages of the books trying to discover it. Grace lived to be 85 years old and is buried in the same tomb as her uncle.

Dean Swift was a governor of the library and did much of his writing in the building, but he heartily loathed Marsh and wrote a purported panegyric which is a masterpiece of ambiguity: "He is the first of the human race that with great advantages of learning piety and station ever escaped being a great man." The interior of the library, with its beautiful dark-oak bookcases, each with carved and lettered gables topped by a miter, and the three elegant wired cages where readers were locked in with rare books, is charming in every degree.

## Christ Church Cathedral

More properly known as the **Cathedral of the Most Holy Trinity**, Christ Church *(map 3 D3, open 10am-5pm except during services: Sung Eucharist 11am, Choral Evensong 3.30pm)*, sits in its pretty little eminence and oasis of greenery at the western end of Lord Edward St. and has, for all its grandeur and bulk, an oddly welcoming air — perhaps because it seems to lie along the flank of its hill rather than soaring above the skyline as do most cathedrals. It is marooned from its neighbors, from the markets and the antique streets, from any approach from St Patrick's, by those dual carriageways.

Founded in 1038, it is, somewhere within its bulk, the oldest building in Dublin, nearly a thousand years old, but it suffered heavily unsympathetic and arrogant restoration in the 19thC. The money to pay for the restoration of Christ Church and St Patrick's Cathedral came from the distiller Mr Henry Roe for the former and the head of the brewing family, Sir Benjamin Lee Guinness, for the latter.

Roe spent £250,000 on Christ Church, and the architect G.E. Street, given his head and these huge funds, practically rebuilt the cathedral and swept away the 14thC choir. (Of course, hindsight is easy; a guidebook published in 1825 describes the choir: "105 foot long by 28 in breadth . . . a most extraordinary and tasteless medley of Gothic and Italian architecture . . . the reading desk is supported by a brazen eagle and is a specimen of the worst possible taste . . . . " The eagle is still there, so judge for yourself.)

The palimpsest that was Christ Church, on which so many generations had left their faint and valuable mark, so that there had built up an atmosphere and shape to the interior, an exhalation of faith that is one of the most valuable, almost evolutionary things we connect with in old churches and cathedrals, was here swept away, so that we walk around an emptiness filled with monuments, which fortunately redeem much by their beauty and sentiment.

Among the most memorable is a superb oak carving of the **tomb of Lady Cecilie Harrington** (1584) in her ruff and farthingale, kneeling opposite her husband Sir Henry Harrington and her father Francis Agar, who was Secretary to the Lord Deputy of Ireland.

Nearby is an altogether more grandiose monument by Henry Cheene containing wonderful social detail of the period of **Robert, Earl of Kildare**, who has just expired with his curls and ruffs all of a flounce. The 19th Earl, who built **Carton** (see EXCURSIONS, page 245) and in rank was the first Lord of Ireland, lies in his ermine, his grieving wife in her buttoned dress with its dropped waistline, her rather plainer daughter, Lady Hillsborough, behind her, and a son, the new Earl (who became the first Duke of Leinster), at his feet, a dandy in cravat and jabot, clasping his hands.

The Earl had four sons and eight daughters, but only these two, preserved in stone, survived him. One dreads to think what he would have done if he could have looked into the future and seen his grandson Lord Edward hunted and shot for his part in an uprising against England.

Among other monuments there is an archetypal Victorian statue of a weeping child with a famous teardrop coursing down its pale cheek, erected by the citizens of Dublin in memory of a pious worthy, who "Was beloved by all, not because he sought it but because he deserved it."

Look for the effigy of **Strongbow, Richard de Clare**, Earl of Stigul and Pembroke, the most powerful mercenary of the 11thC. It is a deeply sinister tomb, black like something out of a movie about futuristic motorcyclists, although oddly enough his legs are crossed in a dainty fashion. Beside him lies another stumpy half-figure, reputedly that of his son, who he is supposed to have sliced in two to cure him of cowardice. This is not the original, which was vandalized centuries ago, but a replica brought down from Drogheda.

In the **Chapel of St Loo** or St Laud to the right of the high altar, there is a most curious object. A little cage hanging on the wall contains a bronze heart-shaped case, which in turn contains the embalmed heart of Lorcan Ua Tuatha or St Laurence O'Toole, Archbishop of Dublin in 1162 and monk of Glendalough (see EXCURSIONS, page 229), the patron saint of Dublin, who became archbishop when he was only 34.

This is the last of the relics that were formerly venerated in this cathedral and which included "a crucifix which had spoken twice; the staff of our Lord; St Patrick's high altar of marble on which a leper was miraculously conveyed from Great Britain to Ireland; a thorn of our Saviour's Crown; part of the Virgin Mary's girdle; some of the bones of St Peter and St Andrew . . . . "

The vaulted **crypt** is both mysterious and banal. The size is impressive, the arches wonderful, and the lighting such as to dispel any mystery whatsoever. But what is illuminated is worth looking at: the 18thC skeleton of a cat found in the organ pipes and looking like something painted by Goya; two bigger-than-life-sized statues with damaged, grotesque faces, wearing chains of office and ringlets, supposed to be Charles II and James II by William de Keysar and bought from the Tholsel, the 17thC Royal Exchange, demolished in 1806; and many urns and fascinating memorials. In one dark recess may be a kettle and the remains of the workmen's lunch circa yesterday. This is quite within tradition; this crypt has not always been a place of reverence. In medieval times markets were held here, and there were taverns on the site in the 17thC.

There are good early music services held here; and in fact the services at matins and evensong are a joy to attend. The *Irish Times* lists the times of special services and special events.

## St Patrick's Cathedral

About 500 yards s of Christ Church is **St Patrick's Cathedral** *(map 3 E3* ☎ *(01) 4754817, open daily),* standing on the oldest Christian site in Dublin (although Christ Church is the older and the mother church). A church has stood here since the 5thC, and St Patrick is traditionally supposed to have baptized his converts at a spot marked by a Celtic Cross in the w end of the nave. The river Poddle once flowed around the cathedral and still flows through a culvert under the church.

In 1191 the Normans built a new church, rebuilt again around 1225, and the massive w tower, which houses the largest ringing peal of bells in Ireland, was rebuilt by Archbishop Minot in 1370 after a fire destroyed the earlier peal. The tower, 141 feet in height, is surmounted by a 105-foot-high spire, and the church itself is the largest in Ireland, 300 feet long. The first public clock in Dublin was placed here in 1560.

St Patrick's was the seat of the first University in Ireland until it was replaced by Trinity. Like Christ Church, the cathedral suffered Victorian restoration from G.E. Street, but since only £160,000 was spent by Sir Benjamin Lee Guinness the damage was perhaps less comprehensive than in its neighbor; who knows, any longer?

All the same, we get an idea of what happened from a book, *Photographs of Dublin,* published in 1867. "The restoration has been most complete and the glorious old pile presents as nearly as possible the same appearance as it did over 600 years ago . . . where the stonework had suffered from the effects of fire, and water, the accidents or neglect of centuries has been recased and is now considered the finest and most complete specimen of medieval architecture in Ireland."

The medieval **Chapter House** has a door with a hole in it dating from 1492, which gives rise to the phrase "chancing your arm." Lord Kildare cut the hole and put his arm through in friendship in order to reassure his fairly suspicious enemy, Lord Ormonde, who was under siege in the Chapter House.

The cathedral is full of interesting and curious details and is the showplace of the Anglo-Irish dead. Its tombs and walls are inscribed with the names of their fallen sons. Here too are the colors of many old Irish regiments and a toll of honor to the 50,000 Irishmen who fell fighting for England in 1914-18. In the choir are the banners, stalls and hatchment of the **Knights of St Patrick's**, a heraldic club which seems to have been founded in 1783 principally to give its members the fun of dressing up in the flowing-robes-and-slashed-bodice school of chivalry.

For centuries there was intense rivalry between the two cathedrals, and after the 16thC, St Patrick's fell into disrepair, being used as a stable by Cromwell's troops and as a barracks by James I.

Jonathan Swift was Dean here from 1713-45. He was a hero of the Dublin working classes during his life because of his savage, vociferous indignation against English misrule, and when he returned to "wretched Dublin in Miserable Ireland" after the publication of *Gulliver's Travels,* church bells were rung and bonfires lit. Swift was a Jove who flung thunderbolts, but he had a tender heart, something he did his best to disguise; not that he had much good to say about Ireland either:

*I never was in haste before / To reach that slavish hateful shore /
With rage impatient makes me wait / A passage to the land I hate*

The historian, Professor Roy Foster, wrote that Swift, Berkeley and Burke form the great intellectual triumvirate of Ascendancy culture. The ambivalence between living in England and hoping to expand a career in England remained a constant in Irish life and was the leitmotif of much of Swift's career. The lines written as he was waiting at Holyhead for a favorable wind to take him back to Ireland and to the dying Stella (who, after he had cruelly mistreated her, cut him out of her will), are expressed with typically rancorous wit and anger:

*Lo here I sit at Holyhead / With muddy ale and mouldy bread: / All
Christian victuals stink of fish / I'm where my enemies would wish /
Convict of lies is every sign, / The inn has not one drop of wine / I'm
fastened by both wind and tide / I see the ship at anchor ride*

This complex, marvelous, melancholic, choleric man wrote like an angel and shaped English/Irish prose, giving it a Classical outline, and eschewing that terrible sweet tooth for language so many Irish writers have. He had a style and lucidity that shines down through the ages, and his prose, driven, hurtles along with the impetus of a cold but compassionate anger. One of his most famous remarks was that the Irish should burn everything English except their coals.

Toward the end of his life, he began to believe that he was mentally ill. One of his last endowments to Dublin was the establishment in the Kilmainham area, in an architecturally fine building designed by George Semple, of a hospital for lunatics, now a psychiatric hospital known as **Swift's Hospital** (a.k.a. St Patrick's Hospital — "St Pat's"). It was begun in 1749, four years after his death, and has lately been restored.

*He gave the little wealth he had / To build a house for fools and
mad / To show by one satiric touch / The nation wanted it so much.*

Swift's grave and that of his beloved Stella (Hester Johnson) are in the cathedral, and the most famous of all epitaphs, written in Latin by himself, is his best monument. The translation by Yeats is in itself a poem:

*Swift has sailed into his rest;*
*Savage indignation there*
*Cannot lacerate his breast.*
*Imitate him if you dare*
*World besotted traveller;*
*He served human liberty.*

To the left of the entrance to the cathedral is an enormous Jacobean **memorial** in black marble and alabaster, to the megalomaniac English bandit and administrator Richard Boyle, Earl of Cork, and his numerous issue. One of the children, on the memorial, is his son, Robert Boyle, who discovered Boyle's Law — that the volume of gas varies inversely as the pressure increases.

Originally destined to loom beside or indeed instead of the altar, the Viceroy, Lord Wentworth was having none of it and ordered it out. He was not prepared to worship "crouching to an Earl of Cork and his lady . . . or to those sea nymphs his daughters with coronets upon their heads, their hair dishevelled, down to their shoulders." It looks somewhat like a set design for an elaborate Venetian opera with bodies piled to the rafters, and is very robust and splendid.

There is an informative booklet and usually a recording of the fine choir on sale in the cathedral.

**St Patrick's Park** was landscaped around the end of the 19thC to give St Patrick's Cathedral a more appropriate setting. The entrance is at a gate near to the cathedral, and just inside is a stone marking the site of St Patrick's Well. On the far garden wall are a series of plaques honoring eight Dublin writers: Beckett, Joyce, Mangan, O'Casey, Shaw, Swift, Wilde and Yeats. The sculpture *Liberty Bell* is by Vivienne Roche (1988).

Near here, along the street called The Coombe, w of St Patrick's Park, is the **Coombe Hospital Memorial**, which is really the portico from the old maternity hospital that used to stand here in the heart of the Liberties. On it is inscribed a list of nicknames of characters who lived here over the years. The Irish have always been good at nicknames; just how good you can see by reading this list. It includes Shell-Shock Joe, Hairy Yank, Jembo No-toes and Nancy Needle Balls.

### From the cathedrals to the brewery

**St Audoen's Church of Ireland** in High St. *(map 3D3)*, the main thoroughfare of medieval Dublin, is dedicated to the Norman saint St Ouen and contains some fine Norman remains. It was once a group of guild chapels and is the only remaining medieval church in Dublin. The church bells are the oldest in Ireland; three date from 1423. In the porch is an Early Christian gravestone known as the "lucky stone," which has been kept at the church since 1309 and is associated with many legends. St Anne's Chapel has been reroofed, and in the crypt is an exhibition of the history of the Viking settlement in this area.

Outside, at the bottom of the winding **Forty Steps**, is **St Audoen's Arch**, the only surviving gate of the old city. There is another **St Audoen's** here, the Catholic church, built between 1841 and 1847 by Patrick

Byrne. Two giant Venus shells serving as holy water containers are an imaginative touch. There is an audiovisual presentation of *The Flame on the Hill*, which tells the story of Ireland before the coming of the Vikings.

A short walk away NE, on the historic site of **Wood Quay**, where Dublin was founded, the best story ever told of the coming of the Vikings was revealed when a rich treasure trove of Viking archeology was uncovered. In spite of a massive public outcry, Dublin Corporation went ahead and built the pair of hulking bunkers that serve as their new administration offices on the very site. The buildings, like abandoned giant helmets, dominate the area, knock everything out of scale and give this oldest of places in Dublin a futuristic fascist look. So much for Viking remains. Nearby on the quays is a sculpture of the half-buried hull of a Viking longboat by Betty Maguire (1988).

**St Catherine's** in Thomas St. *(map 3 D2)*, designed by John Smyth in 1769, was deconsecrated some years ago and turned into a community center, but its interior has been mutilated, its fine organ smashed. The finest Palladian church facade in Dublin is boarded up and looks like a desolation. The Irish Georgian Society try their best to get something done, but the future of the site remains doubtful.

Robert Emmet was hanged in front of the church; a plaque commemorates this event.

Near to here in Francis St. *(map 3 D3)* is the imposing and depressing front of the Classical **Church of St Nicholas of Myra**, built in 1832 by John Leeson to celebrate Catholic Emancipation and set back from the street in a little courtyard, which by hemming the facade in makes it the more looming. The **Pietà** over the altar is by John Hogan, and there is a stained-glass window by Harry Clarke in the Nuptial Chapel, a depiction of marriage with all the wistful, imaginative, febrile beauty that his work always possessed (see FINE ARTS, page 63). The church is open between 10.30am and noon every day.

**Francis Street** *(map 3 D3-E3)* is famous for its antique stores. There is also an extraordinary motorcycle shop and yard, which is always teeming with heavy metal. **Kevin Street** and **Clanbrassil Street** are good for print, antique and bric-a-brac shops, with an emphasis on decorative objects with an Irish provenance.

The **Guinness Brewery** in St James's Gate *(map 3 D1)* is on nearly everyone's itinerary. This was the ancient entrance to the outer city in the 16thC, and this is where Guinness stout has been brewed ever since Arthur Guinness, the eldest son of Richard Guinness of Celbridge, land agent for the Archbishop of Price of Cashel (see EXCURSIONS, page 262), bought an existing old brewery in 1759 and began brewing his stout or porter, which now sells over 10 million glasses each day. (The famous Harp trademark is taken from the O'Neill or Brian Boru harp in the library at Trinity College.)

In Crane St., nearby, is the **Guinness Hop Store**, a 19thC converted warehouse, which houses the **World of Guinness** exhibition, as well as a bar and shop *(Crane St., off Thomas St., map 3 D2, open Mon-Fri 10am-4.30pm excluding bank holidays; last program starts 3.30pm* ▨ *buses 21A, 78, 78A from Fleet St.).*

On the N side of the Guinness Brewery, along the quays, is a sad little plaque commemorating "The Barges and Bargemen that [sic] navigated the Liffey from 1873-1961 carrying stout to the waiting ships at Custom House Quay."

There is an odd little conjunction with Dean Swift and Handel in this area. It was in a building in the curiously named **Fishamble Street**, near Christ Church, that *The Messiah*, which Handel had written in six weeks while staying in Dublin in 1742, was first performed. When Dr Delaney, who, with his wife Mary, was one of the ornaments of Dublin society and an aficionado of great music, heard it for the first time, he sprang to his feet and cried to the soloist, a perfectly respectable lady called Mrs Cibber, "Woman, for this be all thy sins forgiven." (It is not related how the sinner-singer reacted.) Handel was taken by Dr Delaney to call on poor mad dying Swift, who, on realizing it was Handel, cried "Oh! a German and a Genius. A Prodigy! Admit him!." So not that mad.

This area is one of the strangest and most cryptic in Dublin: a mixture of isolation and intimacy, of secrecy and open spaces, of small houses and derelict squares, the greatest of ecclesiastical buildings and the most inconsequential of secular. It is chic and shabby: in short, it is Dublin.

One of the strangest things is to go up to **Francis Street** in the evening. There is very little traffic around at that time: occasionally an old man goes by, a pub door opens, or a cat stalks and leaps up into the precinct of St Nicholas.

Otherwise, this once most teeming of places, alive with people, so much so that Dean Swift felt he should be given a hat-tax in compensation for wear and tear, so often did he have to touch his hat in greeting as he walked by, lies deserted. The population of the inner city has been reduced by half to just over 80,000 in the last 25 years.

When Dublin Corporation set about rehousing the slum dwellers, they built new estates on the sites of some of the old streets, near the city center, putting up buildings that now also look like slums themselves and are of such ugliness that the heart stops. Each block of flats has a peculiar kind of turret or campanile, attached to it by a brick umbilical cord, which apparently houses the staircases, adorned with lozenge-shaped windows, all set in a sea of tarmac.

The planners built huge estates outside the city limits in country villages like Tallaght near the Wicklow hills without making any provision for shopping, church-going, drinking or amusement. A close-knit, indomitable community, a tough proletariat with its own wicked black humor and an unsurpassed nimbleness of tongue, which depended on the fast interchange of the extraordinary close and interwoven life of the street, were siphoned into to an alien place of silence and strangeness.

Brendan Behan, one of Dublin's most famous writers of this century, and his family were moved to one of these garden estates. Dublin legend has it that they walked all the way. "Somehow," he said, "people hated leaving where they had been reared," and he remembered hearing a neighbor moaning to his mother: "Ooh, Mrs Behing, jewel and darling, don't go out to Kimmage, that's where they ate their young." Kimmage was four miles away from where they were speaking.

## Kilmainham

A little farther W from here, about $1\frac{1}{2}$ miles from the city center, is the Kilmainham area, and a complex and extraordinary excursion in its own right that might well be given a day to itself rather than trying to jam it in.

Kilmainham consists of a number of important monuments built for military, civil and charitable purposes and spanning 300 years of construction, neglect, care and chance. (One of the few stray bombs that fell in the Dublin area during World War II came close to the Hospital.)

The astonishing central point is one of Dublin's great classic buildings, a Carolean masterpiece, the **Royal Hospital, Kilmainham** by Sir William Robinson, the Surveyor-General. The Duke of Ormonde, the Viceroy at the time of its building between 1680 and 1684, laid the first stone, and his coat of arms is over the main portal, a memorable edifice in itself. The hospital is two years older than Sir Christopher Wren's Royal Hospital in London and, as there, everything is on a monumental yet felicitous scale. It is extraordinary how beautiful are these hospices, designed as a ghetto for old soldiers, considering that they were built in response to expedient political concerns.

The buildings are constructed around an arcaded courtyard, with enormous passages so that the old soldiers could still take their constitutionals in bad weather.

Visitors' cars and taxis are directed around the S of the building, past the symmetry of a long, dazzling facade, impeccable in its symmetry, with a pedimented pavilion at its center. The central five-bayed pavilion that greets the visitor, with its arched and pedimented portal door, opens to the courtyard, through which can be seen another archway opening to the infinity of the west. Within the courtyard the spaces sing, their vast volume guarded by the **Great Hall** and the **Clock Tower**, with its fine flying steeple.

In the 19thC Francis Johnston made drastic changes to the hospital, which were much disapproved of by purists; and after the last old soldier departed in 1927, the building fell into some disrepair and became part of the *Garda Siochana* headquarters, until in 1970 extensive restoration work was begun.

There has been as much adverse reaction to as praise for how this enormous project has been fulfilled. One distinguished critic wrote, "It was not repaired; but exhumed rather, reconstructed and rendered sterile and inert. The soft texture and the quiet modulation of light afforded by lime plaster was replaced with the hard and sharp line of gypsum and cement. A dramatic change of mood was established as the sensuous qualities of the surface of traditional materials were eradicated to make way for clinical precision." Certainly there is no feeling of age inside the building. All is "smack smooth," as Lady Louisa Conolly once said with satisfaction after she had had her stucco work removed in Castletown (see EXCURSIONS, page 241).

The original buildings cost £24,000. The restoration cost nearly £21 million and is now the **Irish Museum of Modern Art (IMMA)** (see

GALLERIES, page 68 for further details). This must surely be one of the most spectacular and inspired spaces in the world for showing contemporary and performance art. The mixture of rooms with their noble windows and austere long corridors constitute the grandest of galleries, in their truest sense. A 17thC aesthete, talking of galleries in their historical origins, defined them as places wherein "one may walk and exercise the senses in viewing, delighting and censuring." The only problem is that there is no real collection of modern art, as yet, to censure or delight. But there is a remarkable sense of enthusiasm and energy about these wonderful rooms, lacking in many better endowed museums.

Part of the museum's acquisition is the **Madden-Arnholz Collection** bequeathed by Claire Madden in memory of her daughter and son-in-law, who formed this extraordinary representative collection of European masters of the print. This will soon be on permanent show; parts of the collection are on display in various other galleries around the city.

The **Chapel Royal** is a magnificent building with a papier-mâché replica of the 17thC ceiling and oak reredos carved by the French Huguenot sculptor Jean Tabarict or Tabary, who was admitted to the freedom of the Liberties in 1685. The elaborate plasterwork on the ceiling was molded originally onto green twigs of oak, which acted as the bearings, but as they dried out over the centuries they began to snap, so that a hundred years ago, the plaster fruit and flowers came tumbling down on the startled congregation.

The stained-glass window is supposed to contain fragments from the one broken by the wreckers during the Reformation, when the original Temple Priory was destroyed. This was on the site of the graveyard known as **Bully's Acre**, adjoining Kilmainham, where Brian Boru's son and grandson, both killed at the Battle of Clontarf, were buried; the base of an early High Cross stands here. The graveyard was closed when after a cholera epidemic 500 bodies were buried there in the space of ten days. There is another little graveyard here dedicated to the British soldiers killed in the 1916 Rising.

The little twin-towered **Garden House**, the focal point of a walled garden to the N of the Royal Hospital, believed to have been designed by Sir Edward Lovett Pearce, has now been restored, and its 18thC interior re-created. The whole area, whether over-restored or not, is a tribute to those trying to make old buildings work in a new context, and a heartening place for those who despair of Dublin's commitment to her architectural inheritance.

There are educational and community programs in performance art, and theater, concerts and musical events held here, and in the vaults there are various events, like craft fairs and antique fairs, where one sees the resurgence and revival of arts and crafts around Dublin today. These are advertised in the magazines and newspapers.

A short walk from here is **Kilmainham Gaol** (map 1 C1 ☎ (01) 535984, open June-Sept 11am-6pm; Oct-March Mon-Fri 1-4pm, Sun 1-6pm; audiovisual presentation; bookshop; buses 79, 69, 78, 23, 51). This is now the Kilmainham Prison Museum, one of the most forbidding buildings in the city. To walk through it is a unique and remarkable experience, for though it is a museum in name it still feels like a prison, echoing, bleak and hopeless. Over the entrance to the prison gates and doors is a relief of writhing snakes and serpents, as good a symbol of banishment as any.

The "new" jail was built in 1792 and remained in use for 130 years. All the leaders of the 1916 Rebellion were incarcerated and indeed executed here, so that it is a shrine and a pilgrimage for the Irish. The guided tour misses nothing out, including the Killing Courtyard. The yacht *Asgard*, owned by Erskine Childers, which was used for gun-running in 1914, is in one of the courtyards.

After the establishment of the Irish Free State the place was left to molder. Then through voluntary labor it was restored, and it is now in the care of the OPW.

Between the prison and the rear entrance to the Royal Hospital is **Kilmainham Court House**.

Just down the Lane from the Royal Hospital is **Dr Steevens' Hospital**, the city's oldest public hospital, although it is no longer used as such. Dated 1721, it has been restored and is somewhat like a miniature version of the Royal Hospital. Built by Thomas Burgh, the successor to William Robinson as Surveyor-General and most famous as the designer of Trinity College Library, the hospital was a bequest from Dr Richard Steevens, a Professor of Physics who died in 1710.

His formidable sister Grissel, known as Madame Steevens, though she was unmarried, supervised the building and lived in rooms next to the entrance sitting in full view of passers-by, to disprove the rumor that she had a pig's snout for a nose, the result, it was rumored, of a curse placed on her mother by a beggar woman with a tribe of children refused alms and characterized by Mrs Steevens as being like an old sow with her litter. However, since she wore a heavy veil when she walked out, the rumor persisted.

A portrait of Madame Steevens (with a perfectly normal nose) holding the plans for the hospital in her right hand, and the library bequeathed by a governor in 1733, were both given to Trinity College when the hospital closed. There are hopes that these will be restored to the hospital if plans to have the library restored come to fruition. The hospital is now the headquarters of the Eastern Health Board, which hopes to open a museum of medical history incorporating a re-creation of a ward from the 1760s, and the anatomical laboratory belonging to Dr Colles, who is also associated with the hospital.

The hospital is open only by special request.

If you walk toward the river you will come upon the **Irish National War Memorial Gardens** (*Colbert Rd., Islandbridge, map 1 C1, open during daylight hours throughout the year*), designed by Edwin Lutyens and built between 1933 and 1939 as a memorial to the 50,000 Irishmen who died in World War I while serving in the British Army. The symmetrical semicircular design centers on the *War Stone* and two almost silent fountains on the great lawns. There are four granite pavilions, in one of which is enshrined a set of eight large quarto illuminated volumes printed on handmade paper, with designs incorporating Celtic and Art Deco motifs by Harry Clarke (see FINE ARTS, page 63). These contain the names of the men in Irish regiments and Irishmen in British regiments killed in the Great War. This place is both a melancholy reminder of violence and a haven of tranquility from the traffic, which pounds along on every side.

If you have done all this in a day you deserve to take a taxi home.

# Day 4
## The Merrion area and the Pembroke estate

See Dublin City map **4**, and **DAY 4** map opposite.

*For the atmosphere of Anglo-Ireland from the early eighteenth century cannot adequately be represented by the correspondence of the great ladies at houses like Carton, Castletown and Delville, reading* Candide, *building shell-houses and even (in the Duchess of Leinster's case) considering Rousseau as a tutor for their children. It is important to recapture a more gamey flavour . . . an echo of colonial Virginia, or even the Kenya Highlands in the 1920s . . . .*
(*Modern Ireland; 1600-1972*, Roy Foster)

The history of the area begins with the enclosure and allotments of St Stephen's Green in 1664, instigated by Sir William Robinson, Surveyor General of Works and Fortifications in Ireland and the genius to whom we owe the great complex of Kilmainham (see DAY 3, page 157). In about the same era the quays were built, and after the turn of the century, the Library at Trinity, and Parliament House, and the great civic buildings that took the power and glory away from the narrow streets of old Dublin and began the process that transformed the city into such a remarkable cosmopolitan capital.

In a very few years, Dublin was transformed from a small, walled, rough-edged garrison town into a city with a metropolitan stream of culture informing it, or at least informing the elite who lived a life that had no connection with rural Ireland other than using it as the shaky economic base for its extravagances. A visitor, visiting what he had thought was a provincial town, was staggered by the inappropriate grandeur of what he found, "like being at a table with a man who gives me Burgundy but whose attendant is a bailiff disguised in livery."

The second half of the 18thC, the Age of Enlightenment, had its many vices, no doubt, and improprieties, but style and wit are among the chief characteristics of the time, and the contemporary architecture reflect them.

Lord Fitzwilliam of Merrion, head of one of the richest families in Dublin, wanted to build, as the *arriviste* Lord Gardiner had done on the North side with such spectacular success. But his land, Merryon Fields, lay too far away from the fashionable development of the North side and

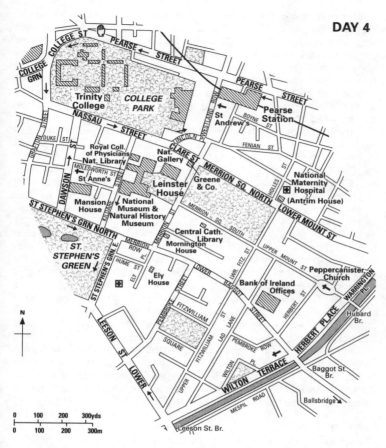

was still all trees and lanes, though it abutted against the new urban area of Dawson and Molesworth Streets.

Then the young James Fitzgerald, Earl of Kildare, bought and leased all the cheap land E of Molesworth St. at Coote Lane, and began to build an enormous palace in 1745 to complement his sense of self-importance. His father, the 19th Earl, had just died, and he was determined to show that he was his own master. (To get an idea of what this headstrong dandy looked like, go to Christ Church Cathedral and look at the monument to his dead father in which the new earl, who later became Duke of Leinster, looks jolly pleased with himself. How much of a master he was at home is something to speculate about. His wife, Lady Emily, daughter of the Duke of Richmond and a goddaughter of George II, was a most formidable woman. In a full life, she had time to bear 20 children, and when the Duke died she married her children's Scottish tutor, who was father of at least three.)

161

The new house, Kildare House (renamed Leinster House), was designed by Richard Castle and instantly became the great focus of the area. No matter that it was practically in the country nor that it was so far out on the unfashionable South side of the river. Kildare's sense of self-importance was, not unnaturally, as Ireland's premier earl, highly developed, and when the advisability of the site was questioned he said, "Wherever I go, fashion will follow me." And indeed, within a few years his house was surrounded by the mansions of the quality, and it has stayed fashionable ever since.

On the whole the South side of Dublin did not suffer the same fate as the North, in those dark years following the Union when it was predicted that grass would grow again in Dublin's streets. Dublin was not only no longer a capital; it was a provincial backwater. Within a few years of the Act of Union, 91 of the great houses were deserted by the owners, most of whom went to England to follow power; others returned to their country houses and carried on an extravagant way of rural social life that had its compensations.

In Dublin fashionable life stopped. Craftsmen, artisans and artists suffered deprivation as the whole elaborate service infrastructure crumbled. Property values fell inexorably. The house in Merrion Sq., for example, that Lord Cloncurry bought for £8,000 in 1794 was sold after the repeal of the Union for £2,500, and a few years later would not have fetched £500. It was only because many of the houses in this area were taken over by clubs and institutions that they were saved from that inexorable downward spiral that so desolated the N of the city, a spiral that became a freefall at the beginning of this century.

Until the end of the 1950s, most of Dublin still looked as though it were caught in a cobweb of time and beauty. Parts of this area, SE of the Liffey, stretching out through leafy avenues and little parks down to Rathmines and Sandymount, along the canals, and down to the Victorian suburbs, still have that same undisturbed quality.

## Georgian Dublin

The terrace houses of Georgian Dublin are among its chief delights. Although they look of a piece, they are all subtly different, and within the same streets their heights might vary considerable from three-story to four-story without breaking the long perspective. The typical pattern is of a red-brick four- or three-story over-basement, with a pitched slated roof, generously proportioned windows with characteristic small-bar glazing and "patent reveal" (a white plaster lining around the window recess, butting beyond the brickwork, which by reflecting light into the glass emphasizes the window's crisp proportions), and wide and handsome granite steps leading up to the fanlighted doors.

Farther from the center, the houses often had ironwork railings dividing the flights of steps and hemming in the front gardens, marking the equitable division of the gardens. Many houses often had long gardens in front and lanes behind backing onto mews and coach houses. And no matter what the external proportions, the rooms inside had an ample and generous span that made them wholly elegant; and all had fine plasterwork and cornices and architectural detail. All of this is to be seen on a traverse around any part of this quarter.

Doorways are of course among the pleasures of Dublin, and those in the **Merrion Square** area are among the best. There are many variations on the characteristic design of these round-headed doors, but they always keep within the proper constraints of the motif invented by Palladio, which first appeared in the gallery arcades of the Basilica at Vicenza. The glazed openings to each side gives the actual doorway a noble width, and makes the interior of the halls light and wide. The segmented fanlights have different patterns and interpretations, and some have a little lantern fitted into the fanlight; lovely examples of these can be seen in Merrion Sq. Look out too for the elaborately carved door furniture, with knockers and handles in the shape of lions or gargoyles.

### From College Green to Leinster House

If you start from **College Green** by **Lincoln Place**, you are a step away from **Westland Row**, dominated by the Greek Revival **Church of St Andrew's** (built by James Boulger 1832-37), with its school and presbytery flanking it on either side. Beside this little ecclesiastical complex is **Pearse Station** (a.k.a. Westland Row Station), the first rail terminus in Ireland, built in 1834 by the railway king of Ireland, William Dargan, but completely reconstructed in the 1890s. Most of the houses along here belong to Trinity College. The modern steel-and-glass building by the architects Scott Tallon & Walker is the **O'Reilly Institute**, part of Trinity.

**Nassau Street** leads into **Clare Street**, named after the unpopular Lord Clare, the Attorney-General and Lord Chancellor, who sold Ireland out in 1800. **Greene & Co's** famous bookshop with its barrows outside and people browsing, subject of many a Dublin photograph, is just here, and a little farther along on the opposite corner is no. 1 Merrion Sq., a noticeable house with its glass-covered and ironwork balconies. For ten years Sir William Wilde, father of Oscar Wilde, lived here, having moved up from Westland Row, on his social ascent, as an antiquarian and eye surgeon. (It was on this corner that James Joyce arranged to meet Nora Barnacle for their first date. She failed to turn up.)

**Leinster House** is an imposing building, spreading its gray length along the W side, with Leinster Lawn in front. When it was being built, Castle designed it to be both a town house and a country seat, though all in all it seems entirely unsuited to be a domestic dwelling in any location. The **Kildare Street** facade was the town entrance, and the **Merrion Square** side-opening onto Leinster Lawn was the country side, so that officially the building has two facades, and two main formal entrances. Leinster Lawn was and remains a fine green sward, and it was from here in 1785 that the first balloon ascent was held in Ireland, when Mr Crosbie floated on high, to the general astonishment of the onlookers.

In 1814 after calamity had overtaken the Kildare family, partly caused by the involvement of Lord Edward Fitzgerald in the 1798 Rising, Leinster House was bought by the **Dublin Society** (now known as the Royal Dublin Society). The society is chiefly known outside Dublin for the Horse Shows held in its showground at Ballsbridge.

But this is a remarkable society founded in 1731, "for the improvement of Husbandry, Manufactures and other useful Arts." Many great national institutions, including the National Library and the National History Museum, were created through its endeavors. Today it continues its scientific and research work in its big headquarters in Ballsbridge, farther out in this area (see page 170). When it bought Leinster House, the society added two wings to the back elevation in Merrion Sq. to house its complex of institutions and museums, and, in a separate and much later building, the **National Gallery**.

After the establishment of the Free State, the Royal Dublin Society sold Leinster House, or rather were pressured into selling it to the new government in 1925, and Leinster House is now the seat of the Irish Parliament, *Oireachtas na h-Eireann*. The **granite memorial** outside commemorates Arthur Griffith, Kevin O'Higgins and Michael Collins, who were the most famous founders of the Irish State.

### Merrion Square

Lord Merrion, given the extraordinary stroke of luck of his grand new neighbor's choice of site, lost no time in starting into developing his land, and work began on what became Merrion and Fitzwilliam Squares, transforming this area of Dublin into the delicate and felicitous city it remained until the process of destruction, foreseen by Yeats, began in the 1960s.

The spacious and elegant area that makes up Merrion Sq. covers about 12 acres and was laid out by Ralph Ward and John Ensor, one of Richard Castle's most talented pupils. The N side was the first to be built in 1762, and Ensor designed it with basement stories of rusticated granite and three upper stories of red brick. It was nearly 30 years before the S and E sides, all in characteristic red brick, were completed.

The oldest and best houses are along the N side, always the swankiest side, where the fashionable inhabitants congregated and promenaded of a summer's evening.

After Leinster House the grandest house was **Antrim House**, owned by the Earl of Antrim, nos. 33-34, the large house that closes off the view from Fitzwilliam St., now part of the National Maternity Hospital. Next door to it is the **LaTouche mansion**.

In 1780 Lord Fitzwilliam leased the land along the E length of the square to Samuel Sproule, who worked for the Wide Street Commissioners, and who was a cousin of Francis Johnston. He designed and built many of the houses on this side and in **Lower Mount Street**, and his cousin, another Samuel Sproule, did much of the fine interior plasterwork.

The finished square was elegant enough to become a new center of fashion, and in the years before the Union in 1800, no less than 22 Members of Parliament lived in Merrion Sq. A correspondent writing in 1783 noted that "every street in this neighbourhood is elegant, superb and regular, this part being the residence of many of the nobility and principal gentry of the kingdom."

To walk along here is a great pleasure, particularly in the morning or evening when the traffic is stilled. All around stretch 18thC vistas, especially along the S of the Square and Upper Mount St., where the view is brought to a lovely close by the church popularly called the **Peppercanister Church**, for obvious reasons, though its official name is **St Stephen's**. It was designed by John Bowden and completed by Joseph Welland in 1824.

The portico is based on the Erechtheion in Athens, and the spire on that same city's Tower of the Winds. It stands on an island site, and behind it, linking Herbert Place and Warrington Place with the pretty terrace of houses called Percy Place, reflected in the canal water, is **Huband Bridge**, built in 1791, one of the oldest bridges in Dublin and crossing one of the most charming stretches of the canal.

The Peppercanister is a pretty and much-loved little temple. There are often events, concerts and poetry readings in the evening. (Look for notices in the *Irish Times* or on the board outside.)

**Merrion Square Park** is open to the public and is surprisingly large. As with most of the gardens in Dublin's squares, it is impeccably kept. Through any of the small gates that open from every side of the square, high-hedged paths lead to sequestered small oases of green and quiet, used almost as outdoor rooms in fine weather: in one, a group of intent performers are enacting a strange balletic outdoor yoga; in another, children are playing on swings and seesaws.

At every turn, pedestrian busts and heads of leaders and heroes loom from their pedestals. There is one of Henry Grattan, which makes him look mad as a coot; a large and beautiful monument to *Eire* by Jerome Connor was presented by a biscuit company to celebrate their centenary. The garden, so crowded on sunny days at lunchtime, is almost deserted in the evenings and is an Arcadian haven, with the felicitous roofline of the surrounding Georgian houses forming the backdrop for the massed high green trees.

This lovely and essential garden was nearly lost when the park was purchased by the Catholic Church with the intention of building a cathedral there. It was officially named Bishop Ryan Park when the Bishop returned the park to the people — but you won't get far asking for directions using that name. (It has been observed that in the plans put forward for Dublin over the years, the developers and planners seem to think that squares and parks are simply acres of empty and wasted land, ripe for development. And there have been various proposals over the years for filling in the canals, which are one of the glories of the city; indeed, the little harbor at Portobello, one of the most picturesque places in Dublin, was filled in to make building land in this century.)

On the NW corner of the square is the grand **Rutland Fountain**, commemorating the popular but long-gone Viceroy, the Duke of Rutland. Parnell Sq. used to be called after him too. He died of a fever when he was only 33. The fountain was erected for the use of the poor people of Dublin, and looks more like a closed-in triumphal arch than a fountain. In the center is a nymph, leaning on an urn from which water flows, or rather is meant to, into a shell-shaped reservoir. On the frieze of the entablature is a medallion on which a gracious Marquis of Granby is relieving a soldier's family in distress; on one side is an inscription setting forth the life and conduct of the Duke of Rutland. *What* a goody-goody. It was designed by Henry Baker, that same apprentice to Gandon who helped build the King's Inns (see DAY 2, page 134).

The fountain was restored recently in memory of a great Dublin lady, Sybil Le Brocquy, but seems to have become unrestored as it lies dusty and unwatered, a reproach to the personages it commemorates. Although very splendid and unifying on that corner of the square, the whole point of the fountain is lost by its being railed in, and its lack of water.

As you walk around Merrion Sq. there is a positively luminous atmosphere from all the famous people who have lived here, or indeed infamous people, like one of the Luttrell brothers who lived at **no. 41** in the late 17thC. The name of the Luttrells lives on in the great estate of Luttrellstown Castle just outside Dublin. They became notorious during the Williamite Wars for taking opposing sides: Simon died with Sarsfield at the battle of Landen; Henry betrayed his background and cause and died ignominiously from stab wounds when returning from a coffee house in a sedan chair. He was described as "a bad man, the father of a bad man, and the grandfather of a bad man," and though £300 was offered for his assassin's arrest, he was never found. The crowds spat at his funeral, and 80 years after his murder, the hatred for him so festered that masked men burst open his tomb and smashed the skull with a pickaxe.

Sir Jonah Barrington, judge, Member of Parliament, diarist and writer, venal and peerless representative of the Ascendancy, lived in **no. 42**, and gave glittering parties and soirees attended by Lord Castlereagh, Henry Grattan and Arthur Wellesley, the future Duke of Wellington. (The Duke of Wellington's father, Lord Mornington, was Professor of Music at Trinity College. The Duke was born at **24 Upper Merrion St.**, one of a peerless little block which for decades were the Land Commission Offices and which, after long neglect, have just been sold.)

Sir Jonah was appointed judge of the Court of Admiralty in 1798, got into debt, and with characteristic insouciance transferred certain of the Court's funds to bail himself out, and then took off for Paris. His book *Historic Memoirs of Ireland* is an entertaining if unreliable account of the times. He divided gentlemen into three categories: "Gentlemen-to-the-backbone, gentlemen every-inch and half-mounted gentlemen." A malicious neighbor, Lady Clonmell, spread the rumor that Lady Barrington, daughter of a silk-merchant, sat in the bay window of her house because she missed being in the front of her father's shop. Sir Jonah promptly blocked up the window, but there were those who observed that the reason Lady Clonmell was so *au fait* with Lady Barrington's motives was because her own family had but lately been in trade.

Daniel O'Connell lived at **no. 58**, Sheridan Le Fanu, the master of the Gothic novel, at **no. 70**, William Butler Yeats at **no. 82**, and George Russell (the painter A.E.) at **no. 84**. These last two lived as neighbors, and the story goes that the two set out to visit each other simultaneously. Yeats' head was in the clouds, Russell's eyes were on the ground, and the two passed without seeing each other. The shadows of these people are still here, in this part of the city, Yeats especially, with his famous trick of appearing to vanish even as he drew nearer. His brother Jack Yeats, the painter, lived in Fitzwilliam Sq., just to the s off Baggot St.

## The National Museums

The great things to visit while in Merrion Sq. are the Natural History Museum and the National Gallery of Ireland, which flank Leinster House. The adjacent **National Museum of Ireland** is on the route of DAY 1 (see page 99).

The **Natural History Museum** *(Merrion St., map 4E5 ☎(01) 6618811, open Tues-Thurs, Sat 10am-5pm, Fri 10.30am-5pm, Sun 2-5pm* 📷*)* is a Victorian museum, designed by F.W. Clarendon in 1856. It has not been modernized and so looks like a period piece in itself, set in an aspic of nostalgia. Bits of it keep being closed off. Thus the exquisite Blaschka glass models of marine invertebrates and molluscs are housed in a top-floor room that is now closed, although it can be opened if you fling yourself on their mercy. The collection of animals, birds and fish is so comprehensive that all Irish vertebrate animals are represented here. It is a fascinating museum, and long may it stay exactly as it is.

The **National Gallery of Ireland** (see GALLERIES, page 68 for further details) was founded in 1854 and opened to the public in 1864. It was designed by Francis Fowke (who also designed the Victoria & Albert in London), with later additions by Sir Thomas Deane. The Dargan wing is dedicated to William Dargan, who helped fund the gallery, and whose huge statue dominates the lawn in front of the gallery, making the statue of the other great benefactor, G.B. Shaw, look like a pixie. There was nothing pixie-like about Shaw's legacy though; he left one-third of his royalties, the **Shaw Fund**, to the gallery in gratitude for the education he felt he had gained there, as a young man desperate for knowledge.

The gallery now has over 7,000 paintings, 250 pieces of sculpture and icons, and is one of the finest small collections in Europe.

This is a gallery simply to enjoy; everything combines to make it pleasurable. Its intimacy, the lack of crowds, the lack of pretension, the level at which the pictures are hung so that there is visual intimacy between viewer and viewed, the attendants who carry on a sotto voce conversation, which makes for an aural intimacy that can be riveting.

And, of course, the quality of the works, with so many revealing so much about the personalities and places of Ireland.

To add to it all, a smell of delicious cooking occasionally wafts from the restaurant. There are lunchtime lectures in the Gallery Lecture Theatre at 1pm on Wednesdays during July and August; admission is free and visitors are welcome. There is a good gallery shop.

Just up the street are the **Government Buildings**, in Upper Merrion St., which are often confused with Leinster House but which are quite separate. These are large Edwardian buildings with a pompous air and a turbulent skyline of urns and statues. The facade has just been cleaned and now glints and sparkles in the sun. They are open at certain times on Saturday mornings for guided tours, which include the newly restored staircases, offices of various ministries and the Taoiseach's office; it all gives a glimpse into the aloof affairs of State. For tickets and times, apply to the National Gallery just down the road.

On the N side is the **Royal Institute of the Architects of Ireland** (8 Merrion Sq. North, map 4 E6 ☎ (01) 6761703, open Mon-Fri 9.30am-5pm), which holds fascinating exhibitions, often of the work of obscure but interesting foreign architects, as well as a permanent exhibition of the work of regional Irish architects.

On the opposite side, the **Irish Architectural Archive** (73 Merrion Sq. South, map 4 E6 ☎ (01) 6763430, open Tues-Fri 10am-1pm, 2.30-5pm) is a collection of articles, books, drawings, models, photographs and prints about buildings from every part of Ireland from 1560 to the present day. It was founded in 1976 by Nicholas Robinson (husband of the President of Ireland) and Edward McParland, rectifying a gap in Ireland's architectural history with the aim of recording the architecture of Ireland through the ages. The visitor can go in and consult or browse in the library on the first floor. This invaluable institution is much used by scholars and students.

On Saturdays and Sundays the railings around Merrion Sq. become an outdoor art gallery where over 100 painters exhibit their work from about 11am to 5pm, depending on the weather (and the demand) The best site is opposite the National Gallery, naturally. (If you fancy displaying your own work, call Dublin Corporation ☎ (01) 8727666.)

### From Merrion Square to Fitzwilliam Square

Leaving Merrion Sq. on the E side leads one along what was until the 1960s the longest unbroken Georgian street in Dublin, a completely integrated Georgian townscape. Then a disastrous decision on the part of the Electricity Supply Board in 1958 to demolish 16 houses in Lower Fitzwilliam St. and build a modern office block in their place defaced it. The injury is further compounded by the condition of the offensive dark brown building that they erected, with ugly windows at exactly the wrong height, many of which have dirty curtains knotted in the center, with rolls of paper and telephone directories lying piled against the glass. It is extraordinary to see such things in a square that is otherwise one of the most perfect in Europe. The wrecking of these houses by a State body opened the gates of destruction to private speculators.

The ESB have since tried to make amends by restoring **no. 29**, the remaining house on the corner of Lower Fitzwilliam St. This is presented as a living museum furnished in the style of an upper-middle-class family of the period 1790-1820. It is certainly worth a visit with its pretty rooms, superb curtains, stenciled floors, fine objects and paintings, and, as so often in Dublin, guides who turn the tour into a delight. But how authentic a guide it is to the ways of life of an 18thC family is a moot point. Much of the furniture is from the collection of the National Museum of Dublin.

**Fitzwilliam Square** is the last of Dublin's Georgian squares to be completed, and its central park is still reserved for residents. Its N side was begun in 1791 and was not finished until 1825; the houses are less grand than in Merrion Sq. in terms of size, but their proportions are as perfect and the square has a lovely aspect. This was the Harley Street of Dublin, but the houses are now almost all used for offices.

### The Pembroke area

To get to Fitzwilliam Sq. you will have crossed Baggot St., a busy commercial road that crosses the canal at Mespil Road. Thomas Davis, leader of the Young Ireland party, lived at no. 67 in Lower Baggot St. The huge offices of the **Bank of Ireland** are here, ruining the skyline. In the Exhibition Hall on the ground floor, parts of the bank's own collection of modern Irish Art is on show.

The **Grand Canal** changes the look of these places, ruralizing them, as it cuts past streets, its waters gleaming. To walk along the towpaths of the Grand Canal from Baggot St. or Leeson St. Bridge during the day will give you an intimate glimpse of the organic life of urban Dublin, as well as revealing views of the back life of grand houses; too many, though, have been replaced by Post-Modernist office blocks standing empty. If you walk it at night, you will meet some of the ladies of the night.

The other great landlord in this area was the Herbert family of Wilton in England, and the names of the streets nearby reflect the provenance: Wilton Place, Herbert Place, Pembroke Rd. The period of building is reflected too, in names like Wellington Rd., Waterloo Rd. and Raglan Rd., broad tree-lined streets with Late Georgian and Early Victorian houses.

Around here too you will find the single-story terrace house, a peculiarity of this district. There are many charming small houses in these suburbs, built in what in England would be called the Regency style but here date from a decade later, from 1830-60.

The poet Patrick Kavanagh lived on the first floor of a house in Pembroke Rd., a busy, tree-lined Victorian street, which he characterized as a jungle, unlikely as it would seem, in one of his poems. At the junction of Baggot St. Bridge and Wilton Terrace is a shop called **Parson's**, which appears in many guide books as a famous literary meeting place, but is now a newsagent. Kavanagh called all this area his Pembrokeshire; "I have been thinking of making my grove on the banks of the Grand Canal near Baggot Street Bridge where in recent days I rediscovered my roots. My hegira was to the Grand Canal Bank where again I saw the beauty of the water and green grass and the magic of light."

A bench near the bridge commemorates the memory of this haunted, irascible, complex poet who is now one of Dublin's legendary heroes, although he only died in 1967. On the opposite bank is another bench to celebrate the memory of Percy French, the painter and songwriter, whose songs are as popular in their way as Moore's Melodies. *The Mountains of Mourne,* for example, has become an Irish classic.

The leafy suburbs of the Pembroke estate preserve a dignity constantly being tweaked by the students and the football and hurling fans who come into the district for the matches, although there is no violence. The said inhabitants are above such low mockery.

## Ballsbridge

Just E of here is the area known as Ballsbridge from the wide bridge built by Mr Ball. The mix of small parks and pubs, hotels and restaurants, offices, houses, terraces and grand streets make it a cross between a village, a town and a city. Its focal point is the sprawling complex that houses the offices, library and showgrounds of the **Royal Dublin Society** *(Ballsbridge, map 1 C3* ☎ *(01) 6680645; library open Tues 10am-5pm, Wed-Thurs 10am-7pm, Fri 10am-5pm, Sat 11am-5pm),* where the famous Horse Shows are held.

The Horse Show in July is the pinnacle of the Dublin season, when the best international teams of riders and horses compete for the Aga Khan cup. The fact that such events are still held in the center of a capital city is one of the joys of Dublin.

There are shows and exhibitions, events and concerts presented at the RDS all the year round, and the library has interesting exhibitions of art and books.

All over this area are many houses of charm and institutions of architectural distinction, such as the **Thomas Prior House** in Merrion Rd., a rambling baronial building, originally the Masonic Female Orphan School, which has been sold by the RDS.

One of the most prominent sights in this area is the **American Embassy**, built on the important corner of Elgin and Pembroke Rd., a building often described as futuristic, but looking more like a tired old science-fiction cartoon. This round building is so out of step with its surroundings and with Dublin that as one walks around it looking at its yellow-brown fascia and oddly shaped windows, one wonders what the architects can have been thinking of when they were designing it. It turns out that the architects, an American, John L. Johansen, and an Irishman, Michael Scott, were apparently thinking to fuse ideas about Celtic ornament and American technology to create a symbiotic building. They created a shocking one.

From here it is a short walk to the grand, leafy suburbs around Herbert Park with their tranquil, rather Edwardian quality, with something of the air of those old photographs when trees and people and houses seem caught in a silver platinum hush of nostalgia. Then the many schools in the area discharge their children and the mood changes.

**The Museum of Childhood** *(20 Palmerston Park, Rathmines, map 1 D2* ☎ *(01) 973223, open July-Aug Sun and Wed 2-5.30pm; Sept,*

*Nov-June Sun only 2-5.30pm, closed Oct* ▓ *bus 13 to terminus at top of park, 14 to Palmerston Park)* in Rathmines is a lodestone for children or those with a *nostalgia de l'enfance*, with its heaped-up collection of bright-eyed, bisque-headed old dolls, its dollhouses, cyclorama and miniature furniture, as well as its signs warning potential malefactors that the house is guarded by a snake. Wholly idiosyncratic, this is the dream child of one enthusiast and is more like an obsessive, slightly surreal nursery than a museum.

An internationally famous library is tucked away down a leafy suburban street. The **Chester Beatty Library and Gallery of Oriental Art** (see GALLERIES, page 67 for further details) was bequeathed to the Irish people by Sir Alfred Chester Beatty, a mining engineer in Denver, Colorado, who made a fortune, came to England as a mining consultant and spent his winters in Cairo, where he began to acquire the Oriental objects and manuscripts that form the core of his collection. The museum contains a beautifully furnished Chinese Library, and houses the Chester Beatty papyri, a group of codices from the 2ndC BC. It also has one of the best small collections of Oriental manuscripts and miniatures in the world, and boasts a rare collection of Western bindings and manuscripts, including some exquisite Continental Books of Hours. Here is the history of civilization from 2700BC to the present day.

There are so many things of sheer beauty to look at in this museum that one doesn't need previous knowledge or scholarly background, just an ability to wonder at man's quest to communicate. There is a good catalog on sale, and in the museum shop the copies of the netsuke and the lacquer make great presents.

Walking through this district is a pleasure. In the words of Maurice Craig: "The Pembroke district in particular, on the Fitzwilliam estate, lying between the Grand Canal and Donnybrook, is a suburb of enviable beauty . . . . In all this building, one principle is constant, whatever the stylistic trimmings. Building associates with building on equal terms; all groupings are free and informal. The formally composed terrace and the geometric layout are almost equally unknown . . . . Dublin rejected this kind of building, cold and passionless and grandiose as it is, in favour of something warmer and subtler."

*Dublin has about it a leisurely, dawdling desinvolture and a certain restless consciousness of its own incompleteness that makes it a fine place in which to live and work. It is at once ambitious and lazy, dissipated and pious, elegant and slovenly, thick-headed and witty, friendly and malicious, knowledgeable and naive, tolerant and ungracious, quizzical and deeply imperceptive . . . it is a city that is half small capital, half provincial town; and but for its superb setting between mountain and sea-coast and for certain lovely 18th century squares and streets, one wonders at times why so many famous poets, dramatists and wits chose it for their birthplace.*

*(From Ireland,* by Micheal Mac Liammoir)

# Phoenix Park

Map 1B1-C2 ☎(01) 8213021 (park), (01) 6771425 (zoo) ➡ 🅿 and zoo shop.
**Park** open daily 6.30am-11pm 🅿 **Zoo** open Mar-Oct Mon-Sat 9.30am-6pm,
Sun 10.30am-6pm; Nov-Feb Mon-Fri 9.30am-4pm, Sat 9.30am-5pm, Sun
10.30am-5pm 🚍 Bus 10 from O'Connell St., 25, 26 from the Bus Station in
Middle Abbey St.

The park dearest to Dubliners' hearts is Phoenix Park, which runs by
the Liffey for 3 miles and is an immense area of 1,752 acres, with a
circumference of 7 miles within the environs of the city, only 2 miles
from O'Connell St.

Its name is the English misinterpretation of the Gaelic name, *fionn
uisge,* meaning "clear water," and it is the largest enclosed park in Europe.
This was originally the great western desmesne of the Knights Hospital-
lers of medieval Kilmainham and was acquired for Charles II by his Lord
Lieutenant, the Duke of Ormonde, in 1671. Originally it was surrounded
by a wall to contain the deer, which still roam in the park, but was
landscaped by Lord Chesterfield, Viceroy in the 1740s, who threw it open
to the public.

You can get to the park on foot, by bus or by car. On the way you will
pass **Collin's Barracks**, the oldest continuously occupied barracks in
the world. The main entrance is by Parkgate, where a magnificent main
avenue called Chesterfield Rd. stretches ahead for 3 miles through
wooded landscape.

There are acres of land to wander over; a polo ground, a race course,
a Victorian bandstand, still used, athletic grounds, a People's Garden,
ponds (including one grandly called the Citadel Pond, but known as the
Dog Pond), and the venerable kiosk tea rooms. There are endless views
and lovely vistas, where cattle and 300 fallow deer still graze. It is a
magical place, and never ever seems crowded.

In 1979, 1.2 million people gathered on the **Fifteen Acres** (which is
actually 200 acres) near the American Embassy for the Pope's visit to
Ireland. A **Papal Cross** was erected to commemorate the occasion.

One of the first things you see is the enormous **Wellington Testimonial**, at 205 feet the largest obelisk in Europe, begun in 1817, wreathed
with plaques cast from cannon captured at Waterloo. It was designed by
Robert Smirke, who won the competition for the design and was paid by
public subscriptions. (Smirke later designed the British Museum in London.) One of the inscriptions reads: "Asia and Europe, saved by thee,
proclaim / Invincible in war thy deathless name, / Now round thy brow
the civic oak we twine / That every earthly glory may be thine."

A more beautiful and less grandiose monument is the much earlier
**Phoenix Pillar**, erected by Lord Chesterfield in 1747. This is a classic
column surmounted by a phoenix rising not very successfully from the
flames, and is generally known as the Eagle. The column was once at the
center of the crossroads, but was moved to make way for motor racing
in the 1930s. Now that traffic through the park has so much increased, it
remains tucked into its less imposing site.

Nearby is the privately run **Dublin Zoo,** one of the oldest in Europe, founded in 1831 and where incidentally that lion that roars out from the MGM logo was born (no one knows why the zoo was so successful in breeding lions, but between 1857 and 1946, 131 litters of lions were born here). The zoo now covers 30 acres and has 900 animals, many of them rare, and concentrates on breeding endangered species, including the clouded leopard, rare tigers and exotic wild fowl. A miniature tram traverses the zoo which was laid out by the famous landscape gardener Decimus Burton.

There are little isolated islands of "private" public estates scattered throughout the park, chief of which is the President of Ireland's official residence, **Aras an Uachtarain**, designed and built in 1751 by Nathaniel Clements, the Warden or Ranger of Phoenix Park, but much altered by Francis Johnston. It is a large, somewhat ungainly house, but in the vast expanse of Phoenix Park, as that miraculous writer V.S. Pritchett points out, it has the scale of a Czar's hunting box. It is not open, but has become a more loved building since the immensely popular President, Mrs Robinson, moved in.

Clements was an amateur architect of great distinction and took his duties as overlord of the park extremely seriously. The *Freeman's Journal* "looked back to his rule with nostalgia, when — "

> . . . *every impropriety was rigorously expelled from the beautiful spot. Ill-looking strollers of either sex could never get admittance at the gate except on public occasions. Cars and noddies were refused passage. But now the gates are opened wide to Tag, Rag and Bobtail. The Sabbath is abused by permitting hurling match to be played there every Sunday evening which is productive of blasphemous speaking, riot, drunkenness, broken heads and dislocated bones, among them thousand of the lower class; and meanwhile the deer are hunted by detached parties of these vagrants and their dogs.*

The **American Ambassador's Residence**, near the Fifteen Acres, was originally a four-roomed lodge, which Colonel Blaquiere, the chief secretary to the Viceroy, bought in 1772, with a potato patch and grazing rights for six cows. He expanded into the park, was sued for "encroaching on the public desmesne," but nothing daunted, enlarged the house. But "the financial strain of his gregarious nature took its toll" and in 1780 it became the official residence of the Chief Secretary to the Viceroy, the most famous of which was Lord Frederick Cavendish. He had just arrived to take up his post when in one of the most shocking incidents of the 19thC he was assassinated with his Under-Secretary T.H. Burke by members of a secret society called The Invincibles. It transpired that they had not meant to kill Lord Frederick but his predecessor, who had moved out a few hours earlier. Four men were hanged for the crime.

**Ashtown Castle**, with its 15thC tower, is the oldest historic building in the park and was for many years the Apostolic Nunciature. It is being restored to its original character by the Office of Public Works and is to be reopened as a Visitor Centre.

The ***Garda Siochana*** (police) headquarters contains a Police Museum showing the history of the police force since it was established in 1922, but can only be viewed by arrangement ( ☎ *(01) 6771156)*.

**The Ordnance Survey** is housed in an 18thC building which was the private residence of Luke Gardiner, father of the first Lord Mountjoy.

Going w in the direction of Chapelizod is the **Magazine Fort**, which stands on the site where Oliver Cromwell's son Henry once lived. About it Swift wrote:

> *Lo, here's a proof of Irish Sense*
> *Here Irish wit is seen*
> *Where nothing's left that's worth defence*
> *They build a magazine.*

There is a Heritage Trail in Phoenix Park highlighting all the historical features of the park. It runs from Parkgate St. near the main entrance to Castleknock. There is a self-guiding booklet to accompany the walk.

# Where to stay

## Choosing a hotel

*When you come to your bedchamber do not expect a canopy and curtains, the wild Irish have no candles on their tables. What! Did I speak of tables? Indeed they have no table but set their meat upon a bundle of grass and use this same grass to wipe their hands. . . .*

Things have changed on Dublin's hospitality scene since Luke Gernon wrote this in earlier days; and indeed things have changed in the last five years. The standard of accommodation is better all over Ireland, although the hideous hotels built in the boom years of the 1970s still dominate their landscapes like Godzillas in a garden.

In the 1960s and '70s, Dublin lost some of its famous great hotels, and with them some of the old traditions. People still regret the loss of the old Russell and the Royal Hibernian; and the Gresham, while still in its old place, has lost its former high glory.

There is no doubt that the food has improved immeasurably in hotels in the last decade, but you have to pick and choose. The ingredients have always been first-class, and a generation of new young chefs are using them properly. An exception to this laudable tendency is the Irish breakfast, which Bord Failte (the Irish Tourist Board), an admirable institution in every other way, seems to interpret constantly as an enormous fry-up.

Remember that in Dublin hotels, nothing is standard, and a different set of rules prevails to those in other capital cities. There are few hotels belonging to the big international chains, so there is, fortunately, no imposition of a uniform look and taste. But, on the other hand, none of the flagship hotels of the big Irish chains even begins to measure up to the standard of a first-class hotel in Paris.

Everything that is written about Irish service and willingness to please is true, but overall standards in hotels fluctuate according to the discernment, taste and skill of the owner/managers. Many believe that they are operating to the highest standard, and are not. But those Dublin hotels that succeed in this aim are truly wonderful.

There are those who argue that if Dublin's hotels were to be brought up to a truly international standard, their spirit and atmosphere would necessarily disappear. Some of the hotels listed below prove that this is not the case.

For a list of hotels approved by the Irish Tourist Board, contact the

**Irish Hotels Federation** *(13 Northbrook Rd., Dublin 6, Republic of Ireland* ☎*(010-353-1) 976459* ⨍⨯*(010-353-1) 974613).*

## HOW TO USE THIS CHAPTER

I have divided the remainder of the chapter into three sections covering Dublin City (a full alphabetical selection), the outskirts of Dublin (examples from Dublin Airport, Dun Laoghaire and Killiney), and alternative styles of accommodation (guesthouses, private houses, and the youth hostel).

**Symbols** denote many categories of information, from ⌂ (quiet hotel) to 👥 (conference facilities). Luxury hotels carry the 🏨 symbol, simple hotels 🏠. Hotels recommended as particularly good value in their class are denoted by the ♣ symbol. A full list of symbols with explanations is provided on page 7.

**Price categories** in the following listings are intended only as rough guides to average prices. There are five bands: cheap ( ▭ ), inexpensive ( ▭ ), moderate ( ▭ ), expensive ( ▭ ) and very expensive ( ▭ ). See HOW TO USE THIS BOOK on page 7 for approximate corresponding prices.

# Dublin City hotels A to Z

### BLOOMS 🏨 ♣
*Anglesea St., Dublin 2. Map 4D4* ☎*(01) 6715622* ⨍⨯*(01) 6715997* ▭ *86 rms, all with bathrm* AE ⊕ VISA ⇌ ⌂ ⊟ □ ⌂
🐾 ⟙ 🌙
*Location: Right in the heart of Dublin in an area that has become Dublin's bohemia— between the Quays, old Dublin and College Green.* This was rebuilt in 1978. With a name like that, one might expect a rather more evocative atmosphere than Blooms manages to provide. What it *does* provide, however, is comfort and good service, a good bar for meeting people in, and a restaurant. It is essential to ask for a quiet room.

### BURLINGTON 🏨 ♣
*Leeson St., Dublin 4. Map 1C2* ☎*(01) 6605222* ⨍⨯*(01) 6605064* ▭ *500 rms, all with bathrm* ▤ AE ⊕ ⊙ VISA 👥 ⇌
⌂ ‡ □ ⌂ 🐾 ⟙ 🌙 ⅋ ⊟
*Location: In the Pembroke area, a short walk from Ballsbridge and the city center.* In a big, ugly building looking more south LA than Dublin, the Burlington has little ambience but compensates with friendly staff and comfortable

rooms. **Annabel's** nightclub in the hotel is among the best in Dublin, with a full bar until about 2am. This is one of the places where fashionable young people in Dublin go later on in the evening; as a result, the hotel is lively but can be noisy.

### BUSWELLS ♣
*Molesworth St., Dublin 2. Map 4D5* ☎*(01) 6764013/6613888* ⨍⨯*(01) 6762090* ▭ *67 rms, all with bathrm* AE ⊕ VISA 👥 ⇌
□ ⌂ 🐾 ⟙
*Location: Between St Stephen's Green and Trinity College, near Leinster House.* Buswells is part of Dublin's fabric. Visiting publishers have always liked it, so it is a traditional meeting place for anxious or aspiring or even successful writers and their masters. The Irish Parliament is nearby, so less anxious politicians use it as a place to gather for a bite or a drink. The decoration is a curious, eclectic mixture of *belle époque* and not-so-belle "eighties epoch." Friendly staff and delightful, idiosyncratic service are its hallmark. Rooms, which have an individual look, can be noisy, so be sure to ask for a quiet one.

## CENTRAL

*Exchequer St., Dublin 1. Map 4D4* ☎(01) *797302* ▥ *70 rms, all with bathrm* ▣
▣ ▣ ▨ ▦ ▦ ▢ ▨ ▨ ▨ ▨
(robotized mini-bar with automatic billing facility).

*Location: Very near to City Hall.* Right in the heart of Dublin, this has been glamorously restored with no frills spared. Nowhere else is quite like it: it has both an international and local feel. There are many bars, with good service, and a restaurant with even better. A useful central rendezvous for Dublin business people.

## CONRAD ▩  Oo353 l6765555

*Earlsfort Terrace, Dublin 2. Map 4F5*
☎(01) 6765555  ▥(01) 6765424 ▥
*197 rms, all with bathrm* ▦ ▣ ▣ ▣ ▣
▨ ▨ ▨ ▦ ▦ ▢ ▢ ▢ ▨ ▨ ▨ ▨

*Location: Just off St Stephen's Green, so extremely central.* Conrad Hotels are an international subsidiary of Hilton USA, so this hotel has a sleek, impersonal look: lots of glass and glitter, conference rooms and suites. The public areas have large expanses of marble, and the foyer area stretches across different levels, with meeting places, a café, tables for drinks, leading to constant, rather agreeable comings and goings. The hotel overlooks the National Concert Hall, so you see musicians (and sections of the audience before and after the event). Bedrooms and bathrooms are decorated in the International Bland style, and are extremely comfortable and well serviced.

## GRESHAM ▩

*23 Upper O'Connell St., Dublin 1. Map 4B4*
☎(01) 8746881  ▥(01) 8787175 ▥
*200 rms, all with bathrm* ▦ ▣ ▨ ▦ ▨
▢ ▢ ▨ ▨ ▨ ▨ ▨

*Location: In the center of Upper O'Connell St., N of the Liffey.* This is one of the most famous of Dublin's hotels and one that has always prided itself on its celebrity regulars, especially movie stars. Now, the Gresham's noisy location is against it, so you should be sure to ask for a quiet room. Inside, you can expect international-style decoration in com-

fortable, traditional rooms without much style; there are also some grand terrace suites. The good service for which the Gresham has always been well known remains.

## JURY'S HOTEL & TOWERS ▩

*Ballsbridge, Dublin 4. Map 1C3* ☎(01) *6605000* ▥(01) 6605540 ▥ *300 rms in main hotel, all with bathrm; 100 rooms in the Towers (supplement payable)* ▦ ▣ ▣
▣ ▨ ▨ *Indoor/outdoor heated* ▨ ▦
▦ ▢ ▢ ▨ ▨ ▨ ▨ ▨

*Location: In the heart of Ballsbridge, near the American Embassy, the Royal Dublin Society showgrounds, and 20 minutes' walk from central Dublin.* A big hotel in an inappropriate architectural style and decor: that strange mixture of gleam and highly colored decoration that some Dublin hotels take for chic. This is a famous meeting place for out-of-towners and has large conference facilities, so its foyer can seem more public plaza than reception area. Rooms are quite comfortable, and service good and friendly. Jury's is famous for its dinner plus cabaret, every evening from April to October (dinner is optional).

## LONGFIELDS

*Fitzwilliam St. Lower, Dublin 2. Map 4E6*
☎(01) 6761367  ▥(01) 6761542 ▥ *26 rms, all with bathrm* ▣ ▣ ▨ ▨ ▢ ▢
▨ ▨

*Location: Situated in one of the finest townscapes in Europe (try not to look at the Electricity Supply Board offices opposite) in the Merrion Sq. area.* A pretty, Georgian frontage, with, behind its traditional door, a charming, comfortable hotel where the decoration, furniture and paintings look as if they always belonged there. The restaurant here is well known for being out of the ordinary — French, light, delicious.

## MONT CLARE ▨

*13/14 Clare St., Dublin 2. Map 4D5* ☎(01) *6616799* ▥(01) 6615663 ▥ *74 rms, all with bathrm* ▦ ▣ ▣ ▣ ▨ ▨ ▢ ▢
▢ ▨ ▨ ▨

*Location: Very central, on the corner of*

*Merrion Sq. and a few minutes from College Green, near to bookstores, galleries, etc.* This old, pretty house, recently redecorated, is a comfortable, central hotel with pleasant staff. It is on the corner of a busy street (near to Oscar Wilde's old house) and Merrion Sq., so ask for a quiet room.

### RUSSELL COURT 血 ♣

*21/23 Harcourt St., Dublin 2. Map* **4E4**
☎(01) 4784991 ▣(01) 4784066 ▥ 42 *rms, all with bathrm* ⇆ *nearby* ▤ ▨ ⬤
▨ ⇌ ‡ ▢ ▱ ⚶ ♈

*Location: Just off St Stephen's Green, 5 minutes' walk from Grafton St. and old Dublin.* This charming, smart hotel occupies a row of converted Georgian houses. It has its own horse-drawn cabriolet, which — while not perhaps everyone's choice of sightseeing transport — lends a certain charm and slows the pace. A hospital nearby causes the noise of ambulance sirens to intrude, so ask for a room at the back. Comfortable with good service. (Parking is in a little parking lot nearby, which does not belong to the hotel.)

### SACHS

*Morehampton Rd., Donnybrook, Dublin 4. Map* **1D3** ☎(01) 6680993 ▣(01) 6686147 ▥ *20 rms, all with shower* ▨
▣ ▣ ▨ ⚶ ⚹ ♈ ▱ ‡ ▢ ▱ ♈ ⬤
♈ ⇐

*Location: In a pretty, leafy part of Dublin not far from the city center.* The river Dodder runs near to this pretty old house with porticoed facade. The hotel is well run, agreeable, and popular with business people as well as visitors.

### SHELBOURNE 血 ⬤ ♣

*St Stephen's Green, Dublin 2. Map* **4E5**
☎(01) 6766471 ▣(01) 6616006 ▥
*166 rms, all with bathrm* ▤ ▨ ▣ ⬤ ▨
⚶ ⚹ ⇌ ▱ ‡ ▢ ▱ R ♈ ▣

*Location: Central Dublin, overlooking St Stephen's Green.* The most famous hotel in Ireland has been on the same site for 200 years. It is one of Dublin's great landmarks, with its four Nubian slave girls holding aloft the lights and guarding the canopied entrance. The

Shelbourne has even had a book written about it by that wonderful Irish writer, Elizabeth Bowen. The faint patina of an old family place, which made this hotel so very special, has gone, but the refurbishments have not altered its style. Bedrooms are pretty, with well-chosen pictures on the wall, and bathrooms are luxurious. The rooms overlooking Kildare St. and the Green can be noisy, even with double glazing. Service is excellent and amiable, and the hotel still has a bellboy who comes paging for visitors. The hall porter is an institution in himself.

**The Horseshoe Bar** is a good place to meet people, and on Thursday and Friday nights it can be so crowded that people spill out into the foyer and the afternoon tea room. The Shelbourne is an essential part of Dublin social life. Popping in for tea and delicious smoked salmon sandwiches is one of life's little pleasures.

### STEPHENS HALL

*14/17 Lower Leeson St., Dublin 2. Map* **4F5** ☎(01) 6610585 ▥ *37 rms, all with bathrm* ⚶ ⇌ ‡ ▢ ▱ ♈

*Location: Near to St Stephen's Green (on busy street).* All-suite accommodation with living rooms and small but well-equipped kitchens in these converted Georgian terraced (row) houses. They provide a way to be independent without renting a house or flat in the center of Dublin. The **Terrace Restaurant** is open to nonresidents.

### WESTBURY 血 ♣

*Off Grafton St., Dublin 2. Map* **4D4** ☎(01) 791122 ▥ *150 rms, all with bathrm* ▤
▨ ▣ ⬤ ▨ ⌂ ⚹ ⇌ ▱ ‡ ▢ ▱ ⚶
♈ ▣

*Location: One of the most central hotels in Dublin, just off Grafton St.* Because this is within a pedestrianized area, many of the rooms are quiet, save for the sounds of Dublin youth making merry on the way home of an evening. The Westbury is a luxurious hotel but, as is the case with so many new Dublin hotels, the public areas are badly proportioned. The decor is glossy, the bedrooms comfortable. Good places to meet friends are the **Polo Bar** or (for tea) **The Terrace**. The Westbury has an innovative approach to food; each year it has an international gourmet food season, which in turn lends an extra fillip to the cuisine after the foreign chefs have departed.

# Outskirts of Dublin

### COURT
*Killiney, Co. Dublin. Map 2E5* ☎*(01) 2851622* ☒*(01) 2852085* ▥ *86 rms, all with bathrm* 🔲 🔲 ▥ 🔲 🔲 🔲 🔲 🔲 🔲 🔲 🔲
*Location: Spectacular setting on Killiney Bay, just a few miles s along Dublin Bay.* There are lots of weddings and 21st-birthday parties in this hotel in a Victorian building, so besides the courtly service you will have a chance to observe south Dubliners *en fête*.

### FORTE CREST
*Dublin Airport, Co. Dublin* ☎*(01) 379211* ☒*(01) 8425874* ▥ *(discounts on weekends). 190 rms, all with shower* 🔲 🔲 🔲 🔲 🔲 🔲 🔲 🔲 🔲 🔲
*Location: Near to the airport, off the new N1 Motorway, 7 miles N of Dublin.* Part of the international Forte Crest group, this is a stopover hotel with all amenities. A courtesy coach shuttles between the airport and the hotel 24 hours a day.

### ROYAL MARINE 🏨
*Marine Rd., Dun Laoghaire. Map 2D5* ☎*(01) 2801911* ☒*(01) 2801089* ▥ *104 rms, all with bathrm* 🔲 🔲 🔲 🔲 🔲 🔲 🔲 🔲 🔲 🔲 🔲 🔲 🔲 🔲
*Location: Overlooking Dublin Bay.* A big white spa-like hotel, its central tower gives it an Edwardian appearance, marred by the modern block added to one side. The Powerscourt wing (for which a supplement is payable) has a Victorian suite with four-poster beds. It is a convenient launchpad for travelers setting out south. Quiet, decent service is the style, unremarkable in the best sense of the word.

0035 318 080 500

# Alternatives

## GUESTHOUSES

### ANGLESEA TOWN HOUSE
*63 Anglesea Rd., Ballsbridge, Dublin 4. Map 1C3* ☎*(01) 6683877* ☒*(01) 6683461* ▥ *7 rms, all with shower* 🔲 🔲 🔲 🔲
*Location: In the pretty Ballsbridge area, near Donnybrook Church off Merrion Rd.* An idiosyncratic little guesthouse with a distinctive style all of its own — almost an Edwardian boarding house in ambience. Everything has been thought out for the guest's comfort.

### BUSH HOUSE
*Northumberland Rd., Dublin 4. Map 1C3* ☎*(01) 6683* ▥ *6 rms, 5 with shower, 1 with bathrm* 🔲 🔲 🔲 🔲
*Location: Comfortable and agreeable rooms in a large Victorian house in Pembroke area; 10 minutes' walk from city center.* Prettily decorated rooms and guest lounge in this family-run guest house. Wonderful breakfasts, a most congenial atmosphere, and a quality of service outside the normal are plus points. Bush House is set back from a busy road, so ask for a room at the back if traffic disturbs you.

### CLARA HOUSE
*23 Leinster Rd., Dublin 6. Map 1D2* ☎*(01) 975904* ☒*(01) 975904* ▥ *10 rms, all with bathrm* 🔲 🔲

*Location: In a busy suburb, near bus stops.* This small Georgian house, very typical of Dublin architecture, provides all the basic comforts.

### GLENVEAGH TOWNHOUSE

*31 Northumberland Rd., Dublin 4. Map 1C3* ☎(01) 6684612 ☒(01) 6684559 ▭ 11 *rms with showers, 1 with bathrm* ▣ ▣ ▢ ▱

*Location: Next door to Bush House.* Quiet rooms (especially at the back), friendly, efficient service, and a good Irish breakfast are what you can expect here.

### KILRONAN HOUSE

*70 Adelaide Rd., Dublin 2. Map 1C2* ☎(01) 4755266 ☒(01) 6782841 ▭ 11 *rms, all with bath/shower* 🄥 ▢ ▱ *Closed Dec 24-Jan 1.*

*Location: Near St Stephen's Green, in a leafy but busy street.* This well run, immaculate guesthouse is highly recommended by regulars. Pleasant service and a wine license are other attractions.

### MOUNT HERBERT GUEST HOUSE ▰ ♣

*Herbert Rd., Lansdowne Rd., Ballsbridge, Dublin 4. Map 1C3* ☎(01) 6684321 ☒(01) 6607077 ▭ 144 *rms, 137 with bathrm* 🄰🄴 ▣ 🄥 ▱ 🆈 ▱ ▢ ▱

*Location: In the middle of the Pembroke area, near pretty little Herbert Park and the Lansdowne Road Rugby Stadium,* well *within walking distance of the city center.* This is a small hotel with undistinguished but friendly decor and a welcoming atmosphere. It was once a temperance hotel but now has a wine license. The same family has been in charge for 35 years. A baby-sitting service is a useful feature for travelers with children.

### ORIEL HOUSE ▰

*62 Lansdowne Rd., Ballsbridge, Dublin 4. Map 1C3* ☎(01) 6685512 ☒(01) 6685845 ▭ 27 *rms, all with bathrm* 🄥 ▱ ▱

*Location: In the Merrion area near the Rugby Club, near to DART station but an easy walk to Ballsbridge and Merrion area.* This large, smart, mid-Victorian mansion, furnished appropriately, makes a congenial place to stay. There is no restaurant, and a wine license only.

### RAGLAN LODGE

*10 Raglan Rd., Dublin 4. Map 1C3* ☎(01) 6606697 ☒(01) 6606781 ▭ 7 *rms, all with bathrm* 🄥 ❦ ▱ ▱

*Location: 5 minutes from the Royal Dublin Society.* Situated in Ballsbridge, an area with some of the prettiest terraces and streets in Dublin, this is a really good guest house. (Riders in the RDS Horse Show stay here.) Victorian high-ceilinged rooms are prettily decorated. Very well run.

## PRIVATE HOUSES

There are various organizations that provide accommodation in private homes and country houses run as hotels and restaurants.

**Irish Country Houses and Restaurants** issues descriptive booklets and price-lists, which are available at most travel agencies and all Irish tourist offices. Correspondence/inquiries to: The Secretary, Ardbraccan Glebe, Navan, County Meath, Ireland ☎(046) 23416 ☒(046) 23292.

**The Hidden Ireland** offers the visitor a stay in private houses of architectural merit. Inquiries to: The Secretary, The Hidden Ireland, Kensington Hall, Dublin 6, Ireland ☎(01) 6686463 ☒(01) 6686578

**Elegant Ireland** can arrange accommodation in unusual or grand houses and castles in and around Dublin. One example is **Luttrellstown Castle** to the NW, in the Castlenock area of Dublin. The castle was owned by Guinness heiress Aileen Plunkett who commissioned the murals, plasterwork and other decorations that adorn this great Irish house. Attractions include shooting, fishing and a helicopter landing pad.

Geraldine Murtagh, who runs Elegant Ireland, can arrange holidays for individuals or groups sharing the same interest (e.g., archeology, genealogy, great paintings, architecture). She will arrange licenses and landing fees and provide an entrée to many houses closed to the public. Among the houses available on short let in the Dublin area are:

- **Chestnut Lodge**, Monkstown, Co. Dublin. Reservations by the week, or on a bed-and-breakfast basis.
- **The Mews**, Dublin 4. A modern house with a garden and parking; close to shops.

For information on both houses, apply to **Elegant Ireland**, 15 Harcourt St., Dublin 2 ☎(01) 4751632/6751665 Ⓕ(01) 4751012.


## DUBLIN ON A SHOESTRING

**The Dublin International Youth Hostel** *(61 Mountjoy St., Dublin 2, map 3 B3* ☎*(01) 301766/301396* ⬜*)* is a few minutes' walk from O'Connell St., N of the Liffey. Accommodation is in rooms or small dormitories. Useful features include a courtesy bus, restaurant, self-catering (efficiency) facilities, left-luggage lockers (checkroom) and a night porter. The hostel is open 24 hours a day and has a supervised parking lot and information desk.

# Eating and drinking

## Food and drink in Ireland

*Nor did their diet have many refinements: herbs, shamrock, water-cress, berries and esculent roots eaten raw, simple milk products, oatcakes, whey, broth, and sometimes barely cooked, unseasoned venison, mutton, or beef were the fare that strangers found exe-crable, although apparently it suited those who were used to it, for they were described as hardy, sinewy and fleet.*

As in so many things, there was a divide in Irish cooking. There was the food in the great Anglo-Irish houses, which could be superb and lavish. In households at the other end of the scale, there were potatoes and buttermilk at every meal.

Reading the history of Dublin can provide an insight into this area. In the minutes of the Kildare Street Club, we learn that Mr Hamilton Stubber had been given a bad egg for breakfast, Mr Tighe doubted the freshness of his herring, and Lord Greville was alleged to have said, "Damn your bloody eyes, do you think I am going to pay three pence for this rotten beef . . . ?"

In his amusing and informative book *The Twilight of the Ascendancy*, Mark Bence Jones writes of Edward Martyn (see DAY 1, page 101) that his tastes were those of an old-fashioned country priest: "oysters (if they were in season), a kipper and a huge steak with onions, washed down with quantities of strong tea . . ."

To read of life in the great country houses is to enter a lost world. At the house of the Martins of Ross in Galway, a sheep was killed every week, a bullock once a month, and the country around provided meat, fowl, game and rabbits. The rivers and the sea furnished salmon trout and other fish. The wine, laces, tea and tobacco, as well as the fineries of household ware such as mirrors, carpets and velvets, were all smuggled in; the corn grown on the adjoining hillside was threshed in the barns; the flax and wool were spun under the mistress's eyes; hide was used to make shoes; candles were made from fat and tallow. There were gangs of people working and living in and out of the large houses, and each house was a citadel unto itself.

Molly Keane, one of Ireland's most loved writers and a brilliant cook herself, gives in many of her books an idea of the food in these houses, perhaps most memorably in *Two Days in Aragon*, in a snatch of dialogue between a starving old aristocrat and the servant who is starving her. They talk: one of the food of her dreams; the other of the food she will serve that night to other people:

> . . . *strong clear soup made of the best shin and reduced to pure goodness, followed by nice salmon leaping fresh from the sea, imagine, and lettuce hearts; and then shoulder of black faced lamb and the first green peas, juicy little Marvel peas, with a little butter and mint . . . .*
>
> *And the sweet — don't tell me, I'll guess . . . bottled plums? . . . rhubarb fool . . . jam puffs and cream? . . . Is it gooseberry tart from the early bush on the left hand side of the asparagus bed?*
> *It is.*

For a long time, there was no chance of emulating such a simple and delicious meal in Ireland in any eating house. You could get salmon but it would be fried black. You could get delicious salad but it would have "salad cream" puddled over it.

Kate O'Brien, in her book *My Ireland,* wrote in despair after her journey through Ireland and her search for good food:

> *I may be a bit afraid of bossy waitresses but I am not at their mercy. And I have tried in quite expensive Irish hotels, to get my own way. I have asked for instance if I could have a minute steak, a plain green salad and a glass of wine. Always no. (I have asked everywhere). I have asked for an apple or a pear at supper. I have asked for honey. I have asked if the sauce bottles could be removed, I have been so driven in experiment as to ask if I could have a linen napkin instead of a paper one.*

She prophesied that "points of judgement and moderation will be picked up as tourist trade widens and experience imposes steadiness on publicists and hotel-keepers alike." And now, 30 years later, everything she begged for would be given to her as a matter of course.

One of the great influences on Irish cooking has been Myrtle Allen, through her inspired meals at her hotel, **Ballymaloe House** in County Cork, and through her writings and books. Her daughter-in-law, Darina O'Connell, herself from a family of brilliant cooks and chefs, runs a cookery school there that is as good as, if not better than, any in Europe, *and* set in the most wonderful surroundings.

All over Ireland, delicious meals are now to be had in hotels and restaurants, and as the wide repertoire of Irish food to be found in private houses (and the spate of Irish cookbooks) has shown, the recipes are there to be exploited. Most of the better restaurants in Dublin specialize in French food based on *nouvelle cuisine;* chefs are grounded in classic French cookery and then take off from there, so successfully, indeed, that many Irish chefs are now working in top hotels in London and Paris.

This would have been unthinkable not long ago. There was never a history of *haute cuisine* in Ireland, if only because many of the people rarely had enough to eat. But there was a history of delicious ingredients and simple recipes, so that today there are restaurants that serve only ethnic Irish food.

Of course, there are countless cafés and pubs and snack bars all over Dublin, serving every degree and nationality of food you could wish for, from the grandest cuisine to a "one and one," which is Dublin argot for a portion of fish and chips.

"The main thing to remember about restaurants in Dublin," wrote one perceptive critic recently, "is that the categories overlap. The pond is so small that the frogs and the frog princes share and share alike."

The best comprehensive guide devoted solely to food and restaurants all over Ireland is the excellent *The Bridgestone Irish Food Guide,* invaluable and as fiercely subjective as all good food guides must be. And half of the fun of being a visitor in a city is finding out where they're playing your meal.

Remember that there is a whacking great Value-Added Tax (VAT) on wine, which makes all wine in restaurants very expensive.

Below are a few of the best places to eat in Dublin, but there are many more.

# Dublin's restaurants A to Z

The following pages focus on different styles of eating and include recommended restaurants a little way out of the city. Each section is arranged alphabetically.

### Dining out in style

#### THE COMMONS
*Newman House, 85/86 St Stephen's Green. Map 4E4* ☎*(01) 4780530, 4780539. Open Mon-Fri 12.30-2.15pm; Mon-Sat 7-10.15pm* **AE CB DC VISA**

A delightful restaurant, although somewhat subterranean in feel. Situated below Newman House (see DAY 1, page 98), this has, since its opening, become one of the best restaurants in Dublin, with food that can be delicious and inspired. If a dish fails, it is because of vaunting ambition rather than the opposite. Attention to detail is unflagging, and the service is good. The restaurant is large, but looks smaller because of the clever division of the big rooms with pillars, flowers and the paintings on the walls. The decoration is unobtrusive but grand, and outside lie Iveagh Gardens to stroll in before or after meals.

#### LE COQ HARDI
*35 Pembroke Rd. Map 1C3* ☎*(01) 6684130. Open Mon-Sat 12.30-2.30pm, 7-11pm* **AE CB DC VISA**

A restaurant with a dark *fin-de-siècle* feel in a voluptuous atmosphere in a large town house, which can be oppressive at lunchtime but may suit the mood of those who want a meal to be an event. Rich food, good wine.

#### DOBBINS WINE BISTRO
*15 Stephen's Lane, Dublin 2. Map 4E6* ☎*(01) 6764679. Open Mon-Sat 12.30-3pm, 8pm-midnight.*

A vintage Dublin restaurant, although its name implies otherwise; the entrance passage is lined with wine bottles, and there is a wide choice of wine, which is perhaps more important than the food.

## L'ÉCRIVAIN
*Lower Baggot St.. Map 4E6* ☎(01)
*6611919. Open Mon-Fri 12.30-2pm; Sat*
*6.30-11pm* AE □ □ VISA

A small, stylish restaurant, below street level down some rakishly steep steps, where the chef/patron Derry Clark is in attendance to dish up more than food. His motto is to produce the best cosmopolitan food with the best Irish ingredients, in an atmosphere predicated on his personality. The atmosphere is as Continental as any in Dublin.

## THE GREY DOOR
*23 Pembroke St. Map 4F5* ☎(01)
*6766890. Open Mon-Sat 12.30-2.30pm,*
*7-11pm* AE □ □ VISA

Interesting, in that it's the only place in Dublin, apart from its sister, the OLD DUBLIN, that serves vaguely Eastern European/Russian food with a hint of the Baltics. The downstairs wine/bar bistro is almost as expensive as the main restaurant and not as good. Pleasant atmosphere, never overcrowded, but an overpriced wine list. Used by Department of Foreign Affairs personnel, perhaps to give them practice.

## LOCKS
*1 Windsor Terrace. Map 1C2* ☎(01)
*543391. Open Mon-Fri 12.30-2.30pm;*
*Mon-Sat 7.15-11pm* AE □ □ VISA

A popular restaurant down by the Grand Canal in the picturesque Portobello area. There is a slightly New England feel to this agreeable, long, low room, with its board-paneled walls hung with so many prints and dotty pictures that it's almost like eating in a private gallery. The atmosphere is as impressive as the food. But it's a nice place to eat at lunchtime, with that strange silver quality of light that comes from reflections off water.

## Informal eating

## COOK'S CAFE
*14 South William St. Map 4D4* ☎(01)
*6790537. Open daily (except Sun dinner)*
*12.30-3pm, 6.30pm-midnight* □ VISA

## THE OLD DUBLIN
*91 Francis St. Map 3E3* ☎(01) 542028.
*Open Mon-Sat 12.30-2.30pm, 7.30-*
*10.30pm* AE □ □ VISA

A Russian/Irish restaurant, with French undertones in the street of antique stores (so, busy at lunch times and deserted at night), is a curious anachronism; but its customers are faithful. Uncle Vanya might have eaten here, grumbling away about the food and Moscow.

## POLO ONE
*5-6 Molesworth Place. Map 4D5* ☎(01)
*6766442. Open Mon-Sat 12.30-2.30pm,*
*7-10.30pm* AE □ □ VISA

A pretty restaurant near to the busy shopping area of Dawson St. French food is cooked with a twist that is individual and delicious, with tasty little starters to whet your appetite. This is the place for a quiet, unwinding, though rather formal meal at lunchtime (people dress smartly for lunch in a place such as this in Dublin); but it's not at all stuffy — rather like eating in a quiet and civilized drawing room.

## RESTAURANT PATRICK GUILBAUD
*46 James Place. Map 4E6* ☎(01)
*6764192.*

This is one of the best restaurants in Dublin, if not *the* best. It is an agreeable, chic space with a Post-Modern look that is at odds with the traditional style of Dublin restaurants. On offer is French grand food adapted to Dublin tastes, impeccably presented, without losing essential flavor. There are good paintings on the walls, many of them by the Irish artist Mary Swanzy. Patrick Gilbaud is French, as are his waiters, and he keeps a strict Gallic eye on things. When he is not there, the service slackens.

One of Dublin's best chefs has opened his own place in the Powerscourt Town House Centre, after years of working in other restaurants all over, including Dublin at POLO ONE. His style of food is Provençal/Mediterranean, lightened by a Californian influence. The restaurant is small: 12 tables inside, six under the awning, where it's most fun. Light, airy atmosphere. Prices are restrained. Always packed out.

### CORA'S

*1 St Mary's Rd., Lower Baggot St. Map 1C3* ☎*(01) 6600585. Open Mon-Fri 8.30am-6pm; Sun 9.30am-3pm. No cards.*

Tucked just off Lower Baggot St., below the big junction at the traffic lights, this restaurant from the outside looks like a relic of the 1950s — a set for a Bogdanovich film, perhaps — and inside is much the same. Formica-topped tables are jammed together, so you will find yourself a very close companion to the couple at the next table, who, fortunately, will be deeply interested in you. Friendly service and lashings of food — filling Italian and Irish dishes. Unsophisticated, easy-going.

### LES FRÈRES JACQUES

*74 Dame St. Map 4D4* ☎*(01) 794555. Open Mon-Fri 12.30-2.30pm; Mon-Sat 7-11pm* AE ● ●● VISA

Les Frères Jacques is an unpretentious and pretty restaurant, serving a mixture of French and nursery food. The atmosphere is informal but there is nothing casual about the food. It is particularly good for lunch.

### LORD EDWARD'S SEAFOOD RESTAURANT

*23 Christchurch Place. Map 3B3* ☎*(01) 542420. Open Tues-Fri 12.30-2.30pm; Tues-Sat 6-10.45pm* AE ● ●● VISA

Dublin's oldest seafood restaurant is at the top of the old pub opposite Christchurch. Enormous meals, traditional in every sense, include that wonderful Irish classic dish, *champ* (creamy potatoes with scallions and buttermilk). A place where serious Rotunda lawyers do serious eating. The idea of *nouvelle cuisine* turns them white at the gills.

### THE MAHOGANI GASPIPES

*17 Manor St. Map 3B2* ☎*(01) 6798138.*

The proprietors lived in New York for years and their ideas about food make this a touch different from other Dublin restaurants: Oriental mixed with Irish mixed with Manhattan. Certainly there is nothing like it in Stoneybatter, to the N of the Quays, where this restaurant, with its little courtyard, is situated. The best fried potato skins I've ever had, and imaginative Oriental rice dishes. A very brave endeavor, this good little restaurant.

### MITCHELL'S CELLARS

*21 Kildare St. Map 4E5.*

This wine bar is almost a full-scale restaurant rather than a pub. It is tucked below street level under the oldest wine merchants in the city and serves bistro food, with a good flavor of Irish cooking. No reservations; you take your chance for a table, but can always sit up at the bar. The atmosphere is convivial. Lots of old coopered barrels and wine memorabilia around, but not just as trappings — they belong here. Very busy at lunchtime, and only open then.

### NICO'S

*53 Dame St. Map 4D4* ☎*(01) 6773062.*

One of the oldest, some swear *the* oldest, Italian restaurants in Dublin. It looks it. "Rossini on the Liffey" might be a good way to sum up its unique character. Or, as someone said, "Ireland's idea of Italy before *La Dolce Vita.*" Red plush, flashing-eyed waiters and Italian food that inclines to the stuffed (ravioli, dauphin of sole), are the trademarks of this most congenial place, where people always seem to linger.

### UNICORN RESTAURANT

*12b Merrion Court, off Merrion Row. Map 4E5* ☎*(01) 6762182. Open Mon-Sat 12-3pm, 6-10pm* AE ● ●● VISA

Just near St Stephen's Green, this is a Dublin institution: people use it as a meeting place, as much as a restaurant. You find a seat where you can at the lunch hour, when it is always packed. On Saturday mornings it has the air of a raffish congregational salon, as everyone knows everyone else. A great place for an Irish-Italian meal, a combination which, as a bemused French visitor observed, *est une genre*.

### DA VINCENZO
*133 Upper Leeson St. Map 1C2 ☎(01) 6609906.*
A bistro/restaurant without pretensions, but because of its congeniality it succeeds at a high level. The atmosphere is inviting, with wholesome decor, checked table cloths and charming staff. It specializes in Italian food with variations: good pizza, delicious spaghetti. One or other of the husband-and-wife owners is usually on the premises checking everything out. Busy at lunchtime.

## Fast food and cafés

### ELEPHANT & CASTLE,
*Temple Bar. Map 4D4 ☎(01) 6793121.*
A good place to eat, if you're with a crowd or on your own; the place is always seething and you may have to wait for a table. If there are long lines of waiting customers, you put your name on a list and repair to the congenial pub across the road (**Flannery's**); or there are many other pubs nearby, since this is in the heartland of Temple Bar. Comprehensive menu of risottos and Creole food, as well as the best hamburgers in Dublin (which is what most people seem to have). Family parties come here, as well as students.

### FITZER'S
*24 Upper Baggot St. Map 1C3 ☎(01) 6600644. Open 8am-11.30pm.*
A branch of the well-run food-bar chain with imaginative, good-to-terrific food to eat in or take out. Their Raglan Road Sandwiches on a bap or French bread are delicious and enormous; so is their BLT. They also make good ragouts, chili con carne and spaghetti. The Fitzer's chain is also in charge of the café at the National Gallery. The staff is exemplary.

### MARKS BROTHERS
*7 South Great George's St. Map 4D4 ☎(01) 6771085.*
The most famous sandwiches in Dublin, and rightly renowned. Also soups and salads. This is ideal for a quick lunch.

### WELL FED CAFÉ
*Dublin Resource Centre, 6 Crow St. Map 4D4 ☎(01) 6771974. Open Mon-Sat 10am-4pm. No cards.*
This is a most congenial place at any hour of the day. There is a vaguely San Franciscan 1960s feel to it, as though at any moment Ginsberg might come in and howl. Notices and posters for current events are pinned up everywhere, and the food is simple and filling with a good selection of vegetarian dishes. These are served at scrubbed tables on pine floors, surrounded by people engaged in more or less serious conversations, which they take up as they walk in with people already there. If you're on your own, the place is an agreeable oasis, where you can brood or dream without being disturbed.

### THE WINDING STAIR
*40 Lower Ormond Quay. Map 4C4 ☎(01) 8733292. Open Mon-Sat 10.30am-6pm.*
Just off the Quay, overlooking the Liffey, through a warehouse entrance and up the stairs, one comes upon floor after floor of books, and coffee bars. You can buy the books and eat the food; it is a most congenial place, and somehow redolent of Dublin — you remember it when you're far away. There are snack meals, including good home-made soups and big sandwiches, served at lunchtime, and coffee, tea and snacks at other times. Outside, from this vantage point, the Liffey flows through the heart of Dublin.

## Indian cuisine

### THE RAJDOOT TANDOORI
*26-28 Clarendon St., Westbury Centre. Map 4D4 ☎(01) 6794274. Open Mon-Sat 12.30-2.30pm, 6.30-11.30pm* AE ⬤ CD VISA
Some say this is the best Indian restaurant in Ireland. It is certainly delicious, this Dublin version of food from Northern India (no wonder the Moghuls were so civilized, living on food like this).

### SITAR
*8 Merrion Row. Map 4E5 ☎(01) 6615095. Open Mon-Sat 6.30pm-1am; Sun 6.30pm-midnight* AE ⬤ CD VISA
An old-established restaurant with no pretensions to anything other than serving Indian food to hungry people who want a hot curry and all the trimmings.

## Museum restaurants

### CHAPTER ONE AT THE IRISH WRITERS MUSEUM
*18/19 Parnell Sq. Map 4B4 ☎(01) 8732266, 8732281.*
Irish food served imaginatively, in the new museum, and Kate O'Brien (see page 183) would have been delighted. Not just green salads, but Irish venison, Fanad salmon, Irish sole, duckling, Wicklow lamb, Loughshinny crab and, of course, Dublin Bay Prawns. No starving artists here.

### NATIONAL GALLERY RESTAURANT
*Merrion Sq. Map 4D5 ☎(01) 6615133. Open Mon-Sat 10am-6pm, Thurs until 9pm; Sun 2-5pm.*
This FITZER's-run serve-yourself restaurant is one of the nicest places to have lunch: mainly salads and vegetarian foods as well as good hot Irish food (Irish stew, cottage pie). A large, airy restaurant, with a little courtyard somewhat hemmed in, but with fragments of Greek reliefs on the high, dark walls. *Very* busy, serve-yourself, so go early or prepare to shuffle along clutching your tray. Not that this is any penance, as National Gallery lunchers are a motley, interesting lot, who talk while they line up.

## Oriental cuisine

### THE CHILI CLUB
*1 South Anne's Lane, South Anne St., off Grafton St. Map 4D4 ☎(01) 6773721. Open Mon-Fri 12.30-2.30pm, 7.30-11pm* AE ⬤ CD VISA
The name, so redolent of hot food (or South America) is a mask: this is a brilliant little Thai restaurant with a choice of five delicious starters and a further esoteric menu. Rumor has it in Dublin that the chef here was formerly employed by the King of Thailand; she certainly cooks fit for a king. It is essential to reserve, and sometimes up to a week ahead.

### CHINA SICHUAN
*4 Lower Kilmacud Rd., Stillorgan. Map 1E3 ☎(01) 2884817, 2889560. Open Mon-Fri noon-2.30pm; Sat, Sun 1-2.30pm; Mon-Sat 6.30-11.30pm; Sun 6.30-11pm* AE ⬤ CD VISA
Someone described this experience as being like eating butterfly food served by

engineers. What he meant was that the exquisite Chinese food here is often served by unsmiling Chinese waiters of the old school of the Long March. However, others find the service here as good as the food is delicious. Especially good for fish dishes. The taxi journey from central Dublin is worth every mile. But be warned and under-order: servings are lavish.

### IMPERIAL CHINESE RESTAURANT

*12a Wicklow St. Map 4D4 ☎(01) 6772580. Open Mon-Sat noon-midnight. No cards.*
A busy Chinese restaurant in a central location near Grafton St. The Chinese eat there — always a good sign. *Dim sum* is served from 12.30-7pm every day. Just the place for a quick and satisfying Chinese meal.


## North of Dublin

### KING SITRIC

*East Pier, Howth, Co. Dublin. Map 2B6 ☎(01) 325235, 326729. Open Mon-Sat 6.30-11pm; Seafood bar 12.30-3.30pm.*
A famous fish restaurant overlooking Dublin Bay. The fish and lobsters couldn't be fresher — practically jumping from the nets to the kitchen. In season, from May to September, there is a seafood bar with a wonderful buffet of oysters, fresh salmon, gravadlax, prawns and more.

### THE OLD SCHOOL HOUSE

*Coolbanagher, Swords, Co. Dublin ☎(01) 402846. Open Mon-Fri 12.30-2.30pm; Mon-Sat 7pm-10.30pm* AE ⊕ ⊚ VISA
Set in an 18thC school, with pretty walled gardens, this restaurant serves imaginatively prepared fish and fresh food with great enthusiasm.


## South of Dublin

### THE AL-MINAR TANDOORI RESTAURANT

*21 Castle St., Dalkey, Co. Dublin. Map 2E5 ☎(01) 2850552. Open Mon-Sat 12-2.30pm, 6pm-midnight; Sun 1.30-3.30pm* AE ⊕ ⊚ VISA
This restaurant has won the highest praise for its Indian food, based on Moghul recipes.


## Treats

Sample barm-brack in **Bewley's Oriental Cafe** in Grafton St.; "brack" means "speckled," and this rich half-fruitcake, half-teacake is delicious.

The best chips are supposed to be at **Burdock's** in Werburgh St., but there was a fire there and the reopened café will have to strive to be as good; the **Fish Inn** at the N end of Capel St., N of the city, also serves delectable fish and chips, but it has arbitrary opening hours. It is certainly open at lunchtime, but other times you must take your chance.

**Le Petit Gourmand Pâtisserie** ( ☎ *(01) 300788),* run by French chef Rene Becher, produces delectable pâtisserie (eclairs, *bavarois, mille feuille*), as well as savory delights. At **Brown Thomas food hall** and, seven days a week, at **The Riverview Centre**, Donnybrook.

189

In **Mother Redcap's Market** ( ☎ *(01) 538306)* are two outstanding shops. At one entrance is Anne Brodie's **Ryefield Food**: Ryefield cheese from her own farm in Co. Cavan, and brown bread, barm-brack, country butter and biscuits, smoked trout, carrot cake, marmalade, all home-made and delicious. Also at the Blackrock Market on Saturdays.

**The Gallic Kitchen** is at the other entrance of the market, just opposite the Tailor's Hall and beside Mother Redcap's Tavern. It is run by Sarah Webb, who was a pastry chef at one of Dublin's best restaurants. This is a wonderful place for quiche, bread, cheesecake, potato cakes and pies. She also does cooking for dinner parties.

# Pubs

It is, of course, a truism that drinking is a way of life in Dublin, and certainly the pub is a kind of tabernacle in Irish life. They are open all day, and once inside you have instant access to conversation, often the second most boring story you've ever heard in your life. The man on your right is about to tell you the first.

As a rule, pubs are for drinking in, more than for eating in, and you too can find the archetypal Irish pub, where groups of inspired and welcoming lunatics dazzle the air with the free flow of their *bons mots*. To stumble on it, literally, you just need a few drinks inside you. (The awful truth is that the legendary characters so beloved of modern mythology could be stupendously boring and pugnacious when they were drunk, which was often.)

One of the most famous and most congenial of bars is **The Horseshoe Bar** in the Shelbourne hotel. (In there, I am always reminded of the notice in a New York bar: "This is a high class bar. Act respectable.")

In most pubs, however, you can act as Bohemian and daft as you like and you won't be noticed.

Some pubs are famous because a writer wrote about them, and they have lived off that reputation ever since. The problem is that once a place becomes famous for being an authentic Dublin pub, it is either demolished or else it blushes all over and tarts itself up. The joy lies in finding your own idea of Dublin authenticity.

In every district there is at least one pub where traditional music-makers and singers gather in the evening for impromptu concerts or *ceilidhs* for the delectation of customers.

Among the nicest of these is **Mulligan's** in Poolbeg St., a genuine little dark pub, with great paint effects inside and out — the kind that decorators spend a fortune trying to emulate, and that actually comes from years of nicotine burnishing the traditional stippled and dragged surfaces. It is famous for its good pints. Journalists tend to gather here and regulars can be welcomingly taciturn. Don't even *think* of asking for something to eat. "Is this the oldest pub in Dublin?" asks an excited tourist, looking around. "No ma'am," the barman says, "that'll be the Brazen Head in Lower Bridge Street. But we have the oldest bar staff."

## AN BEAL BOCHT
*50 Charlemont St. Map 1C2.*
Down near the Grand Canal, this pub has some of the best traditional music events in town.

## BAD BOB'S
*East Essex St., Temple Bar. Map 4D4.*
A pub with country music and a cover fee to hear it, but worth it.

## THE BAILEY
*Duke St. Map 4D4.*
This is one of the places where the people in the fashion business drink, after work. A cosmopolitan place, a famous pub, but be prepared for the thatched cottage outside advertising the Irish restaurant upstairs. The actual door from no. 7 Eccles St., the house in which the imaginary Leopold Bloom of *Ulysses* fame lived, is now here, in a twist that Joyce might have relished. Or not. There is nothing of the local tavern about this bar, and the restaurant is geared to the visitor. Pub lunches are served.

## THE BRAZEN HEAD
*20 Lower Bridge St. Map 3D3.*
For all that this is a famous tourist attraction as the oldest pub in Dublin, it is an attractive place, recently greatly enlarged but not so as to notice, with old photographs, dark stained wood, dark green anaglypta walls, different levels, and gleaming mahogany. "You get a decent enough do at the Brazen Head," mused Leopold Bloom. Sometimes one wishes Joyce could have held his tongue.

## DAVY BYRNE'S
*21 Duke St. Map 4D4.*
Joyce wrote about this "moral" bar in *Ulysses,* and it's still there but changed. Go, if only to say you've been there and rubbed elbows with Leopold Bloom. You'll rub smarter elbows than he ever did, as it is now used as a local by the people working in the fashion business in Grafton St. and the surrounding areas. Lots of tourists, too. Specialities are seafood and salads.

## DOHENY AND NESBIT
*Lower Baggot St.*
Small and smoky, with a snug and lots of atmosphere. Senior civil servants, lawyers and politicians go there, and it becomes crammed and terribly noisy and smoky at night.

## HUGHES BAR
*19 Chancery St. Map 3C3.*
An old Dublin pub with no pretensions, which is magic. It has impromptu (but expected) music sessions most nights and arranged sessions other nights. A star from The Chieftains might come in and play, and they push the tables back and *dance*. There are enough regulars to keep the sets going with some sort of order and it is a good bit of "crack," that cover-all Irish word for what the English call "splendid entertainment." Irish dancing in its competitive set form is an ersatz, soulless, leaping affair, which you might think was invented by De Valera and an Archbishop, its movements designed only to develop calf muscles and to prevent any movement of the bosom, and certainly to prevent any dreaded bodily contact. There is little of that frozen-from-the-waist-up stuff here; this place breaks down any inhibitions you might have about getting up and moving around.

## JOXER DALY'S
*103 Dorset St. Map 4B4.*
South Dubliners think this place has a North Dublin feel, and North Dubliners know only that it is a very good pub, just getting on with its business. Phew, what a relief.

## KITTY O'SHEA'S
*23 Upper Grand Canal St. Map 1C3 ☎(01) 6608050.*
This is decorated, as the name would suggest, with relics, paintings and memorabilia of Charles Parnell and his famous mistress. Perhaps there's a mite too much stained glass separating the booths in this agreeable drinking house, but after all, it's pretty old glass. There is a raised, closed-in terrace at the back where you can get good pub food.

Sunday brunch here is about the best in the city. It is packed out, but waiting is fun. There is traditional music and jazz here in the evenings. Sister pubs (both called Kitty O'Shea's) have opened in Paris and Brussels, where they are a wild success.

### THE LONG HALL
*South Great George's St. Map 4D4.*

A wonderful-looking pub. You could sit for ages realizing what has been lost in the refurbishment of other places by seeing how this place looks by standing still. Mirrors, smoky glass, commemorative plates and clocks that don't tell anything about time other than that it has stopped.

### MCDAID'S
*3 Harry St. Map 4E4.*

Anthony Cronin wrote a mouthwatering description of this old bar: "It has an extraordinarily high ceiling, and high, almost Gothic windows in the front wall, with stained-glass borders. The general effect is church-like or tomb-like according to the mood: indeed indigenous folklore has it that it was once a meeting house for a resurrection sect who liked high ceilings in their place of resort because the best thing of all would be for the end of the world to come during religious service and in that case you would need room to get up steam." McDaid's is just off Grafton St. and has been redecorated to suit its smart setting, and the counter changed from one side to another, which would have confused the old regulars. A pity. The new regulars are a sophisticated lot, though, and not confused about anything.

### MOTHER REDCAP'S TAVERN,
*Back Lane. Map 3D3.*

Near the Iveagh Market is Mother Redcap's Tavern, one of the best places for music of all kinds on Sunday mornings. This is also where you can hear some of the *seannachi* (traditional storytellers) weave their songs and stories. (See local newspapers for details). Good brunch, terrific atmosphere.

### O'DONOGHUE'S
*Merrion Row. Map 4E5.*

This is a small pub in this small bustling street, a pub famous not only for its good pints but also for its entertainment. The Dubliners folk group started here in the 1960s, and there is still live traditional music every night. The place has a busy, un-self-conscious atmosphere, but becomes impossibly crowded on some weekend nights in high season.

### O'NEILLS
*Suffolk St. Map 4D4.*

A student haunt with atmospheric effects and a real sense of vivacity. Tends to get overcrowded.

### THE PALACE BAR
*Fleet St. Map 4D4.*

Here, in Anthony Cronin's words, Patrick Kavanagh, the poet, first came to Dublin, and sat in the haunt of journalists and men of letters "entranced in the inner circle of the local world of letters, and it appeared to him for a while he was part of it."

You can do likewise, with the same misapprehension and equal enjoyment, at the Palace Bar, where journalists, by tradition, have always met. It is close to the offices of *The Irish Times,* the best Irish newspaper, near to where the buses rumble to a near-permanent stop and where students and tourists wander. So, inside you will find an entertaining mix of characters, as well as a good pint.

### SLATTERY'S
*129 Capel St. Map 3C3.*

This is a music pub with Irish music sessions as well as blues, folk and jazz; one of the best known in Dublin. Crowded, enjoyable and authentically Dublin in style and pace.

### THE STAG'S HEAD
*Dame Court. Map 4D4.*

An old pub, not all that easy to find, with built-in nostalgia. Regulars come here for the feel of it, as well as the good pints and atmosphere. If you look up you will see why it is called the Stag's Head. Wrought-iron chandeliers too, and dark mirrors. It serves good pub food, soups, snacks, cheeses, omelets.

## TONERS
*Baggot St. Map 4E5.*

This was once that peculiarly Irish institution, a spirit grocery, where food and liquor were sold under the same roof. It still shows traces of this in its shelves and cabinets. A dark, cozy and relaxing pub, just off one of the busiest streets in Dublin, near St Stephen's Green. Like all Dublin pubs it gets intolerably smoky.

## WILLIAM RYAN
*Parkgate St. Map 1C2.*

Near to the main entrance of Phoenix Park is this bar famous for its Victorian fittings, gleaming brass, engraved glass and snugs. It is a convivial pub, and a favorite with the locals.

## POSTSCRIPT

There's a nice joke told about Dublin barmen (well, there are many jokes but only one good barman — the one behind the bar you are in.) This one goes: An American comes into the bar and says "Hey, Jimmy, I'd like some of this wit I'm always hearing about." "Certainly, sir," Jimmy says, "would you like it dry or sparkling?"

There is something called **The Dublin Literary Pub Crawl**. It is a guide to the hostelries where Beckett, Behan, Joyce and Kavanagh drank. Enjoy, if that's your tipple. Apply to **The Bailey** *( ☎ (01) 540228, May-Sept Sun-Thurs at 7.30pm)*. It's often booked out so call in advance.

One last thing: nearly every pub believes or advertises that it serves "probably the best pint in Dublin." You'd better believe it.

# Entertainments

## Performing arts

### CINEMA

There are large, multi-auditorium movie theaters all over Dublin, showing the latest releases. Program times are published daily in most newspapers. Among the cinemas showing more elusive "art-house" films are:

- **IFC Cinemas** 6 Eustace St., map 4D4, box office ☎(01) 6793477, 6793542. Late-night showings Thursday to Saturday 11pm. This Temple Bar complex (the **Irish Film Centre** — see DAY 3, page 140) also has a bar and restaurant (last orders 11pm).

- **The Lighthouse Cinema** Middle Abbey St., map 4C4 ☎(01) 8730438, booking office open 2.30-7.30pm.

### CLASSICAL MUSIC

The **National Concert Hall (NCH)** *(Earlsfort Terrace, map 4F5 ☎(01) 6711888; for charge/credit card reservations ☎(01) 6711533)* is the principal classical music concert hall in Dublin, with visiting orchestras as well as the **RTE Concert Orchestra** and the **National Symphony Orchestra**, both based there. It also presents jazz, opera and traditional music. The RTE Concert Orchestra, with its large repertoire, plays all over the country and tours the world.

Dublin is not in the avant-garde of modern music, but there are several societies that organize concerts and provide a platform for 20thC music in general and the work of young Irish composers in particular.

**Sundays at Noon** is a series of hour-long concerts on about 30 Sundays in the year, starting at noon, at the **Hugh Lane Municipal Gallery of Modern Art** *(Charlemont House, Parnell Sq., map 4B4 ☎(01) 8741903)*. Their main focus is on new music by Irish composers. Look for them in local listings.

The **Contemporary Music Centre of Ireland** *(95 Lower Baggot St., map 4E6 ☎(01) 6612105, open 10am-5.30pm)* is an archive and resource center which documents and promotes music by modern Irish composers. There is a library, a sound archive and collection of information about all kinds of modern music in Ireland. Its magazine *New Music News* is issued free three times a year.

If you visit that Dublin institution, the large music shop **Waltons** *(5 North Frederick St., map 4B4 ☎(01) 797166)*, just N of O'Connell St., or **McCullough Piggott Ltd** *(11-13 Suffolk St., map 4D4* ☎*(01) 6773138/6773161)*, just off Grafton St., you will find notices of classical and modern musical events including opera, raga, and workshops in and around Dublin. You can join the **Music Association of Ireland** at either of these two shops, which among other things publishes a monthly *Music Diary* of musical events.

The **Opera Theatre Company** is an adventurous and often brilliant young company which has been touring Ireland with a small orchestra since 1986. It commissions new operas, often with Irish themes. One of its venues is the Royal Hospital Kilmainham. See local listings, or ring McCullough Piggott (see above) for details.

The **Royal Dublin Society** *(Ballsbridge)* has for over a century organized a series of recitals open to the public on Mondays from November to March, engaging eminent international artists and ensembles. And there are regular concerts of chamber and piano music at the **Bank of Ireland Arts Centre (The Armoury)** *(Foster Place, map 4D4* ☎*(01) 6711488)*.

Check listings for the following in the local press:

* The **House of Lords** and **Bank of Ireland** hold lunchtime chamber music recitals. Admission is free.
* There are frequent early music concerts and recitals in **Trinity College**, as well as many other forms of music-making.
* There are regular chamber concerts at **St Stephen's Church (Peppercanister)**.
* Look out too for concerts by the **Hibernian Chamber Orchestra**.

## JAZZ

For years there was no jazz scene as such in Dublin, but now there are pubs and clubs where jazz is regularly played. Among the best are **The Purty Loft** *(Dun Laoghaire Harbour, map 2D5* ☎*(01) 2801257)*, **The Barge** *(Charlemont St.* ☎*(01) 4780005)*, and late-night sessions at the **Andrew's Lane Theatre**. There are sessions every Sunday night at the **Harcourt Hotel** *(Wexford St., map 4E4* ☎*(01) 4783677)*.

At **J.J. Smyths** *(Aungier St., map 4E4)* there are jazz concerts, and the **Wexford Inn** *(Wexford St., map 4E4)* has blues and jazz evenings and festivals. **Bad Bob's** *(34-35 East Essex St., map 4D4* ☎*(01) 6775482)* is a famous country and western pub venue.

There are cover charges for many of these events. Look up listings for prices, times and venues.

If you want to hear an international-class jazz guitarist, then go wherever **Louis Stewart** is playing. He is technically brilliant, and as good as you'll hear anywhere in the world.

## ROCK

Rooted in traditional Irish music, Ireland's characteristically anarchic, driven rock musicians have made a huge contribution on the world's stage — a subject explored in MUSIC (see pages 77-8).

The venue for international stars and rock bands is **The Point** ( ☎ *(01)* *363633)*, the huge building so brilliantly converted from warehouses down on the Quays. For younger, less exalted groups, **The Rock Garden** in Crown Alley in Temple Bar *(map  4D4* ☎ *(01)  799114)* is the place to head for.


## THEATER

Classic Irish drama, such as Synge's *The Playboy of the Western World* and O'Casey's *The Plough and the Stars,* still figures strongly in the repertoire of Dublin's legendary **Abbey Theatre**, which played such a vital part in the renaissance of Irish culture at the turn of the century (see IRELAND'S THEATRICAL HERITAGE, page 74 for the full story). The work of such modern Irish playwrights as Brian Friel, Tom Murphy and Sebastian Barry is also regularly performed there. The smaller **Peacock Theatre** is also part of the Abbey complex *(26 Lower Abbey St., map 4C5, booking office* ☎ *(01) 8787222, open 10.30am-7pm)*.

The other "great" Dublin theater, the **Gate Theatre Company** (see page 75), founded in 1928 by Micheal Mac Liammoir, stages classic and international productions and is an integral part of Irish theater life. *(Parnell Sq., map 4B4, information office* ☎ *(01) 6774085, charge/ credit card bookings* ☎ *(01) 8746042, telephone bookings* ☎ *(01) 8744045, discount for groups of 20 or more, box office open Mon-Sat 10am-7pm.)*

The **Dublin Theatre Festival**, in late September or early October, has become a highlight of international drama. Irish literature, poetry and drama is experiencing another renaissance, and many Irish playwrights are producing new work that is universal in breadth, impact and under- standing.

### Other theaters

**The Eblana Theatre** *(Store St., map 4C5, booking office* ☎ *(01) 6798404)* was originally built in the Busaras complex (the bus station), just down from the Abbey Theatre, so that people could watch news reels as they waited for a bus. Take a taxi at night — it is near some very rough areas.

**The Gaiety Theatre** *(8 South King St., beside St Stephen's Green Shopping Centre, map 4E4, booking office* ☎ *(01) 6771717, open 11am-7pm)* is one of Dublin's most loved theaters. Erected in 1871, it has been busy ever since as a showcase for drama, musicals — especially new Irish musicals — and pantomime. The **Dublin Grand Opera Society** was founded in 1941 to present opera here.

The **Lombard Street Studio**, near Westland Row *(map 4D5)*, is a space used primarily for productions from the excellent drama depart- ment of **Trinity College**. It is not open all the year round, so check before you go. Part of the new Pearce St. development within the campus, a 250-seat studio theater and 100-seat dance studio, the **Samuel Beckett Centre for the Performing Arts** *(map 4D5* ☎ *(01) 7021239 9am-5pm* ♿*)*, has opened, presenting a program of productions by the drama department from October to May. The intention is to use the theater during the summer months for varied productions by visiting companies.

**The Olympia Theatre** *(Dame St., map 4D4, charge/credit card booking* ☎*(01) 6777741, booking office open 10am-6.30pm Mon-Sat, group discount),* originally called The Star of Erin and then the Empire Theatre of Varieties, both of which names gave a hint of the joys to come, opened in 1879 as a music hall and became a Dublin institution. Part of the theater collapsed in 1972 during a rehearsal, but it has been restored and is now the home of ballet and revue as well as drama.

**The Project Arts Theatre** *(East Essex St., behind the Olympia in Temple Bar, map 4D4* ☎*(01) 6712321, lunchtime, evening and late-night performances)* is an adventurous company which stages new and experimental plays.

New theater groups and projects have sprung up all over Dublin, among them the **Andrew's Lane Theatre** *(9-17 Andrew's Lane, map 4D4, booking office* ☎ *(01) 6795720),* a small, somewhat uncomfortable studio theater just off Dame St., up Trinity St. and across from Central Bank, and the **City Arts Centre Theatre** *(23 Moss St., map 4C5, box office* ☎*(01) 6770643).*

**The Riverbank Theatre** *(13/14 Merchants Quay, map 3D3, charge/credit card reservation* ☎*(01) 6773370, booking office open Mon-Sat 10am-6pm),* on the s quay at Merchant Quay, is a fairly new theater with a full, ambitious and unpredictable program of productions that places special emphasis on Irish groups and Irish plays. A bonus is the spectacular view across to the Four Courts. The auditorium, restored from an old meeting hall, seats around 400 people comfortably.

Look out also for shows at the following:

* **Lambert Puppet Theatre and Museum**  Clifton Lane, Monkstown, Co. Dublin, map 2E4 ☎(01) 2800974. A huge repertoire of plays (from Oscar Wilde to fairy stories) and over 1,000 puppets.
**Tivoli**  135-138 Francis St., near Christ Church (take a taxi in this area at night), map 3D3 ☎(01) 544472. Visiting companies — everything from Shirley Valentine to *King Lear.* A theater with a fine atmosphere, considering its origins as an old cinema.


## TRADITIONAL IRISH MUSIC

Traditional Irish music is what most people want to hear when they visit Dublin, and there is still plenty of opportunity. The traditional music scene has flourished since emerging from shameful obscurity in the 1950s. Today, it is played and listened to with enthusiasm all over the country. But the pool of talent is vast and varied, and listening to Irish music is an art in itself. What follows are some of the best names to look out for, and some hints on attending that most Irish of cultural events, the session.

### Who to see

A lasting phenomenon is **de Danann**, which many say is the greatest Irish dance band ever, a changeable group that centers around the leader Frankie Garvan. For traditional virtuoso fiddle playing, for rhythmic playing, for the best version of *Hey Jude* you'll ever hear and for *the Queen of Sheba's Arrival* (wait for it) *in Galway,* this is the band. You'll hear nothing like this outside Ireland and nothing better inside.

Over the years, de Danann's vocalists have added something extraordinary to the ensemble — and what is also so extraordinary is that when they leave to go solo they are replaced with another singer who is equally astounding. This is what Irish music is about: iconoclastic, learned, instinctive, virtuosic. When you see de Danann you will marvel that any group can be so good. They are based in Galway but come to Dublin regularly.

**Mary Black**, a great singer and an international star, used to sing with de Danann. Her records are on sale in all record stores.

If you can, see **Sharon Shannon**, the accordionist who looks and plays like an angel: anything from fada to a classical melody to high traditional. People debate endlessly whether she is the best in Ireland or the best in the world.

Because the pub scene in terms of real music is nearly dead, the best thing to do is to follow the people who are great, which is what Dubliners do. So go wherever **Dolores Keane** is appearing with her husband **John Faulkner** (she was also with the group de Danann). You won't see or hear another performer like her in a month of Sundays. The voice soars, the face is beautiful, the performance riveting, she sings everything you can throw at her from *Lili Marlene* to the most moving traditional lament.

The word *Seisiun* (sessions) means a more or less impromptu evening of music and song, and it generally takes place in a pub. The instruments can be anything from an accordion to the *bodhran,* the traditional drum (and it is wonderful to watch a skilled exponent use this instrument), the fiddle and often the spoons or the bones. Everyone can join in, dancing sets or singing. It can be the best entertainment in the world. Many pubs have sessions, including **Hughes**, an old Dublin pub where there are music sessions most nights, some of which are genuinely impromptu, although enough regulars turn up to give some coherence to the scene. Someone from the famous group **The Chieftains** might turn up and play.

But Dublin is still a place where music happens. It is quite possible you will walk into a pub or a gathering and find an exhilarating session: people drinking and listening (or gossiping), while the musicians play intently, only occasionally glancing at each other, yet playing a driven ensemble music with a wild elegance that insists on its separateness.

All this you can hear anywhere, at night in many pubs and halls: people making music to their hearts' content. "You'd think they would need a conductor to keep that rhythm so perfectly," a Dutch visitor marveled to a fiddler after a set. "Ah, we'd eat a conductor," the fiddler told her mildly, and she looked alarmed.

There is traditional music every night at **Whelans** (*25 Wexford St., map 4E4* ☎ *(01) 4780766)* and **An Beal Bocht** (*58 Charlemont St.* ☎ *(01) 4755614).* There are sometimes cover charges for these sessions.

The other thing to do to hear the real thing is to attend an organized session such as those at the **Comhaltas Ceoltoiri Eireann** (*Belgrave Sq.*

*Monkstown* ☎ *(01) 2800925; DART station Monkstown or Seapoint; bus 7 or 8 from city center),* the headquarters of the country's traditional music association. Look out too for notices of events and concerts in the listings of magazines and papers.

The **Irish Traditional Music Archive** *(63 Merrion Sq.* ☎ *(01) 6619699, open by appointment)* is a new national resource center concerned with collecting, preserving and organizing Irish traditional music and making it available to the public. It includes 2,500 books, masses of documents, pamphlets and ephemera, as well as videotapes and over 4,000 sound recordings.

### The art of the "session"

There is a certain etiquette to be observed when listening to a pub session of traditional music. Although it may all seem random and haphazard, it is as measured as any 18thC gavotte. Never use a flash camera, for example, and do not assume you can stick a tape recorder under the musicians' noses. Ask permission to record, and be unobtrusive while you do so. Then buy the musicians a drink.

Approbation is shown by applause, by stamping the foot, by emitting little whoops and shrieks of pleasure throughout the session (these, though, need practice as to tone and timing), and by buying the musicians a drink.

The listener should never sit in with the musicians. Keep a respectful distance and buy the musicians a drink.

# Nightlife

### CABARET

**Jury's Cabaret** in JURY'S HOTEL (see HOTELS) is famous, and not for having star turns, although stars do appear. But often, sopranos who have never made the top notes and were taught by nuns quaver arias; a comedian cracks jokes; a tenor sings *My Way.* This is Irish stage entertainment, cabaret and good clean fun. It's hugely popular. Cabaret starts at 8pm, and dinner at 7.15pm. You can attend the cabaret without having dinner.

The other well-known cabaret with dinner is at the BURLINGTON (see HOTELS).

### CLUBS AND NIGHTLIFE

Because of the disproportionate number of people under the age of 25 in Dublin, many nightclubs are geared to the very young and are dark, airless and noisy. Nightclubs in Dublin, especially in **Leeson St.**, where the clubs are known as **The Strip**, have a very short lifespan and for one to survive more than nine months to a year is something of a miracle. They are more discos than clubs. But the musical scene at night is jumping.

A look in any of the free listings papers (the best is the *Dublin Event Guide*) will give a comprehensive sweep over what is available on what particular night. Two leading examples are:

- **Annabels**, a fashionable disco and nightclub in the underground car park below the BURLINGTON hotel.
- The **Rock Garden** *(Crown Alley, Temple Bar, map 4D4)*, a lively and noisy place to go to hear good new Irish bands, with a restaurant.

Whatever the sound you prefer, from hip-hop to thrash, you can find it playing somewhere, on any night of the week. What follows is a night-by-night guide to some of the best clubs:

### Monday
**The Ju-Ju Club**  Upstairs at the Rock Garden, Crown Alley, map 4D4. Salsa, reggae, ska and African. Open 11.30pm-2.30am.

### Tuesday
**Club Dropout**  Upstairs at the Rock Garden, Crown Alley, map 4D4. A student-style club featuring indie, house and hip-hop music.

### Wednesday
**Club Taboo**  Upstairs at the Rock Garden, Crown Alley, map 4D4. Mixing house, techno. Open 11.30pm-2.30am.
**The Country Club**  Harcourt Hotel, Harcourt St., map 4F4. Country, cajun and bluegrass disco. Open 11pm-2am.

### Thursday
**Anarchy Night Cafe**  Fibber McGees, Parnell St., map 4B4. For radical youth, mix of hardcore tunes, loud guitars, punky reggae and live bands. Open 11pm-2am.
**Funk Off**  The Waterfront, Sir John Rogerson's Quay. Two floors: upstairs funk, hip-hop, 1970s pop; downstairs funk, jazz and hip-hop. Also comedy. Open 11.30pm-2.30am.
**Panic**  McGonagles, South Anne St., map 4D4. Classic indie rock and new sounds. Open 11.30pm-2.30am.
**Tropicana**  Upstairs at the Rock Garden, map 4D4. Dance music from Africa, the Caribbean, Latin America and the Middle East. Open 11.30pm-2.30am.

### Friday
**Dischord**  Fibber McGees, Parnell St., map 4B4. Thrash music from the likes of Therapy, Ministry and live bands. Open 11pm-2.30am.
**The Funky And Fresh Club**  The Cottonwood Café, Johnson's Court, map 4D4. Jazzy, funky music to eat, drink and dance to. Open 11pm-late.
**Junior Metal Bash**  McGonagles, South Anne St., map 4D4. Alternate Fridays 7.30-10pm.
**Shampoo**  The Station, Central Hotel, South Great George's St., map 4D4. Funk and 1970s, full late bar and films. Open 11.30pm-3am.
**The Sweatbox**  Roxey's Bar, Little Green St., map 4D4. Punk, hardcore, indie, techno, thrash and goth, live bands and videos. Open 8-11.30pm.

**Thank Friday It's Crunchy**    McGonagles, South Anne St., map 4D4. Pop music from bands like Betty Boo, the Nymphs and Nirvana. Open 11.30pm-2.30am.

**The Web Rock Night Club**    5th Ave., D'Olier St., map 4C5. Heavy rock with full bar. Open 9pm-2am.

### Saturday
**Flesh**    Spectrum, 26 Dame St., map 4D4. Latest house and garage. Open 11.15pm-3am.

**The Funky and Fresh Club**    The Cottonwood Café. See FRIDAY for details.

**Sonic Boom**    McGonagles, South Anne St., map 4D4. Alternate weeks with **XS**. Indie/rock club. Open 11.30am-2.30pm.

**XS**, McGonagles, South Anne St., map 4D4. Alternate weeks with **Sonic Boom**. Pop, indie and dance music. Open 11.30pm-2.30am.

### Sunday
**Stompin' Georges Rockin' Roots Club**    The Lower Deck, Portobello. Mix of rock'n'roll, cajun, r'n'b, rockabilly. Open 4-7pm.

**World Music Midnight Club**    Fibber Magees, Parnell St., map 4B4. Open midnight-2am.

# Shopping

## A shopping renaissance

When Hugh O'Donnell, the ruler of Tyrconnel, appeared at the English court, he received great honor from Henry VIII. The unusual mien of this liege chief and the outlandish garb and obscure language of his party, with their saffron-colored smocks, narrow trews, rug-like fringed russet mantles, their mustaches, and their hair worn in thick long matted fringes over their eyes, must have aroused considerable comment and curiosity at the Tudor court. Nothing much has changed, and you can see people like this in Grafton St. any day.

The traditional souvenir buys from Dublin are to be found in shops all over the city. They include silver and gold Claddagh rings, Aran sweaters, or glass and crystal from Waterford or other Irish centers.

But there are other things to take home from Dublin: a painting of a Georgian door bought off the railings in Merrion Sq. on a Sunday morning; a bolt of Irish linen; a record from Claddagh Records in Temple Bar; spongeware by Nicholas Mosse, pottery from Stephen Pearce or glass from Jerpoint, all in the Kilkenny Centre; a copy of an old map from the Ordnance Survey Office; handmade Irish chocolates; a sweater from Lainey Keogh or Edel MacBride; a pair of handmade shoes from Tutty's; a linen blouse from John Rocha at Chinatown; or a book printed by one of Ireland's small printing presses. Look out especially for anything by the Dolmen Press, which over the years has produced editions of the works of contemporary Irish poets that are a delight to handle.

### SHOPPING HOURS
Most shops are open from 9.30am to 5.30pm. On Thursday, city center shops stay open until 8pm and suburban shops until 9pm. There are all-night grocery stores dotted around the edges of the inner city, especially in areas with visitors and students.

### TAX-FREE SHOPPING: CASHBACK
Non-EC nationals buying goods for export are entitled to a refund of the 21-percent VAT that is levied on all nonessential goods in Ireland. You must keep the receipt and present it at the special desk marked "Cashback" at the airport. The refund is given there.

# What to look for

## ANTIQUES

There are antiques stores all over Dublin, often in their own little clusters, ranging from little nooks selling bric-a-brac to large, beautiful showrooms selling the grandest furniture. In the past few years, the Irish have woken up to the fact that their country was once a treasure trove of antiques, being plundered by the pantechnicon-load.

Now, the Irish are mad about their own heritage and at least as keen on antiques as any visitor. But times have been hard in Ireland in the past few years and some of the best old shops have disappeared.

The **North Quay** was a wonderful place for the antiques addict, with shabby old places mixed with grand salons, but this has been vandalized by traffic and town planning. There are still some nice shops along here selling Irish furniture, pictures and china; and some, less formal, warehouse-type ones, where you penetrate high into dusty floors to come across acres of chairs. Farther along, in **Capel Street** *(map 3 C3)*, there are large antiques stores that are interesting to browse through, although they tend to stock larger Victorian pieces.

The **Powerscourt Townhouse Centre** has tiny antiques stores selling smaller things — china, jewelry, prints. In the **Dawson Street** area there are more expensive shops including the discreet showroom, **Ronald McDonnell Antiques** *(Kildare House, 16 Kildare St., map 4 E5 ☎ (01) 6762614)*. This is filled with delights: Irish furniture of the highest quality, fine pictures, porcelain and decorative objects. Here you may find a Lely, a piece of 18thC chinoiserie, or Waterford glass.

In the old area of the city known as The Liberties, near Christ Church and St Patrick's Cathedral, is **Francis Street** *(map 3 F3)*, which is lined with antiques stores full of diverse and fascinating furniture, objects, paintings and junk.

Until 1992, **Clanbrassil Street** *(map 3 F3)* was a busy tumble-down thoroughfare, full of Dublin atmosphere and lined with a curious mixture of shops; now a dual carriageway spoils it. **Conlon Antiques** is still there, though, the dealer's dealer: he sells large things rather than objects or pictures.

In **Patrick Street** *(map 3 E3)*, small antiques stores are tucked into the facade of the Iveagh Buildings (if you can reach it, across the stream of cars), including the **Caxton Gallery** *(63 Patrick St., map 3 E3 ☎ (01) 530060)*, which has the best antique prints in Dublin.

## ART GALLERIES

There has been a renaissance in the visual arts in Dublin. The works of young contemporary Irish artists now sell all over the world.

### KERLIN GALLERY
*38 Dawson St., map 4D5 ☎ (01) 6779179 ☒ 779652.*
One of the best places to see the work of young Irish artists who are breaking new ground. Among those they represent are: Guggi, Finbar Kelly, Felim Egan, Richard Gorman, Elizabeth Magill, Brian Maguire and Anne Madden.

### OLIVER DOWLING GALLERY
*19 Kildare St., map **4**E5* ☎*(01) 6766573*
A good selection of contemporary, avant garde and conceptual works by Irish artists.

### ORIEL GALLERY
*Clare St., map **4**D5* ☎*(01) 6763410*
Floor after floor of well-chosen, covetable Irish paintings, with an emphasis on early 20thC work.

### RIVERRUN GALLERY
*82 Dame St., map **4**D4* ☎*(01) 6798606.*
This congenial gallery has an innovative approach to the showing of art; it provides a good hanging space for the work of contemporary Irish artists such as Michael Ashur, Michele Souter and Eithne Jordan. It is open all hours, with a restaurant and a bistro.

### SOLOMON GALLERY
*Powerscourt Townhouse, Clarendon St., map **4**D4*
This agreeable gallery exhibits the paintings, sculpture and ceramics of contemporary Irish artists.

### TAYLOR GALLERIES
*4 Kildare St., map **4**E5* ☎*(01) 6766055.*
Traditional Irish art, as well as work by contemporary artists such as Michael Mulcahy, William Crozier, Charles Brady, Camille Souter and Louis Le Brocquy. Regular shows, together with auctions of Irish art approximately every three months, under the title of **Taylor de Veres**.

### TEMPLE BAR GALLERY & STUDIOS
*48 Temple Bar, map **4**D4* ☎*(01) 6710033.*
This gallery and studios has a special place in the development of awareness and acceptance of the new work of artists in Ireland. Funded by the Arts Council, it occupies an old building converted into studios, with 30 artists working there. There are regular exhibitions and installations of paintings, sculpture and photographs by contemporary Irish artists.


## ARTS AND CRAFTS
The **Kilkenny Shop** *(Nassau St., map **4**D5* ☎*(01) 6777066)* is the retail outlet for the work of over 400 suppliers, artists and craftsmen who work under the aegis of the Kilkenny Design Centre. Here you will find some of the best examples of contemporary Irish design. There is a slightly dated feel to some of the pieces, but the leather bags, the fine porcelain and many other goods have a lovely, clean, satisfactory appearance.

Look out for **Lainey Keogh Knitwear**, jewelry by **Sonia Landweer** and glass by **Jerpoint Glass**, which can also be bought direct from Kilkenny.

A short walk from Trinity College, down Pearse St., is the **Tower Centre** *(map **4**D5* ☎*(01) 6775655)* with its 35 workshops, which shows the best work of both new and established independent artists and craftworkers: jewelry, painting, pottery and much more.

A little farther out of town, at Marlay Park (see EXCURSIONS, page 231), the stables and workshops have been converted into the **Marlay Crafts Courtyard** studios for professional artists and craftsmen working in various crafts: painting, glassware, bookbinding etc. (*Marlay Park, Rathfarnham, map 1 D2*).

## ARCADES AND SHOPPING MALLS

Shopping in Dublin has changed dramatically in the past few years with the appearance of shopping centers and malls all over the city. Young designers, artists, craftspeople and jewelers have found a new outlet in these thriving covered markets, which have a long provenance in Ireland.

The best of them have a feeling of community life akin to that of a bustling, energetic marketplace. One example of the breed that stands out is the **Powerscourt Townhouse Centre**, a converted 18thC mansion, built around a courtyard that has been glassed into an atrium spanning several levels. It is crammed with shops and galleries, including antiques and jewelry stores selling the best of Irish fashions.

Dublin's best shops and arcades are spread all over the city. Some suburban shopping malls, such as **Blackrock Shopping Centre** and the **Merrion Centre**, are extremely good, even if they tend not to have many avant garde or high-fashion shops. Some of the main centers for this type of shopping are **Powerscourt Townhouse Centre**, **Grafton St.**, and the **Temple Bar** area.

Among the old arcades that still exist is the **George's Street Arcade** (*map 4 D4*). It is old and rather seedy, but charming, with a delightful shop called **Jenny Vander** ( ☎ *(01) 6770406*), an oasis of faded color crammed with Victorian and 1920s clothes, feather boas, jewelry and bric-a-brac. It is like being turned loose in the best dressing-up box.

With the restoration of the **Temple Bar** area, right in the center of Dublin, the city has another new shopping area. Here, there are small shops selling everything from idiosyncratic jewelry to second-hand clothing, especially from the 1950s and '70s, as well as record stores where you can buy obscure titles and the best of Irish ones. There are lots of galleries (at least eight at the last count), including the innovative **Temple Bar Studio**, and two theaters.

## AUCTIONS

A step away from the SHELBOURNE hotel (see page 178), **James Adam and Sons** (*St Stephen's Green, map 4 E5* ☎ *(01) 6760261* Ⓕ *680101*) hold auctions of paintings, furniture and silver on certain Wednesdays. It is a fascinating place to browse during viewing hours the day before the auction.

**Taylor de Veres** (*35 Kildare St., map 4 E4* ☎ *(01) 6768300*) hold regular auctions of Irish art approximately every three months. There are three days of viewing before the auctions, which are usually held on a Tuesday.

## BOOKSTORES

Dublin has many delightful bookstores and good second-hand ones that are best for browsing in. Good places to try are **The Winding Stair** (see EATING AND DRINKING, page 187) and **Books Upstairs** *(25 Market Arcade, South Great George's St., map 4D4 ☎ (01) 6710064).*

Other good bookstores are:

- **Creene & Co.** In Clare St. *(map 4D5)*, with its barrows outside where people browse and where, as well as holding general stock, they sell books of Irish interest and second-hand books.
- **Eason's** 40-42 Lower O'Connell St., map 4C4 ☎ (01) 8733811, which is also a publisher.
- **Fred Hanna** 27/29 Nassau St., map 4D5 ☎ (01) 6771255, which has a fine store of posters and old postcards.
- **Hodges Figgis** 41 Dawson St., map 4D5 ☎ (01) 6774754, which stocks a comprehensive list of books on Ireland and will endeavor to get any book you want.
- **Waterstone's** 7 Dawson St., map 4D5 ☎ (01) 791415, efficient and agreeable.
- For specialist Irish-interest bookstores, see READING, page 88.

## CRYSTAL

**Waterford Crystal** is a famous product, and does not vary in price from shop to shop. There are many other types of crystal on sale, including Tyrone Crystal and Derry Crystal. The main issue in choosing is the design, and some are much better than others.

There is some wonderful old Irish glass to be found in antiques stores, and again the design is crucial, only in the past it seems always to have been felicitous.

## CUTLERY

**Reads** *(Parliament St., map 4D4)* is the oldest shop in Dublin, occupied since the 17thC by a firm of cutlers who in former days were sword-makers to Dublin Castle.

## DEPARTMENT STORES

The big department stores each have their own distinctive flavor and price range, depending on location as much as tradition. The best department store in Dublin is **Brown Thomas & Co.** *(15 Grafton St. ☎ (01) 795666, map 4D4),* which sells everything from food to high fashion from all over the world.

This excellent store is one of the two best places for Irish fashion, especially in the section called **Private Lives**, its store-within-a-store, where some of the best names in Irish and international fashion have outlets. These include **Michelina Stacpoole** and the brilliant **Paul Costello**, who for years has been dressing women in his own distinctive look, one that might give Armani a touch of envy.

There is an **Italian Designer Room**, which stocks many of the best-known designers from Italy, such as **Genny**, **MaxMara** and many more. The famous old establishment, **Callaghans**, which sells everything for riding except the horse, is also there. Other Brown Thomas delights are the scrumptious **Food Hall**, and its fine **linen department**, with good Irish linen.

The other department stores are **Switzers**, opposite **Brown Thomas** in Grafton St. (long one of Ireland's most prestigious stores but now owned by an English chain), **Arnotts** of Henry St. and **Clery's** of O'Connell St. These last two are N of the Liffey and are traditional Dublin stores; they are much more budget-conscious than those S of the river. Everybody knows what to meet "UCC" means — Under Clery's Clock. (Clery's, a fine building with an interesting facade, was designed by Ashlin and Coleman to replace the old Clery's warehouse destroyed in the Rising.)

## FASHION

Some Irish designers have become internationally famous, including the legendary **Sybil Connolly** *(71 Merrion Sq. ☎ (01) 6767281, map 4 E6)*, who is still the doyenne. Some ballgowns and long skirts are available in her showroom, but her forte is *haute couture*.

**Pat Crowley** *(3 Molesworth Place., off Molesworth St. ☎ (01) 6615580, map 4 D5)* makes delectably elegant daywear, as well as drop'em dead party dresses and lovely lace blouses. Prices are in the upper range.

**Ib Jorgensen** *(29 Molesworth St. ☎ (01) 6619758, map 4 D5)* has been a leader of Irish fashion for years and has a following of devotees, who love his elegant suits, his understated evening clothes and the chic classic line that is his trademark. Haute couture and ready-to-wear are available at his Molesworth St. shop.

**Richard Lewis** concentrates on cut and fit, the flare of the line, and draping. He uses clinging fabrics that skim the figure. His couture range is available from **Brown Thomas** and his prêt à porter range is available under the **Hand Writing** label from major branches of **A Wear**. His salon is at 26, South Frederick St. *(just off Dawson St., map 4 D5 ☎ (01) 6797016)*.

**Thomas Wolfangel** is an established designer who uses Irish tweeds and leather to make distinctive clothes, both couture and ready-to-wear, for men and women. His salon is at 158 Pembroke Rd., opposite the American Embassy *(map 1 C3 ☎ (01) 6604069)*.

**Kennedy and McSharry** *(19 Nassau St. ☎ (01) 6778770, map 4 D5)* are an old-established (1890) firm of bespoke tailors with devoted clients, including some who come from London to have their tweed suits made here. Their cashmere sweaters for men are bought by canny women.

### Young Irish designers

**The Design Centre** *(Powerscourt Townhouse Centre, Clarendon St., map 4 D4 ☎ (01) 6795718)* is the showcase for young Irish fashion, and among the talented designers who have their outlets here are:

- **Mariad Whisker**, who designs clothes with an original unstructured look that still retains shape.
- **Louise Kennedy**, who has won many prizes for her suits and makes clothes for Mrs Robinson, President of Ireland, including those she wore on the day she was sworn in.
- **Lainey Keogh**, who designs sweaters in cotton, wool and crochet that are sold in many shops in Europe. Many of her designs are based on Celtic themes.
- **Mary Gregory**, who has a subtle and clever way with Irish linen, which she uses for her suits, trousers and dresses with their chic international look.
- **Francobolli**, who designs avant garde knitwear, often using chenille, with his distinctive motif of flowers around the neck.
- **Tony Close**, an excellent tailor, who specializes in well-cut suits and separates.
- **Edel MacBride**, a new young designer with great flair, particularly obvious in her shawls, scarves, sweaters and traditional Irish woolens given a new twist.
- **Michael Mortell** is an inventive and stylish designer with a knowledge of how to make women look good. His raincoats have become a staple item in many Irish women's wardrobes. His clothes are available in **Firenze** in the **Westbury Mall** *(Balfe St., map 4D4)*, and his coats are also available in the coat department of **Brown Thomas & Co.** (see DEPARTMENT STORES) and central **A Wear** stores.

### Fashionable alternatives

**A Wear** stores are highly recommended for their value and style by smart women who go in to pull the best of their stock *(branches in Grafton St., map 4D4 and Henry St., map 4C4)*.

The fact is that all over Dublin you will find shops selling good clothes for men and women. Look out for the work of **Quinn and Donnelly**, who are especially good at using different knitted fabrics. Their label again is to be found at A Wear stores. One of the best-kept secrets is the quality of the underwear at the **Penneys** *(Mary St., map 4C4)* chain store. This is where many Dublin women shop for well-cut undies, at half the price of comparable ones in more expensive stores.

In the **Donnybrook Mall** in the suburbs, you will find **Marian Gale**, a shop with an imaginative range of wonderful evening clothes.

### Footwear

Dubliners seem to be mad about shoes. There are countless shoe stores all over the city, and Grafton St. is like Imelda Marcos's dream. **Thomas Patrick** in Grafton St. has a wide range of shoes in different skins and leathers, with a Bruno Magli room upstairs. Next door, **Fitzpatricks** has a wide range of fashion shoes.

**The Natural Shoe Store**, which would not be Imelda's thing at all, is at 25 Drury St. *(map 4D4 ☎ (01) 6714978)*.

For something really special, **Tutty's** *(Powerscourt Townhouse Centre,* *map 4D4* ☎*(01) 6796566)* have been making made-to-measure shoes for over 50 years. They make a personal last for each customer; a pair of brogues is about IR£180 and classic riding boots IR£300.

## Knitwear

Dublin has always been famous for its knitwear, particularly the traditional Aran sweaters. The same sweater can cost a third less in Dublin than in European and American shops. Among the many specialists are:

*   **Blarney Woollen Mills** 21/23 Nassau St., map 4D5 ☎(01) 6710068
*   **Dublin Woollen Co.** Ormond Quay, map 3D3
*   **The Irish Scene** Powerscourt Townhouse Centre, Clarendon St., map 4D4 ☎(01) 794061

## FOOD STORES

Most fish stores will post a side of salmon overseas. Good examples include:

*   **Hanlons Ltd.**    20/21 Moore St., map 4C4 ☎(01) 8733011/8733017
*   **McConnell & Nelson Ltd.**    38 Grafton St., map 4D4 ☎(01) 6774344

**Cavistons** *(59 Glasthule Rd.* ☎ *(01) 2809120),* just out of the city, at Blackrock, makes the best soda bread in Dublin. Good smoked salmon, Irish cheddar cheese, and a mouthwatering selection of shellfish are other reasons for making the trip.

The best sausages in Dublin are reputed to come from **Mogerleys** *(104 South Circular Rd., Leonard's Corner).*

Brilliant food is cooked by an inventive and talented chef, Sarah Webb, in her little open stall at **The Gallic Kitchen** *(Mother Redcap's Market, 40/48 Back Lane, map 3D3* ☎ *(01) 6761872).* One of the best cheese places in Dublin, with a full range of Irish cheeses, as well as much other homegrown food direct from the Irish countryside, is **Ryefield Foods** (also in Mother Redcap's Market).

## HAIR AND BEAUTY PARLORS

*   **Robert Chambers**, 31 South Anne St., map 4D4 ☎(01) 6719755.
*   **Cherry Coogan** has a beauty parlor and hairdressing salon in the SHELBOURNE hotel ☎(01) 6766471.
*   **Dillons Hair Studio**, South Frederick St., map 4D5 ☎(01) 679726/7.
*   **David Marshall**, 6 Dawson St., map 4D5 ☎(01) 6770106, 711594, has two hairdressing salons, one for women, the other for men.
*   **Tatlers Hair and Beauty Parlor**, Upper Baggot St. ☎(01) 6602845.

Two other good hairdressers are **Pzazz** *(* ☎ *(01) 794194, 794183)* in the Powerscourt Townhouse Centre *(map 4D4)* and **Reds** *(* ☎ *(01)*

*6791596)* in Dawson St. *(map 4 D5)*, where you will be attended to by young, stylish hairdressers. Both these salons have recommended colorists.

**South Street Barber Shop** *(14 South Frederick St., map 4 D5* ☎ *(01) 6795351)* is where men in Dublin who care about their appearance go for their hair cuts; it is terribly busy, considering.

### INTERIORS

- **The Furniture Gallery** *(12 Parliament St., map 4 D4* ☎ *(01) 6719345)* designs, manufactures and sells modern Irish furniture.
- **Van Dam & Co.** *(38 Dame St., map 4 D4* ☎ *(01) 6799053)* is a seductively chintzy interior design and furniture store, one of the very few in Dublin with international chic. It sells pretty, small *objets d'art* and decorative prints and fabrics.

### MUSIC AND RECORDINGS

**Claddagh Records** *(2 Cecilia St., map 4 D4* ☎ *(01) 6770262)* is a dark, intimate little shop that stocks a comprehensive catalog of Irish records from all over: American-Irish, Canadian-Irish as well as Irish-Irish, plus reggae, soul, blues, jazz. If you want it and it's ethnic, they generally have it. Knowledgeable staff.

**Walton's Musical Galleries** *(North Frederick St., map 4 B4* ☎ *(01) 8747805)* is a Dublin institution, selling musical instruments, sheet music and Irish ballads.

### POTTERY AND JEWELRY

Pottery and jewelry are good buys in Ireland. Silversmiths like **Patrick Flood** *(Powerscourt Townhouse Centre, map 4 D4* ☎ *(01) 6794256)* are part of an Irish tradition. **Weldons of Dublin** *(55 Clarendon St., map 4 D4* ☎ *(01) 6771638)* are specialists in antique Irish silver and antique jewelry.

Pottery has long been a skill in Ireland, changing all the time. The new pottery by **Simon Pearce** or the **Shanagarry Pottery**, or **spongewear** mugs and plates, for example, are much loved as gifts. Work by **Sonia Landweer** is into another realm — her jewelry and pottery are works of art. Examples of all of these can be found at the **Kilkenny Centre** *(Nassau St.* ☎ *(01) 6777066, map 4 D5)*.

### STAMPS

**Michael Giffney**, 39 Lower Ormond Quay, map **3** D3 ☎ (01) 370859.

# Recreation

## Sports and activities

Dublin and its surroundings offer any number of activities, for those who want to do something more strenuous than looking around the city. Below is a selection.

### BEACHES
There are sandy, safe beaches N of Dublin at **Dollymount** ($3\frac{1}{2}$ miles from the city), **Claremount** (9 miles), **Sutton** (7 miles), **Portmarnock** (9 miles), **Donabate** (13 miles) and **Malahide** (9 miles).

To the S of Dublin, there are good beaches at **Merrion** and **Sandymount**, both about 3 miles from Dublin.

### BEAGLING
Contact **Kerrs Beagles and Riding Centre**, Bishop's Hill, Ballymore, Eustace, Co. Kildare ☎(045) 64201.

### BOWLING
The best-known Bowling Alley in Dublin is the **Stillorgan Bowl**, with 24 ten-pin bowling lanes. Open daily from 10am. Regular buses from the city center: 46A, 84 and 63.

### CANALS AND RIVERS
Ireland has nearly 600 miles of navigable rivers, canals and lakes. On the way to Sandymount is **Ringsend Basin**, the gateway to the **Grand Canal**, which is gradually being restored all the way to Mullingar in the West Midlands.

The Office of Public Works has opened **The Grand Canal Visitor Centre**, an interpretive center at Ringsend Basin. It illustrates the social history of the canal, and what an extraordinary feat it was to build these canals and basins in the 1790s.

The Ringsend Basin is a good place for water sports. The restoration of the area has been planned with the long-term aim of turning it into a center for water sports and other recreational amenities.

Some contacts for more information on Ireland's waterways:

- **The Inland Waterway Association of Ireland**   Stone Cottage, Claremount Rd., Killiney, Co. Dublin ☎(01) 2852258
- **Irish Boat Rental Association**   55 Braemor Rd., Churchtown ☎(01) 987222
- **Office of Public Works**   Waterways Division, 51 St Stephen's Green ☎(01) 6613111
- **Waterways Division**   Office of Public Works, St Stephen's Green ☎(01) 6613111, ext. 2597

## EQUESTRIANISM

Ireland provides marvelous riding opportunities, too numerous to mention here. Two addresses to contact for information are the **Association of Irish Riding Establishments (AIRE)** *(Daffodil Lodge, Eadestown, Naas, Co. Kildare ☎(01) 955990)* and the **Equestrian Federation of Ireland** *(Ashton House, Castleknock ☎(01) 387611)*. Or simply consult the telephone directory.

## FISHING

There is no closed season for coarse fishing. Sea angling is possible all the year round. **Sea-trout** fishing runs approximately from May to October; **brown trout** angling begins in mid-February and ends in September; the **salmon** season opens on New Year's Day on some rivers and continues until the end of August. Permits and licenses are required, and may be obtained locally or booked with your vacation.

### Fishing licenses

Game anglers require a license for both salmon and sea trout fishing, although only one is needed for both. Licenses are available from the **Central Fisheries Board** *(Balnagowan House, Mobhi Rd., Glasnevin ☎(01) 379206)*, from the appropriate **Regional Fishing Board**, and from various tackle stores. Some salmon fishing is free or available at a nominal charge, but almost all sea-trout fisheries are under private or club control. Contacts:

- **The Irish Federation of Sea Anglers**   67 Windsor Drive, Monkstown, Co. Dublin ☎(01) 2806873/2806901.
- **Irish Trout Fly Fishing Association**   26 St Margarets Rd., Malahide, Co. Dublin ☎(01) 84501911.
- **National Coarse Fishing Federation of Ireland**   43 Shanliss Rd., Santry ☎(01) 6711020/843823.

### Fresh water

The **River Liffey** provides fair salmon and good trout fishing, but fishing rights are generally held by clubs. It is surprisingly easy to fish. Buy a state salmon license from any good anglers' store, and a district license. Helpful shops are **Watts Bros Ltd** *(18 Ormond Quay, map 3D3 ☎(01) 6788574)* and **Rory's Fishing Tackle** *(17a Temple Bar, map 4D4 ☎(01) 6772351)*.

It also holds good pike and perch. For spring salmon the best months are from February to May; the best stretches for brown trout are between Celbridge and Millicent Bridge, near Clane (12 miles W of Dublin).

The **Dublin Trout Angler's Association** exercises fishing rights over much of this water as well as at Sallins and Leixlip. They also have rights on the **River Tolka** (brown trout), which has good fishing in its lower portions, and on the **Poulaphouca** and **Leixlip** lake reservoirs.

### Sea angling

This is an all-year-round sport offering much variety, depending on the time of year. Recommended centers in the environs of Dublin include **Howth**, **Skerries** and **Dun Laoghaire**. Anglers are asked to return as many fish as possible alive to the water.

The Bord Failte booklet *Sea Angling in Ireland* gives details of bait, boats, maps and festivals. It is available from any Irish Tourist Office, or by post from **The Irish Tourist Board Literature Dept.** *(PO Box 1083, Dublin 8* ☎ *(01) 8747733 for price information).* Ask for Bord Failte Information Sheets Nos. 41, 42 and 43 on sea, coarse and game angling respectively.

## GAELIC GAMES

**Gaelic football** and **hurling** are the great rural pastimes on Sunday afternoons in Ireland. The intercounties matches always inspire fanatical enthusiasm among their followers, and the All-Ireland Finals in September bring the country to a standstill. The National League Finals are played in May. At almost any match you can see why Ireland's footballers play in major clubs all over the world.

The **Gaelic Athletic Association** (GAA) ( ☎ *(01) 363222)* is the governing body for Gaelic games; its headquarters are at **Croke Park**, where most of the important matches are played. The GAA has been reproached for being too purist in its approach, but it has kept the games thriving in every sense.

Croke Park has two stands, both considered good (if and when you can get tickets). Of the terraced areas, **Hill 16** is famous for its atmosphere; an afternoon there brings you right into the heart of Dublin at play.

## GOLF

The following golf clubs are within easy reach of the city center.
*   **18-hole Courses**   Castle Golf Club, Rathfarnham, 4 miles; Clontarf Golf Club, $2\frac{1}{2}$ miles; Donabate, 13 miles; Dun Laoghaire, 7 miles; Elm Park, $3\frac{1}{2}$ miles; Grange, Rathfarnham, 6 miles; Hermitage, Lucan, $7\frac{1}{4}$ miles; Howth, 9 miles; Island, Malahide, 9 miles; Milltown, $4\frac{1}{2}$ miles; Newlands, Clondalkin, 6 miles; Portmarnock, 9 miles; Royal Dublin, Dollymount, 3 miles; Woodbrook, near Bray, $11\frac{1}{2}$ miles; Slade Valley, Saggart, 9 miles.
*   **9-hole Courses**   Balbriggan, 20 miles; Carrickmines, $8\frac{1}{2}$ miles; Foxrock, 6 miles; Killiney, 9 miles; Lucan 8 miles; Malahide, 9 miles;

Rathfarnham, $4\frac{1}{2}$ miles; Rush, 19 miles, Skerries, 18 miles; Sutton, 7 miles.

For further information, contact **The Golfing Union of Ireland** *(Glencar House, Eglinton Rd., Donnybrook* ☎*(01) 2694111)*, or the **Irish Ladies Golf Union** *(1 Clonskeagh Rd.* ☎*(01) 2696444)*.

### Pitch and putt

There are numerous pitch and putt courses around the city. Details from the **Dublin Tourist Office**.

## GREYHOUND RACING

Many of the Irish are fanatical about greyhound racing. A leading spectator sport (it attracts more than one million patrons annually), it is held in the **Shelbourne Park Stadium** *(Ringsend, map 1 C3)* on Monday, Wednesday and Saturday at 8pm and at **Harold's Cross** on Tuesday and Thursday at 8pm.

You will often see the greyhounds being walked with their owners and trainers on country roads.

## GYMS AND EXERCISE CENTERS

- **Digges Lane Dance Studios**    Digges Lane, map 4D4  ☎(01) 4784288.
- **Litton Lane Dance Studios**    2 Litton Lane, map 4C4  ☎(01) 8728044.
- **Slender Health Studios**    6 Lower Kilmacud Rd., Stillorgan, map 2E4  ☎(01) 2886871.

## HORSE RACING

Regular meetings are held at **Leopardstown**, six miles from Dublin. Other main racing centers are **The Curragh** (29 miles), at which all the Classic Races are run, and **Naas**, Co. Kildare (32 miles). Annual meetings, which are as much family outings and social gatherings as race meetings, take place in May at **Punchestown**, Co. Kildare (3 days) and Easter at **Fairyhouse**, Co. Meath (3 days).

## HUNTING

Much of Co. Dublin and the neighboring counties of Meath, Kildare and Wicklow are excellent hunting country. The following hunts meet twice or three times weekly: **Ward Union Staghounds**, **Kildare Foxhounds**, **Meath Foxhounds**, **Bray Harriers**, **Fingal Harriers**, **Naas Harriers** and **South County Dublin Harriers**.

## RUGBY UNION

Parts of the population of Dublin are rugby mad. **Lansdowne Road** is the headquarters of Irish rugby and is also the venue for matches played in the Five Nations Championship, including the Triple Crown.

The "Internationals" are played during January, February and March. Stand tickets for home games are difficult to obtain (though that's what makes good hall porters good). If you succeed in obtaining one, you'll have been carried away to another place altogether.

Details of matches are available in daily newspapers, or you can contact the **Irish Rugby Football Union** *(62 Lansdowne Rd.* ☎ *(01) 6684601).*

## SAILING

The oldest yacht club in the world is in Ireland — the **Royal Cork Yacht Club**, founded in 1720. Dublin Bay is one of Ireland's great sailing centers, and has some venerable clubs of its own, including the **Royal Irish Yacht Club**, the **National Yacht Club**, the **Royal St George Yacht Club** and the **Dun Laoghaire Motor Yacht Club**. There are also yacht clubs at Howth, Sutton, Malahide, Swords, Rush, Skerries and Clontarf.

Further information can be obtained from the **Irish Yachting Association** *(3 Park Rd., Dun Laoghaire* ☎ *(01) 2800239).*

Dinghy sailing and keelboat sailing are popular. Contact Bord Failte for details.

Yachts or dinghies may be brought into Ireland for a temporary period without liability for tax or duty. Owners of seagoing yachts must apply to the Harbour Masters of all ports in which they wish to anchor. On arrival at the first port of entry, the flag "Q" should be shown. You should then make contact with a Customs and Excise Officer, or with a Garda.

A full-time secretariat is available to give further information to visiting yachtsmen. Further information from the **Irish Yachting Association** *(3 Park Rd., Dun Laoghaire* ☎ *(01) 2800239).*

Other useful addresses to contact are:
- **Irish Association of Sail Training**   Confederation House, Kildare St. ☎(01) 6779801
- **Irish Cruising Club**   Cairngorm, Baily, Co. Dublin ☎(01) 2884783

## SWIMMING

There are numerous swimming places along the coast both N and S of Dublin. There are public (outdoor) pools at **Blackrock**, **Clontarf** and **Dun Laoghaire** *(open June-Sept).*

## TENNIS

Some hotels and guesthouses have tennis courts, but otherwise only public courts are available.

For advice on finding a court, contact **The Lawn Tennis Association** *(22 Upper Fitzwilliam St.* ☎ *(01) 6606332).*

## WALKING

There are wonderful walks within and outside Dublin. **Dublin Tourism** publishes pamphlets on walking trails inside Dublin that are interesting and comprehensive. They go under such names as the Georgian Heritage Trail, the Old City Trail and the Rock'n'Stroll Trail, which follows the haunts and associations of famous rock and traditional Irish musicians. (See page 26 for further details.)

Outside Dublin the most beautiful walk is the **Wicklow Way**, which stretches for 70 miles, although there are shorter walks within the trail (see EXCURSIONS, page 231). Further information is available from **Bord Failte**, who publish a guide to the Way.

Another source of useful information is **An Oige (Irish Youth Hostel Information)** *(39 Mountjoy Sq., map 4B5* ☎ *(01) 304555* Fx *(01) 305808)*.

It is possible to hire a guide to show you Dublin and its environs for any length of time, either for groups or individuals. Guides are available in most languages including Russian and Japanese. Tourist information (Bord Failte) have names of recommended agencies. Several useful contacts (though there are more than we can list) are given at the end of WALKING TOURS near the top of page 27.


## WINDSURFING

Windsurfing is becoming a popular sport in Ireland, and the Atlantic swells on the west coast of Ireland provide international competitors with heavy thrills. Dublin's water is less of a challenge, but good for enthusiasts, whatever their level of experience. See Bord Failte information sheet No. 35, or contact the following organizations:

- **Glenans Irish Sailing Centre**    28 Merrion Sq. ☎(01) 6611481
- **Irish Boardsailing Association** or **Irish Windsurfing Class Association**    c/o Irish Yachting Association, 3 Park Rd., Dun Laoghaire, Co. Dublin ☎(01) 2800239

# Excursions

## Make haste slowly

There is such an abundance of things to do and see within a short journey from Dublin that one is spoiled for choice. From the beginning, give yourself time. East to west, it can take only three hours to drive. But in those three hours you've missed the spirit of Ireland. And even with a planned itinerary, on the way to your chosen main destination you often find you are passing up things well worth a visit; it is often in the unplanned visit, the impulse, that one finds the most memorable things.

Among the most wonderful objects I ever saw in Ireland were in a roofless church at Kilfenora, in the west of Ireland. Simply as a result of wandering in one early morning on my way to the Burren, I happened upon two small effigies, like Cycladic sculptures, resting modestly, demurely, as they had done for at least a thousand years, on each side of a great open arched window, which, though it was missing its glass, was filled with the stained colors of a blue and cloudy June sky.

Always leave room for a wander. And plan to return to Dublin by a different route, since this will nearly always lead to further imperatives, and certainly give you a different perspective on the city and its environs.

Half the point of traveling anywhere in Ireland is the scenery on the way and the look of the place. There is no point in racing along to fulfil a schedule when around every corner there is a view that makes you want to stop, or a bit of social history either from the past or in the making, even if it's only in the form of two teenager hitchhikers, *not* sticking their thumbs into the onrush of air, but with clasped hands *beseeching* you for a lift. And driving anywhere near water in Ireland, changes the light so much that it is sad not to savor the moisture-filtered light, the curious greeny-gray sift of the air. Driving fast through villages and towns is not only antisocial — you miss what makes them unique, so slow down.

It is rare that you will find anywhere crowded. Compared to other countries, even Ireland's most popular tourist sites suffer less from the inbuilt paradox that the more symbolic or representative of a country any given sight is, the more people will flock to see it, and so the less will be its chances of remaining true to what it originally signified.

All the same, when you are doing the tourist route, remember that this is where people live. A writer who lives in Wicklow once made the observation that "those on the picturesque tour like today's travellers who prefer to ignore the dingy reality of Wicklow's country towns and

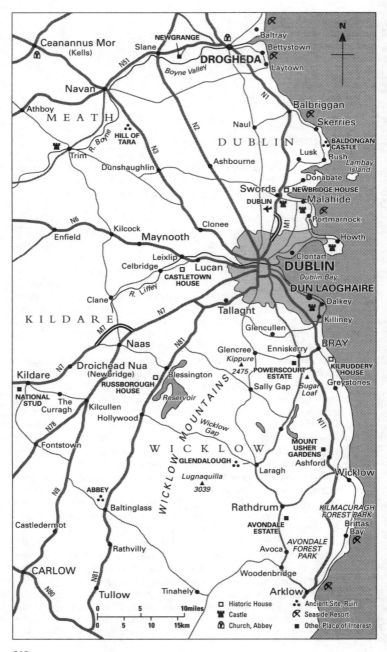

N

Ceanannus Mor (Kells)
Slane
NEWGRANGE
DROGHEDA
Baltray
Bettystown
Laytown
Boyne Valley
N51
N1
Navan
N2
Balbriggan
Athboy
MEATH
Naul
DUBLIN
Skerries
BALDONGAN CASTLE
HILL OF TARA
R. Boyne
N3
Lusk
Rush
Lambay Island
Trim
Ashbourne
Dunshaughlin
Donabate
Swords
NEWBRIDGE HOUSE
Malahide
DUBLIN
Portmarnock
N6
Kilcock
Clonee
N1
Enfield
Maynooth
Howth
Leixlip
Celbridge
Lucan
CASTLETOWN HOUSE
Clontarf
DUBLIN
Clane
R. Liffey
Dublin Bay
DUN LAOGHAIRE
KILDARE
N7
Tallaght
Dalkey
Killiney
Naas
M7
N81
Glencullen
Glencree
Enniskerry
BRAY
Kippure
2475
POWERSCOURT ESTATE
KILRUDDERY HOUSE
Kildare
N7
Droichead Nua (Newbridge)
RUSSBOROUGH HOUSE
Blessington
Sally Gap
Sugar Loaf
Greystones
NATIONAL STUD
The Curragh
Reservoir
W I C K L O W   M O U N T A I N S
Kilcullen
Hollywood
Wicklow Gap
MOUNT USHER GARDENS
N78
Fontstown
W I C K L O W
GLENDALOUGH
Ashford
Lugnaquilla
3039
Laragh
Wicklow
N9
ABBEY
Baltinglass
RATHDRUM
KILMACURAGH FOREST PARK
Castledermot
AVONDALE ESTATE
Brittas Bay
Rathvilly
Avoca
AVONDALE FOREST PARK
CARLOW
N81
Woodenbridge
N60
Tullow
Tinahely
Arklow

| | 0 | 5 | 10miles |
| 0 | 5 | 10 | 15km |

☐ Historic House    ∴ Ancient Site, Ruin

♟ Castle    ⚔ Seaside Resort

⛪ Church, Abbey    ■ Other Place of Interest

bungalow blight, were seldom much concerned with the reality of life for the majority of the country's inhabitants; their attitude to the landscape was exclusively aesthetic — an attitude that is in itself blameless so long as it isn't founded on an insensitivity to needs other than one's own."

Driving through these valleys and mountains, you will make your own discoveries. No guide book could cover all there is to see, or do more than scratch the surface of the old history or the new life. And, of course, no guide book can reveal the real pleasure of traveling in such places, which is the encounters with the people who live and work here, nor the pleasures of stopping off in a pub or hotel or bar that turns out to be delightful, and which you have come upon by yourself.

On a more sober note, remember when crossing fields to a public monument owned by the Office of Public Works or listed in a guide such as this that the land on which it stands may well be private, and landowners may refuse or restrict access over the land.

## THE DUBLIN REGION

The **Dublin Mountains** are part of the **Wicklow Mountain range** and lie remarkably close to the city, holding it in a lovely intimate embrace. As close as ten miles to St Stephen's Green lies their rugged scenery, spectacular in its changing beauty, now part of a national park.

There are three distinct regions within reach of the city center, and many excursions that can easily be done either in the course of a morning or a day. There are good hotels along the routes, if you plan to spend a certain time away. And if you are driving to Cork the choice is huge.

The three areas around Dublin are the **south and southeast**, the **west** and the **north**. They all have their own distinctive air and atmosphere, as though the characteristics evoked by their names were distilled, so that traveling along the N coast, for example, one gets a much sharper, saltier feel than along the S coast: the air somehow feels saltier at **Howth Head** than it does at **Bray**.

All along **Dublin Bay** and **Killiney Bay** to the S, what used to be a series of small villages and towns are now almost linked up with one another, but they still preserve their characters and individuality. These are affluent suburban towns now, but they hardly feel like dormitory towns or conurbations. Each has a distinctive look.

You can go N along the bay as far as **Howth** and S as far as **Bray** on the DART train, getting on and off at stations. This is a smooth and trouble-free way to see the coastal area. The trains run from 6am-11.30pm, with extra trains at rush hours. You can buy a day-ticket that will take you anywhere on the line, getting on and off as often as you wish. And there is a guided tour on the DART: see page 26.

Farther afield, there are bus tours (see page 26) to the **Boyne Valley** in the north, and to the most famous sites in the hinterland of Dublin: **Avondale and the Wicklow Hills**, **Russborough**, **Powerscourt** and **Glendalough**.

Then there are specialist tours which go on pony and horse treks all through the **Wicklow Mountains**; and there are even riding tours that start at Rathcoole and finish at Glendalough, taking six days and seven nights, staying at good hotels along the way. Contact **Calliaghstown Riding Centre** *(Calliaghstown, Rathcoole, Co. Dublin ☎ (01) 589236)* for further information. There are also various focused walking opportunities: one exhilarating example is the **Kildare Way**, a signposted walk through the Bog of Allen and along the banks of the Grand Canal.

But if you wish to venture farther afield into the Wicklow Mountains, you really need a car.

The remainder of this chapter is divided into four sections: **SOUTH OF DUBLIN** (this page); **WEST OF DUBLIN** (page 239); **NORTH OF DUBLIN** (page 247); and **THE NEXT JOURNEY: SETTING OUT FOR CORK** (page 256), which is intended to give the flavor of traveling in Ireland beyond, as it were, the Pale.

Wherever possible there are telephone numbers given for places of particular interest, and it is best to phone ahead and check access and opening hours before you go. Do not assume that anywhere will be open just because you happen to drive up to it.

There are countless other excursions to make from Dublin, and the **Irish Tourist Board**, **Dublin Tourism** and **Historic Irish Tourist Houses and Gardens** will supply information about the many great sites and houses that lie within easy reach. Three useful telephone numbers outside Dublin are **Dun Laoghaire Tourist Office** ☎(01)2806984, **Wicklow Tourist Office** ☎(0404) 69117/8 and **Midlands East Tourism** ☎Mullingar (044) 48650.

The early stages of some of these excursions fall within the area of greater Dublin, the area covered by our maps **1** and **2**. The map of the Dublin Pale on page 218 provides an overview of the entire region.

# South of Dublin

The **Dublin Mountains** to the s and w are regions of outstanding beauty and are the playground for Dubliners. There are lovely views everywhere, both along the coast and on the heights of the hills, and many of the resorts have an extraordinary vital air that seems more Continental than northern.

### The southern outskirts of Dublin

As you drive out along the coast you will see how Dublin lies linked into her famous serene bay. You will see, too, the striped chimneys, like two candles on a flat cake, of the Pigeon House power station, which gets its name from the first caretaker, Pidgeon, who lived in the little wooden house built at the end of the breakwater constructed in 1755 from Ringsend out into Dublin Bay. (The name Ringsend comes from *rinn,* meaning spit or sandbank.)

**Booterstown Marsh** *(map 1 D3),* which is a fine bird sanctuary, links sea to land, and **Monkstown**, with its high terraces, merges into Black-rock, a good shopping town with a coastal park. If, via the one-way system, you divert to the right, you will find a handsome but uneasy obelisk in **Stillorgan** *(map 1 E3)*, with a grotto-like cave underneath designed by Sir Edward Pearce as a mausoleum for the Allen family around 1732. Visible from the road, it is, alas, in poor repair, and carries warning notices.

**Blackrock** *(map 2 D4)* has fine terraced houses overlooking superb sky and sea views which, with their faintly leached air of having been washed onto a backdrop, have the look of watercolors. There is a good, old granite cross in the main street, and the big new Frascati shopping center (one of the best in Dublin) is built on the site of a house where **Lord Edward Fitzgerald** once lived. The monument by the side of the main dual carriageway of straining figures supporting a black rock is by Rowan Gillespie (1986).

If on the way out from Dublin you take the coast road through Ringsend (which for a century or more was the port of Dublin), you will pass **Sandymount Strand** *(map 1 C-D3)*, a magnificent stretch of sand at low tide, with dogs and children running exultantly along the water's edge. Some of the children are "travelers" from the caravans occasionally parked illegally along the strand farther up. There is a Martello tower, with a restaurant within its walls, halfway along. The name Martello comes from the prototype in Corsica, and such towers were erected in 1804 to keep out that great Corsican Napoleon.

Beaches like these are an amazing facility to have within a few minutes' drive of the city center; no other capital city has such a unique lung. However, swimming is not recommended here.

The little park along the Sandymount Strand is where James Joyce set the tumultuous *Nausicaa* passage of *Ulysses:* two hewn sculptures mark the fictitious spot (more real to many people than the ground under their feet) where Leopold Bloom watched Gerty MacDowell lean back and show her drawers, in one of the most erotic and sly scenes in literature.

In real life, if there is such a thing in Dublin, this, too, is where James Joyce and Nora Barnacle went walking on their first arranged meeting on the evening of June 16, 1904 and where, as he said to her, "You made me a man" — the phrase covered a sexual revelation. He immortalized the day, Blooms-day, in *Ulysses* — all the events in which take place on that single day in 1904; and every year in many cities around the world, but especially in Dublin, the events of that day are re-enacted by followers of Joyce who dress up in the costumes of the time, eat the food that Leopold Bloom ate, visit the pubs he visited, in a literary pilgrimage toward the shape and meaning of a novel that for its believers has the intensity of faith.

Farther along the coast is the **James Joyce Museum** *(map 2 E5* ☎ *(01) 809265/808571 on weekdays* ☒*)* in the **Martello Tower** at **Sandycove**, where Joyce lived, again which event he immortalized in the opening chapter of *Ulysses.* The tower is one of 15 squat coastal fortifications, built between Dublin and Bray in the first decade of the 19thC as defense against the feared Napoleonic invasion: 40 feet high, with walls 8 feet thick. The entrance was 10 feet from the ground, so this was defense indeed.

The tower was rented by Oliver St John Gogarty, the Dublin wit and scholar (and later surgeon) whom Joyce immortalized, though not to

Gogarty's liking, as "stately plump Buck Mulligan." In fact Joyce only stayed at the tower for a few days before exiting in terror, fleeing from the obsession of the third occupant, one Samuel Chenevix Trench, who would keep firing pistols at imaginary enemies. Gogarty called the tower the *omphalos* because it resembled a navel, and also because he hoped it might prove "as important to the world as the navel stone at Delphi." He didn't know the half of it.

The tower has had a face-lift and contains Joycean memorabilia, including new material from the estate of his literary executor, his guitar (he had a wonderful sugary singing voice) and his cigar case, as well as letters and documents, a library of his works, related literature, original manuscripts and rare editions. This is an almost sacred place of pilgrimage for Joyce worshipers and scholars. (Incidentally, there is another Joyce museum in Dublin, the James Joyce Cultural Centre in North Great George's St. — see DAY 2, page 125.) And then there's Dublin.

Beside the tower is the famous **Forty-Foot** gentlemen's bathing place, reserved by force of tradition for male nude bathing. Now also part of the tradition is the sporadic invasion by women who know that Right is on their side: in other words, that the Sandycove Bathers Association (a.k.a the Nude Male Bathers) pay 50 pence a year, not for exclusive bathing rights but only for permission to "erect encroachment." The encroachment erectors quiver with outrage, a general free-for-all ensues, and then it's back to the status quo. The name incidentally comes not from gigantic men or even the height of the rocks, but from the gun-battery placement above, manned in the 19thC by the 40th Foot Regiment.

## Dun Laoghaire

Near the entrance to Dublin Bay is the "out-post" of Dublin, **Dun Laoghaire** *(map 2 D5)*, named after an Iron Age king whose capital was here; or else the High King whose might St Patrick defied, by lighting a pre-emptive Pascal fire at Slane before the king had kindled his own blaze at his capital, Tara, on the hill opposite. After George IV's visit (he landed at Howth, speechlessly drunk) it was renamed Kingstown. An obelisk with a big fat crown resting on four balls, all of which Thackeray vilified as hideous, commemorates his departure.

In more recent days the first railway ever built in Ireland, in 1834, linked the town with Dublin. Dun Laoghaire (pronounced Dun Laireah) has a deep-water approach and a fine harbor built by John Rennie, a Scottish engineer, between 1817 and 1852. The town promenade, esplanade and small bandstand are redolent of the days when it was an important package station and naval sanctuary.

It is still a busy ferry port and a pretty town, laid out in terraces, climbing the hills and encircling the harbor, though the symmetry and scale of the buildings is sadly and irretrievably interrupted, as is so often the case in Ireland, by modern buildings housing official bodies, such as the Fisheries Board, or branches of Irish banks. Such institutions, with the Catholic Church, seem to be the chief despoilers of Irish towns.

(The other noticeable thing is the jumble of electric wires overhead; a cobweb of wires fly and net and entangle the skyline. It is curious that they are not buried as in most other European towns; they give a vague air of dereliction to many areas of Ireland.)

Dun Laoghaire harbor is pinched by two piers tipped with lighthouses; and to walk along the East Pier, a mile in length to the lighthouse at the far end, is bracing in the extreme. The Sealink ferry docks here, and the harbor is Ireland's yachting center. There are at least four yacht clubs, so in the spring and summer it is busy with sailboats and yachts.

In the suitably named **Mariners Church** (1837) is the **National Maritime Museum of Ireland** *(Haigh Terrace ☎ (01) 2800969)*, containing nautical exhibits, models, ships, boats and relics of anything and everything to do with sailing, including a curragh from the West of Ireland. Here too is the Bailey Optic, the mariner's light that shone for over 70 years from Howth Head across the bay, to where it now rests. The nave of the church is an ideal setting for the Bantry Longboat captured from the French in 1796.

### Dalkey and Killiney

A few miles s along the coast is **Dalkey** *(map 2 E5)*, originally a medieval walled village, known as the Town of Seven Castles; two now remain, the 16thC Archbold's Tower and what is now the Town Hall. George Bernard Shaw lived in Dalkey for years, in Torca Cottage, but the house is not open to the public.

There is an annual August festival of the crowning of the King of Dalkey, a revival of an old tradition originally banned for being too subversive, which is now a fine excuse for a festival celebration. A small fishing fleet sails from the harbors of Coliemore and Bullock.

Farther s is **Killiney** *(map 2 E5)*, with its wonderful bay, often compared with the Bay of Naples, when that bay was considered the most beautiful in Europe. Dalkey Island lies offshore, with its Martello tower and ruined abbey, and there are boat trips to it from Coliemore in the high season.

Killiney is a complicated, hilly series of streets and winding roads, but Killiney Hill is easily reached, by car or on foot (quite a steep climb). The monument at the summit is *Thus Daedalus Flew* by Niall O'Neill (1987). The obelisk was erected by John Mapas to provide work for the poor after the wickedly hard frosts of 1739-40. The view from here on a clear day is one of life's epiphanies.

One writer, Richard Hayward, went over the top:

*From here the panorama is unobstructed in every direction, and to the northwest the great Bay of Dublin now lies below you in a majestic sweep. Due north across that bay the bold mass of Howth Head rears itself in striking contrast to the level lands of that region, and turning round to the south you will get an eyeful of the Dublin and Wicklow mountains that will make you catch your breath at the glory and wonder of it all. Eastward lies the Irish Sea, betimes roaring like a lion and anon gentle as any dove, argent and fugitive in light and shade beneath a misty sun, or bluff and blue and ridden with white horses when the winds blow the curtains*

*from the casements of heaven. And to the west is the great green
level plain of the Irish waistlands, flat and mysterious as it dissolves
into the blue haze that would carry us on to Galway and the
legendary Hy Brasil beyond in the mighty Atlantic. Indeed, Dublin
is a city girt with beauty of an opulence and variety that would be
difficult to equal and well-nigh on impossible to excel.*

This was written not in the 1840s but the 1940s.

Between it and the cliff face that falls down to the Vico Rd. is a wishing
stone, dated 1852 in Roman numerals. This is in the form of a stepped
pyramid, and lore has it that one must walk clockwise around the seven
levels, moving toward the summit and there, looking over Dalkey Bay,
one must make a wish.

On the hill are the ruins of an early Celtic church, which probably gave
the district its name, *Kill na N-Ingean,* the Church of the Daughters, the
Six Holy Virgins, Sisters or nuns of Saint Colman of Cloyne in the 6thC.
In the little church of **Holy Trinity** is the stained-glass window *Angel of
Peace* by Harry Clarke with its strange attenuated fingers and deep-set
eyes: a beautiful window commissioned as a war memorial to a young
man born in Victoria Castle, Killiney. On Marino Avenue West is **Killiney
Church**, a venerable 11thC church with interesting details and relatively
few later additions.

The huge building called **Killiney Castle** is now a hotel, and climbing
beyond this edifice one finds an area rewarding to walk through. It is a
place with a curiously atavistic Edwardian air. Ancient huge houses,
half-derelict-looking buildings totter at the top of hills. On the streets that
spiral around the descending hills are pretty houses, half glimpsed
behind walls, through wrought-iron gates and laurel hedges. One half
expects to hear the clip clop of horses, carriages, men in livery hurrying
on errands. Instead of which it is curiously deserted, considering that it
is one of the most desirable suburbs to live in.

### Bray, Kilruddery and Greystones

From Killiney the roads are good but busy, to Bray and Greystones,
busy residential resorts with fine views and esplanades.

**Bray** (from the Irish word meaning *Sudden Hill* ) has been called the
Gateway to Wicklow, and Wicklow is an astonishingly beautiful and
varied county for any gate to swing open on. Sheila Wingfield, Lady
Powerscourt, chatelaine during the 1930s and '40s of one of Wicklow's
greatest houses, Powerscourt (indeed, one of the world's great palaces),
once wrote:

*Ireland always looks its best at sunrise or dusk. Early light on an
empty crossroads in Co. Wicklow made even Maguire's Bar and
Saloon appear all innocence and gold.*

There aren't many empty crossroads any more, but there is much
innocence and gold as you drive from view to view in this country of
treasures and beauty.

Bray's chief feature besides dips and hills, astonishingly busy main streets and ungainly, ill-designed shopping centers, is a mile-long esplanade leading toward **Bray Head** with its wide and splendid view from the summit. (When as children we climbed the winding road to the top, it was called the Great White Way, but I have not heard it so called lately.)

In Bray at No. 1 Martello Terrace lived the family of James Joyce before they began their downward peregrinations (the house is not open to visitors.) In the Main St. is the handsome old Town Hall (built in 1881 by Lord Brabazon) and shopping center, with a restaurant, art gallery and craft center. The fire station at the rear has been converted into a Market Court with shops and offices. In Bray too is the **National Aquarium**, which has hundreds of species of fish, and where research on aquatic life is carried out. The **Heritage Centre** of Bray *(☎ (01) 2862539)* is in the newly restored, handsome Old Court House opposite St Paul's Church.

There is a long walk to **Greystones** along the cliffs, and bisecting the horizon are the Sugar Loaf mountains with their unique shape, which appear in so many views of the area and which give the backdrop to so many vistas. (Again, as children we believed that these were extinct volcanoes, but in fact they are quartzite cones.)

Two miles w of Bray is the **Dargle Glen**, a famous beauty spot where the river Dargle leaps and runs in a series of small cascades. There are scenic picnic places signposted to a fault here, and the **Dargle Glen Gardens**, open all year round.

Between Bray and Greystones are the gardens of **Kilruddery House** *(☎ (01) 2863405)*, seat of the Earl of Meath; this is a grand and formal garden, with its 500-foot twin canals, wonderful statuary and fine borrowed views in a romantic setting. There are occasional seminars on great gardens in Europe and learned gardeners here, but numbers are very limited *(contact Persephone FitzGerald ☎ (01) 2803306/2843558)*.

For centuries Wicklow was woody and wild, with uncultivated land, valleys and mountains, secretive and untamed. It was natural and native, and metaphorically important as a wilderness. There is a well-known anonymous painting dated 1780 of the Kilruddery Hunt, its huntsmen in the livery, the hounds bred for the chase, in front of Kilruddery House, its formal garden spread around, dominating, out of all proportion, the wilderness, the outside landscape suitably tamed and naturalized, by the authority of the Big House. It is a fine symbol of The Pale. Such estate-making happened all over Wicklow; and history being what it is, we now pass the shells and ruins of such houses, with nature climbing back in.

### Ashford, Wicklow and Arklow

From here the scenic route s leads to **Ashford**. About two miles NW of the town, and well signposted, is **The Devil's Glen**, a wooded chasm two miles long where the Vartry leaps and tumbles 75 feet down the gorge into the **Devil's Punchbowl**. The paths and walks reveal more and more splendid views, all well marked. The tourist board seems obviously concerned that we might all get lost in the satanic clutches. The name is a Victorian invention and comes from susceptible swooning ladies who found its dark and brooding aspect deliciously sinister.

On a sunny day it seems more heavenly than hellish. (For a view that describes exactly why it is named so, look at the painting in the National Gallery of *The View of the Devil's Glen* by James Arthur O'Connor, the best artistic chronicler of the sights of Wicklow.)

As you drive southward toward Ashford the road passes by **Mount Usher** *(☎ (0404) 840205),* another superb garden. Parts of this low-lying area are a paradise for gardeners, as plants that normally are too tender to withstand northern frosts flourish here, warmed by the soft airs from the ocean. The soil is generous, rich and loamy, fed by rivers and streams, so that everything grows luxuriously verdant.

The gardens, planned around an old mill on a tributary of the Vartry, were founded by the Walpole family in 1868 and remained in their care until 1980. Still privately owned, the gardens are beautifully maintained and among the most spectacular in Ireland, with over 4,000 plants, trees and shrubs spread over 20 varied acres. They are full not just of sights but of sounds, for there are hundreds of birds including waterbirds, and if you are lucky enough you may see the kingfisher do what Seamus Heaney called "rent the veil of the usual."

Edward Hymans, who wrote one of the definitive books on great Irish gardens, described this as "the most perfect example of the romantic-paradise Robinsonian garden . . . which idealizes to perfection a possible natural world." (There is a good informative booklet on this garden on sale in most bookshops in the area and in Dublin.)

**Wicklow**, 32 miles SE of Dublin, situated at the mouth of the Vartry, is the capital town of the county (which is 781 square miles in extent). St Patrick is supposed to have landed here with his companions and been driven off by the local ruler. Patrick's companion lost his teeth in the struggle and from this got his name *Mantan,* meaning toothless; there are churches to St Mantan all over Wicklow.

The 18thC Protestant church stands on the site of a medieval church and in the S porch are remnants of a 12thC Romanesque door. Nearby is the **Round Mount**, a motte that is supposed to be part of the Viking defenses.

Wicklow suffered in 1798 and there is a monument in Market Square to gallant Billy Byrne, who was executed following that terrible and violent rising. The Byrnes of Wicklow were a famous and heroic family whose fortunes were closely interwoven with that of the country. There is also a monument to Captain Halpin of the *Great Eastern,* the ship that laid the first transatlantic cable, who was born here. There are fragments of a 13thC Franciscan monastery at the W end of Main St.

The shattered ruins of the ancient **Black Castle** lie S of the harbor. Built on the earlier ruins of a 12thC castle, it was the stronghold of the Anglo-Norman ruler, Maurice FitzGerald. The fragments look as though they have been cast up from the depths of the sea.

A **Heritage Center** normally located in the Old Gaol is temporarily in the Courthouse *(☎ (0404) 67324).*

At **Wicklow Head** stands the **Wicklow Lighthouse**, a tapering octagonal six-story tower built in 1778 by John Trail. Being on a high promontory, it does not have to withstand the pounding of waves and so looks more like a folly than a practical guide to rocks and bad weather. It has been described as the most grandiose of all lighthouses in the British Isles.

There are actually three lighthouses here. After the first one was built, sailors complained that the light was obscured through half of its sweep by Wicklow Head. So a second lighthouse was planned in the government's Maritime Offices, and built, and opened, and lit, whereupon the seamen reported that although the half previously obscured was indeed now lit, the other half was correspondingly blind. At which point someone actually went to Wicklow Head and chose the site on which the grand lighthouse now stands.

Between Wicklow and Arklow is **Brittas Beach**, $2\frac{1}{2}$ miles of shiny sand backed by dunes, looking like the Hamptons in North America. The beach is often deserted on weekdays but is a playground for families for miles around on sunny weekends, which is entertainment enough in itself.

**Arklow**, 16 miles s along the coast on the R747, has a superb harbor on an almost tideless coast with wonderful beaches. It is on the estuary of the **Avoca** (or the Avonmore). Down the South Strand is **Arklow Rock**, over 400 feet high, which gives fine views in every direction.

Originally a Danish settlement (the suffix *low* means a flame, although another theory is that it is named after Aru-Kell, the Viking chieftain who founded it), Arklow is now a busy seaside town with a special place in Irish history, for it was here that Father Murphy, the leader of the 1798 rebels, was killed as he was leading a charge to try to take the town. It has a special place in modern seafaring history too, for Sir Francis Chichester's yacht in which he sailed around the world was built in a yard here that still functions. The Catholic Church is by Patrick Byrne, one of the best 19thC Dublin architects. Nearby are the ruins of a Dominican friary founded in 1264.

The **Arklow Maritime Museum** ( ☎ *(0402) 32868)* is here, and the **Arklow pottery** ( ☎ *(0402) 32401/32597)*, first founded in 1934, producing a pretty blue-and-white china that is avidly collected. The factory has now been taken over by a Japanese firm.

## Woodenbridge and Avondale

From Arklow there is an easy road leading NW to **Woodenbridge**, on the R755 and R752, where much of the gold for many of the great artifacts of Ireland's Golden Age was mined. It was also the site of a gold rush in 1795, after a nugget weighing $21\frac{1}{2}$ ounces (609 grams) was discovered.

North along the Avoca Valley is where the waters of the Avonbeg and Avonmore join, three miles N of Avoca village, at a spot supposed to have inspired the poet Thomas Moore to write the famous song *The Meeting of the Waters,* long one of the romantic anthems of Ireland. There is less to it than the song promises. "There is not in this wide world a valley so sweet / As the vale in whose bosom the bright waters meet." In fact Moore was using poetic license to a degree and when questioned about the source of the inspiration could not recall precisely where it was. The modern visitor might well have the same problem. There is a famous weaving mill here, **Avoca Weavers** ( ☎ *(0402) 35105)*, open to the public. This area was once a great copper pyrite mining center.

Toward **Rathdrum** is the **Motte** or **Motha Stone**, a glacial granite boulder perched on the top of an 800-foot hill, from which vantage point there are spectacular views. In legend this was the hurling stone belonging to the legendary giant Fionn MacCumhaill, to whom any large natural feature pertaining to the Ice-age is generally attributed, in Ireland.

There are two forest parks in the area. **Kilmacuragh Forest Park**, a wild arboretum off the N11 four miles s of Wicklow, is a quiet haven, with paths and a lake. The better-known **Avondale Forest Park** spreads over 500 acres. Once away from, literally, the beaten track, this forest too is a source of quiet pleasure. It is the old demesne of **Avondale House** *(Avondale House and Estate ☎ (0404) 46111 ▨ ▣)* and has a fine collection of trees (forestry research is carried on there).

Avondale House is where Charles Stewart Parnell was born and lived all his life with his mother (the daughter of an American admiral) and elder brother. Part of the house was built in 1779 for Samuel Hayes, an amateur architect who may have designed it himself (James Wyatt is also associated with the design of the house). Hayes planted many of the older trees. Perhaps because of hindsight and history and what we know of Charles Stewart Parnell, that unremitting giant of a man, this square, unromantic, handsome building is a most stirring place to visit. In 1991, the centenary year of his death, *Coilte Teoranta,* the Irish Forestry Board, completed a refurbishment program that restored much of the house and turned it into a museum devoted to his life and times.

### Glendalough

From Avondale it is an easy drive N via Rathdrum to one of Ireland's National Monuments, **Glendalough**, "The Valley of the Two Lakes" through which flow three small streams.

It is approached from the NE down the R755, or from the NW across the **Wicklow Gap**, the main pass over the mountains between **Hollywood** and **Glendalough**, over which looms **Tonelagee**, nearly 2,700 feet high. This was traditionally called the Madman's Road, and the saint most closely associated with the site, **St Kevin**, is reputed to have taken it on the way to found his monastery, which became a center of learning.

Hollywood itself is on the old pilgrim's road to Glendalough. Both churches in the town are dedicated to him, and a statue of the saint stands high above the village.

South of Hollywood are the **Piper's Stones**, a Bronze Age henge; a legend says they are dancers and their piper, transmogrified as a punishment for dancing on the Sabbath.

**Glendalough** *(Glendalough Monastery ☎ (0404) 45325)* is one of the most beautiful and resonant small valleys in the country. By its very nature it is meant to be a quiet place for contemplation and peace, but sometimes in high season it has more crowds than one comes to expect in Ireland. It is, all the same, a romantic place, high in the hills, with its lakes and streams and verdant broad banks and steep wooded hills encircling the clear water. Several little holy buildings of great antiquity endow the valley with an air of sanctity and significance. Lawrence O'Toole, before he became Archbishop of Dublin (aged only 34), had been an abbot here, but St Kevin was the first begetter of this place as a holy site.

St Kevin evidently had an eye for aesthetics when he chose this place as his retreat from the world in order to live a solitary life in AD545. But as is so often the way with romantic sequestered heroes, he was soon surrounded with acolytes, although it was not till after his death — reputedly at the age of 120 — that it became such a large monastic site.

He seems to have been the St Francis of Ireland, loved by all who knew him, and like St Francis is reputed to have come from a noble family, a royal Leinster tribe. One of the best-known stories associated with him is that as he was reading, with his arm outstretched on the window sill, a blackbird made a nest in the palm of his hand. When the saint finally noticed, he kept his hand in the same position until the fledglings had hatched. He was surely either very absorbed or very unobservant. The other famous legend is that he retreated here to escape the temptations of a beautiful girl called Kathleen. Women are often to blame in Ireland.

After his death the place grew in size and veneration, and although there were Viking raids from the 9thC onward, and destruction by a great fire in 1398, followed by long years of official neglect, the site is remarkably well preserved. The buildings on the upper site are simple and austere, including **Reefert Church**, where the Kings of Leinster lie buried. At the lower site are **St Kevin's Kitchen**, a 9thC high-pitched double-stone-roofed church, with a later belfry (12thC), a high **round tower** (100 feet) dating from the 11thC, and the roofless **cathedral** with its 12thC chancel and fine E window. **St Kevin's Bed** is a table-tomb a little distance away, where he is reputed to have slept in penitence. There is a little monastic poem from the 9thC which might have been written by the tender-hearted monk:

> *A wall of woodland overlooks me.*
> *A blackbird sings me a song (no lie!).*
> *Above my book, with its lines laid out,*
> *the birds in their music sing to me.*

> *The cuckoo sings clear in lovely voice*
> *in his grey cloak from a bushy fort.*
> *I swear it now, but God is good!*
> *It is lovely writing out in the wood.*

In the following centuries, religious repression caused the little monastic community to be disbanded and abandoned. In the 18thC there was a riotous annual assembly here, a mixture of piety, gaiety and slightly debauched carnival, which was suppressed by the Catholic hierarchy, who have never been famous for their sense of fun. Now there is only a spirit of reverence and rubber-necking, a collection of antiquities, and a well-run visitor center, which has an informative audiovisual program.

Glendalough is also a Nature Reserve, part of the **Wicklow Mountains National Park**, but no matter how many people come here, the site retains and preserves a beauty and piety.

What is more, there is no sense of the hand of authority over the land. Many of the famous estates and places of interest in Ireland show deliberate assertions of ownership over landscape, a celebration of the conqueror. In Glendalough, nature was part of the natural glory, a celebration of the native. The park ranges over some of the wildest and most beautiful places in Co. Wicklow, and it is hard to believe one is so close to Dublin when walking in these woods and mountains: among the wild life are deer, peregrine, falcon and ravens.

There are three Nature Trails, all well signposted, each revealing a different aspect of the valleys. The **Green Road** walk is $1\frac{1}{4}$ miles and takes between 30 and 45 minutes. The **Miners' Road** walk is $2\frac{1}{2}$ miles and takes between one and two hours. The **Poulanass Walk** is $1\frac{1}{4}$ miles and takes about 40 minutes: it is steep in parts.

It is possible to ride and trek through these mountains, staying at hotels on the way. See pages 219-20.

### The Wicklow Hills

From here one can drive out at random and find spectacular views and valleys. There are lovely drives up and down the valleys, and through the Wicklow Hills, taking in a variety of sites spanning a millennium and more.

Up to **Glendoo** mountain, for example, or to the **Glenmasole Valley** (the Thrush's Glen), cut deeply by the River Dodder, or over to **Glencullen**, where granite-quarrying over centuries has left its mark (a rock near this road marks the site of a "monster" meeting held by Daniel O'Connell in 1823), or through **Glenealo Valley**, also a nature reserve, with a population of wild deer. Near the mountain hamlet of **Stepaside** are the ruins of the 18thC Kilgobbin Church, with a 12thC granite High Cross. From here there is a drive through a dry valley known as the **Scalp**, which has spectacular views of the whole area.

Nearly four miles sw of Rathfarnham via Ballyboden and Woodtown is **Mountpelier Hill**, the site of a sporting lodge called erroneously the Hell Fire Club, founded in 1735 by those rakes and bloods of Dublin, who had nothing better to do, and renowned as the center for diabolical activities. The devil is supposed to have appeared at one of their meetings, but on the other hand the members did get blind drunk. They once set fire to the building and stayed inside to see what Hell looked like, though it has been observed that they didn't need to bother to light a fire; they should just have looked hard at one another. The building was originally designed as a shooting lodge for Speaker Conolly in 1720 (see page 240).

### Back toward Dublin

Going back via **Rathfarnham** is worthwhile; there is a massive Elizabethan castle there built in the 16thC by Archbishop Loftus, bought by Speaker Conolly in 1723 and later lived in by the "most extravagant man in Ireland," the Marquess of Ely. The interior decoration includes plasterwork by Richard West, and murals and ceiling paintings attributed to Angelica Kauffmann or Giambattista Cipriani. The building, until recently owned by the Jesuits, has been acquired by the Office of Public Works and Dublin County Council and is being fully restored, to be opened to the public.

Rathfarnham is full of history. **The Pearse Museum** ( ☎ *(01) 934208)* is here, in the restored home of the family of patriot Padraic Pearse and his brother Willie and their school, where the arms for the rebellion were kept hidden. The 1916 Uprising and accounts of Pearse's execution, as well as much of the family's photographs and documents, are on show. The museum is in **St Enda's Park**, a charming and atmospheric park with a waterfall and walled garden.

Nearby is the **Loreto Convent**, the headquarters of an order of nuns who have educated generations of Irish girls, which stands in the grounds of the Priory, the house of John Philpott Curran, the cold-hearted lawyer who refused to defend Robert Emmet and whose daughter Sarah was the love of Emmet's short and tragic life. The convent chapel has fine sculptures by John Hogan but is not generally open. (A curious barn known as **Hall's Barn** and modeled on the wonderful barn at Castletown is near here, and is a popular subject for painters.)

Near Rathfarnham is **Marlay Park** *(map 1 E2* ☎ *(01) 934059* ▣ *).* Originally the estate of the Huguenot banker David LaTouche who bankrolled so many grandees, it was recently left to the State to be used as a public amenity, and has become such, with woods, parks, gardens and walks, and a miniature railway. The stables and courtyard have been converted to a craftworkers' center with restorers, clock-makers and potters working on site. The house with its stucco work by Michael Stapleton is being restored.

**Evie Hone**, the 20thC Dublin stained-glass artist and painter, and member of a famous Irish artistic family (the two Nathaniel Hones, the Elder and the Younger, are represented by many paintings in the National Gallery), had her studio here. One of her most famous commissions was *The Crucifixion* and *Last Supper* window at Eton College Chapel (1949), near Windsor, England.

Incidentally, there is a magnificent memorial to David LaTouche, who died in 1785, by John Hickey in the church at **Delgany**, a little town in Wicklow not far away.

### The Wicklow Way

Marlay Park marks the start of the Wicklow Way, the 82-mile walk that finishes at **Clonegall** in Co. Carlow, which covers the Wicklows' eastern flanks, the largest area of unbroken high ground in Ireland and one of the most beautiful. V.S. Pritchett described them better than anyone:

> *Scarcely peopled, blueish, violet or bog-brown, red or green with bracken according to the season, golden or grassy, the Wicklow Hills change their folds at every stroke of light or cloud shadow that passes rapidly over them. The names of the hills announce the*

*mixture of native and foreign: Djouce and Mallaghcleevaun pair with War Hill and Feather Bed; Lugnaquilla with Duff and Sally Gap. Seeing them at sunset the approaching stranger ceases to live on earth.*

**Glencree**, which means "the Glen of the Cattle," is also at the head (or the foot) of the military road that runs straight N-S back to Dublin for 12 miles. These thin military roads across the hills, built at the end of the 18thC, are a sign that English Dublin was always at odds with Wilder Ireland. The barracks here, built to control the insurgents of 1798, are now a center for sectarian reconciliation and headquarters of an Irish geological survey.

An interesting paradox may strike us here. The people who built the houses and towns that we now visit to savor for their beauty, and whose attitude to landscape was aesthetic and territorial, thought nothing of placing huge barracks at strategically important points, which nevertheless were often the most naturally awesome and desolate spots. Nor did they balk at building military roads, the equivalent of motorways, through the loveliest of glens.

There is a military cemetery here, a sad thing, a kind of grotto, in which are buried the bodies of men washed ashore and airmen who crashed during World War II. The Glencree river tumbles through, and near here is the source of the Liffey at **Liffey Head Bridge**, which you have to search to find and which comes out of a hole in the side of a wall of peat. Many enthusiasts, both experienced and inexperienced walkers, do the full 70 curving and meandering miles through three counties, which lead to the mouth of the river at Dublin Bay.

**Sally Gap**, "The Gap of the Willows," is a high pass through the rugged grandeur that is so characteristic of this romantic, archetypal part of Ireland. (The word "Sally" means "willow," and one of the most popular and beautiful of the songs of Ireland is W.B. Yeats' *Down by The Sally Gardens*). On a clear day there are wonderful views.

Among them is **Lough Tay**, the stretch of water to the SE that used to be called, far more romantically, Lough Luggala, "Hollow of the Hill." The beautiful, remote Gothic house at the top of the valley is still called **Luggala**, but it may not be remote much longer, nor may these quiet hills remain so, for the powers-that-be (the Office of Public Works) are bent on opening an interpretive center to lure thousands more people here and to make provision for buses and hundreds of cars, no doubt straightening the sharper bends to help make the journey to the car park the shorter.

Just w is the huge reservoir that serves Dublin: the **Poulaphouca Waterfall** (2 miles N of Hollywood) was once a statutory tourist sight — the Niagara of Ireland — but since the building of the reservoir its 150-foot fall is much diminished. (Puca, or Pooka, a malicious sprite or imp, was said to live in the pool at the bottom of the falls.)

In the distance toward the NE is **Kippure Mountain**; and near here is the **Glen of Annamoe** and the little town of the same name, which means "the Ford of the Cows."

There is a strange and unexpected link with that great writer **Law-**

**rence Sterne**. In his autobiography he writes of how, in Annamoe, he had a wonderful escape — "Of falling through a mill-race whilst the mill was still going and of being taken out unhurt. The story is incredible — but hundreds of common people flocked to see me." Tristan Shandy would never have lived and rollicked through literature if the young Sterne had been ground down.

## Powerscourt

There are two great estates in this area, **Russborough** and **Powerscourt**, both of them superb in their different ways.

**Powerscourt** is 12 miles s of Dublin, at Enniskerry. The gates of the house are opposite the church, and a long avenue, lined with beech, leads up and past the glorious facade of what, heartbreakingly, is only a shell.

**Powerscourt Estate** *(Enniskerry ☎ (01) 2867676)* was one of the greatest houses of Ireland, built by Richard Castle for Richard Wingfield, who became Viscount Powerscourt in 1731. He used granite blocks quarried from Glencree Valley, and the views carved from the wilderness were considered some of the best in the British Isles, though the site had been chosen originally for defense purposes rather than for beauty.

This traditionally was the territory of the O'Tooles, the hereditary kings of Leinster. Dispossessed in the 11thC by the Le Poers, the O'Tooles wrenched their land back 300 years later, but Sir Richard Wingfield, an adventurer from Suffolk, became Knight Marshal of Ireland under Elizabeth I, laid claim to the land and fought it out with the O'Tooles at a place on the demesne called Killing Hollow, to gain possession of this amazing place.

There is a story that when both sides were fighting through these lovely woods and neither side wore uniforms, whenever one of O'Toole's men met a soldier whom he suspected of being the enemy, he would shout, "Say 'dog' in Irish." If the soldier could not, the answer would be "Dog yourself," followed by a swift hanging.

A portrait of Wingfield used to hang in Powerscourt; it showed an old fox of a man with coal-black eyes and a neat white beard, wearing a gauze scarf studded with jewels tied over his armor. A label on the frame read: "The Scarfe which your Majest wears is Sufficient Reward for me" — his reply to the Queen when she asked him what reward he wanted for defeating her enemies. Wily as he was, he knew full well that such an answer would call forth more rewards than had he asked outright for what he wanted, which is what he got: this wonderful demesne outside Dublin, which he then proceeded to tame.

In fact the more a great landowner could tame nature and make her obey the demands of his art, the more the territory came under his sway. Andrew Marvell wrote, "like a guard on either side, the trees before their lord divide." It was a subtle and grand form of colonization and told the very land who was master, never mind the dispossessed on the other side of the wall.

The house was glorious. Today it is just a magnificent husk, a facade with sightless windows, an open roof to the sky and to the rain. From the beginning, of course, it had been a very impractical house. There was no fireplace in the saloon, the main room of the house, for much of its long life, and so it must have been unusable for months on end.

In 1960 Lord Powerscourt sold it to the Slazenger family, and in 1962 the daughter of the family married Lord Powerscourt's son and heir, the present Viscount. They decided to open the house and embarked on a program of restoring and refurbishing. By 1974 the work was completed and the house was restored to full bloom; the Powerscourts gave a lunch party before the opening and lit a fire in the Morning Room, which had not been used for a long time. The chimney caught fire, and was, as it was thought, extinguished. That night the house burned down. It had survived so much, including a near miss in World War II when a land-mine was dropped by the Luftwaffe half a mile to the w and did not detonate. (When it finally did, a neighbor huddling near his fire for warmth was sucked halfway up the chimney by the blast.)

The loss was irreparable; one of the greatest losses to Irish heritage this century, comparable to the fire in the **Four Courts** in Dublin. Every room was rich in history as well as more tangible assets — plasterwork, marble, furniture and fine paintings.

But not only were the furniture and paintings lost. So too were the spectacular interiors: the hall, a strange, shell-encrusted room; the Egyptian Hall, 40 feet wide and high, 60 feet long, with a sumptuous ceiling; the Cedar Room; the pillars of Irish marble; the stone and plasterwork; the murals; the intrinsic decoration of one of the great palaces of Western Europe. (One thinks with longing of the fate of a comparable great house in England, Uppark, burned down one night in 1989, with restoration work begun the *following morning*.) However the terraces and gardens remain intact — for the time being — and these remain incomparable.

Powerscourt is ranked as one of the great gardens of the Western world. This is partly because of its magnificent location and plan, encompassing and drawing in the aloof Sugar Loaf mountains as part of the gardens in a sublimely aristocratic and arrogant device. They form a superb theatrical backdrop.

The garden is wholly contrived. Its prospects and distant views, the five broad terraces that sweep and zoom down the incline (the first terrace is 800 feet long) toward a lake once known as Juggy's Pond, but aggrandized and formalized into a great stretch of ornamental water and rechristened the **Triton Pool**, barred by a grill with rearing *Pegasi* cast in zinc on either side, all were designed, not just to seduce the eye, but to astonish and impress it too and, what is more, to show who was lord and master of these territories and of these effects. Man, not nature, reigned sublime. The fountain jets leaped over 100 feet into the air.

Not everyone was charmed, especially those of a pragmatic and cost-conscious nature. Elizabeth Grant, a Highland Lady in Ireland, wrote in her journal:

> *Such a journey (to Powerscourt), fifty-two English miles. The lawn was extensive, the wooding beautiful, the views all the way up so pretty; then we passed the neat church, then a sort of dressed*

*farmyard, and then came out upon the house, the Customs House on the Quay at Dublin transplanted to the country. I don't myself like this style of architecture, too formal, nor can I endure these palaces with their stiff gravel terraces amid the natural beauties of trees, fields, hills and ocean; but the place as a place is fine, the house as a work of art, handsome, and the anterior of it a show only, for no one with simple happy tastes could endure to live in rooms so gorgeous.*

The designer responsible was the eccentric Daniel Robertson (he once took revenge on an employer he felt had cheated him by opening all his hothouses on a night of deepest frost and then fleeing the country). He supervised the massive earth-moving work at Powerscourt, where over 100 men were laboring at any one time, while sitting in a wheelbarrow drinking sherry with his gouty foot stuck over the side. When he got very drunk, he fell out and work stopped.

One of the most memorable features in a garden landscape filled with things to remember is a terrace balustraded in black-and-gold wrought iron, with an elaborate zodiacal floor worked in pebbles brought from nearby beaches and devised by Francis Cranmer, antiquary to the Royal Academy. Also notable are the statues of the *God of Winds,* which were brought from the gardens of the Palais-Royal in France after the fall of the Second Empire. There is an arboretum, a Japanese garden to the s, and the highest **waterfall** in Ireland, where the Dargle cascades like a helter-skelter down nearly 400 feet of slithering granite escarpment. (There is a romantic and glorious painting of the *Powerscourt Waterfall* by George Barret in the National Gallery in Dublin.)

In her otherwise rather sad autobiography, *Sun Too Fast,* Sheila Wingfield (Viscountess Powerscourt) related:

*The south side of the house had a totally different character. With curves like two breasts in its long facade, it was bathed in sun and looked open, graceful, gay. I surveyed the 40-acre pleasure garden sloping down to Juggy's Pond and the tops of the shrubs, and the trees, and the plum colored hills that nearly ringed the horizon. George V had seen this view from the Powerscourt ballroom, an enormous room known as the saloon when he was in Ireland in 1821 to honor Dun Laoghaire by naming it Kingstown after himself.*

*"What's that over there?" he asked. He had noticed an almost imperceptible roof among far off trees, the only habitation in the whole vista.*

*"Bushey Park," he was told, "belongs to the Boyles."*

*"Great pity. Ought to be removed," he said.*

Incidentally, the king was supposed to have gone up to see the waterfall, and a road was built and a special viewing-stand erected. The waterfall was dammed up, till the royal party was assembled. Fortunately the king fell into a deep sleep and so did not assemble; for when the sluices were opened, the waterfall cascaded down and swept everything away, bridges, workmen, the lot.

At the moment this whole area is under threat from proposed developments, which would change the whole context of the demesne and the house. There is a proposal to turn the house into a hotel and build 350 houses, two golf courses and another hotel within the demesne. The Irish Georgian Society and *An Taisce* (the Irish National Trust), neither of which are State-funded, are doing all they can at least to modify, even if they cannot halt, these proposed plans. The great estate of **Carton House**, not far away, is under the same kind of threat. These houses are like cargoes; they are filled with the freight of history.

**Enniskerry** itself is a charming town with a Victorian clock tower and many shops, inclined toward the antique and craft end of the market rather than its original role as the organic district town; but it is a pleasant place around which to walk and shop.

### Russborough

The other great house to visit while you are in this area is **Russborough House** ( ☎ *(045) 65239),* 2 miles s of Blessington, and 22 miles sw of Dublin. You can reach it easily from Glendalough, and if you do you will get a quick lesson in the respective manifestations of worldly pride and unworldly piety. The more direct journey from Dublin is an interesting but busy drive, through confusing streets and badly sign-posted suburbs. (There is a bus in the summer that leaves on weekdays from the bus station, Busaras, in the center of Dublin, which joins up with a guided tour at the house.)

If you do drive directly from Dublin, take the N81 (N8 on some maps), which takes you around the suburb of **Tallaght**, a small country village until the relocation schemes of 20 years ago turned it into a place which, though it had a population the size of a small city, had none of a city's amenities. Now one of the largest shopping centers in Ireland has been built there, which you skirt on the way.

There is a church at Tallaght by John Semple, built in his curiously spiky style, set in the grounds of an older church.

After Tallaght the road climbs and becomes a little country road again, with astounding views across to the Wicklow Hills. (One thing that jolts any driver into realizing that Ireland is still a different place with different modes and mores is that nearly always there is someone hitching a lift merely to get to the next village, as an alternative form of public transport. Well, the only form at times. Hitchhiking is not fraught with the dangers it is elsewhere.)

One might not guess at Russborough's existence, so badly is it sign-posted, were it not for the notices of the times of opening mounted on the demesne walls. Look out for it after **Blessington**, with its fine broad street, laid out in the 1680s by Archbishop Boyle of Dublin. The drinking fountain across the road from **Downshire House** (once a seat of Lord Downshire, now a hotel) was erected by the same Lord to commemorate his son's coming of age. This marquis, who took £7,000 a year in annual rent out of the town, was once heard to grumble hard and long about the ingratitude of the local poor because they had insufficiently thanked him for a gift of £10 he had given toward clothing them for the winter (£10 for the entire town, not £10 each).

A more satisfactory way to find Russborough is to go from Enniskerry toward Roundwood and up the Sally Gap. This is a refreshing journey in every sense, especially if you stop and look and breathe the air. Thence you go into Blessington, and on to Russborough.

This is one of the great houses of Ireland, perhaps the ultimate example of the Neo-Palladian style in Ireland, again designed by the great Richard Castle. It was built of granite from the nearby Golden Hill quarry, the high mica content of which makes the house in different lights literally sparkle. The large central block linked to the two wings by curving Doric arcades has a most satisfactory unity. The house looks as though it has been very gently stretched and attenuated along its site to gain full advantage of both its site and its location.

The approach is from one side, so that the 700-foot facade allows the view to be discovered gradually, in a way that enhances the final *coup d'oeil.* The general impression is of splendor, which, in its early days, might have seemed ostentatious, were it not for the sheer style and panache of the place, the way it nestles against its backdrop of terraces and trees, and the mellowing process of age. There are crisp and individual details everywhere to snare the eye: the urns along the parapet, the elegance of the roofline, the snarling but rather endearing lions guarding their heraldic shields with tails coiled like snakes around their bodies and looking, it has to be said, rather like English bull terriers, the archways with their little bell towers at each end of the long line of the building.

"No other Irish house is strung out so extravagantly as Russborough," writes Maurice Craig, in the *Architecture of Ireland,* "a piece of theatrical scenery flung across the Wicklow landscape facing the mountain and overlooking a lake as well." Craig, all the same, is a terrible hard man to satisfy. "There is a touch of the jejune about the detailing of the wing, the colonnades are ambiguous in relation to the center and barely strong enough to hold their own against the adjoining masses." Few visitors would be so hard to please (but Craig, above all, has earned the right to criticise).

Russborough was built in the mid-18thC by Richard Castle for Joseph Leeson, first Earl of Milltown, heir to a great Dublin brewing fortune, who later spent years in Rome acquiring treasures to put in his new house. (Many of these paintings are bequeathed to the National Gallery.)

Work started on the house in 1741, but Castle died before it was finished and Francis Bindon supervised the interior, which is outstanding in its variations, richness and curiosity. There are seven ground-floor reception rooms, with magnificent plasterwork, and in some of the rooms such a high mahogany paneled dado that one does a double take, since it makes the marvelous furniture seems slightly scaled down, giving it a miniaturized air, which startles the eye into a new awareness.

The ground-floor rooms are a lofty 20 feet high, with noble propor-tions, marvelous plasterwork, much of it by the two Swiss stuccodore brothers Paul and Philip Lafranchini, who helped to beautify and make fantastical so many of the grand houses in Ireland. The most astonishing plasterwork at Russborough is that on the staircase, where the Irish craftsmen trained by the Lafranchini brothers seem simultaneously to have been given their heads and to have lost them. It is Rococo gone mad — unsuitable, crowded, imaginative and overwhelming. You can just see the workman standing back, head to one side, and then adding a little more. And more. And more.

The Milltowns lived there for years, but the fourth Earl of Milltown was an inveterate gambler and ruined the family fortunes. In that same journal kept by Elizabeth Grant, there are many insights into life at Russborough in the 1840s. "My Lady Milltown began all airs, talking grand, undervaluing everybody and I told her she was wrong and made her confess it. Such nonsense — a brewer for their ancestor, a blanket weaver for one connection, a silk spinner for another. To look down on the son of a silver smith, 'He'll never be noticed by the aristocracy.' 'I can't see any aristocracy hereabouts,' said I."

The chief reason for visiting the house, though, is the collection of furniture, silver, tapestry and, above all, paintings, which have been left to the nation by Sir Alfred and Lady Beit, who, since they bought the house in 1952, have made it into one of the treasure troves of Ireland.

Sir Alfred's uncle (also Alfred), born in Hamburg in 1853, had in his early twenties made a fortune in mining in South Africa. He formed his great collection of paintings in little more than a decade between 1895 and 1906. When he died, his health broken by the years in South Africa, the collection passed to his brother Sir Otto Beit, who added some of the stars of the collection, including *The Portrait of Dona Antonia Zarate* by Goya (a twin of which is in the Hermitage in St Petersburg) and the great Raeburn portrait of *Sir John and Lady Clerk of Pennycuik,* as well as two paintings by Rubens.

The collection includes pictures by Hals, Velázquez, Vermeer, Ruysdael, Raeburn and Goya. Sir Alfred and his wife have added more paintings and, perhaps most felicitous of all, tracked down some paintings which, though intrinsic to the fabric of the house, had been sold off, most notably the Joseph Vernet marine scenes painted for the plaster ovals in the Drawing Room. Reynold's portrait of *Thomas Conolly of Castletown* (see below) hangs here. In 1974 the IRA raided the house and took the greatest paintings for ransom, but they were recovered. In 1987 Sir Alfred and Lady Beit presented 17 great paintings to the National Gallery, but before they were *in situ* a number were stolen from Russborough. Year by year some have been recovered, and there are hopes that they may eventually be brought back.

There is an outstanding collection of Irish silver, which can be seen during a separate tour of the first-floor bedrooms.

There are delightful things to see at every turn, small ceramics, unique fire-places and mantels, a porcelain water spaniel in Egyptian turquoise with huge startled eyes, ravishingly pretty Louis XVI *fauteuils,* extraordinary carpets, some of them Persian, and a wonderful state bed.

The house stands in 200 acres of land, so that the setting remains all it should be, something rare in Ireland where philistine planning decisions have even allowed building estates to be built on the very doorsteps of palaces such as Castletown and the Casino at Marino.

In 1976 Sir Alfred and Lady Beit set up a Foundation scheme whereby the future of the house and its paintings can be assured and held in trust for the nation.

It is heartening that this house been preserved, when so many have been lost. Hundreds of houses that in any other country would form a proud and cherished cultural heritage and architectural backbone have been burned, destroyed or demolished, or have died by inches through neglect, often by the State. Owners who still live in a great house struggle to preserve them as much from a sense of *noblesse oblige* as much as anything else, an attitude and obligation not recognized as valid among certain strata of society in Ireland. These same owners are becomingly increasingly demoralized by the lack of support from men in power who have as much aesthetic sense as Attila the Hun.

# West of Dublin

Driving due west of Dublin takes one on an excursion into an amazing concentration of historical and beautiful places. To drive a dozen miles w out of Dublin on the N4 Galway road and head for **Lucan** and **Castletown House** or **Maynooth** and **Celbridge** and its environs is to be spoiled for choice.

### Castletown

**Castletown House** (*Celbridge, Co. Kildare* ☎ *(01) 6288252* 🖾 ⇌ 🖳 *),* 12 miles E of Dublin on the main Dublin/Galway road (forking left at Lucan), is finally considered to be the finest Palladian private house in Ireland. It certainly is the largest. Nothing so grand had ever been built before and nothing quite so splendid was ever built again, and it became one of the wonders of the world of Ireland. Its center block, restrained, elegant and tranquil, linked by colonnaded curtain walls to the beautifully proportioned twin pavilions, was a startling innovation and became the source of inspiration for aspiring owners all over the country. (At Straffan, for example, not very far away, **Lodge Park**, an enchanting house on a much smaller scale, stretches out like an architectural elastic about to snap, its pavilions and arcades elongated not for architectural imperative but in order that the owner's new residence should be *quite* as long as the one at Russborough.)

The arrangement of house and colonnades and blocks was not just a matter of aesthetics at Castletown, but derived from Andrea Palladio's principles that farm buildings should not be too far away from the main house (the over-seer, as it were) and yet should not be manifest, and that there should be no hint of farmyard smell or noise. In Ireland animals had always been kept within the confines of the keep (or the *bawn,* as it was known in Ireland), and this Palladian arrangement was the perfect solution. The stables and farm buildings were at the end of the long blocks and colonnades; far away, yet part of the whole.

Walking or driving up to Castletown along its avenue leading off the main street in Celbridge is a stirring sight. It was begun in 1722 for **William Conolly**, the ambitious and energetic Speaker of the Irish House of Commons. Conolly was a Donegal man, reputedly an innkeeper's son, and had the natural genius of energy and a fine eye for the main chance. He was an attorney, a Member of Parliament and a Commissioner of the Revenue. Following the Williamite Wars, he dealt in forfeited estates to his great advantage and became enormously wealthy and influential. He lived in splendor in Capel St. in Dublin, but wanted a country estate, and when he came to build it, simply wanted to buy the best, the largest and the grandest.

He turned to the Italian architect, Alessandro Galilei (1691-1737), who had designed the facade for St John Lateran in Rome, and what was good enough for God was good enough for Speaker Conolly. Galilei drew up the plans, but left Ireland before building started.

It is therefore to the Irish genius Sir Edward Lovett Pearce that we owe the curved colonnades, which add so immeasurably to the happy design that is Castletown and which finalizes the sleek, silver-gray 400-foot facade, emphasized by the formal green studs of the conical yew trees and the clipped yew hedges. It is the most perfect machine for showing off a way of life.

Castletown was never intended as a domestic dwelling (Speaker Conolly had enough of those) but was conceived as a palace, like that of a Renaissance prince, an absolute show of richness and strength. It works on that level magnificently, but it works on another level too — of welcome, the feeling of an embrace that comes through the stretch of the arms of the arcades on each side.

Sir John Perceval, a rich Cork landowner, wrote to Bishop Berkeley, who had been consulted about the building. "You will do well to recommend him the making use of all the marbles he can get of the production of Ireland for his chimney, for since this house will be the finest Ireland ever saw and by your description for a prince I would have it as it were the epitome of the Kingdom . . . "

Speaker Conolly died before his great dream was finished, and died childless. His nephew Tom inherited it but died after only two years, and his grand-nephew "Squire" Conolly inherited it. In 1758 he married Lady Louisa Lennox, the 15-year-old daughter of the Duke of Richmond, and her insouciance revivified the house. They commissioned the great staircase from Simon Vierpyl, the brilliant sculptor brought from Rome by Lord Charlemont, and engaged the Lafranchinis for the plasterwork.

Lady Louisa wrote to her sister (the future Duchess of Leinster) at Carton, who also had work done by them. "Mr Conolly and I are excessively diverted at Franchini's impertinence and if he changes anything of that sort to Mr Conolly there is a fine scold in store for his honor." (Incidentally, Mr Conolly would never take an English title; he was proud to be known as Mr Conolly of Castletown, though never as plain Mr Conolly.) Lady Louisa lived at Castletown for over 60 years and died in

1821 as she had wished, seated in a tent on the lawn, looking at the house she had so loved and so graced with her presence.

There are many books on Castletown and much about Lady Louisa, who had such charm, energy and power, as well as an amazing eye, and who was responsible among much else for the famous Print Room, which has alas inspired many a small drawing-room owner ever since. She commissioned the painting of the **Long Gallery** with surfaces and patterns based vaguely on Pompeian frescoes, but imbued with a spirit and freshness of detail unique to the two painters, "a little deformed delicate man" named Charles Riley and Thomas Ryder, who worked on them. Originally there had been stuccowork in the Gallery, but Lady Louisa had them "knocked off smack smooth." She commissioned chandeliers from Venice and when they were unpacked found to her chagrin that they were the wrong blue for the room. She was everywhere, with a hand in everything, a genius whirlwind of energy and taste, who now would be running an international interior decorating firm.

In 1778 Lady Caroline Dawson came to stay:

*We then went to the house which is the largest house I ever was in and reckoned the finest in this kingdom. It has been done up entirely by Lady Louisa and with a very good taste. But what struck me most was a gallery, I daresay 150 feet long, furnished in the most delightful manner with fine glasses, books musical instruments billiard table. In short everything you can think of is in that room and though so large is so well fitted that it is the warmest, most comfortable-looking place I ever saw. They tell me they live in it quite in the winter, for the servants can bring dinner or supper at one end without anybody hearing it at the other; in short I never saw anything so delightful.*

And empty as it is, the room still reverberates to the music of what happened there, in this heartland of Ireland.

A heart, it must be said, that could have stopped beating, for all the powers-that-be cared. When Castletown was sold in 1965, by Lord Carew (whose mother was a Conolly), the Irish Government expressed no interest whatever in saving it, in spite of the national and international importance of the house and the part it had played in Irish history; or perhaps *because* of that part, the impositions such a house made on the native psyche.

The demesne was split up by the developers and the contents dispersed at auction. Kildare County Council gave planning permission for a housing estate right on the line of the avenue, totally despoiling it. The house was left to the mercy of vandals and scrap merchants, and if it had not been for Desmond Guinness, the president of the Irish Georgian Society, a man to whom Ireland owes an immeasurable debt over the years, it would have perished. He bought the house and 100 acres for £93,000, to save it, and turned it into the headquarters of the Irish Georgian Society, who then undertook its restoration. A huge amount was raised by the Society, its supporters, and by friends abroad and in the United States.

Volunteers worked from morning to night over long years till the building was rescued and restored to its glory. (Incidentally, Castletown House is supposed to have been the inspiration, along with Leinster House in Dublin, for the White House in Washington.)

The best description and narration about the house are in two books by Desmond Guinness: *Irish Houses and Castles* (the profits of which went to the society) and *Great Irish Houses and Castles* by Desmond Guinness and Jacqueline O'Brien. And if ever anyone had a right to write these books, it is Desmond Guinness.

There are two famous curiosities in the demesne. One is the enormous 140-foot-high **obelisk** adorned with eagles and pineapples, which can be seen from 20 miles away. The Speaker's widow, Katherine Conyingham, had it designed by Richard Castle in 1740 and built ostensibly as relief work (at a halfpenny a day after the unforgettable hard winter of 1739), although anyone seeing it might be forgiven for thinking there was a hint of self-aggrandizement behind it.

A *most* unlikely motive was attributed to its building by one Henry Jones, who composed *Poems on Severall Occasions:*

> See Grandeur here by social Virtue grac'd;
> The Manner noble as refined the Taste.
> Not Pride, but Piety there strikes our Eyes
> And Meekness lifts yon Pillar to the Skies.

Not much meekness, however, is visible.
Her sister Mary Jones wrote crossly:

> *My sister is building an obleix to answer a vistow from the bake of Castletown House; it will cost her three or four hundred pounds at least, but I believe more. I really wonder how she can dow so much, and live as she duse.*

In fact the obelisk was built on land belonging to the Earl of Kildare at Carton, the neighboring estate, and it was only in 1968 that an American benefactress bought it for Castletown.

Mrs Conolly, who lived in great style until she was 90, continued her good work by building another folly in 1743, the **Wonderful Barn**, a cone-shaped structure, mounted by an external corkscrew staircase, with rooms vaulted in brick, which was used as a grain store. There is a description of the widow Conolly by Mrs Delaney, generally the most charming writer and wit of 18thC Dublin (and indeed of London), as "a plain and vulgar woman in her manner, but had very valuable qualities."

The obelisk can be reached by driving out toward Maynooth and taking the first turning right and bumping along till you see the monument through the gate. The Wonderful Barn is on a private farm and is not open to the public.

Castletown is one of the centers for the **GPA Music In Great Irish Houses** festival held annually in mid-June with a program of international chamber music and visiting distinguished artists. Other wonderful settings include Russborough, Carton and Kilruddery. For information, write to the Festival Office, 14 Ashfield Rd., Ranelagh, Dublin 6 *or* 41 Wellington Place, Dublin 4.

(It costs IR£60 a year to become a Friend of Castletown House, which includes an annual lottery ticket and helps the cause. Write to: Friends of Castletown, Castletown House, Celbridge, Co. Kildare, Ireland.)

## Celbridge and Leixlip

**Celbridge**, 12 miles w of Dublin, is famous for its association with Jonathan Swift and Hester Vanhomrigh (or Esther Van Homrigh), better known as Vanessa, the pet name given to her by Swift, her tutor, some say her lover, her mentor and her idol. She had inherited **Celbridge Abbey** ( ☎ *(01) 6271849)* from her father, a Dutch general, who had come to Ireland with King William and became Lord Mayor of Dublin. Here between 1717 and 1723 Vanessa and Swift continued their relationship, which had begun ten years before in London. The house was only ten miles downstream on the Liffey, which runs through the town, from that of Stella, his other great love. The walks and bowers are, according to Grattan, haunted by their spirits, especially at Vanessa's Bower.

Certainly they are haunted by their latter-day attendants at scholarly lectures and seminars on Swift, his work and his life, which are held annually. (For details write to Celbridge Abbey, Co. Kildare, Ireland.)

The story of Swift, Vanessa and Stella is one of the great romances and tragic mysteries of Ireland. Celbridge Abbey was also the house of the family of Henry Grattan, MP and Leader of the Patriot Party in the 1780s, and the present house was remodeled in the Gothic style in the late 18thC by Henry Grattan's uncle.

The abbey is now occupied by a religious order. The abbey grounds are open, and there is a pets' corner and a model railway. (There are plans to make the abbey and its grounds more accessible to the public.) Conferences are held in the abbey, but at the time of writing, visits are by arrangement only, made in advance. But the **garden** is open from 2-6pm on Sunday afternoons from May to September ( 🔲 ).

In Celbridge Main St. is the lovely **Kildrought House**, which may well have been designed by Thomas Burgh the architect and Surveyor-General in 1700, who was born in Co. Kildare.

On the riverbank, the Neo-Gothic structure is that dreaded institution, the old workhouse, now used as a factory. In the "death-house," standing at right angles to St Mochua's Church on Tay Lane, is a magnificent pedimented monument to Speaker Conolly by Thomas Carter the Elder, in which the Speaker, life-sized and fatly recumbent, lies gazing up at Mrs Conolly. Behind the figures the Speaker's virtues are extolled in marble lettering. The grand pedimented surround is attributed to William Kidwell.

There was another Celbridge house here, known as Oakley Park, built by Archbishop Price in 1724, who employed a decent young land steward, Richard Guinness, among whose duties was the supervising of brewing of beer for the estate workers. Price thought that Guinness made a brew out of the ordinary and of "a very palatable nature." He didn't know the half of it. Richard's son Arthur (named after the Archbishop who was his godfather and left him £100) went to Dublin, bought a small disused brewery in St James's Gate, and the rest is history. The house was later bought by the Conolly family, and here Lady Louisa's sister Sarah lived, who so captivated the Prince of Wales by her beauty that he thought to marry her. The house is now a school.

Not far away the river is crossed by a bridge of four arches built in 1308 by the Mayor of Dublin and said to be the oldest extant bridge in the country. It is called **Newbridge**.

**Leixlip** (the name means *salmon leap*) used to be a quiet little village on the Liffey, but is now a nightmare of traffic and delay, though a by-pass is being built. The castle here is a 13thC building associated with King John and more recently with the Irish Georgian Society, for which it was the headquarters until 1991, when they moved to 42 Merrion Sq., Dublin. It is now a private family home.

## Maynooth and Carton

The **Royal Canal** runs through **Maynooth**, a university town about 15 miles NW of Dublin. For years in Ireland the name was synonymous with priesthood, and **St Patrick's College** was always known simply as Maynooth. This famous seminary, originally founded in 1521, was closed during the Reformation and restored after the Penal Laws were repealed — but only because the authorities felt that if there *had* to be priests, it would be better to keep them back home, rather than have them study in France, where they might imbibe revolutionary ideas. The college buildings exude a feeling of oppressive and didactic piety and are built on the site of an old castle. Inside the main gate is **St Mary's Church**, incorporating ecclesiastical ruins associated with the castle of the Earls of Kildare. (Their latter-day palace, **Carton**, is just up the street.)

The original **castle**, with its gatehouse and hall just to the right of the entrance, is a National Monument.

The buildings of the college are a mixture of Classically-inspired buildings (reputedly designed by Michael Stapleton) and high Gothic Revival, designed by Pugin, who always had the required reverential gift. His work was altered even while it was being built. Whatever else the priests who came out of Maynooth did to and for Ireland, they seem generally to have imposed an appalling standard of taste on their parishes and churches. There is a limestone head of St Patrick by the Cork sculptor Seamus Murphy in the library, which has a large collection of manuscripts and early printed Irish books.

There is an **Ecclesiastical Museum** (☎ *(01) 6285222)* within the university/seminary, but you need to make an appointment to visit. In the museum are vestments worn by the great Irish scribe Geoffrey Keating (see MYTH, page 60), and the electrical equipment used by the inventor Rev. Nicholas Callan (1779-1864), who as Professor of Science investigated and furthered Faraday's work and discovered the principles of the self-induced dynamo.

At the opposite end of the town is **Carton**, sister palace to Castletown, designed by Richard Castle in 1739 for the 19th Earl of Kildare, who considered himself the grandest man in Ireland. The house was built on the site of an existing Tudor building, with a small river, the Rye Water, running through the grounds. Castle used local materials: Mount Mellick flag, granite from Wicklow, Ardbraccan stone and the local blackstone.

The house stood in a wonderful setting, a thousand acres in extent, surrounded by a high wall with many entrances reached through lodges and pillars that were themselves beautiful and gave notice to the passer-by that behind them lay a rich man's creation, an Arcadian dream.

Arthur Young records that in 1776 he went to Carton:

> *The park ranks among the finest in Ireland. It is a vast lawn, which waves over gentle hills . . . and which break and divide in places so as to give much variety, kept in the highest order by 1,100 sheep . . . . The sheep give it not exactly a human touch, but bring it to scale.*

The sheep also bring to mind Le Petit Hameau at Versailles where Marie-Antoinette romped as a shepherdess, and the vogue for great ladies to play at being dairy maids; life at Carton had elements of the same fantasy.

Duchess Emily (the 19th Earl had died in 1744 and his son James, Emily's husband, had been created Duke of Leinster in 1776) subscribed enthusiastically to the idea of simplicity at considerable cost. She tied ribbons round the necks of pretty lambs or cows, and a delightful little marble dairy was created, with rams' heads for spouts and china buckets for cream. She wrote, "Did I ever tell you of my passion for spotted cows? . . . You have no notion of what a delightful beautiful collection I have got in a very short time which is indeed owing to my Lord Kildare who ever since I took this fancy into my head, has bought me every pretty cow he saw."

Lady Emily may have taken pleasure in being a simple country maid while she was *al fresco,* but she needs must shed such artless ways when she went back indoors in her house. It is wonderfully, sublimely, grandly grand. Two rooms remain as they were in her day. The **saloon** rises through two stories, and its ceiling is an intense, wonderfully Baroque example of the Lafranchini brothers at their best. *The Courtship of the Gods* is the theme, and the gods *are* getting on with it. (The organ at one end is a Victorian addition.)

The other memorable room is the **Chinese bedroom**, with its rare scenic wallpaper and lovely gilt fillet work around the cornices and dado rail. The wallpaper was meant to cover all the walls, but when it arrived it was too scant. No doubt Lady Emily (sister to Louisa, who had had to bear the over-blueness of the chandeliers at Castletown) had a word to say; but having said it, she got out her scissors and effected the charming room one sees here.

The building was altered early in the 19thC by Sir Richard Morrison, who straightened the curved colonnades, built protruding blocks to each side and made a new entrance. He designed the **dining room**, 54 feet long and 24 high, with a barrel and vaulted ceiling and beautiful columns.

In the grounds is the **Shell House** made by Duchess Emily (her mother had a similar one at Goodwood); it is absolutely wonderful. There are bridges, and a bower: just what its name describes.

Carton suffered terribly through the foolhardiness of a youngest son with no apparent prospect of being Duke, who sold his birthright to a moneylender in 1910, for £1,000 a year for life. He inherited the Dukedom but without access to the house or to his money, and lived till he was 90. The property was bought by a family who looked after it until the punitive wealth tax of 1975 drove them, with so many others, out of Ireland. The tax was repealed in 1978, after the damage was done.

Now no one knows what is to happen to Carton. Planning permission for a hotel, a golf course, all that is underway. We can only hope it will be saved for Ireland. If only Ireland were like the little village sw across country from here called **Prosperous**, worth a visit just for the name.

### Lucan

Just s of the **Bog of Allen** and abutting onto **The Curragh** is **Pollardstown Fen**, the largest area of marshy ground in Ireland and of prime ecological interest, with rare plants, marsh orchids, rare birds and even mollusks. It is easy, when walking over this ground, to see where **Lucan** gets its name. In Irish it means "marsh-mallow land." The salmon-fishing at Lucan is reputed to be the best on the Liffey, but salmon is ever and ever rarer. The bridge over the Liffey is reputed to have been designed by Isambard Kingdom Brunel.

This is the town to which the great James Gandon chose to retire in **Cannonbrook**, an undistinguished house architecturally speaking but one in which he lived and which he called his Tivoli. It is still there but not open to the public.

The big house here is **Lucan House**, squashed between the Liffey and the main road, and now the Italian Ambassador's residence. The house was designed by Agmondisham Vesey, an amateur architect of distinction, and contains plasterwork by Michael Stapleton. The house and estate is associated with Patrick Sarsfield, who became the first Earl of Lucan, and the ruins of Sarsfield Castle are in the grounds. There is a fine monument by Wyatt, to his memory, which was hidden in the grounds but is now near the house: a triangular carved pillar supported on three tortoises, surmounted by an urn made from Coade stone.

In the gardens is a Gothic "ruined" oratory or hermitage, which is a cold bath fed by the Liffey waters — a grand if tiny swimming pool, in other words, and a reminder that this town was once a fashionable spa. Here the *ton* came to take the waters of the "Boiling Spring," which spewed out hot drafts of mineral water with medicinal qualities, apparently equaled for foulness of taste only by Bath spa water. It was discovered when workmen excavating for the Royal Canal hit the spring. And like the canal we can wend our way home.

# North of Dublin

The region north of Dublin is rich in history, and although the scenery is less spectacular than in other regions, tucked away in the country-side are villages and places that reek not just of history but of prehis-tory; and the coast is often wild and deserted.

## The northern outskirts of Dublin

Nearer to North Dublin the beaches are certainly not deserted. **Dolly-mount Strand** *(map 2 B4)*, for example, has wonderful expanses of sand where ten thousand people can, and do, disport themselves on a sunny Sunday afternoon. So not the place to go for a quiet bathe, but certainly the place to get genuine Dublin life in the raw, as it were.

On the outskirts all around the N city·are various things worth visiting, including the **Dunsink Observatory** *(map 1 B1* ☎ *(01) 387911)*, to the N of Phoenix Park, which is part of Trinity College. Founded in 1783 and one of the oldest observatories in the world, it was designed by George Myers in 1782, with money left by Provost Andrews. It has a 12-inch refractor in the South Telescope built by Grubbs of Dublin in 1863, which is used on "open nights" if the sky is clear. Essentially a research center, it has a collection of memorabilia relating to astronomy. The observatory is open to visitors on the first and third Saturday of every month from September to March, when illustrated lectures and a guided study of the night sky is offered (weather permitting). Admission is free, but tickets must be obtained by sending a stamped addressed envelope to the Secretary *(write to Dunsink Observatory, Dunsink, Co. Dublin, Ireland)*. It is not suitable for children under 12.

In **Glasnevin Cemetery** *(well signposted: map 1 B2)* are many of the graves of the nationalist heroes of Ireland, many almost clustered around the memorial to Daniel O'Connell. Cemeteries in Ireland (usually called graveyards) are well kept, with the graves tended and crowned with flowers (often of a livid plastic). Glasnevin is a remarkable place, a mixture of wonderful monuments and garish headstones, a place that is banal and touching and finally impressive.

Nearby are the **National Botanic Gardens** *(map 1 B2)*, the largest horticultural and botanical institute in Ireland. Founded by the Royal Dublin Society in 1795 to "increase and foster a taste for practical and scientific botany," they fulfil their charter admirably and have always been much loved by Dubliners. Joseph Addison used to walk here when he was Chief Secretary for Ireland (1708-11).

The gardens are so big — over 50 acres (20 hectares) — and so crammed with plants that you would do well to concentrate on the parts that interest you most. The various sections are all clearly marked. There are separate conservatories (one is over 400 feet long), huge yet delicate constructions for orchids, palms, tree ferns, camellias, cacti, succuli and tropical aquatic plants. There is an arboretum, a wild garden, a rose garden and a water garden, fed by the Tolka River.

In 1991 the restoration of the **Curvilinear Range** at the Botanic Gardens, the finest example of cast-iron-and-curved-glasshouse architecture in Ireland, designed by Richard Turner, was begun. When it is finished, the Range will be opened up to allow public access around the houses, giving a new view of the adjoining area.

### The Marino Casino

Threading your way E toward the coast, make for the **Marino Casino** in Clontarf *(Malahide Rd., map 1 B3* ☎ *(01) 331618)*, one of the essential sights of Dublin, designed by Sir William Chambers for Lord Charlemont in 1762. He called it his "marine villa" and it was, so to speak, his beach hut. It was also, so to speak, one of the most perfect buildings of the Renaissance. Charlemont had a large house in Parnell Sq. (now the Hugh Lane Municipal Art Gallery) and a mansion in Co. Armagh, a two-day journey away, and in order to be able to enjoy the clean air of Dublin Bay during the Season, he built this exquisite little jewel of a building.

Looking at it one can see the influence it had on James Gandon, Chambers' pupil, who designed the Custom House. This building has international significance, ranking with Palladio's Rotonda at Vicenza or Inigo Jones' masterpiece at Greenwich, the Queen's House.

Its properties reflect those of the men who built it. James Caulfeild looks uncouth in his portraits, but he had the soul of a gifted and poetic aesthete. (He was also a soldier, commander-in-chief of the Irish Volunteers. Simply *lovely* uniforms.) He may have called his little temple of pleasure a seaside villa, but it was his own homage to the gods of Classicism and culture and agape.

It cost a fortune to build — over £20,000 — and the workmen, who earned but shillings a week, warned one another to be careful "because every broken stone is another townland gone" (a parish in Ireland is divided into townlands).

Every detail of this building, which is as much a sculpture in itself as a building, is felicitous: the benign lions with their curious twisted grins, originally intended as fountains; the statues of *Ceres* and *Bacchus* on the N (or entrance) front, and on the S, *Apollo* and *Venus:* culture and agriculture mixed, as any lover of Italy and Palladio would approve.

The pretty solutions to practical problems add to the pleasure, and indeed the intellectual excitement of looking at and being within this building. The columns, for example, are downpipes in themselves; the garlanded urns on the roof are chimneys; on the flat roof a canopy could be erected.

It took all in all nearly 20 years from conception to finish — and though Chambers himself never came to Ireland, he was lucky that his designs were executed by the genius builder/sculptor Simon Vierpyl (who did the staircase at Castletown and was involved with building the City Hall and the Bluecoat School). It was he who passed on his experience of Roman stone-cutting to the Irish workmen, which skill made such a contribution to Irish architecture; and one of Vierpyl's apprentices was Edward Smyth, the best Irish sculptor, who may well have sculpted the statues and the urns along the roofline.

The Casino, for all its size, is a sumptuous miniaturization of a grand house, with 16 rooms on three stories, and most of the arts and aids to civilized living (not many bathrooms though). The grand entrance hall sets the scene, with its elaborate carved doorframes, fine mahogany doors and a superb inlaid floor. The china closet (which was originally a bedroom) has cobweb-airy plasterwork, a neat little fireplace, and its coved ceiling is a delight. There is a little vaulted kitchen in the basement, a grand master bedroom with a lovely *lit à Napoleon,* and the saloon (the **Apollo Room**) again has extraordinary plasterwork and superb intricate inlaid wooden floors.

Although the Office of Public Works took it over in 1930, for years the architectural jewel moldered and nettles grew in the tarmac around it. I tried to get into it year after year. Once I knocked on the door of a house where I had been told there was a key. The man who opened the door was incredulous at my mission. "That yoke over there," he said staring across at the sad little temple. "Who'd want to get into it?" Then in 1974 major restoration work started. It took years and cost another fortune, and although, alas, the original furnishings disappeared in the 19thC, including the marble and lapis-lazuli chimneypiece, the Casino glows with renewed splendor.

Photographs always show it as sitting in its proper station, isolated, a solitaire in the sun, surrounded by lawn and vistas to the sea. In fact it is in execrable surroundings, behind ugly wire gates, with housing estates crowding nearby and traffic pounding within sight. Not that this is anything new. Not long after Lord Charlemont completed his little treasure casket, a neighbor built a terrace — a handsome terrace, though — in front, to spoil his view.

It is a far cry from the spirit within Lord Charlemont, who left his demesnes open and unwalled so the public could walk as they pleased. The huge building behind the Casino is the **O'Brien Institute**, designed by J.J. O'Callaghan, dating from 1882 and founded by the pious O'Brien twin sisters as a college for boys.

A measure of the meeting of the two minds that resulted in the Marino Casino may be gathered from the epitaph written by Charlemont, on hearing, as he himself lay dying, of the death of Sir William Chambers.

*To, Sir William Chambers, Knight, etc.,*
*Fellow of the Royal Academy,*
*And professor of Architecture,*
*The Best of Men and the First of English Architects*
*Whose Buildings, modelled from his own mind,*
*Elegant, Pure and Solid*
*Will Long Remain the Lasting Monuments*
*Of that Taste*
*Whose Chastity Could Only Be Equalled*
*By The Immaculate Purity of The Author's Heart*
*James Earl of Charlemont, His Friend*
*From Long Experiences of His Worth and Talent*
*Dedicates this Inscription*
*To Him and Friendship*
*Indeed this Lasting monument is one of the glories not just of Dublin,*
*But of the World.*

**Clontarf** *(map 1 B3)* itself was the scene of the famous battle on Good Friday 1014, when Brian Boru broke the power of the Danes. (The legend, or perhaps the truth, is that when he was praying in his tent after his great victory, the Viking sea-king Brodun rushed in and slew him; his two sons had already been slain in battle. So it was a bitter celebration of victory for the Irish that night.)

**Clontarf Castle**, now a hotel, was designed by William Morrison and was built in 1835 on an ancient fortification of the Pale.

**North Bull Island** *(map 2 C4-B5)*, a wildlife sanctuary within the city boundary, is an area of international importance for Brent geese and wildfowl. It is also the home of the Royal Dublin Golf Links.

Back on the mainland, at Raheny, about 2 miles from the city center, is **St Anne's Park** *(map 2 B4)*, 247 acres of public park with an extraordinary show of bedding plants — acres of them — and a large rose garden, which is a center for international rose trials. It is a riot of color in the summer months.

About three miles N of the Marino Casino, off the Malahide Rd., is **Belcamp College** in Darndale. It incorporates an oratory and a house with a fine Dublin plasterwork ceiling, dating from 1765, and some wonderful examples of the work of the great stained-glass artist, Harry Clarke, including 12 representations of the Irish saints, the mysteries of the rosary and two rose windows. The whole building is under threat, since the religious order that runs the college is under severe financial pressure to rent the whole building and is fighting a rearguard action to preserve the windows and the building. Visitors will find the doors closed for security, so ring the bell and wait; with luck, a delightful priest, Father Conellan, passionate about the windows, will show you around. Mass is said in the Oratory on Sunday, but it is not public, so it might be as well to telephone first ( ☎ (01) 8460079).

## Howth

The name **Howth** (map 2 B5-6) comes from the Danish word *hoved*, meaning "head." It is a fashionable town with pretty houses, on the tip of Dublin Bay. Across the isthmus rises the Ben of Howth, a hill of 560 feet topped by a cairn, and from here on a fine day you can see the Wicklow Mountains, and if it is really clear the Mountains of Mourne and Slieve Gullion to the N and even the mountains of Wales across the Irish Sea. On a windy day it is utterly exhilarating, with the seagulls riding the thermals on the wing "for sheer joy played and sang like images took flight . . . "

The islands of **Ireland's Eye** (map 2 A6) and **Lambay Island** (there is a wonderful Lutyens house on Lambay, but the island is privately owned and can only be visited by private arrangement) lie low in the water. An old stone church more than a thousand years old marks the spot where the Early Christians had their monastery on Ireland's Eye (there are boat trips to the island during the summer months).

H.G. Wells called this the most beautiful view in the world. The Irish heroine Maud Gonne, whom W.B. Yeats loved so long and so hopelessly, grew up here at Howth. In her autobiography *A Servant of the Queen* she wrote:

> *No place has ever seemed to me quite so lovely as Howth was then. Sometimes the sea was as blue as Mama's turquoises, more strikingly blue even than the Mediterranean because so often grey mists made it invisible and mysterious. The little rock pools at the bottom of the high cliffs were very clear and full of wonder-life; sea-anemones which open look like gorgeous flowers with blue and orange spots and if touched, close up into brown humps, tiny crabs, pink star fish, endless varieties of sea-snails, white, green, striped and bright buttercup-yellow.*

West of the harbor is **Howth Castle**, home of the St Lawrence family from 1177. A legend relates that Grace O'Malley, the indomitable pirate queen from Co. Mayo, sailed into Howth to replenish victuals and was refused admittance to the castle because the family were at dinner. Enraged, she snatched the son and heir from his cradle and sailed off with him to Mayo. The child, no worse for wear, was returned on the condition that the gates of the castle were always left open at meal-times and that a place was laid for the head of the O'Malleys at all times.

The castle is not open (unless presumably you are the O'Malley chief), but the gardens are, and in due season are awash with rhododendron. In the stables of the castle is the **Howth Transport Museum** ( ☎ (01) 8475623), with trams, buses and fire engines. The bells from **Howth Abbey** in Abbey St. are on the terrace at Howth Castle, and inside this abbey, reputed to have been founded by the Viking king, Sitric, is the 15thC tomb of Christopher St Lawrence and his wife Anna. The graveyard around this church is open from 9am-5.30pm and the church will be opened by request to the attendant, who is there most days.

### From Swords to Bettystown

An alternative route to the area N of Dublin is up the Drumcondra road and out on the new motorway by the airport. On the new Dublin Airport Roundabout on the way to Swords or Donabate is a fine and appropriate granite sculpture by Richard King called *Spirit of the Air,* which won a major competition for the site.

The roads branching off the main road to Derry and Belfast will bring you to **Swords**, a busy, prosaic town with a fortified Bishop's Palace at its N end built at the beginning of the 13thC. There is a Round Tower in the grounds of the Church of Ireland (82 feet high), open only by arrangement, and the remains of a 15thC church.

All around this area are small towns minding their own business and with their own things to see: **Donabate**, with its excellent beach strand; or **Skerries**, the busiest and most popular resort on the N coast of Dublin, with two important bird sanctuaries off its coast. At **Red Island**, which is not an island, legend has it that the indentations in the rocks were made by St Patrick, and on **St Patrick's Island**, reached by boat, are the ruins of an old and historic church. The Martello Tower on **Shenick Island** can be reached at low tide. **Portrane** nearby has an excellent strand, popular with Dubliners. The remains of a 15thC church and castle look suitably romantic. **Portrane House**, now a mental hospital, was the home of Swift's beloved Stella. History has its ironies.

Farther N beyond **Naul** is the prehistoric site of **Fourknocks (Fornocht** in Irish, meaning "bleak place" — they didn't dissemble), where a huge passage grave over 3,000 years old was discovered. The site is kept locked, but the key is obtainable from the house next door.

To walk on the beach at **Bettystown** (where one of Ireland's greatest treasures, the so-called Tara brooch, was found: see NATIONAL MUSEUM, page 73) and **Laytown** (famous for its race meeting in June, July and August, on the beach, between tides) is to step back in time. The train thunders past behind the dunes; the beaches are deserted; Laytown lies locked behind the great railway bridge; a mother and child, its dress tucked up, with bucket and spade, walk the endless rolling sands toward the receding sea; everything is still and golden except for the seagulls. It is hard to believe that one is within such a short distance of a capital city.

### Malahide

Heading S again toward Dublin, the road is signposted **Malahide Castle** ( **☎** *(01) 8452655* **▨** **▨** *)*, nine miles N of Dublin and one of Ireland's oldest and most historic estates.

The castle, an amalgamation of many different periods and styles, with the earliest core being a three-story tower house, thought to date from the 12thC, was lived in by the Talbot family for nearly 800 years from 1185 until 1976. Then the last Lord Talbot de Malahide died and his sister had to sell this casket of Ireland's history to pay for punitive death duties.

The authorities wanted cash instead of history; was there ever a worse bargain than here at Malahide, where for 800 years time had layered up on the castle walls like feathers on a bird's wing, so that the end construction was a working miracle?

The castle and park were bought by Dublin County Council, and at the last moment 35 of the paintings were purchased by the National Gallery and returned on loan. Sadly many other paintings and much of the furniture was dispersed at auction, though some was left in situ, including the wonderful curtains in some of the warm and friendly rooms, which, though grand, are never forbidding and still have their companionable and civilized atmosphere.

The **National Gallery** has contributed greatly to the enjoyment of this historic house by hanging a part of the **National Portrait collection** in it and adding to the collection of 18thC Irish furniture. Among them is the very pretty painting by Mallary (c.1800) of Lady Edward Fitzgerald and her daughter; and what would be nicest of all is if the ravishingly pretty portrait of the Ladies Catherine and Charlotte Talbot transfixed in gathering roses while they play, painted in 1679 by John Michael Wright and now in the National Gallery, came back to rest here. But then, they'd miss it in Dublin. (See also ART GALLERIES, page 69.)

There is an excellent voice-over tape in each room, which is activated by one's entry. The only caveat is that it describes furniture that sometimes is no longer there — perhaps gone for restoration or exhibition elsewhere? — and there is no notice to this effect, so that one is left listening to a mouthwatering description of, say, a gilt console table while staring at a piece of good but dull brown furniture. What is not dull is the wonderful orange color of the drawing room, which is the special "Malahide" orange, much copied, generally unsuccessfully.

Though Malahide is now a museum, it still has a faint air of what it was for so long: a unique family place where people lived ordinary as well as momentous lives.

The name of Talbot is woven indelibly into the fabric of Irish history, so that visiting this house allows one to take a long view back into that history. Perhaps the most moving story from the many connected with the castle is that on the morning of the Battle of the Boyne in 1690, 14 young men of the Talbot family sat down to what was their last meal on earth. Not one survived. When that fateful evening James II, the defeated king for whom they fell, met Lady Tyrconnell (the wife of the Talbot of the day, then called Lord Tyrconnell, and his chief general), he is reputed to have said to her savagely, "Your countrymen can run well." To which she answered, "Not so well as your Majesty, for I see you have won the race."

One of the Talbots married a member of the family of James Boswell, Dr Johnson's brilliant biographer, and large caches of his papers were found in the castle, some in an ebony cupboard, some in a croquet box in an outhouse, after World War II, which caused terrific excitement among the international *literati*. They were bought by Yale University, and since then research into these seemingly limitless papers has fully justified the curiosity and excitement. Boswell emerges as a genius who led a short and irregular life but one in which "he clasped every day, every hour to his greedy heart."

The Talbots are kinsmen of the Shrewsbury family, the premier earls of England, and the Talbot dog, a handsome hound bred by an early Talbot, is used in their coat of arms. The family is also associated with the head of the lion, which appears on furniture all over the house. The writer Laura Talbot was a kinswoman of the house.

The castle is surrounded by a public park, which contains the **Talbot Botanic Gardens** created by the last Lord Talbot de Malahide in the 1950s and '60s, and the **Fry Model Railway Museum** ( ☎ *(01) 8452758* 📷*)*, a rare collection of handmade models of Irish trains, built by Cyril Fry, a railway engineer and draftsman in the 1920s and '30s. As the years passed, what happens to every model train enthusiast happened on a magnificent scale to Cyril Fry: his railway took over every room in his house. It was acquired by Dublin Tourism, and this museum was built to house the grand transport complex, with stations, buses, bridges, trams, the Liffey, the docks and the Hill of Howth. Besides the pleasure, it is a quick surreal geography lesson about Dublin.

Southeast of Malahide, just w of **Portmarnock** with its famous strand, is **St Doulagh's Church**, which claims to be the oldest church in Ireland. The 19thC painter Nathaniel Hone lived in Doulagh Lodge nearby.

### Lusk and Newbridge

Just a few miles N of Dublin is **Lusk**, with its Round Tower, the last relic of a monastery founded in the 6thC by St Cuindid, on a 19thC church which incorporates a 16thC tower. Between them they compose a building that looks like something out of which Rapunzel might lean at any moment. The belfry now houses an exhibition, the **Lusk Heritage Centre** ( ☎*(01) 8721490* 📷*)*, on medieval churches in North Dublin, and also the magnificent effigy of Sir Christopher Barnwell and his wife Marion Sharl.

The Lusk Museum, established in the former church of St MacCullin, has been renamed the **Willie Monks Museum** (📷 *but only open afternoons of first Sun of each month in summer)* after a local antiquarian and depicts rural life over the past 100 years.

**Newbridge House and Victorian Farm** ( ☎ *(01) 8436534* 📷 🍴*)* at Donabate (12 miles from Dublin) is the historic home of the Cobbe family. It was built by Archbishop Cobbe, who bought the demesne in 1736 for £5,136, and designed by Richard Castle. Cobbe was a great friend of Handel, and he and his wife were discerning collectors and, from all the evidence, delightful people. The house, lived in by the Cobbe family until very recently, is filled with fine things. In the account books, diaries and notebooks retained in the house (doubly rare and valuable, since the burning of so much archival treasure in the Troubles) are recorded payments to "Williams the Stucco man" in 1764. He was a pupil of Richard West, and it was this Williams who created the plasterwork in the **Great Red Drawing Room**.

In the 19thC Charles Cobbe built 80 new stone and slate cottages for his tenants, selling much-loved paintings — a Poussin and a Hobbema — to pay for them. He pondered long over losing the Hobbema; in his diary he records that the picture was not looked at much, hanging as it did in a dark corner, whereas a warm, dry stone cottage would present a better picture to everyone concerned. Enlightened landlord! The dwellings were ever after known as "The Hobbema Cottages."

Newbridge, set in 350 acres of parkland, is a ravishing place to visit, an oasis that conveys the sense of life of a quiet, civilized, small estate in Ireland and a view into another kind of life entirely from that lived in those palaces of the very rich or in the dwellings of the peasantry. Here is illustrated the very particular way of life of the Big House, which remained connected to the surrounding countryside.

The fine square cobbled courtyard has been restored and a museum of late 18thC rural life, with a dairy, carpenter's shop, forge and laborer's cottage has been fitted out with the implements and furnishings of the period. There always was a museum in the house, a series of cabinets of curiosities brought back by Cobbe travelers; this is now enlarged, and a recently uncovered bamboo and Chinese wall-covering adds greatly to the charm of the room. Dublin County Council care for this house and have restored it impeccably, replacing the Victorian windows.

### The Boyne Valley and Tara

Among the most fascinating places in Ireland within reach of Dublin are the **Boyne Valley** and **Meath**, where so much history happened and can be traced, and **Tara**, that deserted hillside, the ancient center of Irish power and still the most potently evocative of all Irish places and names. This area is rich in houses and monastic ruins of great antiquity, but most striking of all are the prehistoric sites of **Newgrange**, **Dowth** and **Knowth**, extraordinary megalithic tombs of the Stone Age, older than Stonehenge and the Pyramids.

These tombs are spread right across Ireland but reach their apogee in the sacred burial areas of the Boyne Valley. They are epochal wonders, and in the case of Newgrange, which has been externally restored to conform to its original appearance, almost alarming. They were built centuries before the pyramids, about 2500BC, and at Newgrange and Knowth the richness of design and the execution of the scraped and chiseled carvings and mysterious motifs, which literally carry their secret to the grave, is unequaled in Europe.

The extent and learning of the people who built these tombs was revealed in 1969 when it was discovered that Newgrange tomb was aligned with the position on the horizon where the sun rises at dawn on the winter solstice, and that the roof box over the tomb chamber at Newgrange was placed so that the sun penetrated along the dark passage and into the burial chamber only on that day. There is something so touching about that shaft of light inching its way toward the dark center; metaphors about enlightenment and the Land of Saints and Scholars spring to mind.

The site is open daily from June to September 10am-7pm and October to May 10am-1pm and 2-5pm. The information center is only open during the summer season.

These monuments are worth making a separate journey for, but allow for a whole day away. There are so many things to see all around this area.

# The next journey: setting out for Cork

"There is only one safe rule for travelling in the southern half of Ireland and that is not to cut across the grain of the country from east to west." Only an Irishman would use such an analogy, and it was Frank O'Connor, the Cork-born writer, who delivered this magnificent and proper injunction to the traveler.

The country stretches and sometimes seems to purr north to south along the river valleys, following and making the grain of the country, and since it was the rivers and valleys that brought Ireland the only prosperity it has ever known, along the banks and by these routes, you see the big houses, the lovely villages, the castles, the churches (though some of the houses and the churches are tucked away); and everywhere, of course, that sad, charming and ubiquitous feature of the Irish countryside, the ruins. And remember that you won't have seen Ireland unless you go to **Cork**.

There's a story told by Robert Gibbings in his charming, now historical book about Cork, *Lovely is the Lee,* in which a man at Euston Station in London asked for a ticket from the booking office. "Where to?" asked the booking clerk, somewhat haughtily. "To Cork of course. Where the devil else?"

You can of course arrive in Cork by air, as well as by train, in which case on a fine day you see what a maritime town and county it is; even more so if you come by ferry in the summer months, sailing past the delightful coast of **Cobh**, or by coach on one of many well-organized trips. They all have their little ways.

But many visitors drive to Cork from Dublin, and it is important to spend time in choosing your route; and which route that is to be may well depend on the weather. If it is a clear spring day, prepare to take the N7 to **Kildare** and **Port Laoise**, and then the N8 to **Cashel**, thence to **Clonmel** and **Clogheen**, across through the descriptively named **The Vee**, and then to **Lismore** and via the coast road through **Youghal** to Cork, taking in the **Blackwater Valley** on the way.

If it is a less fine day or heaven forfend *raining,* then plan the more direct route: the N8 again through **Cashel**, over the plains to **Fermoy**, down the new road to **Glanmire** and thence to Cork along the river. This too has its pleasures, but it is a busy road.

## Setting out

The main road out of Dublin has vastly improved in the past few years. Drive along the s bank of the Grand Canal until you come to a T-junction signposted the South-West, turn there, and you are on your way. Beware. The road looks like a motorway *but there are traffic lights on it*. So there you are doing what you think is a statutory seventy miles and ought to be sixty and quite suddenly traffic lights loom up ahead, changing color fast to red. This disconcerting habit stops soon after, but then so does the motorway.

Driving through the small towns of Leinster, through Co. Kildare and Co. Tipperary and down toward Cork, is a great pleasure. A lot of people who have to do this as part of their daily grind or on business curse about the traffic, but since you're on vacation there's no point in having a rigid time-table that is hagridden by container trucks. So take by-roads, or let the traffic pass as you drive. You are opening a wedge through history and you don't want it to close behind you without looking at it.

The very names of the pubs give you a potted history of Ireland as you drive. You see **The Silken Thomas** and remember the strong-willed, impetuous and rash dandy, with courage beyond imagining, his followers dressed in silken fringes, beheaded for his trouble. Catch a glimpse of **The Lord Edward** and remember the doomed, beautiful rake with his hair in a pony tail, the most unlikely nationalist, son of the Duke of Leinster, who died for a different Ireland from the one his father had fashioned and inhabited, and from whose town house Ireland's laws are now enacted. Pass a Round Tower in the middle of a town; a crazy and beguiling shell house alongside the road; see a sign advertising Vesper cake; watch a jockey in well-worn jodhpurs in Kildare bandying along to post a letter.

Other pleasures come from realizing that these towns are unique and individual, and that the sanitized, homogenized infection that afflicts the High Streets of England has not laid these towns low. The tradition of skilled and ornate painted sign-writing makes every shopfront different, and the fairground lettering often bears the old names for the trades: victuallers, haberdasher, tea merchant, chandler. And that heart-lifting tradition of painting the front of the houses different colors so that any main street becomes a long vivid canvas still obtains. Town after town has its own spirit.

You drive into **Port Laoise** and see a huge barracks, the biggest jail in Ireland; see too that the town announces itself as the jazz center of Ireland. You drive through **Monasterevin**, stop to look at the townscape and push past a castle to get over the bridge at **Athy**; stop in **Abbeyleix** because there are so many pretty buildings, notice a big antique store on your right well worth a browse, and find that opposite is one of the most famous pubs in Ireland, apparently not aware of the fact. Morrissey's.

People dream of Morrissey's when they are in far-flung lands. The mustiness, the lie of the light through the old windows, the rows of tea caddies, the biscuit boxes, the chair that is a weighing machine, the Guinness. You certainly wouldn't dream of the coffee or the food, but that's not the point. The point is its atmosphere, and perhaps its porter. I'm not a connoisseur; but I know my coffee and cheese and Morrissey doesn't. Miraculously it hasn't been tarted up to improve the atmosphere so much as to lose it, as has happened, say, to the poor little town of Kinsale near Cork.

As you drive through **Durrow**, home of one of the most famous manuscripts (see DAY 1, pages 113-4), you may well stop because the little square, more of a triangle (and what in the North would be called "a diamond"), is so ravishingly pretty. There is a fine High Cross here (these finely carved sculptures suddenly appeared, fully developed, in the 10thC, ornaments to monastic sites all over Ireland, although here a telephone box has been given more importance). At any one of these places you could stay and ramble and visit any number of amazing buildings and monuments. Every town brings surprises and its own flavor, every mile a new scene.

## Kildare and the National Stud

Driving toward Kildare you cross **The Curragh**, where some of the best racehorses in the world are trained. The racetrack in one form or another has been here at least 2,000 years — indeed the very word means a racetrack or a morass. The Curragh crosses 5,000 acres, the largest stretch of unfenced arable land in the country, and the main road cuts right through it. It is most surprising to leave the little wooded fields with their hedgerows — "hardly hedgerows, little lines of sportive wood run wild" — in the surrounding areas and come upon this amazingly green prairie. If you are driving in the morning or evening you may well see groups of horses being exercised.

The Irish as a nation are horse-mad. There are reckoned to be 55,000 horses in Ireland, of which 15,000 are racehorses. The main bloodstock sales are held in **Kill** (to the E of Kildare), and the National Hunt Sales are in Fairyhouse in Co. Meath. But all over Ireland there are horse fairs worth their weight in gold if you want to observe the Irish going about something they love. Several Irish Classic races are held at The Curragh from June to September.

The **National Stud** ( ☎ *(045) 21251* ✗ *daily Easter-Oct)* is at Kildare. Founded by Lord Waventree, in the early part of the century, the stud, which is a national industry, is owned and run by the Irish government, and among other activities carries out research into bloodstock and provides breeding services.

Lord Waventree's belief in astrology ruled his choice of foal in his stud. If the star chart of the foal portended good, he would keep the foal. His stable did extremely well. In the "lantern" stables, where stallions are quartered, there are still skylights in their roofs so that they can be affected or "touched" by the rays of the sun and the moon.

There is a museum here showing the evolution of the horse and of racing; and — somewhat gruesome — the skeleton of Arkle, one of the greatest and certainly the most loved of steeplechasers.

Lord Waventree also founded the **Japanese Gardens** ( ☎ *(045) 21251, open daily Easter-Oct)* at Tully House, just s of Kildare. Laid out in the first decade of this century by the celebrated gardener Eida and his son Minoru, these gardens lead the traveler through the life of mankind from birth to death, old age to eternity, over a series of metaphorical garden features.

The Curragh also contains the largest army camp in the country, but the road through it is public. Photographs cannot be taken within the precincts.

There are great numbers of prehistoric earthworks and ring-works on The Curragh, one of which contained a ritual victim buried alive. To the w of the Army Camp is **Gibbert Rath**, where 350 United Irishmen were massacred in 1798, after surrendering and laying down arms.

**Kildare** is a small cathedral, garrison and market town, with another of those triangular squares. St Brigid, St Patrick's handmaiden (these two with Columba form the great triumvirate of Irish sainthood), founded a monastery here for nuns and monks, which became the most famous in Ireland. Here burned the Blessed Fire of Saint Brigid (probably a relic from pagan times), kept continuously alight by relays of nuns until it was quenched in 1120 by command of the killjoy Archbishop de Loundres. It was relit and continued to burn until the Reformation. (There is still a great echo of this in the tradition that obtained in all Irish cottages well into this century of never letting the turf fire go out.) The monastery was sacked by the Vikings, though not as badly as it had been by Dermot MacMurrough, King of Leinster, who was also responsible for inviting the Anglo-Normans into Ireland in 1152.

This St Brigid is a great saint in Ireland and sounds lovable with her little penchant for drink (the best maker of ale and mead in Ireland), and it is still a tradition on St Brigid's Day at the beginning of February to weave rush crosses, which are hung over pictures or doors to keep the house holy.

The present cathedral dates from 1686, when the remnants of the old cathedral were rebuilt in the Classical style to serve as the Protestant Cathedral of the diocese. The restoration was done by George Edmund Street, who never restored if he could rebuild (witness Dublin's Christ Church Cathedral). There is a Harry Clarke window of St Hubert in the cathedral, and next to it a remarkably high Round Tower.

These skillfully constructed Round Towers are a curious and distinctive feature in the Irish landscape, and rise with extreme verticality in many a flat landscape. Though they were used as a siege building against the Vikings, they were originally called *cloctheach,* meaning bell-house, so it would seem that their principal purpose was as a steeple. There were never stairs in these buildings; pull-up ladders were used, and since the only door was nine feet up above ground level, they would have served as a safe place from attack.

("These towers," writes Maurice Craig, "have long been regarded and employed as a symbol of Irish nationhood and by the irreverent as a symbol of another kind altogether.")

Kildare, of course, has the closest of associations with the Earls of Kildare and in particular Lord Edward Fitzgerald, who lived here with his beautiful wife Pamela, whose portrait is at Malahide Castle near Dublin (see EXCURSIONS, page 253). Poor Pamela. She was French and had a horrible time in Ireland; Dublin society suspected her, not unnaturally, of harboring republican ideals, and when she went to a ball dressed in the most chic of Parisian fashion, the provincial Dublin women "some of [the] genteelest in Dublin, star'd at her with so much curiosity that she went away crying."

Just NE is the **Hill of Allen**, a steepish 15-minute climb, famous in saga as the seat of Fionn MacCumhaill. The tower on the summit is a folly erected by Sir Gerald Aylmer in the Victorian era on the site of a prehistoric tumulus.

For information about boating on the Grand and Royal Canals, contact **Co. Kildare Tourist Office** ☎(0404) 69117/69118.

## Monasterevin, Port Laoise and Abbeyleix

**Monasterevin** is a pretty little town on the Grand Canal and the River Barrow, with an old drawbridge. The Abbey, founded by St Eimhine, gave the town its name. Gerard Manley Hopkins lived here, and John McCormack the famous tenor bought **Moore Abbey**, gothicized in 1846, the ancient seat of the Earls of Drogheda. The gardens are open and a picnic site is in the grounds. The cross in the Market Place commemorates another victim of that sad rebellion of 1798, Father Prendergast, who was hanged for his part in the rising. The **Monasterevin Festival** takes place during the first week in July.

**Port Laoise** is where Dr Bartholomew Mosse, founder of the Rotunda Hospital in Dublin, was born. Six miles w is **Ballyfin House** (☎ *(0502) 55245)*, one of the grandest houses in Ireland, designed by Richard Morrison, a pupil of James Gandon, built in 1826 by Sir Charles Coote. It is now owned by a religious order and is open only by appointment. Hideously unsuitable furniture is set amid wonderful, rococo decoration.

**Abbeyleix** is a felicitous, well-laid-out town with a sparkle in its air. It was originally centered on a Cistercian monastery, from which it obtains its name. It was built by Lord de Vesci in the middle of the 18thC (his descendant still lives there) and has beautiful houses with fanlights and lime trees, and a lovely market house with Lord de Vesci's arms. All in all it is a lovely, well-laid-out and aspected town, the peace of which is most rudely broken by huge trucks thundering through. The traffic despoils these towns.

In the distance is the 600-square-mile range of **Slieve Bloom**, and though its highest point, **Arderin**, is only 1,733 feet, it looks big in this landscape and means the "Height of Ireland."

Ahead where the Slieve Blooms run into the **Silvermines** and **Slievefelim** mountains is the **Devil's Bit** mountain, which, from many directions, looks as though some giant had taken a bite out of the summit. Legend has it that the giant, not liking what he had bitten off, spat it out as the Rock of Cashel. The Devil's Bit mountain is old red sandstone; the Rock of Cashel is carboniferous limestone. So much for legend, or so much for the giant's gastric juices.

> *There is magic in this region, whether it be the magic of the full blaze of summer's color, the wistful wizardry of the subdued but unforgettably endearing tints of autumn, the sterner browns and deeper greens of winter or the fragile promise of delicate loveliness that comes in early spring, when every small mountainy tree decks itself like a bride and the wild birds begin to send their hopeful songs across the great solitude of the boglands. Get you to the Slieve Blooms at any season and see whether I have spoken truth.*
> (Richard Hayward, *Leinster*)

But on the whole the mountains, though blue and bulking at times, at others a swelling dark green, are not dominant in the landscape and all is flat, the plains of Tipperary like a flung shawl full of honey-colored threads of light, and in the far distance the ramparts, the stage set of the **Galtee** mountains. Everything scenically-speaking is as it should be, and all the buildings one has seen have been lovely, secular and manageably civilized.

## Cashel

And there, ahead of you, is **Cashel Rock** — "the great vision of the guarded mount" rising sheer, transfigured, cleaving a gap in the transparency. It is an extraordinary outward expression of a spiritual urge, of a thrust toward God, and the rearing rock, an arsenal of faith, endows its surrounding countryside with purpose, a sense of meaning. The landscape is pulled irresistibly upward, pleating toward that great organ on the hill. Cashel is an emotional landscape, and in this landscape, where the sky is cloudy, the weather uncertain and the temper of the times was unpredictable, Cashel was indeed the rock, the unchanging symbol of eternity; there ahead lay sanctuary.

When you first see it, whether it be by night when it is gloriously gold, or by day in sun or rain, you realize that that silhouette in the northern light was utterly important, and that whatever else round towers were, they were pointers to heaven.

Frank O'Connor once wrote that "civilization in Ireland is a relative affair." When you look at this series of buildings dating from the 12thC, a living poem to faith, with the lifted finger of the belfry pointing to heaven, and the towers of Cormac's Chapel, you know you are in the presence of the absolute. Nothing else in Ireland bears any resemblance to it; nothing bears comparison, except one, unexpected, monument as profane as Cashel is sacred: the Marino Casino.

"Six centuries of cultural evolution separate these two buildings," writes Sean O'Reilly in his fine commentary on the Casino, "but both remain as monuments to a country at its finest and to countrymen at their best."

Frank O'Connor described Cashel as "an exquisite elaborate model of a Norman church dropped on a bare rock in the middle of Ireland." This, he wrote, was European art with a vengeance. But vengeance is the wrong word, even though it is built on so high, magnificent and fortified a place. It is a great paean to a religious belief in peace and faith that lifts the heart with it. Cashel *deserves* enough time to take it quietly in.

The beautiful little Romanesque building, **Cormac's Chapel**, is currently being restored, with its corbel-roofed nave, arcaded walls and twin square towers, one of which is capped by a pyramidal roof and apse. The chapel lies alongside the **Cathedral of St Patrick** like "a little tender by the Gothic hull" of the cathedral; the building of the cathedral partly swallowed up Cormac's Chapel as it was being built, so that the w windows of the chapel are in the cathedral transept. It is a cruciform shape with a long eastern arm, and the lack of an aisle makes it an astonishing crate full of air. In the 15thC the w front was turned into a castle: it has been twice burned, restored, abandoned and left to disintegrate. It is amazing that any of this building survives, considering its vicissitudes.

The roofless chancel and nave is long — 93 feet — and the chancel is 85 feet high. The adjacent round tower is more than 70 feet high and is well preserved, with its pointed roof piercing the sky, its tiny window like something out of which an angel might lean and drop off the first rung of the ladder to the paradise that the people who built this place must have seen so clearly in their dreams. And when you step outside through the many entrances and arches, you find, as an old poet said, that beauty is contagious to your elbow at every turn.

*If you visit Ireland only to see this astonishing building you will not have crossed the sea in vain. It is the strangest sight to one accustomed to Norman churches in England, built by the Normans — apparently with a chisel in one hand and a drawn sword in the other! Durham Cathedral, which is the greatest Norman church in England, holds something of Flambard's sternness in its stones . . . even small chapels are essentially grim and they appear to have been designed by architects who had just composed a fortress. Cormac's Chapel on Cashel is the only piece of gay Norman architecture I have seen. One might call it Norman architecture with a sense of humour! There is nothing quite like it in the world.* (From *In Search of Ireland*, H.V. Morton)

Cashel was always at the nerve end of history and was the ecclesiastical capital of Munster. The King of Cashel was synonymous with the King of Munster, and it was not till 859 that Munster acknowledged the High King of Ireland at Tara.

The oldest part of the complex is really a testimonial to Cormac Mac Carthy, King of Munster, who died in 1138 and who is reputed to have built the chapel between 1127 and 1134. It was here that a momentous historical meeting that changed the history and culture of Ireland took place: the meeting in the winter of 1171-2 of the Synod convened by Henry II of England, at which he laid claim to the Lordship of Ireland.

In 1495 the church was set on fire by the Great Earl of Kildare because he thought the Archbishop was inside. (At least, this is the reason he tendered to a somewhat bemused Henry VII.)

The church was rebuilt over the centuries and suffered tumultuous events, but remained a church until the philistine Archbishop Price, blockhead and enemy of Swift, stripped it of its roof. (He courted Vanessa without success; on her deathbed she said, "No Price, no prayers.") In the 19thC the E end collapsed, and in 1874 the ruins were handed over to the State to be conserved as a national monument. For years it moldered, and in the old guide books one reads time and again of the hapless astonishment visitors felt at seeing this magnificent monument of international significance left to rot. Not so now. If anything it is under siege from the improvers, and is, in the summer months, busy with visitors ( ☎ *(062) 61437: same number for Rock and Museum)*.

Inside the precincts is the **Cashel Rock Museum** in the Vicar's Choral Hall. Relics of Cashel include **St Patrick's Cross** on a 12thC chain, with a robed figure on one side who is said to be St Patrick. The pedestal on which the cross stands is reputed to be the ancient coronation stone for the Kings of Munster. One of the many legends associated with St Patrick is that when he baptized King Aengus and his son at the stone, he drove the sharp point of his crozier through the King's foot. Asked later why he had not cried out or indeed demurred, the King said that he had thought it a necessary part of the baptism ritual.

**Cashel** itself is a town full of pretty things, including some houses with fanlights to equal anything in Dublin, and the former **Archbishops' Palace** at the foot of the Rock, now the Cashel Palace, a ravishingly pretty house built by Sir Edward Lovett Pearce in 1730.

Beside the Church of Ireland **Cathedral of St John**, built in the 18thC in a pretty old building, is that collection of superb volumes known as the **GPA Bolton Library** *(John St.* ☎ *(062) 61944)*, amassed by the Archbishop of Cashel, Theophilus Bolton, in the early 18thC. This unique collection of 12,000 volumes contains remarkable treasures: there are, for example, two leaves of printing from Caxton's printing press (1486) and a superb illustrated *Nuremberg Chronicle* printed in 1493, as well as early examples of Irish printing from Dublin, Waterford, Kilkenny and Cork. This is a small but wonderful library.

## Cahir

Leaving Cashel to drive s is to set off on a new adventure. The valley of the Suir is famous for its beauty, and the **Comeragh, Knockmealdown** and **Galtee** mountains are around and before you. Cahir is a fine center for exploring this whole area, especially the beautiful glen of **Aherlow**, a long valley on the Tipperary side of Cahir, between the Galtees and Slievenamick. This is rich country. The main dairy area of Ireland — the Golden Vale — is hereabouts.

**Cahir** is a few miles s of Cashel and is most beautifully situated at the foot of the Galtees, where the main roads cross the Suir.

Cahir means "fort," and the **castle** here ( ☎ *(052) 41011)* is the biggest built in Ireland during the 15th and 16thC. It was a stronghold of the Butler family and almost impregnable on its island in the river. This is now a National Monument and has been restored in both the 19th and 20thC to within an inch of its life. You expect Douglas Fairbanks or Harrison Ford to come leaping out, sword between teeth. The curtain wall with its bastions acted as the defenses for the keep, and cannonballs fired by the Earl of Essex's troops in 1599 still remain embedded in the walls. When Cromwell marched into town 50 years later, the castle surrendered without a shot being fired. A famous letter explains why:

*Sir – having brought the army and my cannon near this place according to my usual manner in summoning places, I thought fit to offer you terms honorable to soldiers: that you may march away with your baggage, arms and colors, free from injuries and violence. But if I be, notwithstanding, necessitated to bend my cannon upon you, you must expect the extremity usual in such cases. To void blood this is offered to you by*
    *Your Servant*
    *Oliver Cromwell.*

At one end of the outer wall of its defenses is **Cahir Cottage**, where an audiovisual presentation describes the monuments of the area.

The Gothic Revival **church** was built by the celebrated Regency architect John Nash, more famous for Brighton's Pavilion.

Just N of Cahir are the ruins of **Outeragh**, famous in the Irish annals for having been the parish church of Geoffrey Keating (Seathrun Ceitinn), the great poet, historian and writer, a kind of Chaucer of Ireland, and master of classical modern Irish prose (*c.*1570-*c.*1645). He preached a sermon against vice in high places that so enraged the powerful Earl of Thomond that he had to flee and go into hiding.

Down a lane off the Tipperary Road on the outskirts of Cahir is the Priory of Augustinian Canons known as **Cahir Abbey**, founded in the 13thC and suppressed in 1540. It has wonderful carved heads on the E windows as good as you will see, and a beautiful E window of curious construction with carved strap work.

Just a mile S of Cahir is the delightful little folly and best *cottage orné* in these islands, the thatched **Swiss Cottage** (☎ *(052) 41144* 📧 𝒀 ). Designed in 1810 by John Nash, the Prince Regent's architect for Richard Butler, the 12th Lord Cahir, it sits like Little Miss Muffet on a tuffet in a romantic situation overlooking the River Suir in the middle of the estate of the Earls of Glengall.

Beautifully restored, the colored scenic wallpapers, treasures in themselves, have been replaced and have transformed the interior as they must have done when the glamorous young couple Lord and Lady Cahir brought them back from Paris in 1816.

When the old caretaker died in 1980, the cottage began to deteriorate. A group of people bought it for £35,000, of which sum the Irish Georgian Society paid £10,000. Sybil Connolly, the Irish couturier, who is passionate about houses and gardens, was the decorator who pulled it all together. But it is to the generosity of Mrs Christian Aall and her Port Royal Foundation of New York, who underwrote the expense of restoring the whole thing, that we owe this delightful nonsense, which should be visited if you are in any way interested in the pleasure of beauty for the fun of it.

Incidentally the Cahirs did not build this as a pleasure dome or a folly; they intended to live in it when they visited Ireland, but the lures of fashionable London and Paris left them little time for the hurly-burly of Cahir. Now it is in the care of the Office of Public Works, who also helped with the restoration.

## Across the Blackwater

**Fethard**, **Clogheen** and **Clonmel** are all towns worth at least a morning's visit. Fethard especially is crammed with antiquities: on the town gate is a *sheila-na-gig,* a 14thC stone carving of a squatting female, found in buildings all over Ireland, revealing large sexual organs and probably a fertility symbol. An earlier visitor chronicles that an inhabitant of the town, when questioned about its significance, said, casting his eyes down, "It's a wind fairy."

Southwest of Clogheen is the small village of **Ballyporeen** where ex-President Reagan's great-grandfather was born. From Clogheen there is the twisting, steep, wonderful road that leads over the Knockmealdown Mountains, through **The Vee** and down to Lismore. There is a stopping place at The Vee. Stop. The view stretches for miles, and Ireland becomes a continent.

The only sound is of water gurgling somewhere and the sheep crunching grass as though they were chewing apples. From here on for many miles Ireland becomes a different landscape. Until now the countryside has been pastoral, a beautified landscape and one that bears the traces of man. But moving between these roads, winding down by whin-covered heath and fields that live up to the emerald description, we find we are in rural Ireland, one that is older and has not been groomed and knocked into shape by man. This is the shape of Irish nature.

Then, as we come down the Blackwater to Lismore, we reach the Tennysonian drama of the castle walls of **Lismore**. Crossing the Blackwater, we arrive into another country. This is the southwest of Ireland all right, almost archetypally so, but it has a different history and spirit.

When you travel the road between Dublin and Cork you do more than travel a highway. You have traversed a history and driven between rival capitals.

# Index

- **Bold** Page numbers indicate main entries.
- *Italic* page numbers indicate illustrations and maps.
- The GENERAL INDEX starts opposite.
- See also LIST OF STREET NAMES on page 276.

## INDEX OF PLACES

## GENERAL INDEX

# List of street names

- All streets mentioned in this book that fall within the area covered by our city maps **3** to **4** are listed opposite.
- Map numbers are printed in **bold** type. Some smaller streets are not named on the maps, but the map reference given below will help you locate the correct neighborhood.

Andrews Lane, **4**D4
Anglesea St., **4**D4
Aungier St., **4**E4

Back Lane, **3**D3
Balfe St., **4**D4
Beresford Pl., **4**C5
Blackhall Pl., **3**C2
Bridge St., **3**D3

Capel St., **3**C3-**4**D4
Cavendish Row, **4**B4
Chancery St., **3**C3
Christ Church Pl., **3**D3
Church St., **3**D3-C3
Clanbrassil St., **3**F3
Clare St., **4**D5
Clarendon St., **4**D4
College St., **4**D4-5
College Green, **4**D4
Constitution Hill, **3**B3
Coote Lane, **4**D5
Crane St., **3**D2
Crow St., **4**D4
Crown Alley, **4**D4
Custom House Quay, **4**C5-6

Dame Court, **4**D4
Dame St., **4**D4
Dawson Lane, **O**00
Dawson St., **4**E5-D5
D'Olier St., **4**C4-D5
Digges Lane, **4**D4
Dorset St., **3**B3-**4**B4
Drury St., **4**D4
Duke St., **4**D4-5

Earlsfort Tce., **4**F5-E5
East Essex St., **4**D4
Eccles St., **3**A3-**4**A4
Edward Sq., **3**D3
Ely Pl., **4**E5
Essex Quay, **3**D3
Essex St., **4**D4
Eustace St., **4**D4
Exchequer St., **4**D4

Fishamble St., **3**D3
Fitzwilliam Pl., **4**F5
Fitzwilliam Sq., **4**E5-F5
Fitzwilliam St., **4**F5-E6
Fleet St., **4**D4-5
Foley St., **4**C5-B4
Foster Pl., **4**D4
Francis St., **3**D3-E3

Grafton Arcade, **4**D4
Grafton St., **4**E4-D4
Granby Row, **4**B4

Greater William St., **4**D4

Haddington Rd., **1**C3
Ha'penny Footbridge, **4**C4
Harcourt St., **4**E4-F4
Hardwick St., **4**A4
Hardwicke Pl., **4**B4
Harry St., **4**E4
Henrietta St., **3**B3
Henry St., **4**C4
High St., **3**D3
Hume St., **4**E5

Inns Quay, **3**D3

James's Gate, **3**D1
James's Pl., **4**E6

Kildare St., **4**E5-D5

Leinster St., **4**D5
Liffey Bridge, **4**C4
Liffey St., **4**C4
Lincoln Pl., **4**D5
Litton Lane, **4**C4
Lord Edward St., **3**D3-**4**D4
Lower Abbey St., **4**C5
Lower Baggot St., **4**E5-F6
Lower Bridge St., **3**D3
Lower Dominick St., **3**B3-**4**C4
Lower Fitzwilliam St., **4**E6
Lower Leeson St., **4**E5-F5
Lower Mount St., **4**E6
Lower Ormond Quay, **4**C4

Malahide Rd., **1**B3-**2**A4
Manor St., **3**B2
Marlborough St., **4**B4-C5
Mary St., **3**C3-**4**C4
Merchant's Quay, **3**D3
Merrion Court, **4**E5
Merrion Rd., **1**C2-D3
Merrion Row, **4**E5
Merrion Sq., **4**E5-6
Mespil Rd., **4**F6
Middle Abbey St., **4**C4
Molesworth Pl., **4**D5
Molesworth St., **4**D5
Moore St., **4**C4
Morehampton Rd., **1**C2-D3
Mountjoy Sq., **4**A4-B5
Mountjoy St., **3**B3

Nassau St., **4**D4-5
North Frederick St., **4**B4
North Great George's St., **4**B4

O'Connell Bridge, **4**C4
O'Connell St., **4**B4-C4

Parliament St., **4**D4
Parnell Sq., **4**B4
Patrick St., **3**E3
Pearse St., **4**D5-6
Pembroke St., **4**F5-E5
Poolbeg St., **4**C5

Royal Hibernian Way, **4**D5
Rutland St., **4**B4

St Andrew's St., **4**D4
St Mary's Lane, **3**C3
St Michans St., **3**C2
St Patrick's Close, **3**E3
St Stephen's Green, **4**E4-5
Smithfield, **3**C2
South Anne Lane, **4**D4
South Anne St., **4**D4-5
South Frederick St., **4**D5
South Great George's St., **4**D4
South King St., **4**E4
South William St., **4**D4
Stephen's Lane, **4**E6
Stephen's St., **4**D4
Stoneybatter, **3**B2-C2
Store St., **4**C5
Suffolk St., **4**D4
Synge St., **3**F3

Tara St., **4**D5-C5
Temple Bar, **4**D4
Temple St., **4**A4-B4
The Coombe, **3**E2-3
Thomas St., **3**D2
Trinity St., **4**D4

Upper Fitzwilliam St., **6**F6-E6
Upper Leeson St., **1**C2
Upper Merrion St., **4**E5
Upper Mount St., **4**E6
Upper Ormond Quay, **3**D3
Upper Pembroke St., **4**F5
Upper Rathmines Rd., **1**D2

Werburgh St., **3**D3
Westland Row, **4**D5
Westmoreland St., **4**D4-C4
Whitefriars St., **4**E4
Wicklow St., **4**D4
Wilton Pl., **4**F6
Wood Quay, **3**D3

York St., **4**E4

## CONVERSION FORMULAE

| To convert | Multiply by |
|---|---|
| Inches to Centimeters | 2.540 |
| Centimeters to Inches | 0.39370 |
| Feet to Meters | 0.3048 |
| Meters to feet | 3.2808 |
| Yards to Meters | 0.9144 |
| Meters to Yards | 1.09361 |
| Miles to Kilometers | 1.60934 |
| Kilometers to Miles | 0.621371 |
| Sq Meters to Sq Feet | 10.7638 |
| Sq Feet to Sq Meters | 0.092903 |
| Sq Yards to Sq Meters | 0.83612 |
| Sq Meters to Sq Yards | 1.19599 |
| Sq Miles to Sq Kilometers | 2.5899 |
| Sq Kilometers to Sq Miles | 0.386103 |
| Acres to Hectares | 0.40468 |
| Hectares to Acres | 2.47105 |
| Gallons to Liters | 4.545 |
| Liters to Gallons | 0.22 |
| Ounces to Grams | 28.3495 |
| Grams to Ounces | 0.03528 |
| Pounds to Grams | 453.592 |
| Grams to Pounds | 0.00220 |
| Pounds to Kilograms | 0.4536 |
| Kilograms to Pounds | 2.2046 |
| Tons (UK) to Kilograms | 1016.05 |
| Kilograms to Tons (UK) | 0.0009842 |
| Tons (US) to Kilograms | 746.483 |
| Kilograms to Tons (US) | 0.0013396 |

**Quick conversions**

| | |
|---|---|
| Kilometers to Miles | Divide by 8, multiply by 5 |
| Miles to Kilometers | Divide by 5, multiply by 8 |
| 1 meter = | Approximately 3 feet 3 inches |
| 2 centimeters = | Approximately 1 inch |
| 1 pound (weight) = | 475 grams (nearly $\frac{1}{2}$ kilogram) |
| Celsius to Fahrenheit | Divide by 5, multiply by 9, add 32 |
| Fahrenheit to Celsius | Subtract 32, divide by 9, multiply by 5 |

# KEY TO MAP PAGES

# KEY TO MAP SYMBOLS

## Environs Map

- ■ Place of Interest
- Built-up Area
- Park
- ⊤ ⊤ Cemetery
- Motorway / Superhighway
- Main Road
- Secondary Road
- Other Road
- A201 Road Number
- – – Ferry
- Railway

## City Map

- Place of Interest or Important Building
- Built-up Area
- Park
- ⊤ ⊤ Cemetery
- ✝ Church, Cathedral
- ⊞ Hospital
- *i* Information Office
- ✉ Post Office
- ✋ Garda Station
- 🚗 Garage / Parking Lot
- → One-way Street
- ⧧ No Entry

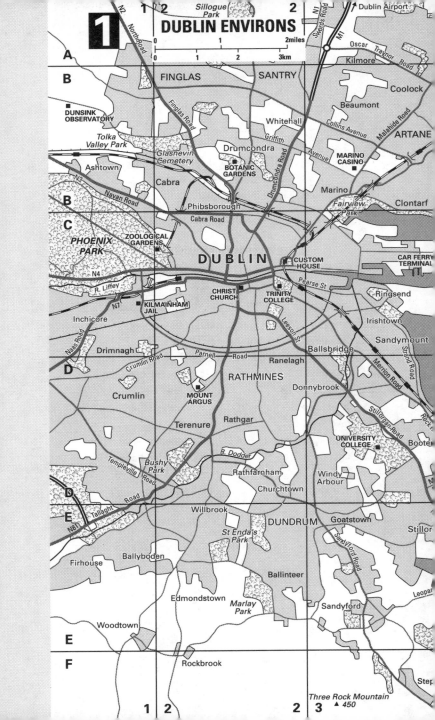

# 1 DUBLIN ENVIRONS

Silloge Park

Dublin Airport

Oscar Traynor Road

Kilmore

FINGLAS    SANTRY

Coolock

North Road

N2

Swords Road

M1

N1

**DUNSINK OBSERVATORY**

Beaumont

Whitehall

Collins Avenue

Malahide Road

**ARTANE**

Tolka Valley Park

Finglas Road

Griffith Avenue

Drumcondra

Drumcondra Road

**MARINO CASINO**

Ashtown

Glasnevin Cemetery

**BOTANIC GARDENS**

Marino

Navan Road

N3

Cabra

Phibsborough

Fairview Park

Clontarf

Cabra Road

**PHOENIX PARK**

**ZOOLOGICAL GARDENS**

**DUBLIN**

**CUSTOM HOUSE**

**CAR FERRY TERMINAL**

N4

R. Liffey

N7

**CHRIST CHURCH**

**TRINITY COLLEGE**

Pearse St

Ringsend

**KILMAINHAM JAIL**

Naas Road

Inchicore

Leeson St

Irishtown

Sandymount

Drimnagh

Parnell    Road

Ballsbridge

Merrion Road

Strand Road

Crumlin Road

Ranelagh

**RATHMINES**

Donnybrook

Crumlin

**MOUNT ARGUS**

Stillorgan Road

Terenure

Rathgar

**UNIVERSITY COLLEGE**

Booter

R. Dodder

Templeville Road

Bushy Park

Rathfarnham

Windy Arbour

Churchtown

Willbrook

**DUNDRUM**

Goatstown

Stillor

Tallaght Road

N81

St Enda's Park

Sandyford Road

Firhouse

Ballyboden

Ballinteer

Leopar

Edmondstown

Marlay Park

Sandyford

Woodtown

Rockbrook

Three Rock Mountain ▲ 450

Step

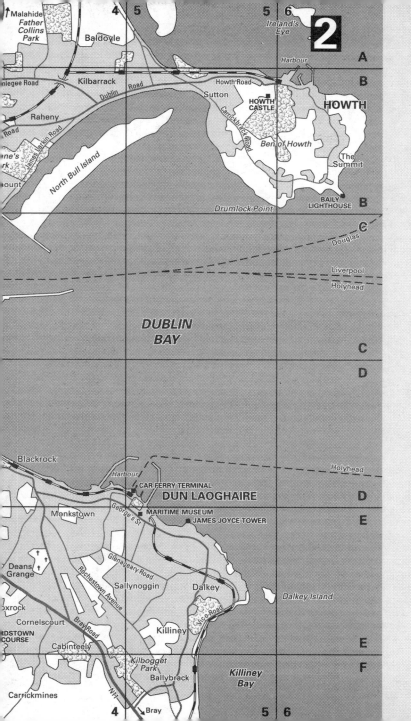

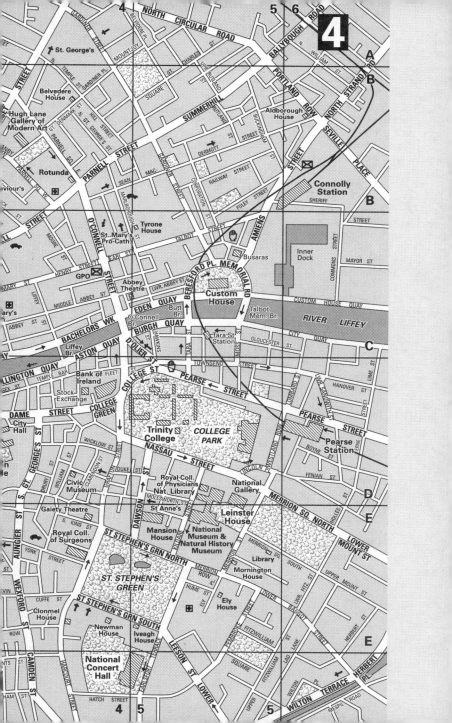

# Clothing sizes chart

## LADIES
### Suits and dresses

| | | | | | | | |
|---|---|---|---|---|---|---|---|
| Australia | 8 | 10 | 12 | 14 | 16 | 18 | |
| France | 34 | 36 | 38 | 40 | 42 | 44 | |
| Germany | 32 | 34 | 36 | 38 | 40 | 42 | |
| Italy | 38 | 40 | 42 | 44 | 46 | | |
| Japan | 7 | 9 | 11 | 13 | | | |
| UK | 6 | 8 | 10 | 12 | 14 | 16 | 18 |
| USA | 4 | 6 | 8 | 10 | 12 | 14 | 16 |

### Shoes

| | | | | | | |
|---|---|---|---|---|---|---|
| USA | 6 | $6\frac{1}{2}$ | 7 | $7\frac{1}{2}$ | 8 | $8\frac{1}{2}$ |
| UK | $4\frac{1}{2}$ | 5 | $5\frac{1}{2}$ | 6 | $6\frac{1}{2}$ | 7 |
| Europe | 38 | 38 | 39 | 39 | 40 | 41 |

## MEN
### Shirts

| | | | | | | | |
|---|---|---|---|---|---|---|---|
| USA, UK | 14 | $14\frac{1}{2}$ | 15 | $15\frac{1}{2}$ | 16 | $16\frac{1}{2}$ | 17 |
| Europe, Japan Australia | 36 | 37 | 38 | 39.5 | 41 | 42 | 43 |

### Sweaters/T-shirts

| | | | | |
|---|---|---|---|---|
| Australia, USA, Germany | S | M | L | XL |
| UK | 34 | 36-38 | 40 | 42-44 |
| Italy | 44 | 46-48 | 50 | 52 |
| France | 1 | 2-3 | 4 | 5 |
| Japan | | S-M | L | XL |

### Suits/Coats

| | | | | | |
|---|---|---|---|---|---|
| UK, USA | 36 | 38 | 40 | 42 | 44 |
| Australia, Italy, France, Germany | 46 | 48 | 50 | 52 | 54 |
| Japan | S | M | L | XL | |

### Shoes

| | | | | | | |
|---|---|---|---|---|---|---|
| UK | 7 | $7\frac{1}{2}$ | $8\frac{1}{2}$ | $9\frac{1}{2}$ | $10\frac{1}{2}$ | 11 |
| USA | 8 | $8\frac{1}{2}$ | $9\frac{1}{2}$ | $10\frac{1}{2}$ | $11\frac{1}{2}$ | 12 |
| Europe | 41 | 42 | 43 | 44 | 45 | 46 |

## CHILDREN
### Clothing

UK

| | | | | | | |
|---|---|---|---|---|---|---|
| *Height (ins)* | 43 | 48 | 55 | 60 | 62 | |
| *Age* | 4-5 | 6-7 | 9-10 | 11 | 12 | 13 |

USA

| | | | | | | |
|---|---|---|---|---|---|---|
| *Age* | 4 | 6 | 8 | 10 | 12 | 14 |

Europe

| | | | | | | |
|---|---|---|---|---|---|---|
| *Height (cms)* | 125 | 135 | 150 | 155 | 160 | 165 |
| *Age* | 7 | 9 | 12 | 13 | 14 | 15 |

## What the papers said:

• "The expertly edited American Express series has the knack of pinpointing precisely the details you need to know, and doing it concisely and intelligently." (*The Washington Post*)

• "*(Venice)* ... the best guide book I have ever used." (*The Standard* — London)

• "Amid the welter of guides to individual countries, American Express stands out...." (*Time*)

• "Possibly the best ... guides on the market, they come close to the oft-claimed 'all you need to know' comprehensiveness, with much original experience, research and opinions." (*Sunday Telegraph* — London)

• "The most useful general guide was *American Express New York* by Herbert Bailey Livesey. It also has the best street and subway maps." (*Daily Telegraph* — London)

• "...in the flood of travel guides, the *American Express* guides come closest to the needs of traveling managers with little time." (*Die Zeit* — Germany)

## What the experts said:

• "We only used one guide book, Sheila Hale's *Amex Venice,* for which she and the editors deserve a Nobel Prize." (Eric Newby, London)

• "Congratulations to you and your staff for putting out the best guide book of *any* size *(Barcelona & Madrid)*. I'm recommending it to everyone." (Barnaby Conrad, Santa Barbara, California)

• "If you're only buying one guide book, we recommend American Express...." (*Which?* — Britain's leading consumer magazine)

## What readers from all over the world have said:

• "The book *(Hong Kong, Singapore & Bangkok)* was written in such a personal way that I feel as if you were actually writing this book for me." (L.Z., Orange, Conn., USA)

• "Your book *(Florence and Tuscany)* proved a wonderful companion for us in the past fortnight. It went with us everywhere...." (E.H., Kingston-on-Thames, Surrey, England)

• "I feel as if you have been a silent friend shadowing my time in Tuscany." (T.G., Washington, DC, USA)

• "We followed your book *(Los Angeles & San Francisco)* to the letter. It proved to be wonderful, indispensable, a joy...." (C.C., London, England)

• "We could never have had the wonderful time that we did without your guide to *Paris*. The compactness was very convenient, your maps were all we needed, but it was your restaurant guide that truly made our stay special.... We have learned first-hand: *American Express — don't leave home without it.*" (A. R., Virginia Beach, Va., USA)

• "Much of our enjoyment came from the way your book *(Venice)* sent us off scurrying around the interesting streets and off to the right places at the right times". (Lord H., London, England)

• "It *(Paris)* was my constant companion and totally dependable...." (V. N., Johannesburg, South Africa)

• "I could go on and on about how useful the book *(Amsterdam)* was — the trouble was that it was almost getting to be a case of not venturing out without it...." (J.C.W., Manchester, England)

• "We have heartily recommended these books to all our friends who have plans to travel abroad." (A.S. and J.C., New York, USA)

• "Despite many previous visits to Italy, I wish I had had your guide *(Florence and Tuscany)* ages ago. I love the author's crisp, literate writing and her devotion to her subject." (M. B-K., Denver, Colorado, USA)

• "We never made a restaurant reservation without checking your book *(Venice)*. The recommendations were excellent, and the historical and artistic text got us through the sights beautifully." (L.S., Boston, Ma., USA)

• "We became almost a club as we found people sitting at tables all around, consulting their little blue books!" (F.C., Glasgow, Scotland)

• "This guide *(Paris)* we warmly recommend to all the many international visitors we work with." (M.L., Paris, France)

• "It's not often I would write such a letter, but it's one of the best guide books we have ever used *(Rome)* — we can't fault it!" (S.H., Berkhamsted, Herts, England)

# American Express Travel Guides

## *spanning the globe....*

### EUROPE
Amsterdam, Rotterdam
  & The Hague
Athens and the
  Classical Sites  * ‡
Barcelona, Madrid &
  Seville  #
Berlin, Potsdam &
  Dresden  * (‡ as Berlin)
Brussels
Dublin
Florence and Tuscany
London
Moscow & St Petersburg  *
Paris
Prague  #
Provence and the
  Côte d'Azur  *
Rome
Venice  #
Vienna & Budapest

### NORTH AMERICA
Boston and New
  England  *
Los Angeles & San
  Diego
Mexico  #
New York
San Francisco and
  the Wine Regions
Toronto, Montréal and
  Québec City  #
Washington, DC

### THE PACIFIC
Cities of
  Australia
Hong Kong
  & Taiwan
Singapore &
  Bangkok  * ‡
Tokyo

---

*   Paperbacks in preparation    #   Paperbacks appearing August 1993
‡   Currently available as hardback pocket guides

## *Clarity and quality of information, combined with outstanding maps — the ultimate in travelers' guides*

### *Buying an AmEx guide has never been easier....*

The *American Express Travel Guides* are now available by mail order direct from the publisher, for customers resident in the UK and Eire. Payment can be made by credit card or cheque/P.O. Simply complete the form below, and send it, together with your remittance.

## New paperback series (£6.99)    # Available from August 1993

☐ Amsterdam, Rotterdam & The Hague
  1 85732 918 X
☐ Barcelona, Madrid & Seville #
  1 85732 160 X
☐ Brussels
  1 85732 966 X
☐ Cities of Australia
  1 85732 921 X
☐ Dublin
  1 85732 967 8
☐ Florence and Tuscany
  1 85732 922 8
☐ Hong Kong & Taiwan
  0 85533 955 1
☐ London
  1 85732 968 6
☐ Los Angeles & San Diego
  1 85732 919 8
☐ Mexico #
  1 85732 159 6

☐ New York
  1 85732 971 6
☐ Paris
  1 85732 969 4
☐ Prague #
  1 85732 156 1
☐ Rome
  1 85732 923 6
☐ San Francisco and the Wine Regions
  1 85732 920 1
☐ Tokyo
  1 85732 970 8
☐ Toronto, Montréal & Québec City #
  1 85732 157 X
☐ Venice #
  1 85732 158 8
☐ Vienna & Budapest
  1 85732 962 7
☐ Washington, DC
  1 85732 924 4

## Hardback pocket guides (£7.99)

☐ Athens and the Classical Sites
  0 85533 954 3
☐ Berlin
  0 85533 952 7

☐ Singapore & Bangkok
  0 85533 956 X

While every effort is made to keep prices low, it is sometimes necessary to increase them at short notice. American Express Travel Guides reserves the right to amend prices from those previously advertised.

---

**Please send the titles ticked above.**                                    **DUB**

Number of titles @ £6.99 ☐         Value:    £

Number of titles @ £7.99 ☐         Value:    £
Add £1.50 for postage and packing             £    1.50

Total value of order:                         £
I enclose a cheque or postal order ☐ payable to Reed Book Services Ltd, or please charge my credit card account:

☐ Barclaycard/Visa     ☐ Access/MasterCard     ☐ American Express

Card number ☐☐☐☐☐☐☐☐☐☐☐☐☐☐☐☐☐☐☐☐☐

Signature _____     Expiry date _____

Name _____

Address _____

_____ Postcode _____

Send this order to American Express Travel Guides, Cash Sales Dept, Reed Book Services Ltd, PO Box 5, Rushden, Northants NN10 9YX ☎(0933) 410511.